OF ELEPHANTS & ROSES

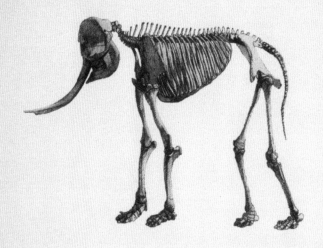

OF ELEPHANTS&ROSES

FRENCH NATURAL HISTORY
1790–1830

SUE ANN PRINCE, EDITOR

APS MUSEUM
AMERICAN PHILOSOPHICAL SOCIETY
PHILADELPHIA, 2013

Memoirs of the American Philosophical Society held at Philadelphia
for Promoting Useful Knowledge
Volume 267

ISBN: 978-0-87169-267-2
US ISSN: 0065-9738

This volume serves as the catalogue for the exhibition *Of
Elephants & Roses: Encounters with French Natural History,
1790–1830* at the APS Museum (March 25–December 31, 2011).
The essays, commentaries, and discussions included consti-
tute the proceedings of an associated symposium held at the
American Philosophical Society on December 1–3, 2011.

The American Philosophical Society gratefully acknowledges
the generous support of the Richard Lounsbery Foundation
for both the symposium and the publication of this volume.

For cover and front matter image credits, see List of Illustrations, p. xx.

. . . .

Library of Congress Cataloging-in-Publication Data

Of elephants & roses : French natural history, 1790–1830 / Sue Ann Prince,
editor.
       pages cm. — (Memoirs of the American Philosophical Society held
at Philadelphia for promoting useful knowledge ; volume 267)
   Catalogue for the exhibition Of Elephants & Roses: Encounters with
French Natural History, 1790–1830 at the APS Museum (March 25–December 31,
2011).
   Includes bibliographical references and index.
   ISBN 978-0-87169-267-2
   1. Natural history—France—18th century—Exhibitions. 2. Natural
history—France—19th century—Exhibitions. 3. France—Social life and
customs—18th century—Exhibitions. 4. France—Social life and
customs—19th century—Exhibitions. I. Prince, Sue Ann, editor of
compilation. II. Title: Of elephants and roses. III. Title: French natural
history, 1790–1830.
   QH147.O34 2013
   508.44—dc23
                          2013014522

Dedication

TO MARY PATTERSON
MCPHERSON AND
THE LATE BARUCH S.
BLUMBERG, FOR THEIR
UNFAILING SUPPORT
OF THIS APS MUSEUM
PROJECT

CONTENTS

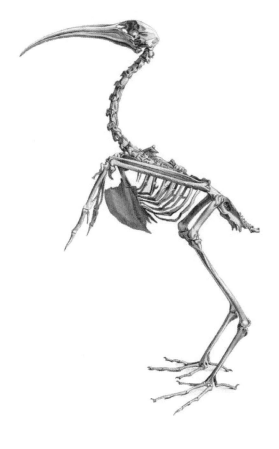

IN ESTABLISHING A NEW MUSEUM IN 2001, the American Philosophical Society (APS) opened the doors of Philosophical Hall to the public on an ongoing basis for the first time since Charles Willson Peale's Philadelphia Museum closed there in the early nineteenth century. Peale's institution was the first successful museum in the United States. Since the inception of the new APS Museum just over a decade ago, it has become the public face of the Society, attracting more than 740,000 visitors to thematic, interdisciplinary exhibitions that showcase treasures of the Society's library and museum collections, along with loans from other institutions.

Like all APS programs, the museum fulfills the Society's mission of "promoting useful knowledge" articulated by founder Benjamin Franklin in 1743. The museum explores the intersections of history, art, and science. Its exhibitions interpret the objects, books, and manuscripts in the APS collections. Exhibition themes for a broad general public are connected to the relevant issues of today through public programs and commissioned artistic projects in a wide range of contemporary visual and performing arts media. In addition, the museum serves Philadelphia-area schools, especially through teacher workshops. Finally, when possible, it publishes exhibition catalogues and organizes scholarly symposia with published proceedings.

The exhibition *Of Elephants & Roses: Encounters with French Natural History, 1790–1830* was on view from March 25 to December 31, 2011. Published in conjunction with the exhibition, this volume serves as both the catalogue for the show and the record of a related symposium titled "Of Pictures & Specimens: Natural History in Post-Revolutionary and Restoration France." During the symposium, which took place on December 1–3, 2011, French and American scholars from different fields explored a wide range of topics that developed and enriched themes considered in the exhibition. Included here are not only the essays presented over the three-day period, revised for publication, but also the commentaries and lively discussions that followed each session. The texts of the essays are also available online on the APS Museum website.

Many individuals, institutions, and funders have collaborated with us in numerous ways, and we thank them for their interest and invaluable support. Without them, this ambitious project—exhibition, artistic projects, interpretive programs, symposium, and book—could not have been realized. Special gratitude is due to Sue Ann Prince for her superb direction of the museum and its activities.

Clyde F. Barker
President, American Philosophical Society

THIS VOLUME is part of a large, multifaceted project proposed and initiated by the APS Museum in 2007. The project was developed over the following five years and ultimately resulted in an exhibition, a series of major interpretive artistic projects and public programs, educational outreach for teachers in Philadelphia schools, a symposium, and finally, this book, which documents both the proceedings of the symposium and the objects in the exhibition.

Numerous people and institutions—scholars, lenders, funders, APS members and staff, and other colleagues—have helped make all aspects of this project possible. It is a great pleasure to offer them my heartfelt thanks for their belief in it and their enthusiastic support.

First, I would like to acknowledge recently retired Executive Officer Mary Patterson (Pat) McPherson for her steadfast support of the museum over the course of her five-year tenure, and more specifically, for her unfailing confidence in the merits of this project, especially during a difficult economic time. I am also grateful to the late Baruch S. (Barry) Blumberg, two-term president of the APS, whose enthusiasm for the exhibition led him on a quest to learn about sites in Philadelphia with a French connection. Intrepid explorer that he was, he was still involved in this pursuit when he passed away shortly after the exhibition opened.

The APS Committee on Museum, chaired by Henry A. (Hank) Millon, was also steadfast in its commitment to the realization of the project. Hank's thoughtful counsel and guidance throughout the project was invaluable, as was the support of other committee members. Over the years of the exhibition's development and implementation, committee members included Elizabeth Cropper, David Brigham, Jonathan Brown, Barbara Grosz, Sheldon Hackney, Sue Johnson, Stanley N. Katz, Jeff Lock, Joseph J. Rishel, Danielle Rice, Charles E. Rosenberg, the late Charles Ryskamp, Keith Thomson, and David Wake.

A special Honorary Committee was formed specifically for the exhibition. Led by the late Barry Blumberg, it included French and American scholars and leaders. My sincere appreciation goes to the members of the committee from France, including Bertrand-Pierre Galey, followed by Thomas Grenon, each one, in succession, Directeur général du Muséum national d'Histoire naturelle; Amaury Lefébure, Conservateur général du patrimoine, Directeur du Musée national des châteaux de Malmaison et de Bois-Préau; Jean-Marc Léri, Conservateur général du patrimoine, Directeur du Musée Carnavalet; Bruno Racine, Président de la Bibliothèque nationale de France; Dominique Brême, Directeur du Domaine de Sceaux, Parc et musée de l'Île-de-France; and Daniel Roche, Professeur au Collège de France and Chaire d'Histoire de la France des Lumières (Émeritus). I am also deeply grateful to the American members of the committee (all APS members) who, in addition to the late Barry Blumberg, included James Billington, The Librarian of Congress; Ellen Futter, President, American Museum of Natural History; Amy Gutmann, President and Christopher H. Browne Distinguished Professor of Political Science, University of Pennsylvania; Philippe de Montebello, Director Emeritus, Metropolitan Museum of Art and Fiske Kimball Professor in the History and Culture of Museums, Institute of Fine Arts, New York University; and Neil Rudenstine, President Emeritus, Harvard University, and Chairman, ARTstor.

Numerous curators, archivists, collections managers, and other colleagues from lending institutions in France and the United States played an essential role in facilitating my work on the exhibition, both providing access to their collections and assisting me in securing loans from their institutions. At the Muséum national d'Histoire naturelle, the largest lender to the show, in addition to Messieurs Galey and Grenon (mentioned above), I would like to thank Myriam Néchad, Ph.D., Déléguée aux relations européennes et internationales, for her interest and support. I am also indebted to Michèle Lenoir, Directrice des bibliothèques et de la documentation, and Alice Lemaire, Conservateur, Service du patrimoine, both of the Bibliothèque centrale du Muséum, for their enthusiasm and cooperation during my many hours of research in their collections; and Anne Nivart, Julie Villemain, Pascal Tassy, and Cécile Aupic for showing me aspects of the Muséum's vast collections of bird specimens, fossils, and herbarium specimens, respectively. Jacques Cuisin offered invaluable assistance in Philadelphia during both installation and deinstallation of the exhibition.

I am grateful to the five other French institutions that also generously loaned objects to the APS Museum, especially the following (in addition to the directors, mentioned above): at the Musée national des châteaux de Malmaison et Bois-Préau, Conservateurs Alain Pougetoux and Elisabeth Caude, and Anne Bouin, Secrétaire de documentation; at the Bibliothèque nationale de France, Isabelle le Masne de Chermont, Adjoint au directeur des collections, and Françoise Simeray, Responsable du Service des expositions extérieures, whose assistance streamlined my work at their institution; Roselyne Hurel, former Conservateur en chef at the Musée Carnavalet–Histoire de Paris, whose enthusiasm and support for the project sustained my work there; Geneviève Lagardère, Conservateur, and Eléonore Jaulin, Chargée de la régie des œuvres, both at the Domaine de Sceaux, Parc et Musée de l'Île-de-France, who were very gracious in helping me access their collections and borrow from them; and finally, Laure Ménétrier, Responsable des Musées des Beaux-Arts de Beaune, for her assistance with the conservation and shipping of a highly prized oil painting. The warm welcome I received in France from all these colleagues was truly extraordinary.

In the United States, I had the pleasure of working with colleagues at several institutions, all of whom were most gracious: George W. Gephart, Jr., President and C.E.O. of the Academy of Natural Sciences of Drexel University, along with Robert McCracken Peck, Curator of Art and Artifacts and Senior Fellow of the Academy, Catherine Wilt, former Director of the Academy's Ewell Sale Stewart Library and Archives, Clare Flemming, Brooke Dolan Archivist and current Interim Director of the Library, and Eileen Mathias, former Information Services Librarian; Executive Director Kate Markert, Liana Paredes, Director of Collections and Chief Curator, Lawrence Waung, Head of Exhibitions and Collections Management, and Ruthann Uithol, former Assistant Director for Collections and Collections Manager at the Hillwood Estate, Museum, & Gardens; Malcolm Rogers, Ann and Graham Gund Director at the Museum of Fine Arts, Boston, in addition to staff members Lauren Whitley, Pam Parmel, Rebecca Tilles, and Thomas Michie; Karin A. Trainer, University Librarian at Princeton University Library, along with her colleagues Ben Primer, Associate University Librarian for Rare Books and Special Collections, and Stephen Ferguson, Assistant University Librarian for Rare Books and Special Collections and Curator of Rare Books. Other colleagues who assisted us greatly include Linda Wood at the Free Library of Philadelphia; Lynn Catanese at the Hagley Museum and Library; Tambra Johnson at the Library of Congress; Ira and David Brind and Mary Ann Meyers of Ira Brind Investments, Inc.; Graham Arader and Lori Cohen at the Arader Gallery in New York and Philadelphia; collector Richard Baron Cohen; and numerous others who assisted with our loans.

My profound thanks goes to exhibition designer Russell Drisch, whose vision and creative solutions for the exhibition displays, attention to detail, and ever-welcome sense of humor resulted in an innovative exhibition layout for the gallery that transcended our expectations. I am likewise grateful to Tamara Block and Anton Stayduhar of Contour Woodworks, who collaborated with Russ in realizing his vision, and proposed and implemented creative solutions for the crafting and fabricating of exhibition cases. The ingenuity of mount-makers William Bucher, Michael Studebaker, and Sebastien LeClerq, along with Bill Severson's skilled framing, added immeasurably to the displays. Finally, graphic designer Ann Antoshak, with whom we have worked for many years, once again produced creative, sophisticated design solutions for the exhibition graphics.

At the APS Museum, I am indebted to the curatorial research staff who helped me select objects and shape the exhibition narrative. Over the course of the exhibition's development, several Research Associates contributed their enthusiasm, dedication, creativity, and impeccable work towards its realization, including Jane E. Boyd, Peter Clericuzio, Erin McLeary, Sylwester Ratowt, and Sarah G. Sonner. Though they were with us at different stages and for different lengths of time, their collective contributions were essential in shaping the show. I am especially grateful to Jane E. Boyd, who returned to the APS as a Research Curator just as we were conceptualizing the exhibition, bringing her multiple talents and her knowledge of French to bear on the development process.

Other museum staff members have contributed their talent and dedication to the cause as well. I thank Associate Director of Collections and Exhibitions Mary Grace Wahl for her skill in masterminding and implementing all loan requests as well as installation and deinstallation; Curatorial Associate Julianna Struck for her multitasking abilities and gracious willingness to pitch in no matter what the task at hand; Curator of Museum Education Jenni Drozdek, for her energetic embrace of the exhibition content, her skill in developing materials for teachers, her creative ideas for programming, and her ability to manage the planning and implementation of The Greenhouse Projects. Finally, I want to thank Associate Director Merrill Mason, whose steadfast contributions in brainstorming, grant writing, planning and implementation of the APS Museum website, coordination of in-house graphic design, and a myriad of other tasks, greased the wheels throughout the entire project.

Many of these same people also carried out functions associated with "The Greenhouse Projects: Five Takes on an Exhibition," an initiative that included three artistic projects—a commissioned greenhouse by architect, designer, and artist Jenny Sabin in the APS's Thomas Jefferson Garden, original music by composer and musician Kyle Bartlett, and a theatrical performance by Aaron Cromie, Mary Tuomenon, and Geneviève Perrière. Two other projects—one a series of five podcasts about French cuisine by radio producer Lari Robling and the other, a geocaching treasure hunt implemented by Erin McLeary—were also commissioned. All five projects were an integral part of the museum's interpretation strategy for the exhibition, linking issues in the stewardship of nature in post-revolutionary and Restoration France to relevant concerns today. The Greenhouse Projects were larger-than-life initiatives that taxed our small staff but proved highly successful as a means of interpreting historical materials and making them relevant to contemporary horticultural and environmental practices today. I am deeply indebted to both the artists and others who participated in the Greenhouse Projects and to the entire museum staff whose herculean efforts made this initiative a success.

Many of the people mentioned above also played a role in realizing the symposium "Of Pictures & Specimens" and this publication. I am grateful to them, and also to the following people who were engaged to carry out specific responsibilities, particularly Corinna Schlombs, whose research and creative thinking contributed to a terrific lineup of symposium speakers. She was followed for a short time by Lisa Uddin, who also provided expertise that widened our scope of speakers. I'm grateful to Lyndsey Rago Claro for her transcriptions of the discussions that followed the sessions. I especially want to thank Sarah G. Sonner, who served not only as a curatorial researcher, as noted above, but was also in charge of rights and reproductions for both the exhibition and the book; she was also project manager for the symposium and the development phase of the book. When she left in the spring of 2012, Catherine (Katie) L. Skeen stepped in to follow through on Sarah's work, quickly learning all aspects of the ongoing project. Tara Miller took on responsibilities that went far beyond her role as Volunteer Coordinator and Education Assistant, managing myriad details that kept the project moving smoothly over many months. Andrew Lopez carefully analyzed the entire volume to prepare the invaluable index. I am greatly indebted to Jane E. Boyd, who, after leaving the museum to do freelance work, served as project editor and translator; her skills are evident on every page. Finally, I was fortunate to be able to engage Marc Blaustein as the graphic designer for this book, and his masterful and elegant layouts throughout have surpassed all our expectations.

Other APS staff members served invaluable roles. I am grateful to Anne E. Downey, Head of Conservation for the APS Library, and Denise Carbone, Book Conservator, whose work on preparing documents and books for display was, as always, stellar. I also extend my thanks to APS Director of Philanthropic Resources Nanette Holben, with whom we worked closely on acquiring the necessary funding; her expertise and development savvy were essential. Mary C. McDonald, Editor, APS Publications Department, helped develop the budget and contracts for the project and provided all necessary functions in the final editing and production stages. I also thank APS Editorial Assistant Celeste Bivings for her meticulous proofreading.

I would be remiss if I did not acknowledge all the outstanding scholars whose essays and commentaries appear in this book. Their work collectively produced a truly stimulating symposium, and their contributions to the study of French natural history and its relationship to art, science, and culture will be of enduring value to future scholars.

The complexity of the wide-ranging *Of Elephants & Roses* project was a challenge that we would not have been able to meet without the generous support of numerous funders. For the exhibition, we are indebted to John Young and the late Mary Young of The Florence Gould Foundation, whose early enthusiasm for the overall concept for the show led to a crucial planning grant that allowed us to do further research and develop our ideas; later, the Foundation provided an even more generous implementation grant for which we are ever so grateful. The Youngs' embrace of the show and thoughtful encouragement sustained us throughout.

Another foundation, the Crystal Trust, also provided crucial support for implementation, including the costly and exacting business of arranging, packing and shipping loans from both the French and the American institutions. It was a generous gift that reflected and honored longstanding ties between the APS and the du Pont family. We are also greatly indebted to The Gladys Krieble Delmas Foundation, established by APS member G. K. Delmas and her husband Jean Paul Delmas. Their foundation provided essential support specifically for the costs associated with borrowing specimens, objects, and manuscripts from the Muséum national d'Histoire naturelle in Paris, the largest lender to the show.

I also would like to acknowledge Margaret Bearn, whose enthusiasm for the exhibition resulted in a gift from the Alexander G. Bearn Memorial Fund for a full-color booklet and guide to the exhibition. Alexander (Alick) Bearn, former Executive Officer of the APS, was not only instrumental in the founding of the APS Museum during his tenure, but also was a bon vivant and Francophile. The booklet, dedicated to him, provided us with the perfect opportunity to honor his vision, commitment, and enduring contributions to the American Philosophical Society.

"The Greenhouse Projects: Five Takes on an Exhibition"—a series of creative, interpretive projects associated with the exhibition—was fully supported by The Pew Center for Arts & Heritage through the Heritage Philadelphia Program (HPP). With the support of the Center's staff members Paula Marincola, Bill Adair, Laura Kolowsky, and Jacque Liu, HPP became an extraordinary partner in these projects, encouraging us to use creative and innovative approaches in our interpretation of the exhibition for diverse audiences.

Finally, I would like to offer my heartfelt thanks to the Richard Lounsbery Foundation, which fully funded the symposium and this publication. I especially want to acknowledge its President, Ambassador David M. Abshire, and also wish to express my gratitude to Maximillian Angerholzer III, whose keen embrace of the symposium's potential for creating an exciting intellectual and interdisciplinary exchange among French and American scholars not only led to the Foundation's support, but inspired us all along the way. Included in this volume are the formal essays and commentaries, post-session discussions, a complete listing of all objects in the exhibition, and more than one hundred full-color images. The Foundation's generous support also allowed us to enlarge the potential readership for the material presented here by making the essay texts available in perpetuity on the APS Museum website. As it is not always possible for us to undertake such a symposium or produce a large publication such as this one, we remain deeply appreciative of the opportunity Lounsbery provided us to further cross-disciplinary scholarship in the field of French natural history on the occasion of this exhibition.

Last but not least, I thank my family and friends, who have heard more about French natural history than they ever wanted to know. I am grateful for their moral support, encouragement, and good humor over the years. I also want to acknowledge my grandchildren—Aidan, Daniel, Elise, and Zoë—all born during this project. May they grow up to love both elephants and roses!

Sue Ann Prince
Founding Director and Curator, American Philosophical Society Museum

Bernadette Bensaude-Vincent is a philosopher and historian of science. She is currently a Professor at Université Paris I Panthéon-Sorbonne, where she received her doctorate. A member of the Institut universitaire de France, she is also Director of the Centre d'étude des techniques, des connaissances et des pratiques (CETCOPRA, Center for Research on Contemporary Technology), and a member of the French Académie des technologies. Her research topics span from the history and philosophy of chemistry to materials science and nanotechnology, with a continuous interest in science and public issues.

Göran Blix studies the tradition of nineteenth-century French prose writing in the context of major historical and political developments. His interests include romanticism, realism, literary aesthetics, the historical imagination, and the relationship between democracy and literature. He has published articles on Balzac, Hugo, Michelet, Flaubert, Tocqueville, the Goncourt brothers, and Zola, among others. His book on romantic historicism, *From Paris to Pompeii: French Romanticism and the Cultural Politics of Archeology* (2008), examines the impact of the nascent science of archeology on modern secular attitudes to death, memory, and immortality. He earned a B.A. in Literature from Harvard College, a DEA from the École des hautes études en sciences sociales in Paris, and a Ph.D. in French from Columbia University. He joined the Department of French and Italian at Princeton University in 2003. His recent research interests focus on the fraught relationship between literature and democratization in nineteenth-century France, especially how literary and political forms of representation overlap. His current book project, *The Heroism of Modern Life*, examines literary democratization by looking at changes in the modern conception of the heroic.

Richard W. Burkhardt, Jr. is Professor of History Emeritus at the University of Illinois at Urbana-Champaign. A historian of biology, he has been interested in the Muséum d'Histoire naturelle in Paris ever since making the evolutionary theory of Jean-Baptiste Lamarck the subject of his doctoral dissertation at Harvard University. This became the basis for his first book, *The Spirit of System: Lamarck and Evolutionary Biology* (1977, 1995). He has also written on nineteenth- and twentieth-century animal behavior theory and evolution. His book *Patterns of Behavior: Konrad Lorenz, Niko Tinbergen, and the Founding of Ethology* (2005) won the History of Science Society's Pfizer Prize in 2006. He is currently writing a book on the history of the menagerie of the Muséum d'Histoire naturelle. He is a past Fellow of the John Simon Guggenheim Foundation and a Fellow of the American Association for the Advancement of Science.

Bernard Chevallier, born in Paris, holds a doctorate in art history from the Université Paris-Sorbonne. He was Conservateur (curator) of the Musée national du château de Fontainebleau from 1973 to 1980, Conservateur of the Musée national des châteaux de Malmaison et Bois-Préau from 1980 to 1989, and was named Conservateur général du patrimoine in 1997. From 1989 to his retirement in 2008, he was the Director of the Musée national des châteaux de Malmaison et Bois-Préau and its affiliates: the Musée de la maison Bonaparte in Ajaccio, the Musées de l'Île d'Aix (Musée napoléonien and Musée africain), and the Collections des domaines français de Sainte-Hélène. He organized twenty-one exhibitions at Malmaison and was in charge of numerous exhibitions abroad on Napoleon, Josephine, and the First Empire, which were viewed by over two million visitors in Europe, America, and Asia. He is a specialist in furniture and objets d'art from the First Empire and in Sèvres porcelain from 1800 to 1870.

His publications include dozens of articles on Sèvres porcelain, decorative arts during the Empire, the history of Malmaison, and eighteenth-century French architecture, as well as many works on Empress Josephine, Malmaison, Sèvres porcelain at Fontainebleau, the art of living in Josephine's era, the splendors of the Empire, and Napoleonic centers of power, as well as numerous exhibition catalogues.

Claudine Cohen teaches the history of science at the École des hautes études en sciences sociales (EHESS) in Paris, where she has served since 1997 as a Director of the research program "Biologie et société." She is also Directeur d'études at the École pratique des hautes études (EPHE) in Paris. In addition to degrees in philosophy and paleontology, she holds a *Doctorat ès lettres* (Université Sorbonne Nouvelle–Paris 3) and an *Habilitation à diriger des recherches* in epistemology and the history of science (Université Paris-Sorbonne). Cohen has written extensively on the history of paleontology, prehistoric archeology, and the related sciences. Her works in French include *La Femme des origines: Images de la femme dans la préhistoire occidentale* (2003, new edition 2006), *La Méthode de Zadig: Le trace, le fossile, la preuve* (2011), and *Science, libertinage et clandestinité à l'aube des Lumières: Le transformisme de Telliamed* (2011). Her books in English include *The Fate of the Mammoth: Fossils, Myth, and History* (2002) and the first English edition of Gottfried Wilhelm Leibniz's *Protogaea* (with André Wakefield, 2008).

Denise Z. Davidson is Associate Professor of History at Georgia State University. She is the author of *France after Revolution: Urban Life, Gender, and the New Social Order* (2007) and co-author, with Anne Verjus, of *Le Roman conjugal: Chroniques de la vie familiale à l'époque de la Révolution et de l'Empire* (2011). Her articles have appeared in *French History, French Historical Studies, Annales Historiques de la Révolution française,* and *The Journal of Family History*; a forthcoming article, co-written with Anne Verjus, will be published by the *William and Mary Quarterly* (2013). She is currently writing a book that makes use of private correspondence to discuss bourgeois families and their survival strategies during and after the French Revolution. She received her Ph.D. in History from the University of Pennsylvania. Funded by a Burkhardt Fellowship from the American Council for Learned Societies, she spent the 2010–11 academic year as a resident fellow at the National Humanities Center in North Carolina. Her other awards include a Fulbright Research Grant for France and a Chateaubriand Fellowship from the French government.

Andrea Goulet is Associate Professor of French and Undergraduate Chair of Comparative Literature at the University of Pennsylvania. Goulet received her Ph.D. in French Literature from Yale University. She is the author of *Optiques: The Science of the Eye and the Birth of Modern French Fiction* (2006) and is completing a second book manuscript entitled *Legacies of the Rue Morgue: French Crime Fiction's Spatial Imaginary,* which traces discourses of paleontology, geology, and cartography in popular crime novels by authors from Émile Gaboriau to Fred Vargas. She has co-edited special journal issues on "Crime Fictions" (*Yale French Studies*) and "Visual Studies" (*Contemporary French Civilization*) and was recently appointed as co-chair, with Corry Cropper of Brigham Young University, of the international Nineteenth-Century French Studies Association.

Sara Gronim is an Associate Professor of History at Long Island University. She received her Ph.D. from Rutgers University. A scholar of early American science and medicine, she has published articles on the history of cartography, smallpox inoculation, and astronomy in almanacs. Her book *Everyday Nature: Knowledge of the Natural World in Colonial New York* (2007) is a study of the reception of the scientific revolution among the literate but non-learned public. Her article "What Jane Knew: A Woman Botanist in the Eighteenth Century," published in the *Journal of Women's History*, won the Margaret W. Rossiter Prize for the History of Women in Science from the History of Science Society (2008).

Daniel Harkett is an Assistant Professor in the Department of History of Art and Visual Culture at the Rhode Island School of Design. After completing his Ph.D. dissertation on exhibition culture in Restoration France at Brown University, he held a post-doctoral fellowship in the Society of Fellows at Columbia University. He has published an essay on Jacques-Louis David and an article on Louis Daguerre's Diorama, as well as book and exhibition reviews in *caa.reviews* and *Nineteenth-Century Art Worldwide*. He is working on a book on the visual culture of sociability in post-revolutionary Paris.

Elizabeth Hyde, Assistant Professor in the Department of History at Kean University, received her Ph.D. in History from Harvard University. Her book, *Cultivated Power: Flowers, Culture, and Politics in the Reign of Louis XIV* (2005) explores the collection, cultivation, and display of flowers in early modern France and their political uses by Louis XIV. In 2007, the book received the Elisabeth Blair MacDougall Award of the Society of Architectural Historians for the most distinguished work of scholarship in the history of landscape architecture or garden design. Her current research reflects her ongoing interest in cultural history, garden history, and the history of France. She is researching the cultural and political dimensions of transatlantic botanical exchange in the eighteenth century and is also writing a cultural history of "how-to" books in the early modern period.

Antoine Jacobsohn was born in the United States to European parents and studied agronomy at Cornell University. He then pursued graduate work on the history of food production and consumption at Université Paris 8 Vincennes–St. Denis and at the École des hautes études en sciences sociales (EHESS) in Paris. In 2004, he began work at the Potager du Roi (King's Kitchen Garden) at Versailles, becoming Director in 2007. This 22-acre garden, a national historic monument, is under the auspices of the École Nationale Supérieure de Paysage (ENSP) in Versailles, the national landscape architecture school. The garden's mission is to preserve and teach about historic growing practices and varieties of fruits and vegetables. Jacobsohn's numerous publications include *Anthologie des bons jardiniers: Traités de jardinage français du XVIᵉ siècle au début du XIXᵉ siècle* (2003) and the exhibition catalogues *L'Épopée des courges: Cultures et consommations en Europe* (2005); *Fruits du savoir: Duhamel Du Monceau et la pomologie française* (2007); and *Du fayot au mangetout: L'Histoire du haricot sans perdre le fil* (2010).

Dorothy Johnson is Roy J. Carver Professor of Art History at the University of Iowa. She received her Ph.D. from the University of California, Berkeley and specializes in eighteenth- and nineteenth-century European art. She has published essays on Chardin, Rousseau, David d'Angers, Delacroix, and Jacques-Louis David among other subjects, and has published several books on David. Her most recent book, *David to Delacroix: The Rise of Romantic Mythology* (2011) developed from the Bettie Allison Rand Lectures given at the University of North Carolina, Chapel Hill. Professor Johnson was a Camargo Foundation resident fellow and has taught as visiting professor at the University of California,

Berkeley. She served on the Board of Directors of the College Art Association and was Director of the School of Art and Art History at the University of Iowa from 1995 to 2009. Her current research centers on the confluence of the visual arts and the natural sciences around 1800 in France.

Pierre-Yves Lacour is Assistant Professor (Maître de Conférences) of early modern history at the Université Paul-Valéry / Montpellier 3. For his Ph.D. at the European University Institute of Florence, he worked on French natural history at the end of the Old Regime and during the revolutionary era. His work is especially concerned with cabinets as well as with botanical gardens. The Muséum national d'Histoire naturelle is publishing his thesis under the title *La République naturaliste* (Collection Archives). He has begun a project called "Encyclopedism, Mapping Knowledge and the Making of Disciplines: Europe, 1780–1830." A paper analyzing the tables of contents of the *Magasin encyclopédique* is forthcoming in *La Révolution française, Cahiers de l'IHRF.* Another paper dealing with boundary objects, items that received different meanings and were used in different ways among the Parisian network of national collections, will be submitted to a French journal.

Anne Lafont is Professor (Maitre de conférences) in the History of Modern Art at the Université Paris-Est Marne-la-Vallée. She received her doctorate in the History of Art from the Université Paris IV–Sorbonne. Since 2007, she has been Conseillère scientifique at the Institut national d'histoire de l'art (INHA) in Paris. Lafont is interested in the visual culture of science in the eighteenth and nineteenth centuries, particularly in the construction of "otherness" and the representation of black peoples in the art of the modern era. She edited a publication titled *L'artiste savant à la conquête du monde moderne* (2010) and directed research at INHA that resulted in an exhibition and book on the world of art and natural science around 1740 through the study of Dezallier d'Argenville, an exemplary collector and historian of painting and shells. The book, titled *1740: Un abrégé du monde*, was published in May 2012 to coincide with the exhibition in the Roberto Longhi Gallery at INHA.

Paula Young Lee is a Faculty Fellow at Tufts University. She holds a Ph.D. from the University of Chicago and has published widely on the history of animal representation and captivity in the *Art Bulletin, Journal of the Society of Architectural Historians, Science in Context, Journal for Eighteenth-Century Studies*, and numerous other venues. Her most recent books include *Gorgeous Beasts: Animal Bodies in Historical Perspective* (edited with Joan Landes and Paul Youngquist, in press) and *Game: A Global History* (forthcoming). She is currently completing a much-anticipated book on the seventeenth-century Ménagerie at Versailles.

Alain Lescart is Professor of French Studies and Literature at Point Loma Nazarene University, San Diego. His degrees include an M.Div. from the Académie de Versailles, an M.A. from the Faculté universitaire de Théologie protestante in Brussels, and a Ph.D. in French Literature from the University of Connecticut, Storrs. His book *Splendeurs et misères de la grisette: Évolution d'une figure emblématique* (2008), a cultural study of the representation of poor seamstresses in nineteenth-century French literature, was based on his doctoral dissertation. He is the author of numerous articles on nineteenth-century French and Francophone literature and also specializes in fantasy literature. His interest in the topic of censorship led him to analyze the representation of the first giraffe in France in 1827.

Elise Lipkowitz is a Postdoctoral Fellow in the Michigan Society of Fellows and Assistant Professor in the History Department at the University of Michigan in Ann Arbor. She received her Ph.D. in History from Northwestern University. Her book manuscript, titled *The End of Cosmopolitan Science: The Transformation of the European Scientific Community in the Era of the French Revolution*, traces the eclipse of the ideals and practices of the early modern scientific Republic of Letters amid the French Revolution and the Napoleonic Wars. A related article, "Seized Natural History Collections and the Redefinition of Scientific Cosmopolitanism in the Era of the French Revolution," is forthcoming in *The British Journal for the History of Science*. Previously, she authored "The Physicians' Dilemma in the Eighteenth-Century French Smallpox Debate" in *The Journal of the American Medical Association* (2003) and edited *From Concept to Completion: A Dissertation Writing Guide for History Students* (American Historical Association, 2008).

Madeleine Pinault Sørensen holds diplomas from the École du Louvre and from the École Pratique des Hautes Études (course in History of the Book). Until her retirement, she was in charge of research in the Départment des Arts Graphiques at the Musée du Louvre. She is a specialist in scientific illustrations and the connections between science, literature, and art, on which she has published widely. She was the recipient of a Mellon Fellowship at the American Philosophical Society Library in 1991. She has organized more than thirty exhibitions, including *Dessin et sciences* at the Louvre (1984) and *Dessiner la nature* at the Fondation Electra, Paris (1996). She published *Le peintre et l'histoire naturelle*, which won the Prix Nature (1991) and was translated into English as *The Painter as Naturalist from Dürer to Redouté*. She is currently working on a biography and a catalogue of the works of the painter Jean Houël for Éditions Arthena.

Sue Ann Prince is Founding Director and Curator of the American Philosophical Society (APS) Museum. Prior to her position at the Society, she served at the Smithsonian Institution as Midwest Regional Director for the Archives of American Art and Director of Public Information for the National Portrait Gallery. She has also served as art critic for *The Seattle Times,* written for art journals and other publications, edited and partially authored *The Old Guard and the Avant-Garde: Modernism in Chicago, 1910–1940* (University of Chicago Press, 1990), and edited two volumes produced in conjunction with exhibitions she curated for the APS Museum: *Stuffing Birds, Pressing Plants, Shaping Knowledge: Natural History in North America, 1730–1860* (2003), and *The Princess & the Patriot: Ekaterina Dashkova, Benjamin Franklin, and the Age of Enlightenment* (2006). She also initiated and curated more than twenty projects for the Museum in contemporary visual art, theater, music, dance, and other performing arts media. Prince holds M.A. degrees in French Literature and in the History of Art and a Ph.D. in the History of Art from the University of Pennsylvania. She received an honorary doctorate from LaSalle University in 2009 and was a visiting scholar for two months in 2011 at the Institut national d'histoire de l'art (INHA) in Paris.

Carol Solomon is author of *The Empress Josephine: Art and Royal Identity* (2005) and curator of the 2005 exhibition of the same name at the Mead Art Museum, Amherst College. An art historian and curator specializing in nineteenth-century French and contemporary art, she received her Ph.D. in Art History from the University of Pittsburgh. Currently Visiting Associate Professor of Art History at Haverford College, she has also taught at Amherst College, Smith College, the

University of Massachusetts Amherst, Mount Holyoke College, and McGill University. From 2002 to 2008, she was Curator of European Art at the Mead Art Museum. Solomon has published and lectured on topics ranging from Napoleon and Josephine to Cézanne and issues of identity and globalization in contemporary art. Recent exhibitions organized by Solomon include *Mapping Identity* (2010), *The Third Space: Cultural Identity Today* (2008), *A Room with a View: The Photography of Abelardo Morell* (2007), *The Pain of War* (2004), *The Myth and Madness of Ophelia* (2001), and *The Hanged Man: Cézanne and the Art of the Print* (1999). In 2009, as curator collaborating with the Algerian-French artist Zoulikha Bouabdellah, she received the Abraaj Capital Art Prize, a competition open to artists from the Middle East, North Africa, and South Asia. Solomon has been awarded a 2012–13 Fulbright Scholar grant to do research on contemporary art in Morocco and Tunisia.

Susan Taylor-Leduc is Assistant Art History Professor for Trinity College in Paris, where she has taught since 2006. Professor Taylor-Leduc received her M.A. and Ph.D. from the University of Pennsylvania. Taylor-Leduc was Lecturer at the Fondation national des sciences politiques (Sciences Po) in Paris, at Columbia University's Paris Program, and at the American University of Paris. She is the author of "Reassessing Fruit Trees in the Marquis de Fontanes' Poem 'Le Verger'" for *Invaluable Trees: Cultures of Nature, 1660–1830*, edited by Laura Auricchio et al. (2012). Other essays include "Thomas Jefferson's Paris Years: A Franco-American Affair" and "Napoleon and Joséphine: Public and Private Images" for the exhibition catalogue *Jefferson's America and Napoleon's France* (New Orleans Museum of Art, 2003); and the articles "Luxury in the Garden: *La Nouvelle Héloïse* Reconsidered" (1999) and "A New Treatise in Seventeenth-Century Garden History: André Félibien's 'Description de la Grotte à Versailles'" (1998), both in *Studies in the History of Gardens & Designed Landscapes*. She also served as the European curator for the Benjamin Franklin Tercentenary traveling exhibition, *Benjamin Franklin: In Search of a Better World* (2003–8).

John Tresch is Associate Professor in History and Sociology of Science at the University of Pennsylvania. He studied social science and philosophy at the Universities of Chicago and Cambridge and the École normale supérieure (ENS) in Paris and has held fellowships at Columbia and Northwestern Universities, the Max Planck Institute, and the New York Public Library. His work examines the relations between science, technology, and their broader cultural settings, including politics, philosophy, and the arts. His book, *The Romantic Machine: Utopian Science and Technology after Napoleon* (2012), set in Paris, explores the ways in which the new technical devices and protean fluids of the early Industrial Revolution were enmeshed with the aspirations and aesthetics of romanticism, and how the alchemical conjunction of romanticism and industrialization set the scene for the worker's revolution of 1848. He has written widely about the history of photography, cybernetics, anthropology, surrealism, and neuroscience. His current research examines the changing nature of communication in early nineteenth-century America and its effects on the public authority of science, as read through the scientific satires and technological obsessions of Edgar Allan Poe.

2.1   J. R. Brascassat, *Passage de la girafe à Arnay-le-Duc*, 1827, oil on canvas. Musée des Beaux-Arts de Beaune. Photo: J.-C. Couval

2.2   An early illustration of the "provisional menagerie" of the Muséum d'Histoire naturelle. Date and illustrator unknown. © Muséum national d'Histoire naturelle, Dist. RMN-GP / image du MNHN, Bibliothèque centrale

2.3   The skeleton of a sacred ibis, from a mummy taken from a tomb in Thebes. From Georges Cuvier, "Mémoire sur l'Ibis des anciens Égyptiens," *Annales du Muséum national d'Histoire naturelle* 4 (1804), pl. 1, p. 116. © Muséum national d'Histoire naturelle. MNHN, Bibliothèque centrale

2.4   The "Festival of Liberty" of 1798. *Entrée triomphale des monuments des sciences et des arts en France; fête à ce sujet. Les 9 et 10 thermidor an 6ᵉ de la République.* Engraved by Berthault after a drawing by Girardet. © MNHN, Dist. RMN-GP / image du MNHN, Bibliothèque centrale

2.5   J. P. Hoüel's illustration of how the elephants caressed each other upon first hearing music played for them. From J. P. Hoüel, *Histoire naturelle des deux éléphans, mâle et femelle, du Muséum de Paris* (Paris, 1803), plate XV. © MNHN, Bibliothèque centrale

2.6   While the elephant's skin was stuffed for exhibition in the natural history galleries, the elephant's bones were reassembled to become part of the comparative anatomy collection. From Georges Cuvier, "Sur les éléphans vivants et fossiles," *Annales du Muséum national d'Histoire naturelle*, vol. 8 (1806), plate 1, p. 154. © MNHN, Bibliothèque centrale

2.7   Kangaroos, emus, and black swans at Malmaison. François Peron and C. A. Lesueur, Title page illustration, engraved by Frères Lambert, from atlas vol. of *Voyage de decouvertes aux terres australes*, by C. A. Lesueur and N. M. Petit (Paris, 1807). Malmaison. RMN / Art Resource, N.Y.

2.8   Atir and the giraffe in the giraffe's stable. Engraved by Andrew, Best, and Leloir after a drawing by Karl Girardet. From M. Boitard, *Le Jardin des Plantes: Descriptions et mœurs des mammifères de la ménagerie et du Muséum d'Histoire naturelle* (Paris, 1842), p. 440. APS

2.9   The new "ménagerie des animaux féroces." Engraved by Andrew, Best, and Leloir after a drawing by C. Marville. From M. Boitard, *Le Jardin des Plantes: Descriptions et mœurs des mammifères de la ménagerie et du Muséum d'Histoire naturelle* (Paris, 1842), p. 162. APS

......

Part II. About Gardens and Gardening

pp. 33–34   Pierre-Joseph Redouté, Josephine's March Lily (*Brunsvigia josephinae*, "Amaryllis de Joséphine, Amaryllis Josephinae"), 1802–5, watercolor on vellum (details), study for *Les Liliacées*, vol. 7 (Paris, 1813). David Brind (see Fig. 3.4)

3   EMPRESS JOSEPHINE AND THE NATURAL SCIENCES

3.1   Plates from Service des plantes exotiques porcelaine de Berlin. Drei Teller aus dem Service für Kaiserin Josephine mit Blumen-Darstellungen (Lotusblume, Taglilie, Geranie), KPM, 1807. Stiftung Preußische Schlösser und Gärten Berlin-Brandenburg, KPM-Porzellansammlung des Landes Berlin / Photograph: Wolfgang Pfauder

3.2   Auguste Garnerey, *Vue intérieure de la serre-chaude à Malmaison*. Watercolor. Malmaison. RMN / Art Resource, N.Y.

3.3   *Rosa gallica purpurea*, from P. J. Redouté and C. A. Thory, *Les Roses*, vol. 1 & part of vol. 2 (Paris, 1817–21). The Academy of Natural Sciences of Drexel University, Ewell Sale Stewart Library

3.4   Pierre-Joseph Redouté, Josephine's March Lily (*Brunsvigia josephinae*, "Amaryllis de Josephine, Amaryllis Josephinae"), 1802–5, watercolor on vellum, study for *Les Liliacées*, vol. 7 (Paris, 1813). David Brind

3.5   Pierre Dandelot, after Léon de Wailly, *Cygnes noirs* (Black Swans from the Bass Straits). Malmaison. RMN / Art Resource, N.Y.

3.6   Antoine-Marie Héron de Villefosse, Cours de minéralogie pour l'impératrice Joséphine. Malmaison. RMN / Art Resource, N.Y.

INTRODUCTION AND SYMPOSIUM KEYNOTE ADDRESS

PART I
INTRODUCTION AND SYMPOSIUM KEYNOTE ADDRESS

Previous page and detail, left J. R. Brascassat, *Passage
de la girafe à Arnay-le-Duc*, 1827, oil on canvas. Musée des
Beaux-Arts de Beaune. Photo: J.-C. Couval (see Fig. 2.1)

INTRODUCTION:
OF ELEPHANTS & ROSES

SUE ANN PRINCE

AS A CURATOR, it is always rewarding to take an idea and shape it into an exhibition. *Of Elephants & Roses* is a case in point. The inspiration for it arose in 2002, several years before the actual work began. At that time, the museum program at the American Philosophical Society was still quite new, and I was working with museum staff on our second exhibition, *Stuffing Birds, Pressing Plants, Shaping Knowledge: Natural History in North America, 1730–1860*.[1] As curator, I wanted to include objects that would help contextualize the practice of natural science in the New World. To achieve that goal, we selected for display a handful of the most important European natural history books of the period. To my surprise, most of these publications were French.

Although we were aware of the substantial scholarship on French natural history in and of itself—by APS member Charles Gillispie and by Dorinda Outram, for example—historians of the Atlantic World generally focused on the British context and its relationship to North America rather than on French and American connections.[2] Yet primary sources in the

Fig. 1.1

Jean-Baptiste Hilair, Jardin du Roi: Greenhouses, 1794, watercolor. BnF

Fig. 1.2

Auguste Garnerey, *Vue extérieure de "la Serre Chaude" à Malmaison*, watercolor. Malmaison. RMN / Art Resource, N.Y.

APS Library and elsewhere attested to strong and important links between eighteenth- and early nineteenth-century French naturalists and the burgeoning scientific community in early Philadelphia. Thus was born the idea for a show that would not only highlight the importance of natural history in post-revolutionary and Restoration France but also enrich the story of science in early Philadelphia, where the APS played a central role as the first scientific institution in North America.[3]

The 2011 exhibition *Of Elephants & Roses: Encounters with French Natural History, 1790–1830* was therefore a kind of sequel to the earlier show. First, we intended to set forth the new scientific theories that emerged in France in this era, using an interdisciplinary approach supported by specimens, manuscripts, and artworks. Second, we wanted to consider how the plants and animals arriving from around the world were acclimatized and assimilated into French culture, simultaneously influencing and reflecting cultural life, politics, and social mores. Inspired by Lorraine Daston's and Peter Galison's milestone book *Objectivity*, we were also eager to use their thesis as a starting point in our investigation of natural history texts and imagery in France.[4] Finally, we hoped to flesh out the exchanges of specimens and scientific information that took place between French naturalists and Philadelphia's APS members such as Thomas Jefferson, Charles Willson Peale, Benjamin Smith Barton, and John and William Bartram.

The topic was enormous, but our gallery space is small. Of the many possible narratives—from the story of chocolate and tobacco in the French colonial context to the North American adventures of French naturalists such as Ambroise Palisot de Beauvois and Constantine Samuel Rafinesque—we ultimately decided to use two specific French sites as the backdrop for our investigations and to choose stories related to them. We settled on the Muséum d'Histoire naturelle in Paris and Empress Josephine's garden at Malmaison just outside the city, arguably the two most important natural history gardens in France at the time (**FIGS. 1.1** and **1.2**). After careful consideration, we chose five stories or "encounters" that we believed would offer windows onto the breadth and the depth of French natural history during the period in question.

Fig. 1.4 (right)

Black Swan (*Cygnus atratus* or *Chenopis atrata*), collected in Australia ca. 1802, sent to Empress Josephine at Malmaison in 1803, died 1814. © MNHN–Patrick Lafaite

Fig. 1.3 (above)

Partial lower jaw, American mastodon (*Mammut americanum*), from Big Bone Lick, Boone County, Kentucky, collected by William Clark, 1807, Thomas Jefferson Fossil Collection, The Academy of Natural Sciences of Drexel University, gift of the American Philosophical Society, Philadelphia, ANSP 13103

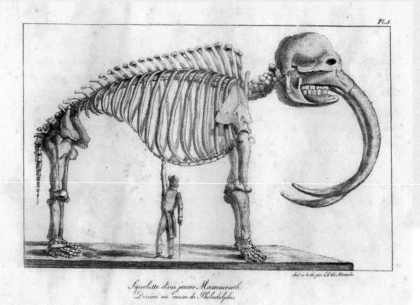

Fig. 1.7 (left)

Édouard de Montulé, *Squelette d'une jeune Mammoth, Dessiné au musée de Philadelphie.* Engraving from De Montulé, *Voyage en Amérique en Sicile et en Egypte,* atlas vol. (Paris, 1821). APS

The displays were drawn from objects in French and American institutions, including the APS Library. Of the 105 objects on view, sixty-five were from France; to our knowledge, none of these had ever before been shown in the United States.

The first section of the exhibition, titled "Music for Elephants," told the story of two famous elephants, Hans and Parkie, whom the revolutionary government confiscated from Holland and shipped to Paris as spoils of war in 1798. Hans and Parkie were the guests of honor at a public concert during which musicians played a revolutionary anthem in a failed attempt to persuade them to mate. The objects on display in this section also included fossil remains of other pachyderms (**FIG. 1.3**), such as the teeth of a mammoth and the jawbone of a mastodon sent by Thomas Jefferson to French naturalist Georges Cuvier. Such gifts supported the French scientist's own research and led to the birth of a new scientific field that came to be called paleontology. In addition, this section featured drawings of the two nearly complete mastodon skeletons exhumed by Charles Willson Peale and his sons. One of these skeletons was displayed in Peale's Philadelphia Museum, which was housed for many years in the APS's Philosophical Hall, the site of our own exhibition (**FIG. 1.7**).

The second encounter, "Hunting for Trees," showcased artifacts related to the work of French explorer André Michaux, whom Louis XVI sent to North America in 1785 to search for trees that could be useful to France. We selected two types of trees as examples, each one prized in

France for a different reason: the American oak, much sought after for its utility, and the rare Franklinia or Franklin tree (*Franklinia alatamaha*), named for Benjamin Franklin and esteemed for its beauty. On view in this section were dried herbarium specimens of both these trees, along with engraved and painted images of them. The Franklinia, discovered in the colony of Georgia and then cultivated by Philadelphia botanists John and William Bartram, eventually made its way to France through André Michaux and botanists in Britain. At Malmaison, Josephine prized her Franklinia for its rarity and beauty. The displays included a juxtaposition of Franklinia images by William Bartram in Philadelphia and Pierre-Joseph Redouté in Paris (**FIGS. 1.5** and **1.6**). We believe this was the first time the work of these two well-known artist-naturalists had been compared, revealing the very different contexts in which they worked. Whereas the Bartram image was an engraving intended for science but never published, Redouté's rendering not only appeared in a scientific publication but was also copied onto a lovely Sèvres porcelain ice cream cooler owned by Josephine. In the context of the French Empire, natural history imagery was not only important for science but also found its way onto luxury objects for the elite.

In another section, the exhibition highlighted Empress Josephine as the first person to breed black swans in captivity outside Australia. On view in "Black Swans for an Empress," the swans became symbols of her taste, wealth, and power—and they also exemplified the period's love for exotic birds (**FIG. 1.4**). The displays in this section also showcased Pauline de Courcelles Knip, whose

Fig. 1.5

William Bartram, Franklinia (*Franklinia alatamaha*), ca. 1786, engraved by James Trenchard. APS

Fig. 1.6

Sèvres Porcelain Manufactory, *Seau à glace forme Hébée* (Ice-Cream Cooler), with Franklinia (*Franklinia alatamaha*, "Gordonie pubescente") and Blue Water Lily (*Nymphaea nouchali*, "Nénuphar bleu"), from Service of Plants of Malmaison and Lilies, 1804–5, hard paste porcelain with colored enamel and gilded decoration. Museum of Fine Arts, Boston, Gift of Mr. and Mrs. Henry R. Kravis. Photograph © 2013 Museum of Fine Arts, Boston

detailed paintings of birds from the collections of the Muséum d'Histoire naturelle were valued both as scientific documents and as works of art (**FIG. 1.8**). Knip was something of a "rare bird" herself—a successful female artist and the only woman to be employed by the Sèvres Porcelain Manufactory. She not only painted watercolors as the basis for engravings in scientific books but also insisted on rendering, in her own hand, scientifically accurate images of birds on porcelain plates and vases.

The fourth section of the exhibition, "A Flower Blooms," illustrated the aesthetic and practical dimensions of the worldwide exchange of flowering plants. It included images by Pierre-Joseph Redouté, who became most famous for his exquisite, highly detailed paintings of exotic plants at Malmaison (**FIG. 1.9**). This section featured his watercolors and stipple engravings, as well as images based on them that were painted on dinner and dessert plates made by porcelain manufacturers in Paris and Berlin. Once again, we juxtaposed images of a rare flowering plant by Bartram and Redouté, and likewise included a herbarium sheet with a dried specimen of the plant and an image painted on porcelain (**FIG. 1.10**). These depictions of the Venus flytrap (*Dionaea muscipula*) highlighted their different styles. Bartram's individualized flytrap, with a "mouth" or trap about to capture its prey, stood in stark contrast to Redouté's more idealized "truth-to-nature" approach (**FIGS. 1.11** and **1.12**). Letters and other documents on view in this section also revealed Josephine's interest in improving plant science as a means of boosting agricultural productivity. Indeed, she propagated many plants for their economic value and sent seedlings all over the country "to enrich the soil of France."[5]

The final encounter, titled "Everything Giraffe," told the story of a female giraffe shipped to France in 1826 as a political gift for King Charles X from the viceroy of Egypt. Upon arriving, the giraffe wintered in Marseille and then was led to Paris on foot by Étienne Geoffroy Saint-Hilaire, one of the most famous scientists at the Muséum d'Histoire naturelle. She became an immediate sensation, creating a consumer-propelled fad made possible by changes in the public audiences for science and in French society in general. Crowds gathered to meet the giraffe all along her walk to Paris, and her image found its way onto political cartoons, broadsides, and a plethora of everyday items from fans and beaded purses to clothing irons and fireplace grilles.

Collectively, these five "encounters" gave us the opportunity to explore the material and visual practices of French natural history over forty tumultuous years, from the French Revolution to the July Monarchy. The encounters also gave rise to the topics addressed in "Of Pictures & Specimens: Natural History in Post-Revolutionary and Restoration France," a symposium held at the APS in December 2011 that convened French and American scholars from different disciplines. Their work, which probes the exhibition content more deeply, is assembled in this volume, along with the commentaries and discussions that followed each session.

Richard Burkhardt, in his keynote essay, draws a parallel between the process of controlling, deploying, and civilizing natural history specimens and the production of good citizens in the new French republic. Just as the Muséum d'Histoire naturelle, founded in 1793, was to be of great utility to the nation both economically and morally, the appreciation of nature was believed essential to the moral development of the French people. "Controlling nature," he writes, "was taken as an index of civilization." Several other essays also consider how the order of nature, the order of society, and the public role of science intersected at this time.

The exhibition's focus on the gardens at the Muséum and Malmaison inspired essays that further examine activities at both sites. A salient theme that emerges in "About Gardens and Gardening" is the desire to improve agriculture, especially food production. Bernard Chevallier and Susan Taylor-Leduc both discuss Josephine's role as a promoter of agriculture as well as a connoisseur of flowers. Leduc also argues that Josephine exploited Malmaison

Fig. 1.8

Plate with Paradise
Tanager (*Tangara chilensis*,
"Septicolor"), from South
American Birds Service,
1819–20, hard paste por-
celain; bird by Pauline Knip,
border and perch by J. F. C.
Leloi. Hillwood Estate,
Museum & Gardens,
Washington, D.C. Bequest
of Marjorie Merriweather
Post, 1973. Photo by
E. Owen

as an emblem of national identity by providing a vibrant example of land ownership and prosperity. Paula Young Lee brings to life debates over whether the Muséum was to be a site for agriculture or botany. Her essay explores a little-known, unrealized architectural project that would have displaced the working poor of the Sans-Culottes neighborhood near the Muséum in order to annex more land—acreage that would have been used for an experimental model farm. As with Malmaison, the intent was to improve the ability of France to feed its people and to make the country more prosperous. A final essay, by Antoine Jacobsohn, explores the practical impact of the discovery of plant sexuality. He distinguishes the work of botanists, who focused on identifying new species, from that of gardeners and commercial fruit and vegetable producers, whose goal was to meet the needs of the masses through varietal stability and crop reliability.

In "Cultivating Useful Knowledge," two essays consider transnational activities and their complex relationship to ever-shifting political and cultural differences. Each speaker presents a case study in a context that differs sig-nificantly from the settings most frequently discussed in recent literature on French natural history as a colonizing activity. Elizabeth Hyde considers André Michaux's botanizing mission in North America, revealing his skill in deploying "a cosmopolitan and scientific identity" in the New World. Her work clarifies another theme implied in letters and other documents shown in the exhibition: the increasing importance of the New World as a source of information and knowledge for European scientists. Elise Lipkowitz presents another view of transnational scientific activity in her examination of the French seizure of natural history collections in Holland during the 1790s. She argues that a new ideology linking natural history to moral reform and political regeneration gave revolutionary-era French naturalists the license to seize natural history objects as war booty.

Representations of flora and fauna in this period stood at the cross-roads of art and science. Then as now, visual imagery was an essential part of natural history practice, and the investigation of its methods, styles, and uses in both the exhibition and the symposium revealed underlying scientific and aesthetic assumptions of the time. The essays in "Making Art, Communicating Science" thus offer fruitful new insights into natural history renderings of the period, whether addressing the illustrations in the Muséum's *Annales du Muséum national d'Histoire naturelle* or the influence of Redouté on high art painting. Pierre-Yves Lacour analyzes the severe black-and-white illustrations of the *Annales*, which convey the maximum amount of information in the most

economical way, showing how "truth" trumped beauty in images destined for the scientific community. Dorothy Johnson explores the flourishing of botanical representations and their influence on still-life and mythological painting. Her argument revolves around Redouté, whose unique contribution, in her words, was to unite "careful scientific or objective description and observation with the dazzling beauty of art." Because his depictions of flowers transcend the principal objectives of botanical illustrations and give the impression that they are portraits of individual blossoms, his work inspired painters such as Jacques-Louis David, François Gérard, Anne-Louis Girodet, and Jean Baptiste Isabey. In an essay about the representation of animals, Madeleine Pinault Sørensen analyzes several examples of artworks that capture the personalities and behaviors of mammals such as lions and elephants. She explores how artists' newfound interest in observing live animals resulted in images of greater empathy.

Finally, two other scholars, Anne Lafont and Daniel Harkett, address representations of the "Other." Lafont considers drawings of Aboriginal

Fig. 1.9

Pierre-Joseph Redouté, Blush-Colored Crinum (*Crinum erubescens,* "Crinum rougeâtre"), 1802–5, watercolor on vellum, study for *Les Lilacées*, vol. 1 (Paris, 1805). Arader Galleries

peoples encountered in Australia during the Baudin expedition of 1800–4. She situates these images within Daston's and Galison's history of the notion of objectivity, but ultimately argues that their credibility resided in the relationship between the images' producers and recipients. This leads her to conclude that "objectivity" itself was a "communal social construction, a common language" from which to build an exchange or knowledge about the "Other." In another essay, Daniel Harkett analyzes the ever-changing roles played by the African keepers that are pictured in representations of the Egyptian giraffe in 1826 and 1827. He discusses how both the giraffe and her keepers became interchangeable stand-ins for a variety of ethnic "Others," including the six Osage Indians who were also in Paris in 1827.

In "Natural History and French Culture," scholars consider the impact of natural history on political, social, and cultural life. In another essay on the giraffe, Alain Lescart reveals how, in the face of King Charles X's move to censor the press, the famous giraffe herself became a mouthpiece for freedom of the press in numerous politically charged prints and pamphlets. In an essay about the birth of the social sciences, John Tresch argues that the Enlightenment notion of the "Great Chain of Being," though already superseded by new, nineteenth-century ideas about the history of life on earth, was still very much alive. He explores various proposals for remaking society in the early to mid-nineteenth century, from the Saint-Simonian reform movement to the new science of sociology. Tresch shows how the emerging field of "social science," in its blueprints for human progress, employed concepts such as the Chain of Being and other ideas and methodologies from natural history, notably those of classifying and serializing.

Denise Davidson's essay directly addresses the audience for natural science at the time, examining in particular the explosion of interest in the giraffe—a phenomenon distinct from previous scientific fads. She proposes three reasons for this difference: the expansion of the press and changes in popular culture; the beginning of the modern "consumer revolution"; and new attitudes toward exotic "Others," now encapsulated in the term "Orientalism." Finally, just as Dorothy Johnson's essay links natural history imagery in France

Fig. 1.10

Venus Flytrap (*Dionaea muscipula*), collected by André Michaux in North Carolina in 1797, herbarium sheet. MNHN

to paintings displayed in the annual Parisian Salons, Claudine Cohen and Göran Blix examine how modalities of natural history practice were embodied in French literature, poetry, and historical writing as well as in scientific illustration. Cohen analyzes the impact of paleontology and geology, two new sciences dealing with prehistory, on French writers in the first several decades of the nineteenth century. Discussing the profound impact of "deep time" and citing a wide range of authors, from François-René de Chateaubriand to Louis Bouilhet to Jules Michelet, she explores the contradiction between the rational understanding of the history of life developed by naturalists at the time and the imaginary and irrational visions such writers often evoked. This contradiction, she notes, even appeared in the work of Georges Cuvier himself, a scientist who wanted to equal Isaac Newton but who wrote poetic texts that conjured imaginary worlds in the name of science.

Göran Blix explores Honoré Balzac's understanding of natural history methodologies and the impact it had on his description of "the various social species that peopled nineteenth-century France." Drawing on numerous

Fig. 1.11

William Bartram, Venus Flytrap (*Dionaea muscipula*), ca. 1803, colored engraving after engraving by James Roberts, after drawings by John Ellis. APS

examples in *La Comédie humaine*, he argues that despite the author's lifelong praise of Cuvier and his own mania for classifying, Balzac never appropriated Cuvier's "fixist" viewpoint. Rather, the "unity of life" set forth by Cuvier's rival Geoffroy Saint-Hilaire gave Balzac license to look beyond strict divisions and to capture the "infinite variety" of human character. Blix proposes that for Balzac, natural history did not provide a perfect model for categorizing the human social condition, but rather served as a rich literary tool for creating an infinite variety of characters—Parisian "species" that could be tentatively classified but never contained. These characters, Blix concludes, resemble more "a cabinet of curiosities than a well-ordered museum of natural history."

In addition to the presenters, the session chairs— Carol Solomon, Sara S. Gronim, Paula Young Lee, and Andrea Goulet—offered provocative responses to the speakers' papers and moderated the interdisciplinary discussions that followed each session. Edited versions of these commentaries and discussions are included in this volume. At the end of the symposium, Bernadette Bensaude-Vincent and Anne Lafont presented their reflections on the issues raised by the symposium as a whole. Their remarks are published here under the title "French Natural History: Reflecting Back, Looking Forward." Historian of science Bensaude-Vincent raises questions about the exact meaning of the word "popularization" in the context of science in post-revolutionary and Restoration France. Using Empress Josephine's botanical pursuits and the giraffe craze as examples, she proposes that the scientific practices in question merged aspects of later, Victorian-style popularization with an eighteenth-century "culture of curiosities," confounding the two genres as they are usually defined. Lafont, an art historian, focuses in part on the interdisciplinary tools natural historians mobilized in postrevolutionary France. She proposes considering the symposium's arguments about collaboration between scientists, artists, and politicians in relation to Bruno Latour's provocative comment "we have never been modern," a statement complicating the idea that modernity entailed the atomizing of knowledge into contained disciplines.

Collectively, the essays, along with the perceptive commentaries and discussions, contain new scholarship on the golden age of French natural history and propose new challenges for future exploration. The authors and discussants reveal the complex intersections of material and visual culture in natural history practice at the time. They also examine numerous reciprocal influences between scientific work and the contexts in which it took place, both in France and around the world, including North America. It is our hope that their work will foster an expanding range of interdisciplinary approaches to the study of nature in this period and its relationship to the larger, multi-faceted milieus and cultures in which it operated.

Fig. 1.12

Royal Porcelain Manufacture, Berlin (KPM), Plate with Venus Flytrap (*Dionaea muscipula*), ca. 1809, porcelain (plants after P. J. Redouté). Twinight Collection

Note on the text: All translations from the French are by the individual authors or the translator unless otherwise indicated. For the most part, eighteenth- and nineteenth-century spelling, accents, punctuation, and capitalization in French and English quotations have been retained, though some minor typographical errors have been corrected silently. The discussions for each section, derived from transcripts of the question and answer sessions during the symposium, have been edited for length and clarity.

SUE ANN PRINCE

1 For essays, illustrations, and a checklist of the exhibition, see Sue Ann Prince, ed., *Stuffing Birds, Pressing Plants, Shaping Knowledge: Natural History in North America, 1730–1860* (Philadelphia: American Philosophical Society, 2003).

2 Gillispie and Outram have written highly influential histories of the social and political dimensions of French natural history in this period. See Charles Gillispie, *Science and Polity in France at the End of the Old Regime* (Princeton, N.J.: Princeton University Press, 1980) and *Science and Polity in France: The Revolutionary and Napoleonic Years* (Princeton, N.J.: Princeton University Press, 2004); and Dorinda Outram, "Politics and Vocation: French Science, 1793–1830," *British Journal for the History of Science*, 13, no. 1 (March 1980): 27–43, and *Georges Cuvier: Science, Vocation and Authority in Post-Revolutionary France* (Manchester: Manchester University Press, 1984). There are a few exceptions to this generalization about the emphasis on the British context for North American natural history. James E. McClellan III's work on science in France's American colonial possessions is a notable example, especially his 1992 book *Colonialism and Science: Saint Domingue in the Old Regime*, since reprinted with a new introduction (Chicago: University of Chicago Press, 2010). A later McClellan article is particularly relevant to Michaux: "André Michaux and French Botanical Networks at the End of the Old Regime," *Castanea: Occasional Papers in Eastern Botany* 2 (December 2004): 69–97. However, as of 2002, most sources that described connections between the French and American communities of science did not make these connections their primary focus. See, for example, British historian E. C. Spary's *Utopia's Garden: French Natural History from Old Regime to Revolution*

(Chicago: University of Chicago Press, 2000).

3 The recent book *Knowing Nature*, foremost among scholarly works on science in early Philadelphia, is an excellent starting point for researchers exploring the topic. Amy R. W. Meyers, ed., *Knowing Nature: Art and Science in Philadelphia, 1740–1840* (New Haven, Conn.: Yale University Press, 2011).

4 We wished to locate the French images within the changes in scientific image-making that Daston and Galison document from the late eighteenth through the mid-nineteenth centuries. They describe it as shift from a "truth-to-nature" epistemology, with a goal of picturing an ideal type or norm for each species, which requires a subjective interpretation on the part of the artist, to a quest for "mechanical" objectivity, with the intent of recording the particularities of an individual specimen as presented to the eye, presumably with no subjective intervention. Chapter 2 of *Objectivity* is particularly relevant to this exhibition. It outlines the characteristics of the "truth-to-nature" framework and mentions conflicts between naturalists and artists regarding proper methods of depicting specimens. Lorraine Daston and Peter Galison, *Objectivity* (New York: Zone Books, 2007).

5 "Veuillez faire récolter pour moi une grande quantité de graines des végétaux de l'Amérique Septentrionale . . . car vous n'ignorez pas que la culture des plantes étrangères fait mes délices. Mr Roux Bordier est un botaniste plein de zèle; il veut enrichir le sol de la France des plus précieuses productions végétales des Etats-Unis, et doit m'adresser les collections des graines qu'il formera." Josephine Bonaparte to Jean-François Soult, 3 thermidor an 12 [July 22, 1804], Archives du Musée de Malmaison,

MM.40.47.2751, printed in *L'Impératrice Joséphine et les sciences naturelles* (Rueil-Malmaison: Musée national des châteaux de Malmaison et Bois-Préau; Paris: Éditions de la Réunion des musées nationaux, 1997), 198.

02

KEYNOTE ADDRESS: CIVILIZING SPECIMENS AND CITIZENS AT THE MUSÉUM D'HISTOIRE NATURELLE, 1793–1838

RICHARD W. BURKHARDT, JR.

ON THE TWENTY-FOURTH OF MAY, 1827, four days after leaving Marseille with the first live giraffe ever to set foot on French soil (**FIG. 2.1**), Professor Étienne Geoffroy Saint-Hilaire of the Paris Muséum d'Histoire naturelle was pleased with how well his trip back to Paris was going. He expressed his satisfaction in a letter to the Comte de Villeneuve, the prefect in Marseille who had served as the giraffe's host over the winter. Well acquainted with the giraffe and its exotic handlers (and having helped make the arrangements for the giraffe's safe transport to Paris), Villeneuve understood precisely of what and of whom Geoffroy wrote when Geoffroy allowed that it would be difficult to proceed better: "Each knows what he has to do, and each is at his station. I say this of all the animals and people. . . . [This morning] as soon as the giraffe saw the cows start to leave, she herself started off before the order from her chief groom, Khassen, who himself is glorious as a peacock holding the lead rope."[1]

Geoffroy explained that the Arab Khassen had feared that the lead position might be given to Barthélemy, a stable hand from Marseille. Instead, Barthélemy had been put in charge of the rear rope on the giraffe's left side, while Atir, a black African (and former servant of the French consul in Cairo) held the rear rope on the right. A fourth stable hand, a young black French-Egyptian named Youssef, led the cows. As Geoffroy contentedly noted: "This order is followed very exactly. Each is properly at his post; each, beast and man alike, has taken well to the spirit of his state as a traveler."[2]

Having animals and people in their proper places appealed greatly to Geoffroy. This was a concern he had shared with his fellow professors at the Muséum d'Histoire naturelle in Paris ever since its founding in 1793. From the start, each of the twelve professors was responsible for teaching a course on his particular subject. Each was also responsible for organizing and developing the collections under his charge. Collectively, the twelve professors administered the Muséum's diverse operations.[3]

Natural history was viewed with favor during the Revolution not only because of its economic utility but also because of the perceived moral power of nature's images. Through observing well-ordered *tableaux* of nature's productions, it was believed, French citizens would gain a deeper appreciation of their own place in nature and the social order, and their moral and social sentiments would be elevated accordingly.[4] The Muséum's efforts to create order were made visible to the public in the institution's gardens, greenhouses, and galleries. As of the fall of 1793, the Muséum also had a makeshift menagerie. The main structure that housed the animals was quickly labeled as "provisional," perhaps reflecting the recognition that seeing animals reduced to miserable existences in cramped, unhealthy cages was more likely to degrade a citizen's moral sentiments than enhance them (**FIG. 2.2**).[5] While the professors took care to nurture ideas regarding the Muséum's economic and moral value to the Republic, they also pursued other, less immediately utilitarian enterprises of classifying nature's diverse products and seeking to understand its basic processes. But whether the Muséum was improving the rural economy, elevating the morals of the citizenry, classifying nature's productions, or understanding nature's operations, one basic activity was crucial to its successful functioning. This was the control of specimens. Through a variety of interrelated practices, specimens were made more and more suited to the needs of science and society. In effect, they became increasingly *civilized.*[6]

The progressive control and civilization of specimens involved diverse operations, including acquiring (in the Muséum's early history this often meant *confiscating*), transporting, identifying, naming, describing, classifying, preserving, portraying, dissecting, reconstructing, arranging, displaying, distributing, exchanging, planting, taming, training, multiplying, acclimatizing, domesticating, and interpreting.

The connection between the development of civilization and the civilizing of specimens was understood to work at several levels. In the mid-eighteenth century, the great naturalist Georges Louis Leclerc, the Comte de Buffon, maintained that a nation's level of civilization could be gauged by its success in adapting the products of nature to its own needs: the more

Fig. 2.1

J. R. Brascassat, *Passage de la girafe à Arnay-le-Duc*, 1827, oil on canvas. Musée des Beaux-Arts de Beaune. Photo: J.-C. Couval

Fig. 2.2

An early illustration of the "provisional menagerie" of the Muséum d'histoire naturelle. Date and illustrator unknown. © MNHN, Dist. RMN-GP / image du MNHN, Bibliothèque centrale

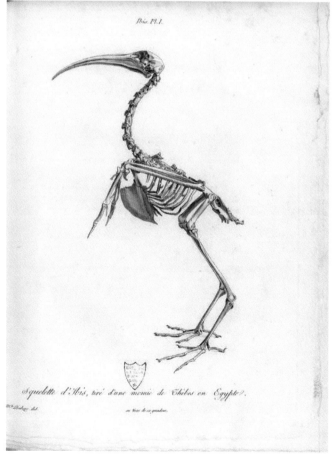

Fig. 2.3

The skeleton of a sacred ibis, from a mummy taken from a tomb in Thebes. From Georges Cuvier, "Mémoire sur l'Ibis des anciens Égyptiens," *Annales du Muséum national d'Histoire naturelle* 4 (1804), pl. 1, p. 116. © MNHN, Bibliothèque centrale

a people succeeded in domesticating plants and animals, the greater their distance from the state of savagery.[7] During the Revolution, leaders asserted (as noted above) that exposure to the right sort of images of nature would have a civilizing effect on a citizenry that remained in need of moral improvement. On yet another level, the development of the world's greatest natural history collection came to be viewed not simply as a matter of national pride but also as testimony that France had become the new leader of world civilization.[8] Significantly, when the French confiscated natural history specimens in other European countries, they not only celebrated these spoils as trophies of war. They also rationalized their prizes as objects liberated for the benefit of all humankind.[9] When one of the menagerie's lionesses gave birth in 1800 to three cubs, this too was hailed as a triumph of civilization. The lion keeper linked the cubs' births with France's military prowess by naming the cubs Marengo, Jemmapes, and Fleurus after the sites of three important French military victories.[10]

Specimens Geoffroy Saint-Hilaire brought back from Napoleon's scientific expedition to Egypt provide an additional, striking example of the "civilizing" process. When Geoffroy's colleagues assessed his collections, they observed that his successes had been made possible by French military might on the one hand and the peculiar superstitions of the ancient Egyptians on the other.[11] Of the ancient Egyptians the Muséum's naturalists wrote: "These bizarre people, in embalming with so much care the creatures they had made the objects of their stupid adoration, have left us nearly complete zoological collections in their sacred grottoes."[12] This fortuitous circumstance would allow scientists of the present to ask "whether species change form over the course of time."[13] In brief, objects assembled for the strange and different purposes of a people of the past would, under the eye of modern scientists, shed new truths about nature—truths then to be shared with the whole civilized world (**FIG. 2.3**).

Offering broad claims about the relations between the ordering of nature and the development of civilization was one matter, but making specimens conform to the needs of scientists and citizens was quite another. In numerous mundane ways, specimens resisted the demands made upon them. Live plants or animals could fail to survive and reproduce in the places where naturalists or governments tried to establish them. Domesticated plants or animals could revert to their wild forms. Live animals could also bite, kick, inflict grievous damage with a swipe of their claws, transmit diseases, behave in ways that their viewers regarded as obscene, or simply run away. Dead specimens could lose their forms or colors. They could decompose. They could stink. They could suffer the ravages of insects. They could lose much of their scientific value if information once associated with them, such as where they came from, went astray. Specimens could also become matters of dispute with respect to who owned them, who had the right to work with them, where to display them, or how they were to be understood. The zoologist Jean-Baptiste Lamarck famously disagreed, for example, with the anti-evolutionary conclusions that his colleague Georges Cuvier sought to draw from the mummified specimens Geoffroy brought back from Egypt.[14] In the realm of politics, furthermore, specimens became the occasion more than once for authors to express seditious sentiments.[15]

As these last examples suggest, controlling citizens could be as problematic as controlling specimens. Beyond the problems associated with simply handling the large numbers of visitors who flocked to see special creatures like the elephants or the giraffe, the Muséum had to instruct visitors not to pick the flowers, not to feed the animals or throw stones at them, and not to encourage their dogs to chase the herbivores in their pens. Unauthorized food vendors and unscrupulous *conducteurs* (guides) had to be banned from the grounds. The animal keepers had to be forbidden from extorting bribes from the public to see the animals up close or outside of regular viewing hours.

Even the professors occasionally had to be reminded not to abuse their positions. In the fall of 1796, the animal anatomist Mertrud warned his colleagues that in a time of great scarcity it was a scandal to hear that professors and staff of the Muséum were feeding their own domestic animals with the fodder the government had intended for the animals of the menagerie.[16] As for the Muséum's dealings with the government, these required a continuous process of negotiation and mutual instruction. Such exchanges usually proceeded smoothly enough, but the professors bristled whenever it seemed that the government was threatening to limit the powers of self-government originally granted to the Muséum in 1793.[17] They also protested when Lucien Bonaparte, as interior minister, insisted in 1800 that the Muséum make the public pay to visit the natural history galleries and to see the elephants.[18]

These brief examples serve to remind us that a host of diverse interests intersected at the Muséum. The general public, the professors, the staff, government representatives, artists, authors, and a wealth of other actors ranging from pickpockets to foreign princes came to the institution with diverse agendas. In the best of situations, this intersection of interests led to the kinds of symbiotic relations where each party had a civilizing influence on the other. In other situations, the different parties simply followed their own inclinations. If a basic level of order was maintained and the Muséum's own interests were not jeopardized, the institution could be content.

A closer look at several different cases in the Muséum's history will help illuminate the theme of civilizing specimens and citizens. We begin with the special, two-day "festival of liberty" held in Paris on 9–10 Thermidor, Year VI of the Republic (July 27–28, 1798), the fourth anniversary of the fall of Robespierre. Like other festivals of the revolutionary period, this festival was designed to offer a great spectacle that would raise the spirits of the citizenry and inspire feelings of patriotism and social solidarity. Although the festival's broad theme was liberty, its more immediate purpose was to celebrate the triumphal entry into Paris of the treasures of science, literature, and art ceded to France upon Napoleon's military victories in Italy. The festival dramatically signaled the change in control of objects and, more generally, the establishment of France as the new center of civilization and culture.[19] The art treasures from Italy were truly extraordinary. While the natural history specimens were not nearly as consequential—certainly not as important as those confiscated from the Stadholder in Holland several years previously—they featured very prominently in the overall *tableau*.

The festival began with a neo-Roman victory parade (**FIG. 2.4**) that assembled on the left bank of the Seine, outside the Muséum d'Histoire naturelle, where the crates of treasures just arrived from Italy had been held in safekeeping for a week and a half.[20] Leading the *cortège* were a troupe of cavalry and a military band. Right after the band, under a banner bearing the words "Histoire Naturelle," came the professors of the Muséum. They were followed by students and other friends of natural history and ten wagons loaded with natural history specimens, including minerals, fossils, the seeds of foreign plants, some live exotic plants, three African lions, a bear, agricultural tools from Italy, and two blocks of crystal. Between the wagon carrying the bear and the wagon carrying the tools walked a pair of camels and a pair of dromedaries. Interestingly enough, none of the live exotic plants and animals had been acquired on the Italian campaign.[21] Their conspicuous display in the parade served nonetheless as testimony to the reach of France's power.[22]

A second division of six wagons carrying manuscripts, rare books, medals, and more followed the natural history division. Then came a third division of twenty-nine wagons carrying the treasures of art. The first two of the wagons of the third division bore the famous bronze horses of San Marco. Accompanying these two divisions were more professors and students, plus actors, artists, and choirs singing patriotic hymns. The whole procession marched slowly from the Muséum d'Histoire naturelle to the Champ de Mars where, in what remained of that day and throughout the next day, solemn ceremonies and military exercises were held. There was also the ascent of an *aérostat*—a balloon decorated with garlands and inscriptions and trailing the tricolor flag. In the evenings there were music and dancing.[23]

The Muséum's professor of agriculture, André Thouin, had been one of the commissioners responsible for collecting the objects of science and the arts in Italy, and he had played a major role in urging that the trophies of the Italian campaign be displayed in a festival of this sort. Thouin officially presented the trophies from the Italian campaign to the minister of the interior when the procession arrived at the Champs de Mars.[24] One can well imagine that he and his colleagues took considerable satisfaction in marching at the head of the parade. They had reason to believe that the government regarded the successful pursuit of natural history as an integral part of France's claims to national glory and to being the leader of world civilization. Citizens observing the parade could be expected to understand the same.

Nonetheless, some of the Muséum's naturalists may well have felt that the government funds spent on this lavish festival could have been better directed towards addressing the institution's most pressing needs. Just two months earlier, Muséum director Antoine de Jussieu had written a long letter to the Executive Directory explaining that the institution was "menaced with imminent destruction."[25] In his words, "the rich and immense collections which give [the Muséum] its preeminence and its utility, these precious properties of the Republic, these glorious trophies of our victories, are close to being annihilated."[26] The Muséum lacked the facilities, he said, to keep alive the various living plants and animals that were continually arriving. Meanwhile, countless dead specimens remained in boxes because the new natural history gallery was not yet finished. Their preservation was in jeopardy. Humidity and insects were taking their toll. The Muséum desperately needed funds for preparing and preserving specimens, completing the new gallery, and making its collections visible to the public. It also needed a new menagerie, one with ample parks and cages for the Muséum's animals, in particular the two elephants that had just come from Holland and various other exotic creatures soon to arrive from Africa. All these animals

Fig. 2.4

The "Festival of Liberty" of 1798. *Entrée triomphale des monuments des sciences et des arts en France; fête à ce sujet. Les 9 et 10 thermidor an 6e de la République*. Engraved by Berthault after a drawing by Girardet. © MNHN, Dist. RMN-GP / image du MNHN, Bibliothèque centrale

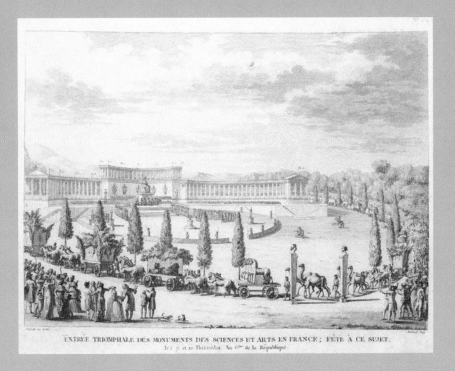

Fig. 2.5

J. P. Hoüel's illustration of how the elephants caressed each other upon first hearing music played for them. From J. P. Hoüel, *Histoire naturelle des deux éléphans, mâle et femelle, du Muséum de Paris* (Paris, 1803), plate XV. © MNHN, Bibliothèque centrale

were likely to perish soon, Jussieu warned, if better living conditions were not provided for them.[27] When the festival of liberty took place two months later, the Muséum's multiple problems were far from being resolved.

As it happened, it was only six days after Jussieu wrote to the Directory about the danger of the elephants dying that the two animals put on a display of behavior that had onlookers thinking that the animals might soon be reproducing (**FIG. 2.5**). This behavior was elicited by a remarkable experiment.[28] Fourteen musicians from the Conservatoire de musique, the Théâtre des Arts, and the Théâtre Pideau came to the Muséum to perform a concert for the elephants. These were highly accomplished artists. Among them was François Devienne, the flutist and composer regarded as "the French Mozart."[29] The interest the musicians showed for the elephants was in no way farfetched, given that the elephant was reputed to be the most intelligent of all the animals (other than humans). The elephant was said to

RICHARD W. BURKHARDT, JR.

have a sense of decorum as well. It was alleged to be so modest that it took care to hide its lovemaking away from the eyes of prying observers. Scientists did not even know which mating position it adopted. As an intelligent and emotionally sensitive creature, the elephant was a plausible candidate for a study of music's impact on a non-human being. The musicians' intent was to see whether the elephants experienced different emotions depending on the character of the music and the key in which it was played.[30]

The elephants provide a particularly good example of the myriad interests that people brought to their engagement with the Muséum's specimens. Reminiscent of the ancient parable of the three blind men who each touched a different part of an elephant, leading to three strikingly divergent accounts of the kind of animal they had encountered, various people were attracted to the Muséum's elephants in diverse ways. Georges Toscan, the Muséum's librarian, was most interested in how the music seemed to awaken the elephants sexually. Toscan, the author of a number of articles designed to develop a love of nature in citizens, described the elephants' romantic responses to the concert in some detail. He also offered the encouraging news that several nights after the concert the elephant's keeper heard a noise in their enclosure and quietly came in to check. The keeper found the female lying on her back on the ground with the male standing above her, his legs apart and making a motion. "As soon as they were discovered," Toscan recounted, "the male very adroitly disengaged his legs [and] made a half turn to the side, making it easy for the female to get up."[31] Toscan concluded that this news, together with the postures the female had displayed in the course of the concert, established the elephants' true mating position beyond doubt. He went on to speculate on the romantic conditions under which the elephants might be induced to mate: a new park, more freedom, ample food, "the joy of seeing each other after a more or less extended separation," "the season of spring, which invites all beings to lovemaking," a moonlit night, and then, when all else was quiet, the sound of music.[32]

Others attracted to the elephants included the artist J. P. Hoüel, who devoted two months to studying and drawing the animals and eventually published a long book about them.[33] Meanwhile, at the Théâtre du Vaudeville, a troupe of performers put on a play entitled *Le Concert aux Éléphans*.[34] The Muséum's naturalists, in contrast, did not hurry to make the elephants a special topic of study. They did not test the animals' intellectual abilities, record detailed observations of their behavior, or offer suggestions about how to get them to mate in captivity.[35] Not until 1801 did any of them write about the elephants. What is more, the article Georges Cuvier wrote in 1801 served to undermine Toscan's most interesting claims. Cuvier related that an Englishman named Corse had published a paper reporting that the coupling of elephants "is entirely like that of the horse and lasts approximately the same time."[36] Cuvier further noted that while much had been made of how excited the Muséum's elephants became during the concert played for them, they displayed the same behavior when they were provided with a new bathing pool. The effects of music on elephants, Cuvier remarked, were in any case no greater than the effects of music on dogs.[37] Cuvier did express the hope, however, that the elephant might one day be domesticated and bred.

For most of the Muséum's naturalists, and for Cuvier in particular, specimens only became worthy of scientific study after they died. When the Muséum's male elephant died on the morning of January 7, 1802, Cuvier was given charge of turning the menagerie's misfortune into a scientific opportunity (FIG. 2.6). The putrefying cadaver had to be rendered useful for the purposes of science and civilization. Under Cuvier's direction, his assistant Pierre Rousseau spent nearly forty days dissecting the body while Nicolas Maréchal, the Muséum's animal artist, withstood the horrible stench of the process to produce more than eighty illustrations of the elephant's diverse parts.[38] The animal's skin was detached from its body and sent away for

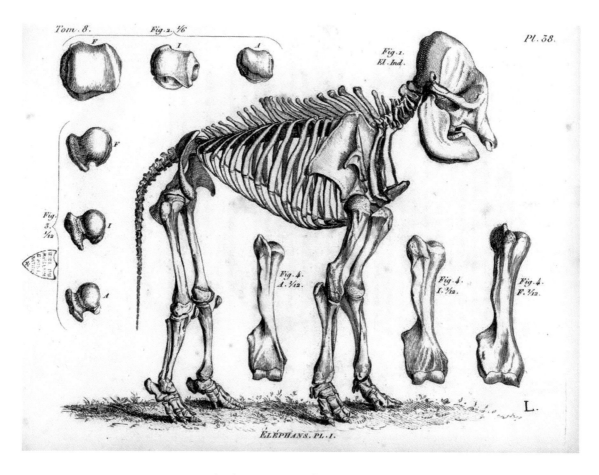

Fig. 2.6

While the elephant's skin was stuffed for exhibition in the natural history galleries, the elephant's bones were reassembled to become part of the comparative anatomy collection. From Georges Cuvier, "Sur les éléphans vivants et fossiles," *Annales du Muséum national d'Histoire naturelle*, vol. 8 (1806), plate 1, p. 154. © MNHN, Bibliothèque centrale

preservation by a tanner. Its bones were cleaned by putting them in maceration barrels where chemicals ate away the remaining flesh. Lassaigne, the Muséum's carpenter and machinist, set about building a wooden frame on which to mount the skin. In the fall of the following year, Geoffroy Saint-Hilaire announced to his colleagues that the elephant's skin had been placed on the wooden manikin and that the result was a perfectly life-like illusion.[39] A month and a half later, Geoffroy reported that the elephant was "completely prepared" and asked for authorization to have it placed in the natural history galleries. The professors approved his request, inviting him "to take the swiftest measures to let the public enjoy the sight of this great animal."[40] The elephant's reincarnation as a stuffed specimen for the public's pleasure and edification had taken two full years.

Guidebooks to the Muséum afford additional perspectives on the civilizing of specimens and citizens. When a minor flurry of small guidebooks began appearing near the turn of the century, the Muséum declared these were unauthorized, detrimental to science, and not to be sold within the gates.[41] But visitors wanted more guidance than a specimen's Latin name, which was typically all the Muséum provided.[42] It thus fell to the unauthorized guidebook writers to offer the broader "histories" of different species, or to tell stories about particular specimens—such as the pair of wolves that ate their pups every year. The books not only directed visitors to where the specimens were located; the guides also told people what to think about the specimens and the establishment that housed them. An anonymous guidebook of 1803 even spelled out for visitors the particular *emotions*—such as curiosity, patriotism, surprise, fear, joy, delight, admiration, gratitude, and awe—they could be expected to *feel* on their visits to the Muséum.[43]

Comparing Muséum guidebooks from successive years allows one to track the arrival of specimens and their movement from one place to another. Such comparisons illuminate different stages in the control of specimens and also reveal occasions when specimens escaped the Muséum's grasp. One such instance involved the pair of kangaroos the Muséum purchased in England in 1802. These animals were heralded in two different guidebooks of 1803, but no mention of them was made in the menagerie guide that Frédéric Cuvier published in 1804.[44] Cuvier did not mention them because they were no longer there. They had been transported to Malmaison, the estate of Josephine Bonaparte (**FIG. 2.7**).

The bare outlines of this story are as follows. When *Le Géographe*, the second of the two ships of the Baudin expedition to Australia, returned to France in the spring of 1804, the Muséum sent Geoffroy Saint-Hilaire to the port of Lorient to ascertain the nature and condition of the collections, to take care of the necessary formalities and paperwork, and "to take the surest means of seeing that all these objects arrive at the Muséum in the best state of conservation possible."[45] When Geoffroy arrived at Lorient, however, he learned that not all the specimens would be going to the Muséum after all, because Josephine, the wife of First Consul Napoleon Bonaparte, had laid claim to some of them.[46]

Some of the specimens arriving on *Le Géographe* had actually been destined for Josephine in the first place. Among these were several panthers, a gnu, and a zebra, all put aboard ship at the Cape of Good Hope. Josephine did not want the panthers, but she did want the gnu, the creature that in Geoffroy's eyes was "the most beautiful animal of this expedition, the most inconceivable with respect to its form."[47] She also decided to take the zebra. In addition, she laid claim to the entire collection of forty or so tortoises.

Fig. 2.7

Kangaroos, emus, and black swans at Malmaison. François Peron and C. A. Lesueur, Title page illustration, engraved by Frères Lambert, from atlas vol. of *Voyage de decouvertes aux terres australes*, by C. A. Lesueur and N. M. Petit (Paris, 1807). Malmaison. RMN / Art Resource, N.Y.

What she had wanted most of all from the Baudin expedition, however, were live kangaroos to populate the grounds of Malmaison. At one point, while still in Australian waters, *Le Géographe* had eighteen live kangaroos on board, but by the time the ship reached the port of Lorient only three of them remained alive. One died before it could be disembarked. Another was loaded onto one of the wagons for Malmaison but expired en route. That left but a single live kangaroo from the whole expedition, which was obviously insufficient for the project of naturalizing and propagating kangaroos at Josephine's estate.

Soon after the gnu and the zebra reached Malmaison, Josephine decided to give both creatures to the Muséum. Recognizing the need to make a magnanimous gesture in return, the Muséum opted to give Josephine its two live kangaroos.[48] Chemist Antoine François, the Comte de Fourcroy, then director of the Muséum, wrote obsequiously to Josephine to tell her that the kangaroos were on the way to her and that she, in taking them and establishing them at Malmaison, would be doing natural history—and the kangaroos—a great favor. "Everything leads me to believe, Madame," Fourcroy wrote, "that the new abode will render them infinitely more interesting for natural history than [did] the one that they inhabited up to the present. For this all they need is a larger space and a little tranquility."[49]

The Muséum, however, was not genuinely thrilled by this arrangement. Although the institution took care to praise Josephine profusely in all of their mutual dealings, it regarded the transfer of the kangaroos to Malmaison as a loss to science. In this particular instance of the control of specimens, the Muséum did not get what it wanted. Nor had it gotten what it wanted the year before, when the first ship from the Baudin expedition returned to France with a pair of black swans on board. Josephine claimed the swans for herself. The Muséum was unhappy about this, but it did not get first choice.

Josephine died on May 29, 1814. Three days later, at their first regular meeting after Josephine's death, the professors decided to inform Aimé Bonpland, Malmaison's head botanist, of the Muséum's continued interest in the Australian animals.[50] The *procès-verbal* (minutes) of the professors' meeting a week later states: "Measures will be taken to try to obtain from the proprietors of Malmaison the kangaroos and the black swans that are deposited there and that had belonged to the Muséum."[51] In the end, however, their efforts failed.[52]

That same year and especially the following year, after Napoleon's defeat at Waterloo, the professors of the Muséum found the shoe on the other foot as the agents of various countries sought to reclaim the specimens the French had taken from them during the previous two decades of military conquest. The most worrisome of these demands came from the Dutch. Elise Lipkowitz has illuminated how the French succeeded in deflecting the Dutch demand for the return of the Stadholder's collection, offering them duplicates from the Baudin expedition instead while pushing the cosmopolitan claim that the collections in Paris in fact existed for the benefit of *all* civilized society.[53]

On balance, France's military defeat proved to be a boon for the Muséum rather than a loss because the cessation of hostilities led to the restoration of the freedom of the seas. This allowed for reconnection with various parts of the world in which France and the Muséum were keenly interested. The Muséum's publication in 1818 of a standard set of instructions for French colonial officials, sea captains, and other citizens identified the kinds of specimens the Muséum especially wanted. It also described how to collect them, preserve them, make notes about them, and send them safely to France.[54] This initiative, interestingly enough, came from the government. So too did the suggestion of founding a special school for naturalist voyagers, where the Muséum would train young men to be effective collectors abroad.[55]

A pair of events from 1837–38 provides a fitting conclusion to this analysis of the control of specimens and citizens. One event was the firing of Atir, the black African who since 1827 had served as the giraffe's keeper (**FIG. 2.8**).[56] The other was the transfer of control of the menagerie from the professorship of mammals and birds to a new professorship of comparative physiology.

On January 1, 1838, Frédéric Cuvier, the Muséum's new professor of comparative physiology, took away Atir's keys to the menagerie and forbade him further entry. Cuvier did so on the grounds of Atir's "extreme negligence" and his life of debauchery ("la vie crapuleuse"). Cuvier asked his colleagues to confirm the decision. As he explained, Atir's service to the Muséum over the previous two years had become increasingly derelict. More and more frequently, he failed to show up for work. When he did show up, he was often drunk. He had also been getting into trouble outside of the Muséum. Cuvier had tried every-thing, he said—"friendly advice, severe reproofs, threats"[57]—but nothing could stop Atir's degener-ate slide. By Cuvier's account, Atir lived a decadent existence in the company of "the most vile and abject people in our *faubourgs*."[58] Late in the fall of 1837, after Atir went missing for two days and then came back beaten and bruised from a brawl with the men and women of the port, Cuvier issued an ultimatum. He told Atir that the next time there was any cause for complaint, he would have to recommend his dismissal. Feeling pity for the giraffe's keeper, however, Cuvier looked the other way as Atir's failings continued.

The last straw came on the first of January 1838, when Atir, in the company of four or five other *débauchés*, entered the Rotonde drunk and disorderly, frightening the members of the public then present. Cuvier concluded that Atir had to be fired. Atir did not dispute the decision. As Cuvier described it, "The poor fellow feels the feebleness of his character and the impossibility of tearing himself away from his fateful habits. He himself asks to be returned to Egypt, convinced that as long as he remains in Paris, he will only plunge deeper into the corruption [*la crapule*] where his bad connections have led him."[59] The professors agreed Atir had to be dismissed.[60]

How does the story of Atir's firing relate to the theme of civilizing specimens and citizens? It is one more episode to illustrate the limitations of the Muséum's power. Whatever civilizing influence the Muséum wanted to have on those who visited there, it could never be the only influence to which individuals were subjected. Atir had scenes of an ordered nature all around him at the Muséum. In some of these scenes, indeed, he played a part. But this was not enough to counteract the temptations of life outside the walls. Significantly, Cuvier did not represent Atir as someone incapable of civilization. Rather, he depicted the keeper as someone who had suffered a moral *downfall*, a *démoralisation* as the result of coming into contact with the wrong elements of Parisian life.

This paper began by citing the happy letter of 1827 in which Geoffroy Saint-Hilaire voiced his pleasure about seeing people and animals in their proper places. A decade later, his mood was completely different. During the 1830s, he had become increasingly alienated from his colleagues at the

Fig. 2.8

Atir and the giraffe in the giraffe's stable. Engraved by Andrew, Best, and Leloir after a drawing by Karl Girardet. From M. Boitard, *Le Jardin des Plantes: Descriptions et mœurs des mammifères de la ménagerie et du Muséum d'Histoire naturelle* (Paris, 1842), p. 440. APS

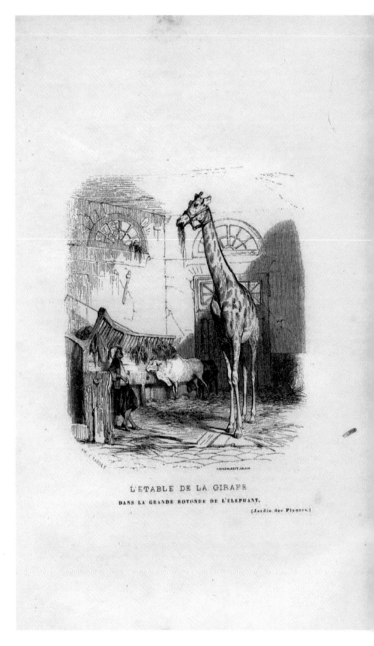

L'ETABLE DE LA GIRAFE

DANS LA GRANDE ROTONDE DE L'ELEPHANT.

(Jardin des Plantes.)

Fig. 2.9

The new "ménagerie des animaux féroces." Engraved by Andrew, Best, and Leloir after a drawing by C. Marville. From M. Boitard, *Le Jardin des Plantes: Descriptions et mœurs des mammifères de la ménagerie et du Muséum d'Histoire naturelle* (Paris, 1842), p. 162. APS

LOGES DES ANIMAUX FÉROCES
(Jardin des Plantes.)

Muséum. Quarrels about the control of specimens featured prominently in his unhappiness.[61] The worst blow came at the end of 1837, when Frédéric Cuvier, who had served as superintendent of the menagerie under Geoffroy's direction since 1803, was appointed to a new chair of comparative physiology and the responsibility for the menagerie was switched to his chair from Geoffroy's.[62] In anger and agony Geoffroy wrote to his fellow professors saying, "You have destroyed me."[63]

Frédéric Cuvier did not have long, however, to enjoy his new position. He died unexpectedly, after a short illness, in the summer of 1838. The task of overseeing the menagerie was returned to the professorship of mammals and birds. Étienne Geoffroy Saint-Hilaire's son, Isidore, serving as his father's naturalist-assistant, superintended the menagerie. Three years later, after the elder Geoffroy become blind, Isidore succeeded to his father's post. He went on to distinguish himself by promoting the study of acclimatization, a quintessential form of civilizing specimens.[64]

Through all these developments the Muséum continued to be regarded as a site for civilizing specimens and citizens. Pierre Boitard's 1842 volume on the Jardin des Plantes offers numerous images of well-behaved citizens enjoying the grounds and galleries of the institution.[65] The illustration of the menagerie of the *animaux féroces* (wild or ferocious animals) for example, shows a well-ordered citizenry in front of well-ordered cages (**FIG. 2.9**). It bears noting, however, that it had taken more than a quarter of a century to replace the provisional, embarrassingly inadequate structure that from

1793 onward had housed the menagerie's *animaux féroces*. Architect Jacques Molinos drew up various designs before a structure was finally completed in 1821. The great, rocky crag that Molinos originally planned was shelved as too impractical and too expensive. The Rotonde, intended at first for the *animaux féroces*, was destined even before it was finished for the elephants and camels. Napoleon rejected another structure proposed by Molinos as insufficiently magnificent.[66]

The difficulty of replacing the early, "provisional" menagerie building with a new, "definitive" one reminds us that the civilizing of specimens and citizens was never easy, nor was it always realized in the ways originally imagined. The elephants were never induced to mate in captivity. The Muséum never recovered the kangaroos and black swans sent to Malmaison. Dogs continued to cause periodic mayhem in the Muséum's gardens and animal pens, and the animal keepers' penchant for taking bribes recurred periodically. New professors competed with old ones over the control of specimens. On a more positive note, the first *authorized* guidebook to the whole of the Muséum and its collections was published in 1823.[67] The galleries, gardens, and animal quarters were also steadily improved.

Back in 1803, André Thouin, the professor of culture, had published a description of what he called his "school of plants useful in the rural and domestic economy" in the Muséum's *Annales*.[68] One of his lessons was that domesticated plants quickly degenerate to their savage state or die out entirely if not steadily subjected to the procedures of crop rotation, maintenance of racial purity, and all the other cultivation practices that have made them useful over time.[69] What Thouin recognized for cultivated plants is akin to what the Muséum experienced with respect to civilizing specimens and citizens from the time of the Revolution through the Restoration and beyond. For any advances gained, constant vigilance and continued efforts were required to maintain them. Civilizing specimens and citizens would of necessity be an ongoing enterprise.

....

Acknowledgments

The author gratefully acknowledges support from the National Science Foundation (Awards 96011390 and 0441935) and the Research Board of the University of Illinois for their support of the research on which much of this paper is based.

1 "Il est difficile de mieux marcher. Chacun sait ce qu'il a à faire et chacun est à son emploi. Je dis cela de toutes bêtes et gens.... Dès qu'elle [la girafe] eut vu les vaches dans le mouvement de départ, elle partit elle-même ayant précédé l'ordre de son chef palefrenier Khassen, glorieux comme un paon de tenir la corde de tête." Gabriel Dardaud, "L'extraordinaire aventure de la girafe du Pacha d'Égypte," *Revue des Conférences françaises en orient* 15 (January 1951): 1–72 (quote from 63–64).

2 "Cet ordre est suivi très exactement. Chacun est bien à sa poste. Chacun, bêtes et gens, ayant bien

pris l'esprit de sa condition de voyageur." Ibid., 64.

3 On the Muséum's founding see Ernest Théodore Hamy, "Les derniers jours du Jardin du Roi et la fondation du Muséum d'Histoire naturelle," *Centenaire de la fondation du Muséum d'Histoire naturelle, 10 juin 1793–10 juin 1893* (Paris: Imprimérie Nationale, 1893), 1–163; E. C. Spary, *Utopia's Garden: French Natural History from Old Regime to Revolution* (Chicago: University of Chicago Press, 2000); and Charles Coulston Gillispie, *Science and Polity in France: The Revolutionary and Napoleonic Years* (Princeton: Princeton University Press, 2004), 165–83.

4 Spary, *Utopia's Garden*.

5 On the history of the Muséum's menagerie see especially Gustave Loisel, "Histoire de la ménagerie du Muséum," *Revue scientifique* (1911), 262–77, 301–4; Yves Laissus and Jean-Jacques Petter, *Les*

Animaux du Muséum, 1793–1993 (Paris: Muséum national d'Histoire naturelle, 1993); and Richard W. Burkhardt, Jr., "La ménagerie et la vie du Muséum," in *Le Muséum au premier siècle de son histoire*, ed. Claude Blanckaert, Claudine Cohen, Pietro Corsi, and Jean-Louis Fischer (Paris: Éditions du Muséum national d'Histoire naturelle, 1997), 481–508.

6 I stress the Muséum's concern with controlling specimens in Richard W. Burkhardt, Jr., "The Leopard in the Garden: Life in Close Quarters at the Muséum d'Histoire Naturelle," *Isis* 98, no. 4 (December 2007): 675–94. The specific phrase, "civilizing specimens," is perhaps new in the present paper, but there is a large and growing literature on the efforts by which scientists and museums make objects amenable to their purposes. On the history of taxidermy, see Paul Lawrence Farber,

"The Development of Taxidermy and the History of Ornithology," *Isis* 68, no. 4 (December 1977): 550–66. More recent works include Sue Ann Prince, ed., *Stuffing Birds, Pressing Plants, Shaping Knowledge: Natural History in North America, 1730–1860* (Philadelphia: American Philosophical Society, 2003) and Samuel J. M. M. Alberti, *The Afterlives of Animals* (Charlottesville: University of Virginia Press, 2011). The development of model organisms in the twentieth and twenty-first centuries can be seen as a modern version of "civilizing specimens." One of the Muséum's *aide-naturalistes*, Louis Dufresne, was the leading taxidermist of his day. See his "Taxidermie," *Nouveau dictionnaire d'histoire naturelle*, 2nd ed., vol. 32 (Paris: Deterville, 1819), 522–89.

7 For Buffon's ideas on domestication, see Richard W. Burkhardt, Jr., "Le

comportement animal et l'idéologie de domestication chez Buffon et les éthologistes modernes," in *Buffon 88: Actes du Colloque international pour le bicentenaire de la mort de Buffon,* ed. Jean Claude Beaune et al. (Paris: J. Vrin, 1992), 569–82; and E. C. Spary, *Utopia's Garden.* The ambiguities of Buffon's ideas on domestication are discussed in Jacques Roger, *Buffon: A Life in Natural History* (Ithaca: Cornell University Press, 1997), 299–304.

8   Likewise, the zoologist Lacepède maintained that the history of menageries paralleled the history of civilization. He promised that when the Muséum's new menagerie was established, it would reflect "the highest degree of perfection to which the present state of civilization can give rise." See Burkhardt, "La ménagerie et la vie du Muséum," 489.

9   See Elise Lipkowitz, "Seized Natural History Collections and the Redefinition of Scientific Cosmopolitanism in the Era of the French Revolution," *British Journal for the History of Science* (forthcoming); and Pierre-Yves Lacour, "Les Amours de Mars et Flore aux cabinets: Les confiscations naturalistes en Europe septentrionale," *Annales historiques de la Révolution française,* no. 358 (October–December 2009): 71–92.

10 The names of the cubs are given in E. J. B. Vignier, *Phénomène d'histoire naturelle: Récit de la deuxième gestation de Constantine, une des lionnes de la Ménagerie du Jardin des Plantes* (Paris: Quillau, an IX [1800–1]). In a parallel from the British side, a lion at the Exeter 'Change in London was named "Victory" in conjunction with the claim that it had been born in Algeria on August 1, 1798, the day Admiral Nelson defeated the French navy at the battle of the Nile. We can view the naming of animals as a popular way

of humanizing them and, in the particular cases just noted, of incorporating them as actors in a nation's enterprises. Significantly, the pet names of individual animals were mentioned with some frequency in the popular literature of this period but rarely if ever in the scientific literature.

11 Georges Cuvier, Jean-Baptiste Lamarck, and B. G. E. Lacepède, "Rapport des professeurs du Muséum sur les collections d'histoire naturelle rapportées d'Égypte," *Annales du Muséum national d'Histoire naturelle* 1 (1802): 234–41.

12 "Ces hommes bizarres, en embaumant avec tant de soin les êtres bruts dont ils avoient fait des objets de leur stupide adoration, nous ont laissé dans leurs grottes sacrées des cabinets de zoologie presque complets." Ibid., 235–36.

13 "Depuis long-temps on desiroit de savoir si les espèces changent de forme par la suite des temps." Ibid., 235.

14 See Richard W. Burkhardt, Jr., *The Spirit of System: Lamarck and Evolutionary Biology* (Cambridge, Mass.: Harvard University Press, 1975), 148–50.

15 In 1827 numerous publications about the giraffe, recently arrived in Paris, offered semi-veiled critiques of the censorship exercised by the reactionary government of Charles X (see the essay by Alain Lescart in the present volume). Almost three decades earlier, the bears appropriated by French armies from the bear pits of Berne provided the occasion for conflict between the right-wing press and the Executive Directory. In May 1798, when the bears first arrived in Paris and were being transferred to their new quarters, one of them broke free long enough to attack a spectator, who was said to be a deputy (see *Gazette des Deux-Ponts,* no. 1278, May 4, 1798, n.p.). The following day a piece in *Le Cercle ou Journal des Arts et*

des Plaisirs stated that "the bears of Berne have declared war on the Jacobins of Paris" ("les ours de Berne ont déclaré la guerre aux jacobins de Paris") and that "it would only be an act of justice" if several hundred Jacobins per week were delivered to the bears in retribution for the victims the Jacobins had sent to the guillotine ("Quand on liverait à ces animaux sauvages quelques centaines de jacobins par decade, ce ne serait qu'un acte de justice qu'on pourrait se permettre en expiation des victimes qu'ils ont livrées à la guillotine pendant le tems de leur regne"). The government responded immediately by banning the journal and decreeing that the author and printer of the journal be denounced before the criminal tribunal and "pursued as provocateurs of murder" ("poursuivis comme provocateurs au meurtre"). See "Arrêté du Directoire exécutif, qui prohibe le journal intitulé Le Cercle ou Journal des Arts et de Plaisirs," *Collections des lois du corps legislatif, et des arrêtés du Directoire exécutif,* vol. 8 (Paris: Gratiot, n.d.), 196–98.

16 Jean Claude Mertrud, Letter to the professors of the Muséum, 11 brumaire [an 5], Séance of 14 brumaire an 5, Archives nationales de France [henceforth AN], Minutes des procès-verbaux des assemblées des professeurs [henceforth MPV], AJ/15/580.

17 The professors were particularly upset in 1800 when Lucien Bonaparte, as Minister of the Interior, wanted each of the institutions under his jurisdiction to have a director general who reported to him. The professors saw this as a reinstitution of the old position of Intendant, which they vehemently opposed. This is briefly discussed in J. P. F. Deleuze, *Histoire et description du Muséum d'histoire naturelle: Ouvrage rédigé d'après les ordres de l'administration du Muséum* (Paris: Royer, 1823), 93–96.

18 The professors resisted the minister's demand, maintaining that charging the public to see any parts of the Muséum's collections was beneath the dignity of a great nation. See Séances of 24 prairial, 4 messidor, and 14 messidor an 8, AN, MPV, AJ/15/584.

19 Art historians have noted that Napoleon's taking of art pieces as trophies of war reflected "the longstanding French desire to replace Rome as the center of culture and civilization." See Patricia Mainardi, "Assuring the Empire of the Future: The 1798 Fête de la Liberté," *Art Journal* 48, no. 2 (Summer 1989): 155–63 (quote from 156).

20 See Yvonne Letouzey, *Le Jardin des Plantes à la croisée des chemins avec André Thouin, 1747–1824* (Paris: Éditions du Muséum, 1989), 502–5.

21 The lions and camels were freshly arrived from an expedition to North Africa undertaken by the Muséum's head animal keeper. The bear had been brought to the Muséum two months earlier, one of three bears taken by French troops from the bear pits of Berne, Switzerland. The two dromedaries had been appropriated three years earlier from a royal estate in Belgium. Not present were the two elephants that had recently arrived in Paris after a long trip from the Stadholder's menagerie in Holland. Had the elephants been easier to manage, they no doubt would have featured in the parade as well. The live, exotic plants came from Captain Nicolas Baudin's voyage to the Antilles.

22 Given that most of the treasures of art and the humanities were crated up and out of sight, the live plants and animals featured especially prominently in the overall spectacle.

23 The information on the arrangement of the procession and the following festivities comes from the official program of the event,

Fêtes de la liberté, et entrée triomphale des objets de sciences et d'arts recueillis en Italie: Programme (Paris: Imprimérie de la République, thermidor an VI [1798]). See also Letouzey, *Le Jardin des Plantes*, and Mainardi, "Assuring the Empire of the Future."

24 Letouzey, *Le Jardin des Plantes*, 502–5; Mainardi, "Assuring the Empire of the Future," 157.

25 "... menacé d'une destruction prochaine." Séance of 4 prairial an 6, AN, Procès-verbaux des assemblées des professeurs [henceforth PV], AJ/15/98, 170.

26 "Les riches et immenses collections qui lui donnent sa préeminence et utilité, ces précieuses propriétés de la République, ces glorieux trophés de nos victoires, sont près d'être anéantis." Ibid., 170.

27 Ibid., 169–72.

28 There are at least two published, eyewitness accounts of the concert: Georges Toscan, "Du pouvoir de la musique sur les animaux, et du concert donné aux éléphans," *Décade philosophique*, no. 18 (thermidor an VI [1798]), 257–64, 321–29; and Gotthelf Fischer, *Das Nationalmuseum der Naturgeschichte zu Paris*, 2 vols. (Frankfurt: Esslinger, 1802), vol. 2, 55–59. Hoüel also suggests that he witnessed the concert, but his account relies primarily on that of Toscan, as do almost all other subsequent descriptions of it. See J. P. Hoüel, *Histoire naturelle des deux éléphans, mâle et femelle, du Muséum de Paris, venus de Hollande en France en l'an VI* (Paris: L'auteur, 1803). Both Fischer and Hoüel indicate that music was played to the elephants on more than one occasion. For more on the initial concert, see Burkhardt, "La ménagerie et la vie du Muséum." That account, to the best of the author's knowledge, is the first to have called attention to the musicians' manuscript

report of the concert in Séance extraordinaire du 27 prairial an 6, AN, MPV, AJ/15/581.

29 Also present was the well-known singer Adrien the elder. Four years earlier, Adrien and Devienne had collaborated in writing music for Robespierre's Festival of the Supreme Being.

30 Séance extraordinaire du 27 prairial an 6, AN, MPV, AJ/15/581. Unfortunately, the musicians drew no conclusions from this first concert, and when they expressed a desire to play another concert, the Muséum asked them to defer it until after a new park for the animals was completed and the male elephant recovered from a minor ailment. AN, PV, AJ/15/99, 197.

31 "Aussitôt qu'ils se virent découverts, le mâle, fort adroitement, dégagea ses jambes, fit un demi-tour de côté, et donna à la femelle la facilité de se lever: ce qu'elle fit promptement." Toscan, "Du pouvoir de la musique sur les animaux," 328.

32 "... la joie de se revoir après une séparation plus ou moins longue, et la saison du printemps qui invite tous les êtres à l'amour." Ibid., 329.

33 Hoüel, *Histoire naturelle des deux éléphans*.

34 Reviews of the production appeared in *Décade philosophique*, no. 30 (30 messidor an 7 [1799]), 175–77; and *Magasin encyclopédique*, 5ᵉ année, vol. 2 (1799): 237–39.

35 One reason for this inattention to the elephants on the part of the Muséum's naturalists may be that the professor of mammals, Geoffroy Saint-Hilaire, left Paris just two weeks after the elephants arrived in the capital and was then away from France for nearly four years as part of Napoleon's expedition to Egypt.

36 "Cet accouplement est entièrement semblable à celui du cheval et dure à-peu-près autant de temps."

Georges Cuvier, "L'éléphant des Indes," in Lacepède and Cuvier, *La Ménagerie du Muséum national d'histoire naturelle, ou description et histoire des animaux qui y vivent ou qui y ont vécu* (Paris: Miger, 1801), 6.

37 Ibid., 11.

38 Cuvier states how long the dissection took and how many drawings Maréchal made in Georges Cuvier, "L'éléphant des indes, femelle," in Cuvier and Lacepède, *La Ménagerie du Muséum national d'Histoire naturelle*. J. P. F. Deleuze, "Notice sur le citoyen Maréchal," *Annales du Muséum national d'Histoire naturelle* 2 (1803), 65–74, mentions how Maréchal devoted himself to the task of sketching the elephant's anatomy despite the cold of winter and the "horrible stench" ("l'infection horrible") of the elephant's remains.

39 Séance of 26 vendémiaire an 12, AN, PV, AJ/15/105, 24.

40 "L'assemblée l'invite à prendre les mesures les plus promptes, pour fair jouir le public de la vue de ce grand animal." Séance of 8 frimaire an 12, AN, PV, AJ/15/105, 50. After the carpenter Lassaigne had an engraving made of the wooden manikin, the administration decided to have the engraving framed and placed under the elephant as a way of instructing the public about the art of taxidermy. Séance of 13 nivôse an 12, AN, PV, AJ/15/105, 82.

41 Séance of 7 fructidor an 9, AN, PV, AJ/15/102, 63.

42 See J.-B. Pujoulx, *Promenades au Jardin des Plantes, à la ménagerie et dans les galeries du Muséum d'Histoire naturelle*, 2 vols. (Paris: Guilleminet, 1803), vol. 1, 6–7. I thank Pierre-Yves Lacour for an exchange of information regarding how the Muséum labeled its specimens. Neither of us has found archival or other evidence to suggest that the Muséum provided anything more than

the scientific names of specimens when labeling them for the galleries.

43 Anonymous, *Le guide au Jardin des Plantes, ou description de tout ce que les galleries, serres, etc. du Muséum d'Histoire naturelle de Paris, renferment de plus curieux* (Paris: Glisau, an XI [1803]).

44 *Notice des animaux vivans de la ménagerie* (Paris: Levrault, Schoell, et Comp., an XII [1804]). The volume appeared anonymously, but Frédéric Cuvier's authorship of it is certain.

45 "... de prendre les mesures les plus sûres pour faire parvenir au Muséum, tous ces objets, dans le meilleur état de conservation possible." Séance of 10 germinal an 12, AN, AJ/15/105, 147.

46 The details of Geoffroy's mission to Lorient and Joséphine's claims on specimens from the Baudin expedition are to be found in AN, MPV, AJ/15/592. I discuss the distribution of the Baudin expedition's live animals in Richard W. Burkhardt, Jr., "Akteure und Interessen in der Pariser Menagerie," in *Mensch, Tier und Zoo: Der Tiergarten Schönbrunn im internationalen Vergleich vom 18. Jahrhundert bis heute*, ed. Mitchell G. Ash (Vienna: Böhlau, 2008), 111–31. I discuss other problems regarding the control of Baudin expedition specimens in Richard W. Burkhardt, Jr., "Unpacking Baudin: Models of Scientific Practice in the Age of Lamarck," in *Jean-Baptiste Lamarck, 1744–1829*, ed. Goulven Laurent (Paris: Éditions du CTHS, 1997), 497–514.

47 "... le plus bel animal de cette expédition, le plus inconcevable relativement à ses formes." Geoffroy Saint-Hilaire, Letter to the professors of the Muséum, 18 germinal an 12, Séance of 28 germinal an 12, AN, MPV, AJ/15/592.

48 On the kangaroos at Malmaison see *L'Impératrice Joséphine et les sciences*

naturelles (Paris: Éditions de la Réunion des musées nationaux, 1997), 135–38. Fourcroy's letter is quoted on p. 136.

49 "Tout me porte à croire, Madame, que le nouveau séjour les rendra infiniments plus intéressants pour l'histoire naturelle que celui qu'ils ont habité jusqu'à present. Ils n'ont besoin pour cela que d'un espace plus grand et un peu de tranquillité." Ibid., 136.

50 Séance of 1 June 1814, AN, PV, AJ/15/114, 140. See also *L'Impératrice Joséphine et les sciences naturelles*, 144.

51 "Il sera pris des mesures pour tâcher d'obtenir des propriétaires de Malmaison les kanguroos & les cygnes noires qui y sont dêposés & qui avaient appartenu au Muséum." Séance of 8 June 1814, AN, PV, AJ/15/114, 143. See also *L'Impératrice Joséphine et les sciences naturelles*, 144.

52 *L'Impératrice Joséphine et les sciences naturelles*, 144–45.

53 Lipkowitz, "Seized Natural History Collections."

54 "Instruction sur les recherches qui pourroient être faites dans les colonies, sur les objets qu'il seroit possible d'y recueillier, et sur la manière de les conserver et de les transporter," *Mémoires du Muséum d'Histoire naturelle* 4 (1818): 193–239.

55 On the instructions for colonial officials and on the school for naturalists, see Richard W. Burkhardt, Jr., "Naturalists' Practices and Nature's Empire: Paris and the Platypus, 1815–1833," *Pacific Science* 55, no. 4 (2001): 327–41; and Lorelai Kury, *Histoire naturelle et voyages scientifiques (1780–1830)* (Paris: L'Harmattan, 2001), 138–39, 169–78.

56 Atir's firing from his job as the giraffe's keeper has not been mentioned previously in the historical literature, to the best of this writer's knowledge. Dardaud, in "L'extraordinaire aventure de la girafe," mentions Atir's return to Egypt but not his firing. Michael Allin, *Zarafa* (New York: Walker, 1998) does not mention Atir's fate at all. Olivier Lebleu, in *Les Avatars de Zarafa* (Paris: Arlea, 2006), misses Atir's firing for derelict behavior, noting simply for the year 1838 that "After ten years of good and loyal services to the giraffe, Atir returns to Egypt" ("Après dix ans de bons et loyaux services à la girafe, Atir rentre en Égypte"), 173.

57 "Les conseils bienveillans, les remontrances sévères, les menaces rien n'a pu arrêter le développement de son penchant à la vie crapuleuse." Frédéric Cuvier, Letter to the professors of the Muséum, 3 January 1838, Séance of 9 January 1838, AN, MPV, AJ/15/655.

58 "Il vit dans la débauche avec ce qu'il y a de plus vile et de plus abject dans nos faubourgs." Ibid.

59 "Le malheureux sent la faiblesse de son caractère et l'impossibilité où il est de s'arracher à ses funestes habitudes. Il demande lui-même à retourner en Egypte, mais convaincu que tant qu'il restera à Paris, il ne fera que se plonger de plus en plus dans la crapule où ses mauvaises liaisons l'ont conduites." Ibid.

60 The following week Cuvier reported that it would cost 500 francs to send Atir back to Egypt. On January 20, 1838, Atir departed Paris via stagecoach for Marseille. He arrived in Marseille in time to get passage on a *paquebot* that was sailing directly to Alexandria. The Muséum's agents in Marseille instructed the boat's captain to make sure Atir was well cared for throughout the crossing. See Séances of 16 and 30 January 1838 and 6 February 1838, AN, MPV, AJ/15/655.

61 Soon after the death of his famous rival Georges Cuvier in 1832, Geoffroy found himself quarreling with Henri de Blainville, Cuvier's successor, over access to specimens. First it was about the distribution of animals that died at the menagerie. See Séance of 11 September 1832, AN, PV, AJ/15/130, p. 147. Then it was about the practice, begun by Georges Cuvier, as Geoffroy described it, of sequestering for anatomical researches specimens that were not yet properly represented in the zoology galleries. (I discuss this in Burkhardt, "Naturalists' Practices and Nature's Empire," 335–36.) In 1833 and again in 1836 Geoffroy told his colleagues that his unhappy interactions with them in the professorial assemblies had led him to fear he was about to have a stroke. His heart, he said in 1836, could not support the "outrages" to which he was always being subjected. See Geoffroy's letters to the professors of the Muséum, 18 January 1833, Séance of 28 January 1833, AN, MPV, AJ/15/645, and 6 July 1836, Séance of 5 July 1836 (Geoffroy evidently misdated his letter by a day), AN, MPV, AJ/15/652.

62 On the tensions and the breakdown, over time, of relations between Geoffroy Saint-Hilaire and Frédéric Cuvier, see Laissus and Petter, *Les Animaux du Muséum*, 130–34. Geoffroy publicly lamented his loss of the menagerie in the chapter entitled "Vieillesse outragé" in his *Fragments biographiques, précédés d'études sur la vie, les ouvrages et les doctrines de Buffon* (Paris: Pillot, 1838), 137–57.

63 "Vous m'avez detruit [sic]." Geoffroy Saint-Hilaire, Letter of 15 January 1838 to the commisssion to examine the work to be done on the zoology galleries, Séance of 23 January 1838, AN, MPV, AJ/15/655.

64 On Isidore Geoffroy Saint-Hilaire and acclimatization see Claude Blanckaert, "Les animaux 'utiles' chez Isidore Geoffroy Saint-Hilaire: La mission sociale de la zootechnie," *Revue de Synthèse* 113, nos. 3–4 (July–December 1992): 347–82; and Michael A. Osborne, "Zoos in the Family: The Geoffroy Saint-Hilaire Clan and the Three Zoos of Paris," in *New Worlds, New Animals: From Menagerie to Zoological Park in the Nineteenth Century*, ed. Robert J. Hoage and William A. Deiss (Baltimore: Johns Hopkins University Press, 1996), 33–42. It bears noting that when Frédéric Cuvier's chair of comparative physiology was created for him, the study of acclimatization was identified as one of the purviews of that chair.

65 Pierre Boitard, *Le Jardin des Plantes: Description et mœurs des mammifères de la ménagerie et du Muséum d'histoire naturelle* (Paris: J.-J. Dubochet, 1842).

66 The aborted plans for the *rocher*, the decision to have the Rotonde house the *animaux herbivores*, and Napoleon's interest in having a magnificent structure for the animals are treated in Loisel, "Histoire de la ménagerie du Muséum," 271–72.

67 Deleuze, *Histoire et description du Muséum d'Histoire naturelle*.

68 André Thouin, "De l'école des plantes d'usage dans l'économie rurale et domestique, établie au Jardin national des plantes de Paris," *Annales du Muséum national d'Histoire naturelle* 2 (1803), 142–62.

69 Ibid., 160–61.

PART I

SYMPOSIUM KEYNOTE ADDRESS

SYMPOSIUM DISCUSSIONS

CIVILIZING SPECIMENS AND CITIZENS
AT THE MUSÉUM D'HISTOIRE NATURELLE,
1793–1830
Richard W. Burkhardt, Jr.

Question: It seems that the gallery at the Muséum was full of stuffed animals, so it was a kind of intermediary between living specimens and dry bones. What exactly was the role of taxidermy and was it a valued practice at the time?

Richard W. Burkhardt, Jr. (RWB): One story that historians of science could write beautifully using the Muséum's archives would be about Louis Dufresne's activity; he was essentially the head taxidermist and the director of the zoology laboratory at the museum. There are wonderful collections and reports by him indicating the tremendous number of things that were getting stuffed as a result of the Baudin expedition to Australia, and wonderful descriptions of old buildings, where the construction of an elephant or a giraffe has to be taken apart so they can move it from one place to another.

But your question is more about the meaning of the stuffed animals, and the professors are at least saying they want the elephant there for the public's enjoyment. There is clearly a sense that the public will be more excited or more comfortable seeing stuffed skins rather than bones. And I think we can reflect on this together. If we look at the black swan in the exhibition, it would be easy for us to say, "there's the black swan that belonged to Josephine." When, in fact, what we are looking at is a bird skin that has been somehow subjected to wonderful taxidermic practice and inside is some kind of stuffing. Probably if you looked at the skeleton of that black swan, you wouldn't say "that's the black swan that belonged to Josephine," you'd say, "that's the skeleton of the black swan that belonged to Josephine."

So taxidermic practice is very important at the time for making something look more lifelike. But in order to pull it off—and this is part of what I wanted to say in somewhat playfully using the term "civilizing specimens"— a tremendous amount of work has to go into preserving the appearance of the animal after it is dead. Because we know that the forces of corruption and decomposition—all the things that are required to preserve a specimen, not just to set it up as a nice specimen, but also to keep it from deteriorating over time—these were the constant business of Dufresne and all his associates. There is a remarkable amount of information if one wanted to tackle this art of what went on at the Muséum.

Question: You began with a great quote from Geoffroy Saint-Hilaire about seeing the humans and animals in their proper order, and we've seen quite a bit about the care of both the living and the stuffed specimens. Can you say something about the order of the collections within the Muséum and the Ménagerie? Who was responsible for that, and who was putting them in their places? What order ruled over those collections?

RWB: The immediate answer is that each professor was in charge of the collection relative to his particular field, so that Lamarck, for example, was in charge of the invertebrate collection. The vertebrates, primarily birds and mammals, would be among Cuvier's collection.

One of the nice things about the various guides that started getting published is that you can actually follow them and in essence "walk through" different galleries to see what was there in, say, 1803. Cuvier of course had his own special collection, and it was a while before it became a public gallery, but eventually his gallery of comparative anatomy was specially arranged according to his principles. Now, you'll recognize that there was competition among the professors regarding the natural order. I think what you'll find is that one order would be represented in one place and another would be represented in a different place.

There were also problems with respect to size; you may know the Muséum today and all the effort that went into building the new Grande Galerie de l'Évolution around the giant whale skeleton. They had large pieces that ended up in places better suited to display them rather than naturally fitting their relations with other animals; so there were compromises.

Question: I was struck by one of the images, the one of Félix Cassal, the guardian of the lions. Is it a coincidence that his physiognomy resembles that of a lion, and vice versa? And I'm wondering if it is a coincidence, or if it is just me interpreting it this way. So if you're talking about connections and the ways in which the animals may have influenced the humans' behavior, or the other way around, that might be something interesting to consider.

RWB: In terms of physiognomy, I don't really want to even hazard a guess. I would say that Cassal turns out to be an extraordinarily interesting figure. Most of the people who write about him, like Toscan, say he is a wonderful man, judging by how well the lions love him. As Frédéric Cuvier later reports, however, he gained that love through an extremely cruel program of breaking the lions' spirits, and the lion Marc had scars on his flanks from whipping. Cassal himself was eventually fired from the Muséum. Atir, the giraffe's keeper, was by no means the only animal keeper to have been dismissed from the Muséum; but Cassal was fired for trying to arrange to have another member of the Ménagerie staff killed. So he is a person who deserves more attention.

PART II

ABOUT
GARDENS AND
GARDENING

PART II

ABOUT GARDENS AND GARDENING

Previous page and detail, left Pierre-Joseph Redouté,
Josephine's March Lily (*Brunsvigia josephinae*, "Amaryllis de
Joséphine, Amaryllis Josephinae"), 1802–5, watercolor on
vellum (detail), study for *Les Liliacées*, vol. 7 (Paris, 1813).
David Brind (see Fig. 3.4)

03

EMPRESS JOSEPHINE AND THE NATURAL SCIENCES

BERNARD CHEVALLIER

WHERE DID JOSEPHINE BONAPARTE'S PASSION for the natural sciences come from? We do not know who introduced her to this science, so unusual for her gender (see **FIG. 4.1**). She went on to excel in it, to the point that the professors of the Paris Muséum d'Histoire naturelle almost considered her as one of their own. No source in the archives or in her correspondence attests to Josephine having the least interest in botany, and still less in zoology, until the moment she bought Malmaison on April 21, 1799. Her husband Napoleon Bonaparte's coup d'état gave her the means to prove herself. From then on, she placed her scientific spirit, in all its method and rigor, in the service of the natural sciences. Her gardens of Malmaison, which she never stopped improving, became her laboratories.

BOTANY

Josephine had always been more interested in the plant kingdom than the animal kingdom. Though this was not the first time a French ruler had attempted to acclimatize exotic plants, the movement had unprecedented growth under her leadership. To begin, she engaged scientific personnel who not only organized plant exchanges with other establishments, but also managed her estates of Malmaison and of Navarre in Normandy, the latter added to her holdings in 1810 after her divorce from Napoleon. The position of superintendent for Malmaison was created in 1803; Charles François Brisseau de Mirbel, a distinguished botanist, was the first to carry out this delicate function. In Josephine's absence, Mirbel had complete power to oversee the estate's farming and botanical establishments. His work included compiling plant catalogs and corresponding with other botanical gardens. Displeased with Mirbel's administration, Napoleon recalled him in 1806, replacing him with Jean-Baptiste-Louis, Comte Lelieur de Ville-sur-Arce, a specialist in horticulture and arboriculture. As Lelieur was already the administrator of the imperial parks, his excess of work made him neglect Malmaison. In 1808, therefore, Josephine named Aimé Jacques Alexandre Bonpland in his place. Bonpland remained in her service until her death in 1814. The superintendents had a head gardener under their orders, who was responsible for planting and maintaining the gardens.[1]

At the same time, Josephine became connected to the greatest botanists of the era. At her request, they described the plants in her greenhouse that celebrated flower painter Pierre-Joseph Redouté (**FIG. 11.3**) would then immediately portray. Étienne-Pierre Ventenat was the first botanist to occupy this post. After Ventenat's death in 1808, Bonpland succeeded him, thus combining the functions of botanist and superintendent.[2] Botanists also authored all the works published under the empress's auspices with her financial support:

- *Jardin de la Malmaison* (Garden of Malmaison): 120 plates delivered in eighty *livraisons* (installments or fascicles) in 1803 and 1804, forming two volumes with only 200 copies printed. Ventenat wrote the text and Redouté drew the plates.
- *Les Liliacées* (The Lilies): 486 plates published in eighty *livraisons*, comprising eight volumes that appeared from 1802 to 1816, the last not published until after Josephine's death. Augustin Pyramus de Candolle wrote the text of the first four volumes, François de la Roche wrote the following three, and the last was by Alire Raffeneau-Delile; Redouté was the artist for all the plates.
- *Description des plantes rares cultivées à Malmaison et à Navarre* (Description of Rare Plants Cultivated at Malmaison and at Navarre), sixty-four plates in eleven *livraisons* produced between 1812 and 1817. Bonpland wrote the text, and Redouté signed fifty-four plates out of the sixty-four.
- *Les Roses* (The Roses), thirty *livraisons* published from 1817 to 1824. Even though the work came out under the Restoration, it had been started under the Empire when Josephine asked Claude-Antoine Thory to write the text. Redouté drew all the plates.

We can thus certify the essential role Josephine played in the publication of the most sumptuous works of botany ever issued under the Empire.[3]

As for porcelain, the Sèvres Porcelain Manufactory made two table services with botanical decoration for Josephine, following the example of the celebrated Flora Danica service commissioned by the King of Denmark in 1790. Both services were ornamented with flowers, all drawn scientifically, and each piece had an inscription on the back providing the plant's Latin name according to Linnaean nomenclature.

In the fall of 1802, knowing Josephine's taste, Alexandre Brongniart, the new Sèvres administrator, had his artisans begin making a dessert service with a reddish-brown background (see **FIG. 1.6**). The service, comprised of 116 pieces including twenty-four plates, reproduced plants copied from three recent collections: Candolle's *Histoire des plantes grasses* (History of Succulent Plants, published from 1799 up to 1837); the first volume of *Les Liliacées* (1805), also by Candolle; and *Jardin de la Malmaison* by Ventenat (1803–4), all with illustrations signed by Redouté. The service was delivered to the empress at the Palais de Saint-Cloud in March 1805, but she kept it for only one year before offering it to Stéphanie de Beauharnais (her cousin by her first marriage and Napoleon's adopted daughter), who had just married the heir to the Grand Duchy of Baden. Today, the pieces are dispersed among private collections, the Museum of Fine Arts in Boston, and the Musée de Malmaison.[4]

Even more important was the service created by the Königliche Porzellan-Manufaktur (KPM), the German royal porcelain manufactory in Berlin (**FIG. 3.1**). Its 222 pieces, of which 178 were plates, had been executed in 1807 under French occupation after Napoleon vanquished Prussia at Jena in October of 1806. For this service, the Berlin artisans again mainly reproduced illustrations from the just-published *Jardin de la Malmaison*, which constituted a sort of homage to the sovereign. Shared with Josephine's daughter, Queen Hortense of Holland, the service was quickly dispersed. Its pieces are in various private and public collections, such as the Charlottenburg Palace, and at Malmaison.[5]

Then, after the divorce, the empress had the Palais de l'Elysée in Paris at her disposal. In 1810, she had a dessert service with flower bouquets

Fig. 3.1

Plates from Service
des plantes exotiques
porcelaine de Berlin. Drei
Teller aus dem Service
für Kaiserin Josephine
mit Blumen-Darstellungen
(Lotusblume, Taglilie,
Geranie), KPM, 1807.
Stiftung Preußische
Schlösser und Gärten
Berlin-Brandenburg,
KPM-Porzellansammlung
des Landes Berlin /
Photograph: Wolfgang
Pfauder

delivered there, which the Sèvres Manufactory had made the previous year.
This service has a completely different spirit than the two preceding ones.
Its plates display in their centers natural flower bouquets composed of roses,
violets, campanulas, and other flowers of the field, without any inscriptions
on the back to identify them. The service is currently dispersed in numerous
collections; the Musée de Malmaison has five of the plates.[6]

As a plant collector, Josephine kept up ties with the greatest scientists
of her time, such as Augustin Pyrame de Candolle, Alexander von Humboldt,
and Alire Raffeneau-Delile. While residing at Malmaison, she wrote a true
profession of faith to Raffeneau-Delile in March of 1804: "We do not yet
know all the plants capable of being cultivated in Europe that North America possesses." Referring to bald cypresses, she added instructions to "write
to the Citizens Arcambal in Baltimore, Le Quinio in Newport and Florent
Guyot in Philadelphia, they will collect seeds in Pennsylvania, Delaware, and
Maryland, provinces that contain vast marshes entirely covered with this
superb cypress."[7] Desiring each *département* in France to possess a rare plant
collection supplied from her Malmaison garden, she had a portion of her
estate laid out as a nursery for cultivating exotic shrubs. Josephine inundated
French representatives in the United States with letters, clarifying that "I want
to multiply in France the plants of this country, which, by its temperature, has
such close ties with ours."[8] But rare plants arrived from the entire world, from
Turkey, from Morocco, from Mauritius, from the Canary Islands, from Guiana;
there was no consular agent, merchant, traveler, or botanical amateur that did
not pay homage to her with unknown plants.[9]

Most of the French and foreign horticulturalists of the era also supplied her with plants, seeds, or bulbs, notably the famous London nurserymen
Lee and Kennedy. Despite the rupture of peace with England, they benefited
from a passport permitting them to continue to deliver enormous quantities
of plants for Malmaison. Science came before war; Napoleon had written to
Josephine in July of 1801, "I received for you from London, plants that I sent
to your gardener."[10] She herself, after the breakage of peace in June 1803, urged
caution to Lee and Kennedy to continue "similar shipments as in the past by
sending all the shrubs you intend for me to Calais and through neutrals."[11]

In addition to plant deliveries, Josephine associated herself with this English firm to fund half the salary of a young Scottish botanist dispatched to South Africa to send her the first specimens of proteas and heathers. Because of the blockade, he sent his deliveries on English ships passing through Amsterdam or Copenhagen.[12]

Josephine carefully followed Napoleon's conquests, deploring the war with England that kept her from asking King George if he would consent to give her some plants from his lovely garden at Kew.[13] Plant acquisitions became easier when French troops occupied the territories of the Electors of Hesse and of Hanover, of the King of Prussia and the Emperor of Austria. She then used the indispensable Pierre, Comte de Daru, who was responsible for drawing up the lists of plants at these various establishments and sending the plants directly to Josephine.[14]

In this way, nearly two hundred new plants flowered for the first time in France at Malmaison, including the celebrated purple magnolia, the tree peony, hibiscus, phlox, camellias, and dahlias. Most grew in the famous large greenhouse, a unique building that surpassed the greenhouse of the Paris Muséum. Here, growing plants attained the same development and the same beauty as in their native lands (**FIG. 3.2**). Fifty meters long (nearly 165 feet), the greenhouse was heated by twelve large coal stoves. This was the first time glass had been used on so large a surface. Besides an orangery, the estate also included several other greenhouses, temperate and cold.[15]

But the memory of Josephine remains particularly associated with a particular flower, the rose, which was also linked to the celebrated work of Redouté (**FIG. 3.3**). She did not possess a rose garden on the model of those

Fig. 3.2

Auguste Garnerey, *Vue intérieure de la serre-chaude à Malmaison*. Watercolor. Malmaison. RMN / Art Resource, N.Y.

we know today. Some roses grew in the form of bushes dispersed throughout the park, and others in the flower garden were intended to be cut for bouquets, but most comprised an enormous collection of shrubs in pots that were only taken out at the moment they flowered. Her collection of roses became the most celebrated in Europe, supplied by the greatest nurserymen of the time, such as Descemet and Du Pont in France, Van Eeden in Holland, and the essential Lee and Kennedy in England. Far exceeding the first estimates made in the early 1900s, which included approximately 250 species and varieties, it is now believed that Josephine's collection may have numbered between 500 and 800 kinds of roses. But she also developed other botanical collections, including pelargoniums and heathers, whose numbers increased to eighty species in five years.[16]

Josephine was not miserly with her botanical treasures and did not hesitate to distribute them around her. Different prefects of the Empire benefited from her largess, as did many individuals such as Corvisart, the emperor's doctor; the comedy actress Mademoiselle Raucourt; or Madame de Chateaubriand, who received a magnificent magnolia with purple flowers. There were fruitful exchanges with botanical establishments and Napoleon's conquests did not fail to enrich Malmaison. During the 1806 occupation of Berlin, six hundred plants were sent directly to the empress; three years later, in 1809, the greenhouses of Schönbrunn were stripped of eight hundred plants, but Josephine, always generous, sent the director a ring valued at two thousand francs to soften the blow.[17]

Wishing to honor their benefactress, botanists gave her name to newly acclimatized plants; thus was born the amaryllis or March lily of Josephine (*Amaryllis josephinae*, now called *Brunsvigia josephinae*; **FIG. 3.4**), a magnificent bright red umbrella of blossoms; *Josephinia imperatricis*, a modest plant nearly forgotten today; or the *Lapageria rosea*, recalling her maiden name of Rose de La Pagerie, a splendid vine that is now the national flower of Chile.[18]

ZOOLOGY

The acclimatization of animals was another important part of Josephine's program. She kept only domestic species or species that could be domesticated; animals judged dangerous were sent to the Jardin des Plantes in Paris. The menagerie of Malmaison was formed very early and she took advantage of every occasion to give it an exceptional impact. From 1800, there were llamas, soon joined by gazelles and small horses from the island of Ouessant (Ushant in English) off the coast of Brittany. She received animals from around the world. In 1804, General Janssens, the governor of Cape Town in South Africa, sent her a gnu and a tame zebra that could be harnessed like a horse. She mated the zebra with a donkey, resulting in a mixed breed that she immediately had painted by Léon de Wailly, who along with Nicolas Huet painted vellums portraying the animals in her menagerie. In March 1808, a female orangutan arrived at Malmaison, the gift of General Decaen, governor of the French Indies. Once tamed, the animal wore a dress and ate its meals at a table. This orangutan is now preserved at the Muséum d'Histoire naturelle in La Rochelle on the west coast of France. One of the attractions was evidently the presence of kangaroos, animals unknown to the great naturalist Georges-Louis Leclerc, the Comte de Buffon, who had died in 1788. The kangaroos were not kept in a cage behind bars, but roamed in partial liberty in a wide enclosure, a very modern concept that foreshadowed the spirit of our present-day zoos.[19]

Fig. 3.4

Pierre-Joseph Redouté, Josephine's March Lily (*Brunsvigia josephinae*, "Amaryllis de Josephine, Amaryllis Josephinae"), 1802–5, watercolor on vellum, study for *Les Liliacées*, vol. 7 (Paris, 1813). David Brind

Fig. 3.5

Pierre Dandelot, after Léon de Wailly, *Cygnes noirs* (Black Swans from the Bass Straits). Malmaison. RMN / Art Resource, N.Y.

But the great fortune of the Malmaison menagerie was the expedition organized by Captain Baudin to Australia on the ships *Le Géographe* and *Le Naturaliste*. Departing from Le Havre in 1800, the ships returned in 1803 and 1804 after having gathered considerable collections of plants and living animals. Immediately informed of their return, Josephine sent her emissary to Lorient. He arrived before the Muséum's emissaries and swiftly sent thirty-five animals to Malmaison, including the kangaroos mentioned above, deer, a gnu, parrots, cassowaries, and the famous pair of black swans (**FIG. 3.5**) that the empress was the first to successfully breed in captivity. They were celebrated throughout Europe and multiplied at Malmaison, their number growing to seven in 1814. But even more rare in the eyes of the scientists was a pair of black emus, the only ones then known in the world (see **FIG. 2.7**). They died at the Jardin des Plantes in 1822, the last survivors of a species completely extinct today. Their preserved skins are among the Muséum's greatest treasures.[20]

Josephine, however, very quickly renounced developing her menagerie; a period of slow decline began after 1805, as the animals were not replaced when they died. She transferred her passion for mammals to birds instead, for after flowers these were certainly the productions of nature that interested her the most. Living birds invaded the vestibule of the château where eight aviaries contained small songbirds from the Americas, along with cockatoos, a gray parrot, macaws, and above all, a pair of lovebirds that delighted visitors. In addition, the environs of the château and the pheasant house sheltered a multitude of birds, principally golden pheasants from China that Josephine

enjoyed feeding herself. The celebrated taxidermist Louis Dufresne, who served as the depository for the Malmaison collection, preserved most of the birds after their deaths. When Josephine passed away in 1814, her cabinet of natural history included more than 600 stuffed birds.[21]

If Redouté specialized in painting flowers, Pauline de Courcelles Knip devoted herself to representing birds, following her teacher Jacques Barraband. The apartments at Malmaison contained several rare watercolors by these two bird artists, but neither had an official position under Josephine. Nevertheless, in the inventory made after her death in 1814, there are several references to original vellums of South American songbirds (tanagers, manakins, and todies) by Knip, as well as a number of drawings of pigeons and other bird species.[22]

Along with the acclimatization of new species, Josephine developed model agricultural establishments on her estate, including a cowshed and a sheepfold located near the Saint-Cucufa lake (see **FIGS. 4.3** and **4.5**). The cowshed was paired with a house for the herdsman and with a dairy that provided milk, cream, and fresh butter to the Château. These dairy products came from a herd of Swiss cows, a gift to Madame Bonaparte (as she was then) from the Canton of Berne. The sheepfold, located halfway up the slope toward the pond, was a building ninety meters long (three hundred feet) that could hold more than two thousand merino sheep, which provided revenue to the estate.[23]

MINERALOGY

Though Josephine did not bring the passion she showed for botany to mineralogy, it is surprising that she had also some knowledge of the art of mining. She owned at least two different collections of minerals. Alexandre Charles Besson, a mining engineer, had formed the most important collection of the two, which Josephine bought from him in 1808. Composed almost exclusively of minerals and rocks, it totaled 2,409 specimens contained in twenty-one cases. Stored in the neighboring Château of Bois-Préau, the cases had not even been opened when the empress died, and it is unclear what happened to the collection after that.

The second collection, with a more didactic character, was kept in thirty boxes, each containing twenty-four compartments (**FIG. 3.6**). Each box is bound in glazed calf and looks like a book on the outside, and all are preserved in the Musée de Malmaison. The collection was created between 1810 and 1814, for the flyleaf of the first volume bears the inscription "Her Majesty the Empress Josephine," a title she used only after the divorce. Antoine-Marie Héron de Villefosse, an inspector of mines who ended his career as vice president of the Conseil des Mines, had gathered and organized the minerals, certainly at the empress's own request.[24]

One of the loveliest homages rendered to Josephine after her death in 1814 came from the professors at the Muséum d'Histoire Naturelle in Paris. They wrote to her son Prince Eugène to say: "We have been very fortunate in the relations Empress Josephine permitted us to have with the storehouse of the natural sciences that her enlightened taste for the arts had impelled her to build. We always had the pleasure, and found a great advantage, in placing our most beautiful duplicates, and often [our] unique objects, with Her Majesty."[25]

Translated from the French by Jane E. Boyd

1   *L'Impératrice Joséphine et les sciences naturelles* (Rueil-Malmaison: Musée national des châteaux de Malmaison et Bois-Préau; Paris: Éditions de la Réunion des musées nationaux, 1997), 22.

2   Ibid., 22–23, 48–61.

3   Ibid., 44–47, 54–61, 73–80, 170–75.

4   Ibid., 182–83.

5   Ibid., 180–1, 184–88.

6   Ibid., 189.

7   "Nous ne savons pas encore tout ce que l'Amérique Septentrionale possède de végétaux susceptibles d'être cultivés en Europe. . . . Ecrivez aux citoyens Arcambal à Baltimore, Le Quinio à Newport et Florent Guyot à Philadelphie, ils feront récolter des graines dans la Pennsylvanie, le Delaware et le Maryland, provinces qui renferment des marais immenses entièrement couverts de ce superbe cyprès." Letter from Josephine to Alire Raffeneau-Delile (French consul in Wilmington, North Carolina), Malmaison, 7 germinal an 12 [March 28, 1804]; excerpted in ibid., 198.

8   "Je veux multiplier en France les végétaux de ce pays, qui, par sa température, a de si grands rapports avec le nôtre." Letter from Josephine to Cazeaux (sous-commissaire in Portsmouth, New Hampshire), Paris, 1 frimaire an 12 [November 23, 1803], Musée de Malmaison, inv. MM. 59.2.1; reproduced in ibid., 195.

9   Ibid., 23–24; 27–28; 193–202.

10 "J'ai reçu pour toi, de Londres, des plantes que j'ai envoyées à ton jardinier." Letter from Napoleon Bonaparte to Josephine, Paris, 27 [illeg.] an X [1802]. Reproduced in *Lettres de Napoléon à Joséphine, pendant la première campagne d'Italie, le Consulat et l'Empire; et lettres de Joséphine à Napoléon et à sa fille*, vol. 1 (The Hague: G. Vervloet, 1833), 75.

11 "Les mêmes expéditions que par le passé en adressant à Calais et par la voie des neutres tous les arbustes que vous me destinez." Letter from Josephine to Lee and Kennedy, Saint-Cloud, 12 prairial an 11 [June 1, 1803], Musée de Malmaison, inv. 2002.8.1.

12 *L'Impératrice Joséphine et les sciences naturelles*, 81–86.

13 "Aussitôt que l'accord sera parfaitement établi entre les deux nations je réclamerai encore vos bons offices. Ne pensez-vous pas que le roi d'Angleterre pourrait consentir à me donner quelques unes des plantes de son beau jardin de Kew, repousserait-il cette idée si elle lui était présentée par vous avec la délicatesse que vous saurez assurément y mettre. Je vous prie de déterminer vous-même le temps et les moyens de lui laisser entrevoir ce désir." Letter from Josephine to Louis-Guillaume Otto, 19 vendémiaire an 10 [October 11, 1801], private collection; reproduced in ibid., 194.

14 *L'Impératrice Joséphine et les sciences naturelles*, 200.

15 Ibid., 90–94.

16 François Joyaux, *Les Roses de l'Impératrice: La rosomanie au temps de Joséphine* (Brussels: Éditions Complexe, 2005); *L'Impératrice Joséphine et les sciences naturelles*, 60–61.

17 *L'Impératrice Joséphine et les sciences naturelles*, 54–59.

18 Ibid., 28.

19 Ibid., 112–40.

20 Ibid., 135–41, 142–47.

21 Ibid., 68–72, 112–29.

22 Ibid, 164–69.

23 Ibid., 148–61. See also Susan Taylor-Leduc's essay in this volume.

24 Ibid., 176–79.

25 "Nous étions si heureuse des relations que l'impératrice Joséphine nous permettait d'avoir avec la succursale que son goût éclairé pour les arts lui avait fait ériger aux sciences naturelles, que nous avions toujours plaisir et trouvions un grand avantage de placer chez Sa Majesté nos plus beaux doubles et souvent des objets uniques." Letter from the professors of the Muséum d'Histoire naturelle to Eugène de Beauharnais, July 29, 1814; quoted in ibid., 34.

JOSEPHINE AS SHEPHERDESS: ESTATE MANAGEMENT AT MALMAISON

SUSAN TAYLOR-LEDUC

BARON ANTOINE-JEAN GROS's full-length portrait from 1809 of the Empress Josephine depicts her as a fashion icon at Malmaison; her Empire-style white dress, embroidered with palm motifs, is draped under her gold-laced bodice, which is accented with a red scarf (FIG. 4.1). A transparent veil, also trimmed in gold, falls from her hair and across her right shoulder; a voluminous cashmere shawl is draped over her left shoulder, tumbling to the floor. She turns towards a bust of her son, Eugène Beauharnais, suggesting the letter she has been reading was written by him, the torn envelope marked with red sealing wax discarded in the foreground. On the table to her right, a vase marked with her own imperial coat of arms (JB), holds hydrangeas or hortensia, a reference to her daughter Hortense. Josephine's dedication to her children, emblems of her fertility, decorates this canvas. Pulled back, the baroque drapery of the background reveals her most productive enterprise: the gardens of Malmaison, where we see a pond with black swans, utilitarian buildings, and beyond, the aqueduct at Marly suggesting that her estate is timeless, like an ancient Roman landscape. Her hand rests on a folio volume inscribed *Flore*, recalling the luxury volumes of her plant collections illustrated by Pierre-Joseph Redouté.[1] Josephine's legacies—fashion, family, and gardens—are commemorated in this portrait.

Gros's depiction of a self-confident and graceful Josephine suppressed the realities of her tumultuous biography. Born on a sugar plantation in Martinique, married to a French nobleman and then widowed, Josephine was a French Revolutionary prisoner, a stylish *merveilleuse*, the wife of a military hero, a *Consuleuse*, and finally an empress.[2] As Bernard Chevallier has astutely observed, Josephine intuitively understood that fashion could promote prosperity.[3] This essay will suggest that Josephine crafted another image for herself, that of shepherdess, which she explicitly linked to her estate at Malmaison.

The image of the shepherdess was complex at the end of the eighteenth and beginning of the nineteenth centuries when traditions of the pastoral, popularized by the translations of Virgil's *Georgics*, clashed with erotic fantasy (FIG. 4.2). Representations of pastoral pleasure, such as Charles Nicolas Cochin's illustration, implied that a shepherdess could neglect her responsibilities in favor of more sensual entertainments.[4] The rococo shepherdess pervaded

Fig. 4.2

Nicholas Cochin, Engraving from the *Georgics*. From *Les œuvres de Virgile, traduites en françois, le texte vis-à-vis la traduction, ornées de figures en taille-douce* (Paris: Quillau, 1743). Courtesy of the Ryan Memorial Library, Saint Charles Borromeo Seminary, Wynnewood, Pennsylvania

paintings, fabrics, and porcelains throughout the ancien régime, but unlike the eroticized pictorial types, Josephine was a shepherdess in reality, over-seeing an extensive flock as an estate manager at Malmaison. Josephine created and maintained a merino sheep farm, knowing that their fine wool could be exploited as a commodity. Moreover, this essay will demonstrate that the merino sheep farm at Malmaison both promoted and reflected the evolution of attitudes towards landownership from the ancien régime until the institution of the Napoleonic Codes. Josephine did not play at being a shepherdess. Rather, she explicitly constructed her sheep farm for revenue, revealing a vision of landownership that I argue was also inspired by her intimate knowledge of the plantation economies of her native Martinique.[5] Josephine's investment in merino sheep exposes another aspect of her patronage of natural history, less well known than her interest in botanicals, roses, or exotic animals and birds, but nonetheless significant for the creation of her personal and national identity.

Josephine and Napoleon purchased Malmaison in 1799 as their country house.[6] Although Napoleon bought Malmaison, the property became Josephine's estate and was included in her divorce settlement in 1809.[7] Josephine's early interest in estate management can be gleaned from her patronage of Jean-Marie Morel, the patriarch of ancien régime garden theory. Morel dedicated the second edition of his *Théorie de jardins, où l'art des jardins de la nature* (1802) to Madame Bonaparte.[8] Morel's dedication to Josephine was not fortuitous, as he was actively seeking her patronage. His strategy was successful and she employed him at Malmaison from 1803 to 1805.[9] Despite Morel's limited tenure at Malmaison, his theorization of the *ferme ornée*, or ornamental farm, seems to have influenced Josephine's conception of her estate.[10]

Morel wrote of the significance of the ornamental farm in 1802:

> *Of all types of gardens, the farm is the only one that unites rural amenities with real utility; it is in the garden of France that these two objects are combined without prejudice, garden and farm both benefiting from their mutual association. Indeed, in a well-ordered farm, all plantations designed for pleasure can be profitable, and all cultures that have a useful purpose can provide a pleasing appearance.*[11]

Thus for Morel the ornamental farm was a useful modern space associated with the nation, the garden of France, which integrated utility and pleasure. Moreover, a profitable farm would assure a flourishing garden.

Between 1803 and 1804, at the adjoining property at the edge of the lake of Saint-Cucufa, Josephine commissioned Morel to build several farm buildings: a *vacherie* or cowshed, three *laiteries* (pleasure dairies), and a house for the cow herders (**FIG. 4.3**).[12] Morel's buildings were specifically designed for agricultural exploitation and were thus different from Queen Marie-Antoinette's pleasure dairies at the Hameau at Versailles.[13] Josephine certainly appreciated the butter produced at Malmaison, and encouraged promenades to visit the dairy, but she never expanded the dairy on the same scale as her sheep farm or *bergerie*.[14] According to Marie-Jeanne-Pierrette d'Avrillion, Josephine's

Fig. 4.3

Auguste Garneray, *Douze vues du domaine de Malmaison: Vue de la vacherie dans le bois de Saint-Cucufat [sic]*, 1815, watercolor. Malmaison. © RMN / Daniel Arnaudet / Jean Schormans

première dame de chambre, she received cream for her coffee every day from her dairy but did not fashion herself as a milkmaid.[15] Unlike earlier generations of female garden patrons in France, who, as Meredith Martin has demonstrated, exploited the milkmaid as a form of female political agency, Josephine assumed the role of the shepherdess.[16]

Morel did not build the sheep farm, but he praised sheep farming and the role of the shepherdess as a model for the ornamental farm when he wrote: "The Farm, whose main purpose is economy and utility, announces its rustic air, natural and unpretentious, like a shepherdess who is naïve and without art, her simplicity her only ornament."[17] Josephine reformulated the pastoral performances and practices of the ancien régime by turning her sheep farm into a profitable enterprise. In fact, Josephine's merger of farm and garden reflected the desires of a new class of landowners.[18]

As Thierry Lentz has explained, in the Consular period after 1802, Napoleon encouraged agriculture as a means of restarting the French economy.[19] Under the Consulate, more than thirty thousand hectares of land (about seventy-four thousand acres) were cleared for production, and more than forty thousand properties were sold between 1800 and 1804.[20] Josephine and Napoleon's acquisition and transformation of Malmaison served as an exemplar for this new class of bourgeois landowners. As the Consulate became the Empire, the post-revolutionary bourgeoisie viewed their landed estates as guarantees of financial success and security.

According to Christophe Pincemaille, both Josephine and Napoleon fervently desired to become property owners:

> *Josephine's acquisition of Malmaison owed nothing to chance. It resulted primarily from the very strong, almost visceral need felt by the couple to own land. Napoleon and Josephine were both exiled from their native islands, and they both descended from noble families with modest means. . . . They desired to mark their personal success directly on the land, thus establishing their roots in the heart of a new society. Buying a beautiful property accomplished this need because it gave them a status of lords, not of the gentry of the old régime, penniless and clutching their seigneurial prerogatives, but of new, young, and talented masters, profiting from the sale of national assets, thus replacing the former landed aristocracy.*[21]

In fact, Napoleon had been seeking to acquire *biens nationaux* (national properties) since 1800 and settled on Malmaison by default, succumbing to Josephine's insistent maneuverings that led to his purchase of the estate.[22] Significantly, Malmaison was the seat of government when Napoleon, as First Consul, issued the first decrees that would redefine the judicial status of land ownership. In April 1802, the Sénat Conservateur (one of three legislative bodies under the Consulate) issued an amnesty allowing the émigrés who had fled France during the Revolution to return to reclaim their properties, not including woods and forests, although they could not demand reparations for damages to their estates.[23] This *sénatus-consulte* (an act with the force of law) in fact legitimized property sales that occurred in the revolutionary period and justified the abolition of feudal practices, allowing new possibilities for land acquisition. In this light, Josephine conceived of Malmaison as an estate that could be transformed into an icon of land ownership, a status accessible for the post-revolutionary bourgeoisie whose self-image was no longer derived entirely from landed wealth, but who still wanted an association with ancien régime values. Thus Josephine transformed Malmaison into an ornamental farm, coupling a garden with agricultural productivity, so that the estate metaphorically functioned as a symbol of domestic prosperity.

Malmaison was not only an emblem of bourgeois landownership. As Pincemaille has suggested, Josephine and Napoleon were born on islands, and thus were both keenly aware of the necessity for trading in raw and manufactured goods. Although Josephine's father was not a successful sugar-cane planter, he belonged to the aristocracy of Martinique planters who valued both trade and plantation management (even if this included slave labor) as an economically viable investment. Jill H. Casid has established that colonial plantations and eighteenth-century picturesque gardens shared landscape engineering practices.[24] Further, Casid argued, eighteenth-century garden patrons showcased their colonial investments, notably botanicals and tropical woods, in their gardens.[25]

Josephine returned to her native Martinique in June 1788, then in the throes of its own slave revolts. After she came back to revolutionary Paris in September 1790, she was apprised of the events in Martinique through correspondence with her family until her mother's death in 1807. She also had her own memories of the precariousness of the island's economy. Both Napoleon and Josephine supported the continuation of slavery on Martinique in 1803, exactly when she began to acquire merino sheep.[26] Josephine's self-invention as a wise shepherdess managing her estate and a promoter of agronomy in France served to divert attention from the consequences of Napoleon's disastrous colonial policies, especially in the Caribbean.[27] Further, Josephine's ornamental sheep farm symbolically displaced French anxiety about colonial economies; her flourishing garden and estate seemed far removed from the harsh realities of slavery, conquest, and colonization.[28] Josephine's investments in wool and her acclimatization of botanical species bolstered Napoleon's domestic investments, securely connecting her personal projects to the national policies of the emperor.

LES MÉRINOS

Merino sheep were popular in the agronomy of the late ancien régime and the Revolution.[29] In 1786, Louis XVI imported the first merino sheep for the royal sheep farm at Rambouillet, southwest of Paris. Proving the diplomatic importance attached to the purchase of merinos, the king requested 380 sheep from his cousin Charles III, King of Spain, who stringently controlled the exportation of the breed, as it was considered essential for Spanish textiles. Upon the advice of the naturalist Louis-Jean-Marie Daubenton, the *mérinosation* of French flocks produced the French Rambouillet breed (**FIG. 4.4**).

The creation of the *bergerie* at Rambouillet reflected the desire of Louis XVI and his minister the Comte d'Angiviller to improve French sheep stock and the quality of woolen textiles. This royal *bergerie*, created in the

Fig. 4.4

Horace Vernet, *Étude pour une tête de bélier*. Musée des Beaux-Arts, Béziers.
© RMN / Gérard Blot

vernacular style, reinforced agricultural and georgic traditions, securing paternal order for the state and establishing a model for agricultural husbandry. The Rambouillet sheep farm signified a fusion of agricultural and seigneurial ideals that provided an enduring legacy. During the French Revolution, all the sheep at the *bergerie* were protected. Following the Revolution, in recognition of the importance of the sheep for the textile industry, Napoleon's interior minister Jean-Antoine Chaptal was instructed to resume bringing a significant number of merinos to France as early as 1801.[30]

Josephine first encountered sheep farming during the revolutionary decade when she took refuge at Croissy in suburban Paris from 1793 to 1794. After the execution of her husband Alexandre de Beauharnais in July of 1794 and her own imprisonment from April to August of that year, her lover Paul François Jean Nicolas, Vicomte de Barras, paid the rent for her Croissy house and even supplied her with a cow, two horses, and a carriage.[31] This sojourn had several implications for her obsession with acquiring Malmaison. Firstly, she could view Malmaison from Croissy, as the *seigneurie* of La Malmaison was directly across the Seine. Thus Josephine had topophilic associations with the site, linking suburban Paris with security, despite the fact that her sojourn at Croissy was a time of personal instability and profound political upheaval.

At Croissy, when food and agriculture were a question of survival, Josephine appreciated the importance of local agronomics. Josephine became friendly with her most prominent local neighbor, Jean Chanorier, who had owned a *seigneurie* at Croissy since 1779.[32] Chanorier, who had been a *receveur principal des finances* (tax collector) under Louis XVI, was interested in experimental farming. He purchased forty merinos at auction from the royal flock at Rambouillet to increase his own flock at Croissy.[33] Forced into exile in 1794, he returned to France and regained his Croissy estate in 1796.

Josephine obviously knew Chanorier well, since he served as her intermediary for the purchase of Malmaison. Chanorier also counseled Josephine about her reputation, suggesting that estate management and the role of the shepherdess in particular might change her image.[34] Chanorier wrote to Josephine in March of 1799: "If you were as rich as the public believes, I would only speak to you about a pleasing property that I know, but you must make a useful purchase."[35] Acting as a perfect agronomist, he added, "the property is the best example of a place that reunites both pleasure and profit," and continued "the house is large and the farm is excellent."[36] The original purchase at Malmaison was sixty hectares of land (about 150 acres), yet Josephine greatly enlarged her estate to accommodate her farms. Upon her death in 1814, the domain encompassed more than 726 hectares (nearly 1,800 acres).[37]

Josephine acquired merinos at Malmaison as early as 1803, when Chanorier advised her that "one could estimate having at least 300 sheep for wool production at Malmaison that could add to the value of the purchase."[38] In 1804, she explicitly asked for one thousand merinos from Spain to supply Malmaison and her son Eugene's estate at the Ferté-Beauharnais in Sologne, along with the government's request for merinos for Rambouillet. Morel was creating the *ferme ornée* in 1804 when Josephine wrote to Napoleon that she had successfully acclimated the merino sheep and would soon be able to hold a public auction of wool. Given her request for more Spanish merinos, the *bergerie* was enlarged in 1806 and 1807 to accommodate the flocks that increased steadily to more than two thousand animals in 1812 (**FIG. 4.5**).[39]

Alexandre de Laborde remarked on Josephine's sheep farm at Malmaison in his *Description des nouveaux jardins de la France et de ses anciens châteaux* (1808), a volume dedicated to linking the ancien régime to the new Napoleonic aristocracy. He published a plan of the estate (**FIG. 4.6**) and wrote about the *bergerie*:

> *Descending from the fine plantation of lofty trees of which we have often spoken, you cross a valley[,] the hills of which, formerly bordered with vines on each side, are now planted with ever-greens. Upon the first elevation you behold the building of the sheepfold, which contains one of the finest flocks in France. The sheep are annually sold by public auction, and they for the most part bring as high prices as those of Rambouillet. It is extremely gratifying to see persons in power giving the example of a kind of industry, so beneficial to the country, and which at the same time is a delightful ornament to a park.*[40]

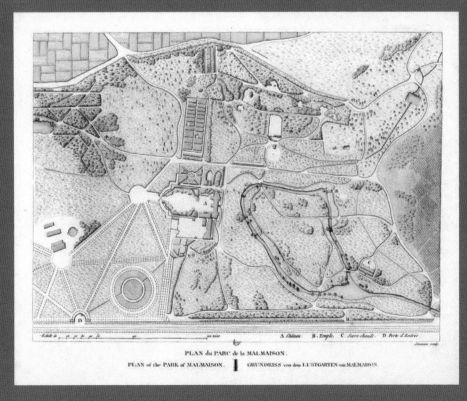

Fig. 4.6 Alexandre Laborde, Plan of Malmaison. Institut national d'histoire de l'art, Bibliothèque, collections Jacques Doucet

Thus by 1808 Empress Josephine's role as a shepherdess of merinos was a model for French prosperity. Josephine's success echoed Morel's theory:

> It seems that the minister governing a large state, the trader who drives a great commerce, the landowner who runs a large farm, all competing for the common good, though by different means, should be equal in the eyes of reason. The minister masters events by his foresight, the trader his fortune by speculation, and the landowner cultivates nature through his industry and work.[41]

Fig. 4.7 Pierre-Paul Prud'hon, *L'Impératrice Joséphine*, 1805, oil on canvas. © RMN (Musée du Louvre) / Gérard Blot

SUSAN TAYLOR-LEDUC

Morel suggested that gardening and agriculture together create an economic force, equal to the concerns of heads of state and men of finance. At Malmaison, Josephine acted like a minister of state on her own domain, usurping the paternalistic georgic tradition and managing her farm as an industrialist. She speculated on the profits from her wool and assured that her investments had market value.

Bernard Chevallier has clearly demonstrated that Josephine was never able to manage her budget.[42] Whatever profits she may have accumulated from her sheep auctions would not have begun to redress her expenses; nonetheless, the increasing number of sheep over the entire period of her occupancy of Malmaison suggests her commitment to sheep farming. Furthermore, her desire to send merinos to her son Eugène's estate at Ferté-Beauharnais implies her advocacy of sheep farming. Certainly Napoleon, who was also constantly searching for a means to link Enlightenment and ancien régime agronomic practices to the economic policies of his reign, supported Josephine's interest in wool through her *bergerie* as a viable agronomic experiment and as a productive image of France under imperial government. Most importantly, though, the investment in wool linked the Consulate and the Empire to the French textile industry.[43]

WOOL

When Napoleon first came to power, the cotton and linen for the dresses that were the favored fashions of the Directory and Consulate were not produced in France, but imported from the Americas or British India. In the last year of the Directory (1798–99), the importation of cotton, wool, linen, and hemp amounted to 96 million *livres*; the following year, the figure had risen to 133 million.[44] Consequently, Napoleon's interest in fashion was an imperative economic necessity requiring him to promote local agriculture to supply raw materials for textiles. When Napoleon became First Consul at the same time that he purchased Malmaison, he turned to uniforms—not only for the military, but also for the legislature and for members of the court—as a means to stimulate the French textile industry.[45] As emperor in 1805, Napoleon required all uniforms to bear the label "made in France" ("étoffe de manufactures française").

As a fashionable *merveilleuse* accustomed to imported cotton, muslin, and silk, Josephine certainly appreciated the need for raw materials, especially wool. Her understanding that wool was a valuable commodity came from her insider's knowledge of military uniforms.[46] During the Consular period, Josephine could not draw on her husband's salary, but Napoleon allowed her to recommend her protégés, notably for the supply of his troops. To make money, she quickly established a network of merchants and manufacturers and speculated in "les marchés des fournitures" (supply markets) that included military uniforms, munitions, and foodstuffs.[47] Investing in merinos for Malmaison was a logical choice, as she could be assured that there would always be a market for her wool production. Josephine, recast as a shepherdess, thus symbolically endorsed Napoleon's domestic policies and military campaigns and promoted the imperial court costume.

Another example of Josephine's interest in wool was her explicitly fashion-conscious promotion of cashmere scarves. The cashmere scarves Josephine draped around her shoulders were considered a luxurious accessory. The French passion for these shawls began in 1799 when General Bonaparte offered his wife a sumptuous hand-embroidered cashmere shawl upon his return from Egypt.[48] But unlike merinos, the attempts to raise cashmere goats in France were not successful, so Napoleon encouraged his manufacturers to create alternative fabrics.[49] Already in 1800, entrepreneur Christophe-Philippe Oberkampf, who printed cottons at his Jouy-en-Josas factory near Paris, was experimenting with imitation cashmere scarves. By 1803, as Josephine was expanding her sheep farm, Baron Guillaume Louis

Ternaux created French cashmere scarves using a blend of merino and goat wools. Several of Ternaux's creations were exhibited at the 1806 Exposition industrielle nationale. In 1807 Napoleon awarded Oberkampf and Ternaux, then exclusive "fournisseurs à la cour impérial" (suppliers to the Imperial court), the Légion d'honneur for their imitation shawls.[50] During the Empire, and especially during the Continental Blockade that forbade the importation of English fabrics, the interest in domestic merino wool increased, thus further legitimizing Josephine's estate management at Malmaison.

THE FERTILE GARDEN

Josephine had been a mother in her first marriage, but she could not produce an heir for Napoleon Bonaparte. This unfortunate twist of fate was an obsession throughout her marriage, suggesting one of the reasons Josephine focused on her gardens—a symbolic topos for fertility—for her patronage. The celebrated portrait of Josephine at Malmaison by Pierre-Paul Prud'hon does not show her gardens; rather, she has spread one of her signature cashmere shawls onto an artfully contrived rock seat, thus molding her carefully fashioned body to the "natural" landscape (**FIG. 4.7**). Josephine's ability to fertilize the gardens at Malmaison signified a fecund body of state; her feats of acclimatization for plants, exotic animals, and livestock (including sheep) implied that everything she touched was abundant and productive.

Josephine's bountiful garden provided cultural capital that outlived her relationship to Napoleon. Josephine's plan to marry her daughter Hortense to her brother-in-law Louis Bonaparte was an effort to project her own fertility into the Bonaparte bloodline. Her grandson Charles-Louis-Napoleon Bonaparte, the future Napoleon III, became the fruit of Josephine's political ambitions. Gros's portrait of Hortense and the infant Louis-Napoleon (**FIG. 4.8**) imitates the representation of Prud'hon's portrait of Josephine. Hortense echoes her mother's pose, sitting on the same rock seat, a red shawl spread beneath her, proudly presenting her son as if he too had sprung forth from the fertile gardens of Malmaison.

Louis-Napoleon spent the summer of 1813 (May to September) under his grandmother's care; she even brought an elephant to Malmaison to amuse her grandchildren, although she later complained that it had ruined the grass.[51] He bought Malmaison in 1861, certainly inspired by memories of his grandmother; he recalled eating sugarcane in her greenhouse. It is possible that after Josephine's death, Malmaison remained a symbol of how gardens reflected and served the French nation. This concept may have influenced Napoleon III's decision not only to endorse extensive garden planning for nineteenth-century Paris, but also to support the French textile industry, notably at the Bergeries Impériales.[52]

Acknowledgments

I would like to thank Sue Ann Prince for encouraging me to develop this topic for this symposium. An earlier version of this paper was presented at a symposium dedicated to Jean-Marie Morel, "Jardin, Parc, Pays: Jean-Marie Morel (1728–1810): Un Paysagiste entre Sensibilité et Lumières," Dijon, November 2005, organized by Joseph Disponzio. I would like to thank Christine Baltay, Joseph Disponzio, Meredith Martin, Susan Sidlauskas, and Patricia Taylor for their insightful comments on earlier manuscript versions of this paper. I would also like to express my thanks to Bernard Chevallier, whose generosity and exemplary scholarship have consistently encouraged art historians to build on his impeccable archival research.

1   Although the title on the folio volume depicted in this painting is *Flore de Malmaison*, this title does not refer to a specific volume. Josephine underwrote E. P. Ventenant's *Jardin de la Malmaison*, 2 vols. (1803–4), illustrated by Pierre-Joseph Redouté. Josephine's patronage of illustrated botanical books is summarized in *L'Impératrice Joséphine et les sciences naturelles* (Rueil-Malmaison: Musée national des châteaux de Malmaison et Bois-Préau; Paris: Éditions de la Réunion des musées nationaux, 1997), 20–24. On Ventenant and Redouté see ibid., 44–47, 73–77. Dorothy Johnson's essay on Redouté in this volume offers a new interpretation of his botanical illustrations.

2   Bernard Chevallier and Christophe Pincemaille, *L'Impératrice Joséphine* (Paris: Payot et Rivages, 1996).

3   Bernard Chevallier, *L'Art de vivre au temps de Joséphine* (Paris: Flammarion, 1998). See also Ewa Lajer-Burcharth, *Necklines: The Art of Jacques-Louis David After the Terror* (New Haven, Conn.: Yale University Press, 1999), in particular the chapter entitled "Necklines: Directorial Self-Fashioning," in which she argues that the increased concern with fashion in the post-Thermidor period was a testimony to the social recognition of the individual body not only as seat of the self, but as a site where the self could be fashioned (181); Christina Barreto and Martin Lancaster, *Napoléon et l'Empire de la mode* (Milan: Skira, 2010); and Jean-Marie Bruson and Anne Forray-Carlier, *Au temps des Merveilleuses: La société parisienne sous le Directoire et le Consulat* (Paris: Paris-Musées, 2005), 76–110, 126–47.

4   Representations of the shepherdess theme in eighteenth-century painting are beyond the scope of this paper, but the notion of a frivolous shepherdess was well established in Denis Diderot's critiques of François Boucher's pastoral paintings. See Georges Brunel, "Boucher, neveu de Rameau" in *Diderot et l'art de Boucher à David: Les Salons, 1759–1781*, ed. Marie-Catherine Sahut and Nathalie Volle (Paris, Éditions de la Réunion des musées nationaux, 1984), 101–9, 136–43. Porcelain figures of the shepherd and shepherdess themes were popularized after Boucher's paintings. See *François Boucher, 1703–1770* (Paris: Éditions de la Réunion des musées nationaux, 1987), particularly *Le berger galant*, a white glazed soft-paste porcelain figurine made in Vincennes in 1752 (354–55, cat. 97).

5   Chevallier and Pincemaille describe Josephine's French Antillais heritage and her youth among the planter aristocracy in *L'Impératrice Joséphine*, 11–20. Josephine returned to Martinique in June 1788 and remained there until 1790, when she fled the revolutionary revolts on the island. Despite the uprisings in Martinique, she received funds from her mother during the Terror in Paris. Ibid., 58–60, 94–98. This paper attempts to place Josephine's colonial plantation experiences in the larger context of transatlantic economic and colonial history. See R. Darrell Meadows, "Engineering Exile: Social Networks and the French Atlantic Community, 1789–1809," *French Historical Studies* 23, no. 1 (Winter 2000): 67–102.

6   The Bonapartes and Napoleon's banker visited Malmaison in the beginning of 1798 and made an offer to purchase the estate, but it was refused. For the details of the purchase of Malmaison, see Bernard Chevallier, *Malmaison: Château et domaine des origines à 1904* (Paris: Éditions de la Réunion des musées nationaux, 1989), 35–40.

7   Ibid., 44–45.

8   Jean-Marie Morel, *Théorie des Jardins, ou, L'art des jardins de la nature*, 2 vols. (Paris: Panckoucke, 1802).

9   Chevallier and Pincemaille, *L'Impératrice Joséphine*, 242–72.

10   For Morel at Malmaison and at other garden sites see Joseph Disponzio, "Jean-Marie Morel: A Catalogue of his Landscape Designs," special issue, *Studies in the History of Gardens and Designed Landscapes* 21, nos. 3–4 (July–December 2001); and *L'Impératrice Joséphine et les sciences naturelles*, 148–53.

11   "De tous les genres de jardins, celui de la ferme est la seule qui réunit aux agréments champêtres une utilité réelle; c'est dans le jardin de la France que ces deux objets se combinent sans se préjudicier, qu'il tirent avantage de leur association et se prêtent un mutuel secours. En effet, dans une ferme bien ordonné, toutes les plantations destinées à l'agrément peuvent être fructueuses, et toutes les cultures qui ont un but d'utilité, peuvent offrir un

aspect agréable." Morel, "De la Ferme," in *Théorie des Jardins*, 2:103.

12 Chevallier and Pincemaille, *L'Impératrice Joséphine*, 244.

13 On Marie-Antoinette's Hameau, see Meredith Martin, *Dairy Queens: The Politics of Pastoral Architecture from Catherine de' Medici to Marie-Antoinette* (Cambridge, Mass.: Harvard University Press, 2011), 160–67, 199–213.

14 Christian Jouanin and Guy Ledoux-Lebard, "Histoire des troupeaux de mérinos de Joséphine à Malmaison et d'Eugène à la Ferté-Beauharnais," *Bulletin de la Société des amis des Malmaison* (1993): 48–55; and *L'Impératrice Joséphine et les sciences naturelles*, 154–61.

15 *L'Impératrice Joséphine et les sciences naturelles*, 149.

16 My perspective on female power and the pastoral is inspired by Meredith Martin's *Dairy Queens*.

17 "La *Ferme*, dont le principal objet est l'économie et l'utilité, s'annoncera par son air champêtre, négligé & sans prétention; ainsi qu'une bergère naïve & sans art, sa simplicité sera son seul ornement." Jean-Marie Morel, *Théorie des Jardins* (Paris, 1776), 37.

18 The interest in sheep farming can be gleaned from a number of treatises published at the end of the eighteenth century and during the revolutionary decade. See, for example, *Remarques sur l'Instruction de monsieur Daubenton, Pour les Bergers & pour les propriétaires de Troupeaux*, (Paris: chez Gueffier, 1785); and Ministère de l'intérieur, *Avis aux cultivateurs et propriétaires de troupeaux sur l'amélioration des laines* (Paris: Imprimerie de la République, prairial an VII [1799]).

19 Thierry Lentz, *Le Grand Consulat, 1799–1804* (Paris: Fayard, 1999), 334–35, 405–6. The decision to grant amnesty to former émigrés who could not reclaim their lands was promulgated under the law of April 26, 1802. In preparation for the closed decision that resulted in the *sénatus-consulte*, an extraordinary meeting was held at Malmaison on April 16, 1802.

20 Ibid., 406–7.

21 "L'acquisition de Malmaison par Joséphine ne doit rien au hasard. Elle résulte d'abord du besoin très fort, presque viscéral, qu'éprouve le couple Bonaparte de posséder une terre. Napoléon et Joséphine sont deux insulaires exilées de leurs îles natales, tous deux issues de familles nobles mais modestes. . . . Ils aspirent à marquer d'une empreinte au sol leur réussite personnelle et à enraciner leur installation au coeur de la nouvelle société. L'achat d'une belle propriété peut y pourvoir, parce qu'elle va leur conférer un statut de châtelains, non pas de ces hobereaux d'ancien régime désargenté et agrippées à leurs prérogatives seigneuriales, mais de ces nouveau maîtres jeunes et talentueux qui profitant de la vente des biens nationaux se sont substitués à l'ancienne aristocratie terrienne." Christophe Pincemaille, *Il y a 200 ans, Joséphine achetait Malmaison* (Rueil-Malmaison: Société des amis de Malmaison, 1999), 4.

22 Ibid., 9–10, 13–14; Lentz, *Le Grand Consulat*, 406–7.

23 "Senatus consultus relatif aux émigres, du 6 floréal an X de la République," in Senate Consultus, *Bulletin des Lois*, tome 6, 3ᵉ série (1802), no. 1401, p. 107.

24 Jill H. Casid, *Sowing Empire: Colonialism and Landscape* (Minneapolis: University of Minnesota Press, 2005), 27–41. Casid focuses primarily on Santo Domingo and does not include Josephine in her interpretation of the picturesque garden as a "displacement" of colonial policy, but I have found her thesis particularly relevant for my interpretation of the sheep farm at Malmaison.

25 Ibid., 45–48. Casid describes this displacement of colonial economies into the aesthetic sphere as "imperial picturesque." Exploitation of colonial woods in eighteenth-century furniture design similarly negated the Caribbean colonial trade in favor of the exotic. See Madeline Dobie, "Orientalism, Colonialism, and Furniture in Eighteenth-Century France," in *Furnishing the Eighteenth Century: What Furniture Can Tell Us About the European and American Past*, ed. Dena Goodman and Kathryn Norberg (New York: Routledge, 2007), 13–36.

26 On Josephine's longstanding networks on Martinique, see Rebecca Hartkopf Schloss, *Sweet Liberty: The Final Days of Slavery in Martinique* (Philadelphia: University of Pennsylvania Press, 2009), 17–45. See especially 32–34 on the Tascher de la Pagerie family correspondence with Josephine about maintaining slavery on their sugar plantation in 1806. See also Pincemaille, *Il y a 200 ans*, 8–9, concerning Josephine's financial ties to Santa Domingo.

27 Philippe R. Girard, "Rêves d'Empire: French Revolutionary Doctrine and Military Interventions in the Southern United States and the Caribbean, 1789–1809," *Louisiana History* 48, no. 4 (Fall 2007): 389–41. France traded with Tobago, Guadeloupe, Martinique, and Santo Domingo for sugar, coffee, cotton, and indigo, exporting manufactured goods. With the French Revolution, the colonial revolts, and then the Continental Blockade, France could not count on her trade with the colonies; thus domestic production was primordial throughout the Empire.

28 Anne Lafont's commentary in this volume draws our attention to the contextual use of the terms "acclimatize" and "appropriate" when discussing colonial history.

29 *L'Impératrice Joséphine* et les sciences naturelles, 154–61, informs my summary of the acquisition of merinos at Malmaison. See also Pierre-Yves Lacour, "La naturalisation des mérinos," in "La République naturaliste: Les collections françaises d'histoire naturelle sous la Révolution, 1789–1804" (Ph.D. diss., European University Institute, 2010), 1:320–28.

30 *L'Impératrice Joséphine et les sciences naturelles*, 154–61; Jouanin and Ledoux-Lebard, "Histoire des troupeaux de mérinos," 78–79. In 1795 the Treaty of Basel included a secret article that guaranteed the French republic's right to import as many as one thousand female and one hundred male merinos for five consecutive years, but from 1795 until 1800 this contract was not honored. In 1800 the agricultural bureau, under the direction of interior minister Jean-Antoine Chaptal, sent Adrien Francastel to Spain to bring the merinos back to France. The first sheep actually arrived in 1801 under the sponsorship of the Société d'Agriculture de la Seine.

31 Chevallier and Pincemaille, *L'Impératrice Joséphine*, 74–75, 77–80; Pincemaille, *Il y a 200 ans*, 4–5. On Chanorier, see Charles Bonnet, *Chanorier, dernier seigneur de Croissy: La Fédération, l'émigration et Brumaire: Extrait de Croissy Saint-Léonard, un village sous l'ancien régime*, Centenaire de 1789 (Saint-Germain-en-Laye: Doizelet, 1889). Chanorier's early friendship with Josephine is discussed on 33–36.

32 Pincemaille, *Il y a 200 ans*, 61–62, 5n8. Also see Gérard Hubert, *Malmaison* (Paris: Éditions de la Réunion des musées nationaux, 1980), 14–16, which reproduces most of Chanorier's letter.

33 Pierre-Yves Lacour, "La naturalisation des mérinos," 325.

34 Ibid.

35 "Si vous étiez aussi riche
que le public le croit, je
ne vous parlerais que des
agréments de la plus joli
habitation que je connaisse,
mais il faut vous fassiez
une acquisition utile." Jean
Chanorier to Josephine
Bonaparte, Croissy, 11
ventôse [March 1, 1799],
quoted in Pincemaille, *Il y
a 200 ans*, 15; and Hubert,
Malmaison, 14–16.

36 "La propriété est tout que
j'ai vu de mieux dans le
genre utile et agréable . . .
La maison est grande et la
ferme superbe." Quoted
in Hubert, *Malmaison*,
16. Josephine bought the
property on April 21, 1799,
but Bonaparte settled the
final accounts in 1810. The
property actually belonged
to him until he officially
gave it to her in their divorce
settlement in 1809.

37 Chevallier, *Malmaison*, 49.
Originally, there were "387
arpents de bois, de vignes,
et de prés en fermage, de
vaches, de moutons, de
cochons d'une basse-cour."

38 ". . . que l'on pouvait avoir
à Malmaison 300 bêtes à
laine et que cet objet bien
conduit peut s'ajouter au
revenu de la terre." Quoted
in *L'Impératrice Joséphine
et les sciences naturelles*,
155. See also Hubert,
Malmaison, 16.

39 See *L'Impératrice Joséphine
et les sciences naturelles*,
154–61, which details
Joséphine's intense interest
in selling and renting her
sheep as well as a certain
awareness of the kilograms
of wool per animal. See also
Chevallier, *Malmaison*, 147–
48. It is also interesting to
note that Chanorier wrote a
treatise about his success in
dyeing merino wool, further
suggesting that Joséphine
would have understood
the exportation of wool as
a commodity. See *Extrait
du rapport fait à l'Institut
national des sciences, et des
arts par Citoyen Daubenton,
Fourcroy et Desmarets, du
Mémoire du C^en Chanorier,
membre associé, sur le drap
bleu teint en laine et fabriqué
avec les toisons du troupeau
de race pure d'Espagne
établie à Croissy-sur-Seine,*

*département de Seine-et-
Oise, en 1786, par Citoyen
Chanorier* (Paris: Imprimerie
de la République, thermidor
an VII [1799]).

40 "En sortant de la belle
futaie dont nous avons
parlé souvent, on traverse
un vallon dont les coteaux,
jadis bordés de vignes des
deux côtés, sont aujourd'hui
plantés d'arbres verts. Sur
la première élévation on
découvre le bâtiment de
la bergerie, qui sert à un
des plus beaux troupeaux
qui soient en France. La
vente s'en fait tous les ans
publiquement, et les prix
s'élèvent à peu près à ceux
de Rambouillet. Il est beau
de voir des personnes
puissants donner l'exemple
d'un genre d'industrie, si
avantageux au pays, et qui
de plus est un très-grand
ornement dans un parc."
English translation and
French text from Alexandre
de Laborde, *Description
des nouveaux jardins de
la France et de ses anciens
châteaux* (Paris: Delance,
1808), 66.

41 "Il me semble que le ministre qui régit un grand Etat,
que le négociant qui conduit
un grand commerce, que le
propriétaire qui dirige une
grande culture, concourant
tous au bien commun,
quoique par des voies
différentes, devraient être
égaux aux yeux de la raison.
L'homme de l'Etat maitrise
les évènements par sa
prévoyance, la négociant, la
fortune par ses spéculations,
le cultivateur, la nature par
son industrie et son travail."
Morel, *Théorie des jardins*,
1802, 2:196n.

42 Chevallier and Pincemaille,
L'Impératrice Joséphine,
273–300.

43 Jean Tulard, *Nouvelle
Histoire de Paris: Le
Consulat et l'Empire, 1800–
1815* (Paris: Association pour
la publication d'une histoire
de Paris, 1970), 67–86,
explains the importance of
industry and manufacturing,
especially cotton and wool,
to Napoleon's domestic
policies.

44 Barreto and Lancaster,
*Napoléon et l'Empire de la

mode*, 166.

45 Ibid., 116–17; *L'Impératrice
Joséphine et les sciences
naturelles*, 155.

46 Barreto and Lancaster,
*Napoléon et l'Empire de la
mode*, 120–27.

47 Chevallier and Pincemaille,
L'Impératrice Joséphine, 135–
37. As Chevallier remarks,
"En qualité d'épouse du
général en chef de l'armée
d'Italie, Joséphine est
particulièrement exposée à
la sollicitude des munition-
naires. . . . Ainsi [elle]
contrôle la chaîne complète
de l'attribution des marchés,
depuis les commis de
bureaux de Paris jusqu'aux
aides de camp de Bonaparte"
(136). See also Lentz, *Le
Grand Consulat*, 376–79.

48 On Josephine's passion
for cashmere shawls, see
Barreto and Lancaster,
*Napoléon et l'Empire de la
mode*, 125–27.

49 Ibid., 122.

50 On Oberkampf and
Terneaux, see Jean Tulard,
ed., *Dictionnaire Napoléon*,
rev. ed. (Paris: Fayard,
1989), 1256; and Baretto
and Lancaster, *Napoléon et
l'Empire de la mode*, 119–20.

51 Chevallier and Pincemaille,
L'Impératrice Joséphine,
392–94.

52 Ibid., 387–95.

OF CABBAGES AND KINGS: THE POLITICS OF PLANTING VEGETABLES AT THE REVOLUTIONARY JARDIN DES PLANTES

PAULA YOUNG LEE

IN 1775, BRITISH DIARIST HESTER THRALE visited France on her honeymoon and was invited to "the King's Musæum, where the famous Mr. D'Aubenton [sic] waited to attend us and display the natural Curiosities deposited in this Suite of Rooms & lately arranged by Mr. Buffon himself."[1] There, she saw precious stones and taxidermied fauna, including "the Yellow Parrot of Cuba, the Jabiru, a Large Fishing Bird from China, twice the size of the biggest Stork I know, & the Promerops of Guinea." She was visiting the Cabinet du Roi, a natural history collection located on the grounds of the historic King's Garden (Jardin du Roi) in Paris. There was no obvious reason for her to call the place a "musæum," as that word was not commonly invoked in any context at the time. Nonetheless, in 1790, as revolutionary furor threatened to destroy institutions of higher learning, it was "musæum" that chief gardener André Thouin proposed as the appropriate new name for the entire Jardin du Roi, just as resident naturalist Louis Daubenton subsequently argued before the Assemblée Nationale that the Jardin du Roi could be transformed into "a true Musæum" by extending its programmatic scope to include all branches of natural history.[2] The only person who objected to the new title was Auguste Charles César de Flahaut de La Billarderie, Buffon's replacement as the new director (intendant), who insisted that the name should remain "Jardin du Roi" (King's Garden) or "Jardin royal des plantes" (Royal Plant Garden), as both affirmed the institution's historical debt to the kings of France as well as the priority it placed on plants.[3]

La Billarderie complained that Thouin, Daubenton, and the other professors were affecting a sort of total amnesia ("oubli absolu") by changing the name, for it required willful denial to forget that the Jardin du Roi had been founded by a French king and continuously supported by the largesse of kings right up through "le Roy regnant," Louis XVI.[4] For La Billarderie, the word "musæum" razed this illustrious past while wrongly focusing attention on the "accessory" collections of natural history. Accused shortly thereafter of "abusing" the institution's finances, La Billarderie resigned his post. But his accusations were not entirely wrong, because the renaming of the Jardin du Roi as the Muséum d'Histoire naturelle transferred all attention to the collections of natural history, while obscuring a political agenda that planned to transform the institution into a place of plants, and specifically into an experimental farm dedicated to agriculture.

On January 9, 1790, English writer Arthur Young went to breakfast at the Tuileries in Paris, where he heard a memoir presented by the Société d'Agriculture on the means of improving agriculture in France. There were three chief points of recommendation: a greater attention to bees; the importance of "panification," the means by which flours were transformed into bread; and the teaching of the "obstetrick art," presumably in reference to livestock. Young concluded: "On the establishment of a free and patriotic government, to which the national agriculture might look for new and halcyon days, these were objects doubtless of the first importance."[5]

Following the arguments of the Physiocrats, eighteenth-century economic theorists who argued that all wealth originated from the land, the new French government began to advocate for a strong system of agriculture as essential to improving the bankrupt nation. From 1793 to 1794, Abbé Henri Grégoire, the former president of the National Convention, proposed a series of national *métairies* to be dispersed through the country. The French system of *métayage* is known elsewhere as sharecropping, an arrangement in which the farmer shared an agreed amount of his crops with the landowner in exchange for the use of the land. Grégoire proposed that these agricultural posts would be centrally coordinated through the newly created Muséum d'Histoire naturelle in Paris. Per his plan, the Muséum would provide these "houses of rural economy" with the botanical and zoological expertise of its faculty. The institution would also supply these outposts with breed types conserved in its cabinets and galleries, while actively collecting exotic plant and animal specimens that might be "usefully" naturalized on French soil. In this way, he concluded, the Muséum could fully realize its mandate of teaching, commerce, and the arts.

The Convention's response to its president's ideas was droningly positive. "Commerce in France needs only to be the agent of agriculture. It is the solid foundation of French industry," pronounced Camille Teisseire. "From there, [the country's] strength, solidity, and happiness will result."[6] Teisseire went on to outline a profit-driven program of "rustic economy" in which important parcels of land would be reserved for commercial cultivation. This land would be "seeded" in Noah-like two-by-twos with native and foreign plants and animals representing the strongest and purest of their "race," the explicit goal of the breeding project being the "perfection and civilization of all that might be useful" to the nation. As elaborated by Joseph-Antoine de Boisset, a member of the Comité de commerce, the program of perfection, domestication, and education might be expanded by placing a "Jardin des plantes" within every department.[7] The public's understanding of botany would thereby be facilitated, and their resulting fascination with plants would bring them "closer to nature." Being simultaneously dedicated to agriculture, these gardens would transform terrains once "regarded as sterile" into fertile soil, offering a direct lesson in the power of cultural regeneration. On a practical level, the results would not only be deliciously edible but would also contribute to commerce.

The key to this program would be the establishment of *métairies* centered on the Muséum d'Histoire naturelle, which was already functioning in this double capacity of serving "botany and agriculture." The Jardin des Plantes at the Muséum, Boisset explained, was already in a condition to furnish the plants necessary to form the foundation of any serious garden. Having established a variety of "correspondences" with other scientists and institutions, it had long been in the practice of obtaining plants from Asia, Africa, and Central America. Some of these species, such as cherry trees, apricot trees, peach trees, fig trees, tuberoses, lilacs, green beans, lentils, melons, and the "tastiest" peas, had already been successfully naturalized in France with great success. Boisset bluntly dismissed those who raised ideological objections to the "soiling" practice of naturalization, for the plants indigenous to France were "tasteless legumes, insipid fruits, and disagreeable flowers." The central clearinghouse for all these useful, naturalized plants had been, and would remain, he insisted, the Jardin des Plantes of the Muséum d'Histoire naturelle in Paris. Through its work, "agriculture will be renewed."[8]

Remarkably, the members of the Convention nationale seemed to agree that the Muséum was the best place to carry out agricultural experiments on behalf of the nation. These experiments required large blocks of time and a varied terrain, and it would take years before viable yields could be established. It was not a task that could be accepted by a farmer, whose job was to cultivate crops that would answer to hunger.[9] It made good sense for the Muséum to initiate the process of naturalizing foreign plants, and to establish their viability in the soil of France. Instead of "useless" plants inside the king's garden, there would be new varieties of artichokes, onions, and cabbages. Once naturalization had been confirmed, the Muséum would send the specimens to farms in France and its colonies, where they could be confidently planted as food or forage crops that would, from then on, directly benefit the people.

Given that the Muséum played such a vital role in this land-based plan of moral and economic regeneration, it is unsurprising that during the first months of its existence the institution was regularly referred to as the "Muséum des plantes."[10] This titular substitution of green and growing things for the text-based study of natural history signaled where the operative emphases lay for the public. The people of France had not misunderstood the new institution's purpose. As outlined by Jean-Baptiste Dubois for gardens in general and the Muséum d'Histoire naturelle in particular, all such "experimental farms" destined for "the perfection of culture" would serve as "depots" of grains and living animals destined to be propagated in neighboring countries. This work would augment the project's overall utility by creating a collection of native and foreign machines and agricultural instruments for the purposes of "instruction."[11]

As official decrees and administrative budgets allocated increasingly large sums for the Muséum's gardens, a variety of architectural projects addressed the institution's central position in the "culturing" of France. Here, it is useful to examine a relatively unknown "Musaéum [sic]" designed by the revolutionary architect Claude Nicolas Ledoux (FIG. 5.1).[12] At first glance, it is, as architectural historian Michel Gallet proposed, an "ideal museum inside a mysterious garden." Crucially, however, this land is not so pristine or arbitrary as it appears. Lightly dotted lines define disjointed paths, the river Seine flows at the foot of the drawing, and the upper quadrant pops obstinately outside of the image's square frame. Bothered by the irregularities of the real, these secondary indications reveal that the "garden" is a cadastral plan of a contested area of working-class Paris known alternately as the section Sans-Culottes, or as the section Jardin-des-Plantes. In short, Ledoux has anchored his imaginary "Musaéum" on the grounds of the existing Muséum d'Histoire naturelle, still located today in what is known as the fifth *arrondissement* of Left Bank Paris.

The ground floor of Ledoux's four-level, circular "Musaéum" (FIG. 5.2) included a chicken coop, stables for horses and cows, a milking room, a kitchen, an oven room, a pantry, laundry rooms, and general storage rooms. A mezzanine featured two multi-room lodgings, residential quarters for household servants, extensive linen closets, and an area for storing fruit. The next floor held six study rooms with beds. These rooms rimmed an imposing two-story central granary meant to store winter provisions such as straw, hay, oats, wheat, and barley. At the uppermost level, a centralized pavilion featuring an "Apollo rotunda" offered three branching arms respectively assigned to painting, natural history, and sculpture. This last was specifically a "sculpture salon, agriculture model" ("sallon de sculture, modele agriculture [sic]").

Unprecedented, misspelled, and offering no further basis for elaboration, the caption's meaning remains vague. Possibilities range from the organization of fine-art objects according to a Linnaean system of classification (as implemented at the then newly created museum of art installed in the Palais de Louvre), to the straightforward display of agricultural machines as "type" models that could be studied by working farmers.[13] Nonetheless, it is evident that the functional program of this "musaéum" has little in common with art museums such as the Louvre; nor does it resemble cabinets of curiosity such as the Cabinet du Roi toured by Mrs. Thrale. Instead, the program recalls the features of "maisons d'économie rurale" (houses of rural economy), as set forth by Grégoire and announced as a competition (*concours*) on 13 Floréal Year II (May 2, 1794). Ledoux had responded with a design for an actual farm:

> *Following the invitation extended to artists to occupy themselves with useful and agricultural establishments, citizen Ledoux offers plans, sections, and elevations of a farm that answers to all needs, a large-scale sheepfold of known applications and utility; it is known that few wools are as fine as those of Spain or England. A public market brings together subsistences of first necessity at the frontiers. Granaries for surplus. . . . In any case, Nature who sees everything with the same Eye does not vary in her principles.[14]*

Given that Ledoux interpreted "house of rural economy" to mean "sheep farm," his circular "Musaéum" begins to fall inside a larger pattern of agricultural thinking. In Year II (1793–94), this vision enjoyed exceptional political currency. Notably, the specific urban sectors activated by Ledoux's plan echo a series of political proposals initiated in May 1794 that would have augmented the grounds of the Muséum d'Histoire naturelle from fifty to an astonishing 270 *arpents*.[15] Thus becoming the "most beautiful garden in the universe," this "vast garden of Natural History" would henceforth present a completely realized microcosm of the "physical world, just as regenerated Paris" (changed tactfully to "France" in the second version of the written project) "will be that of the moral world."[16]

For the professors of the Muséum, the proposed expansion would provide space for "plants of botanical interest, plants that feed humans and animals, fruit-bearing trees, and plants used in industry."[17] Listing botany first was consistent with the institution's pre-revolutionary mission. But it is disingenuous to suggest that the professors added the bits about fruit trees and crop plants merely to pacify external political interests. As I have noted elsewhere, the faculty not only accepted the agricultural program but enhanced it, enthusiastically proposing in this same document that "the opportunity must be taken to newly construct a farming complex [at the Muséum d'Histoire naturelle] which might serve as a model of the genre."[18] They specifically referenced the famous experimental farm in Denainvillers (near the town of Pithiviers) established by the agronomist Henri-Louis Duhamel Du Monceau. One of the most important agronomists of the eighteenth century, Duhamel was well known to the members of the Convention nationale. He had used his farm to establish the relationship of the soil to plant production and to experiment extensively with silviculture. The farm itself included housing for the farmer and his family, as well as cowsheds, sheepfolds, stables for horses, and large granaries. Implicitly, the proposed expansion of the Muséum's grounds would make it possible to establish these kinds of agricultural buildings as well.

For several months the expansion project had been proceeding smoothly, with no hints of trouble or resistance. By the end of June, the proposal had successfully passed all the preliminary stages, including the approval of all required committees, the rewriting of several drafts, and the resolution of specific articles to be named in the decree. But the open call to artists never went out, and the designated terrains were not annexed until the following century when Napoleon consolidated power, and then at a much-reduced

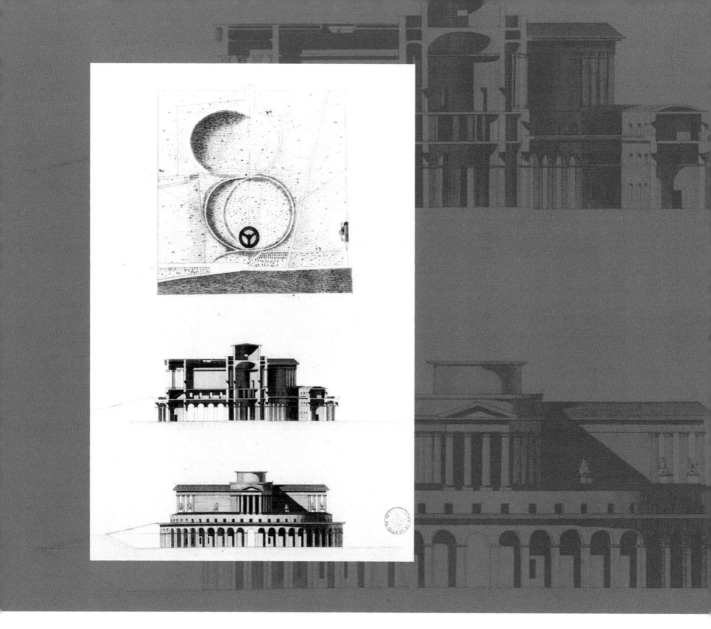

Fig. 5.1 (above)

Claude Nicolas Ledoux, *Musaéum* (site plan, section, and elevation, undated). Courtesy of Fine Art Library, Wellesley College

Fig. 5.2 (opposite)

Claude Nicolas Ledoux, *Musaéum* (plans, undated). Courtesy of Fine Art Library, Wellesley College

scale. Apart from the usual demurrals regretting the deplorable insufficiency of funds, the specificity of Ledoux's vision suggests another reason why these ambitious plans were aborted. Speculatively, we might say that his project was not glorious but ghastly in its barren enormity.

Inconveniently, the political plan to place this area "under culture" required the ruthless displacement of the working poor, whose lives and livelihoods would be sacrificed to an ideological vision. The Sans-Culottes/ Jardin-des-Plantes sector was "extremely" working class, as members of various revolutionary committees noted, and was filled with "industrious citizens."[19] As unsentimentally envisioned by Ledoux, the Latin Quarter's haphazard bricolage of residences, shops, markets, public squares, and streets would be sacrificed to the recuperation of "workable ground" suitable to being transformed into fields of coffee plants and fruit trees. But until such foreign plants could be established, the land promised everything but offered nothing.

Ledoux's "Musaéum" spirals inside an empty expanse of arid ground, relieved only by a few tight rows of trees so dwarfed in scale as to appear to be shrubs. It was, perhaps, a too-literal description of the quotidian sacrifice demanded in the name of a future agricultural good. By Year III, as the political winds shifted, the challenges proved too large to resolve, and the plans to create an agricultural utopia at the Muséum d'Histoire naturelle faded from history. But the remnants of this vision can still be discerned in the huts built in Year II to house exotic sheep, camels, and goats. They are now part of the Muséum's Ménagerie.

PAULA YOUNG LEE

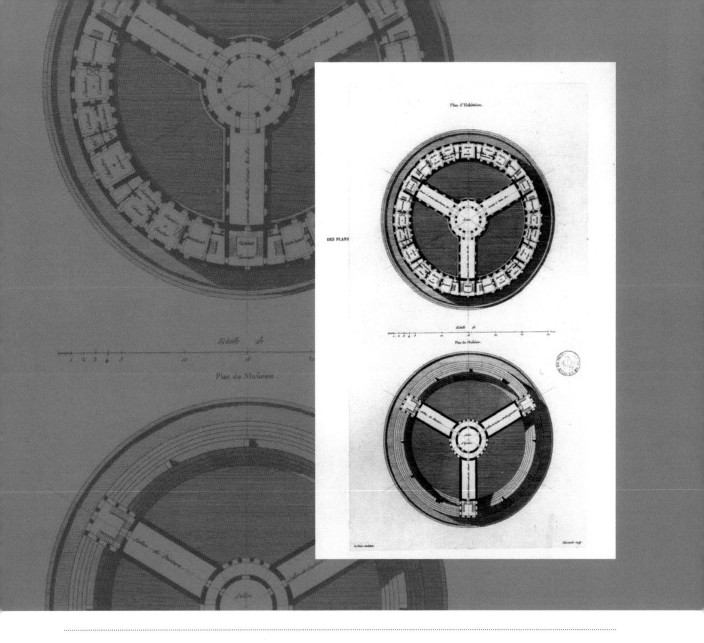

1 *The French Journals of Mrs. [Hester] Thrale and Doctor [Samuel] Johnson*, ed. Moses Tyson and Henry Guppy (Manchester: Manchester University Press, 1932), 111.

2 Louis Daubenton et al., "Seconde adresse et projet de règlemens, présentés à l'Assemblée nationale par les officiers du Jardin des Plantes," in *Adresses et projet de règlemens présentés a l'Assemblée nationale par les officiers du Jardin des plantes et du Cabinet d'histoire naturelle d'après le décret de l'Assemblée nationale, du 20 août 1790* (Paris: chez Buisson, 1790), separately paginated.

3 [Auguste Charles César de Flahaut de La Billarderie], "Jardin du Roy," [1790], remarks on the subject of the "Projet des règlemens" cited in n2. Archives nationales (hereafter AN)

F17/1310; a copy is also found in AN 01/2126, dossier "Jardin du Roi 1790."

4 [Auguste Charles César de Flahaut de La Billarderie], "Observations sur les adresses et projets de règlements de Messieurs les officiers du Jardin du roi, no. 18," [1790], AN F17/1310, in which he offers a point-by-point critique of that founding document. Regarding article I, "L'établissement sera nommé Musaeum d'histoire naturelle," he responded: "Il semble que l'ancien titre du jardin Royal des plantes serait plus convenable puisque le jardin est l'objet principal dont le cabinet n'est qu'un accessoire."

5 Arthur Young, *Travels in France During the Years 1787, 1788, 1789*, ed. Matilda Betham-Edwards (London: George Bell, 1909), 292.

6 "Le commerce en France ne doit être que le commis de l'agriculture. Elle est le fondement solide de l'industrie française. . . . De-là résulteront sa force, sa solidité, son bonheur." Camille Teisseire, *Observation sur le projet d'établissement d'une métairie nationale . . . présenté par le citoyen Grégoire* (Paris: chez R. Vatar, 1793), 1.

7 Joseph Antoine de Boisset, *Rapport et projet de décret du 15 floréal an II* [May 4, 1794] *relatifs à l'établissement des jardins des plantes dans les départements* (Paris: Imprimerie nationale, n.d. [an II (1794)]), 2–4.

8 Boisset, *Rapport . . . relatifs à l'établissement des jardins des plantes*, 7.

9 For example, these same views appear in Jacques Isoré, *Rapport sur l'agricul-*

ture fait à la Convention nationale le 3 floréal par Isoré, cultivateur (Paris: Imprimerie nationale, floréal an II [1794]). Isoré does not specifically mention the Jardin des Plantes in his report; however, his comments clearly informed Boisset's report to the Convention, made just twelve days later, which assigns to the Muséum the role of "experimentation" for all the reasons outlined by Isoré.

10 For example, a letter from André Thouin, chief gardener of the Muséum, to his colleague the chemist Antoine Fourcroy, who was also a member of the Comité de salut public, was receipted as "un paquet adressé audit Comité [de salut public] par le Muséum des Plantes," 4 messidor an 2 [June 22, 1794], MNHN Ms. 308. References to the

"Muzeum nationalle des Plantes" appear in the *Procès-verbaux de la Commune générale des arts de peinture, sculpture, architecture et gravure*, ed. Henry Lapauze (Paris: J.-E. Bulloz, 1903), 362, 363; and in the *Procès-verbaux du Comité d'instruction publique de la Convention nationale*, ed. M. James Guillaume, 8 vols. (Paris: Imprimerie nationale, 1891–1958), 5:513, 6:428, etc., as well as in a host of assorted memoirs well into the 1800s.

11 Jean-Baptiste Dubois, *Vues générales sur l'amélioration de l'agriculture* (Paris: Imprimerie de la Feuille du Cultivateur, an III [1794–95]), 37–39.

12 The unique copy of the third volume of "L'Architecture" by Ledoux is held at the Bibliothèque historique de la Ville de Paris (hereafter BHVP), and has been issued in facsimile as *Claude-Nicolas Ledoux: Unpublished Projects* (Paris: Les Editions du Demi-Cercle, 1991), with historical essays by Michel Gallet.

13 In 1793, André Thouin had such a collection. See Thérèse Charmasson, Anne-Marie Lelorrain, and Yannick Ripa, *L'enseignement agricole et vétérinaire de la Révolution à la Libération* (Paris: Institut national de recherche pedagogique, Sorbonne, 1992).

14 "Sur l'invitation faite aux Artistes de s'occuper d'établissements utiles et agricoles, le Citoyen Ledoux offre les plans, coupes, élévations d'une *ferme parée* qui renferme des besoins de tout genre, d'une *Bergerie* d'un grand produit, dont les principes et l'utilité sont démontrés. On peut citer des Laines aussi belles que celles d'Espagne et d'Angleterre. *D'un marché* public qui rassemble aux frontiers les subsistances de première nécessité. Des Greniers de surabondance . . . Quoi qu'il en soit, la Nature qui

voit tout du même Œil, n'a pas variée dans ses principes." Claude Nicolas Ledoux, 1 thermidor an 2 [July 19, 1794], AN F17/1047, transcribed in Werner Szambien, *Projets de l'an II* (Paris: École nationale supérieure des beaux-arts, 1986), 185–86.

15 According to the *Trésor de la langue française*, one *arpent* designated anywhere from 20 to 50 *ares*; and one *are* equaled 100 square meters. Per *Harrap's Dictionary*, by contrast, one *arpent* equaled 0.4 hectares, or approximately one acre. Per Sir John Sinclair, in his *Statistical Account of Scotland* (1791–92), one English acre equaled 1,135 *toises*. Thus 270 *arpents* represented anywhere from 540,000 to 1,350,000 square meters.

16 "Projet d'arrêté présenté par la Commission des travaux publics au Comité de salut public relativement à un Jardin national des plantes," [1794], Bibliothèque centrale du Muséum national d'Histoire naturelle (hereafter MNHN), Ms. 457/3; and "Suite du Rapport sur le Jardin national des Plantes," BHVP CP 3846.

17 [Professors-administrators of the Muséum], "Rapport sur le projet du C[itoyen] Molinos pour l'emploi des terrains compris entre les Fossés-Saint-Bernard et le Marché aux chevaux," sent to Jacques Molinos on 9 messidor an 2 [June 27, 1794], dated "Juillet 1794." Two draft states, both in AN AJ15/523; formerly MNHN Ms. 309 II.

18 Ibid. On Duhamel's farm, see Paula Young Lee, "Pisé and the Peasantry: François Cointeraux and the Rhetoric of Rural Housing during the Revolutionary Decade," *Journal of the Society of Architectural Historians* 67, no. 1 (March 2008): 58–77.

19 "Extrait du Registre des Délibérations de l'Assemblée des Artistes chargés de

la Division des Grandes Propriétés Nationales situées dans l'étendue du District de Paris," 15 prairial an 2 [1794]; see also Barère and Collot-d'Herbier, "Jardin nationale des Plantes," 3 messidor an 2 [1794], both located in AN F13/873.

SEED ORIGINS: NEW VARIETIES OF FRUITS AND VEGETABLES AROUND PARIS AT THE TURN OF THE NINETEENTH CENTURY

ANTOINE JACOBSOHN

ACCOUNTING FOR VARIETY

The interest in and experimentation with plant varieties by European botanists and horticulturalists was widely influenced by the discovery of the sexuality of plants, which occurred between the end of the seventeenth century and the beginning of the eighteenth century. In this time period, botanists and gardeners were greatly concerned with distinguishing between species and varieties. H. F. Roberts, in 1929, and Conway Zirkle, in 1935, provide us with many examples of how European and American botanists and gardeners grappled with the problem of the variation of plants before and after the discovery of plant sexuality.[1] For example, Zirkle points out how in 1728, Henri-Louis Duhamel Du Monceau immediately understood the implications of cross-pollination for the creation of fruit varieties and devoted himself to eliminating the supposition that the mutability of a fruit variety could be the result of grafting.[2]

Plant sexuality also affected taxonomy. Joseph Pitton de Tournefort's late seventeenth- and early eighteenth-century classification was essentially founded on the taxonomic level of genus, or related group of plants. Beginning in the middle of the eighteenth century, however, the classifications proposed by Carolus Linnaeus, the Comte de Buffon, Antoine Laurent de Jussieu, and later, Michel Adanson, were based on the creation of a single, basic unit: the species. Distinguishing between a species and a variety was based on two criteria: viable sexual reproduction, in order to isolate one species from another; and the stability of one unit (the species) versus the potential mutability of another (the variety). According to Marc Ratcliff, the fact that Linnaeus and his followers had rejected "varieties out of botany was a sort of political and theological act that eliminated variation from the botanist's cabinet." Thus, they could "lock up the myth of the fixity of the species—or genus."[3] The Enlightenment natural philosopher or botanist studied God's work and described its eternal perfection. But what of the eighteenth-century gardener, the practical horticulturalist constantly confronted with plants that changed? How were these changes explained?

In addition, social factors shaped developments in plant research. The upper class of a society, as always, was generally interested in acquiring and consuming the exceptional specimen. The great majority of the population, however, just wanted to have something to eat, if possible something good, and preferably enough of it. Concerning fruits and vegetables, there was a divergent interest in this period between the elite's search for a new variety that possessed some special characteristic and the majority's desire for a variety (old or new) to be stable and dependable.

COUNTING FRUIT VARIETIES

Since fruit varieties are clones and trees or plants are relatively long-lived, it is quite simple to distinguish new and old varieties and to establish a collection. In principle, a fruit variety is stable because it is reproduced asexually. Pomologists (fruit specialists) debate the identification of one variety or the authenticity of another, but in general, fruit varieties have been reproduced since antiquity by grafting branches of one plant (the scion) onto the stock or rootstock of another. Grafting creates a tree or shrub with genetic material identical to that of the scion plant and is thus a form of cloning. Why then did the number of fruit varieties increase so rapidly at the beginning of the nineteenth century? One reason was a desire to catalogue, to inventory what existed, as illustrated by the creation of the fruit variety collection at the Jardin de Luxembourg during the French Revolution.[4] In this essay, I will explore another reason: the changing relationship of gardeners and botanists to the stability of a plant variety or even to the fundamental sameness of a plant of a given species.

		La Quintinie, 1690	Pitton de Tournefort, 1700	Duhamel Du Monceau, 1768	Le Berriays, 1785	Nouveau Duhamel, ca. 1819	Noisette, 1825
CHERRY		6+	29	35+	44+	70	86+
PEACH		41	23	45	36	47	77
PEAR		172+	88	119	92	180	227
APPLE		24	37	44	42	96+	176
PLUM		50	28	48	26+	80	99
TOTALS		293	205	291	240	473	665

Table 6.1 Numbers of fruit varieties listed in selected French horticultural texts, 1690–1825

The table presented here, based on the five most widespread fruit species, does not illustrate a simple linear increase during the eighteenth century (TABLE 6.1). In fact, it seems to indicate a certain stagnation before a dramatic rise at the beginning of the nineteenth century.[5] Although other sources are available, the ones used in Table 6.1 have been chosen for their great influence or reputation and because they contain the most complete fruit variety lists of their time. Nonetheless, these sources did not claim to be exhaustive; they listed a selection of varieties that their authors considered the best for table use. Varieties of apples or pears destined principally for cider or perry have not been included.

Jean-Baptiste de La Quintinie, founder and first gardener of Louis XIV's Potager du Roi (King's Kitchen Garden) in 1678 of Versailles, is still considered the father of French horticulture by many people. Nonetheless, his list of fruit varieties is less important than those of some of his seventeenth-century contemporaries.[6] The inclusion of *Institutiones Rei Herbariae* by Pitton de Tournefort, one of the most influential botanists of the early eighteenth century, may surprise botanists and pomologists alike. Seeking to prove the validity of his plant groups, Tournefort used many plants that are now considered "cultivars" (cultivated varieties). Duhamel's *Traité des arbres fruitiers* (1768) is possibly the first scientific pomology, an attempt to bring order to the passionate world of fruit collectors. When the book was reworked some forty years later by a group of authors (principally Charles-François Brisseau-Mirbel, J. L. M. Poiret, and especially J. L. A. Loiseleur-Deslongchamps) associated with the Muséum d'Histoire naturelle in Paris, the number of varieties was increased dramatically, even more so than in the other contemporary revised edition by Antoine Poiteau and P. J. F. Turpin (begun in 1804 and published between 1807 and 1835; not included in the table).[7]

Both of the last two sources used in Table 6.1 are nursery catalogues. As of its second edition in 1785, René Le Berriays's *Traité des jardins ou le nouveau La Quintinie* presented itself as the sales catalogue of the Vilmorin-Andrieux seed company.[8] Le Berriays's assertion is perhaps overshadowed by the fact that he is known as the principal collaborator, if not author, of Duhamel's treatise on fruit trees. The probable origin of many of the varieties in that work was the Chartreux nursery in Paris. Its fruit variety catalogues (1736, 1752, 1775, republished in 1785), most likely among the best known of their kind in Europe, are well-represented in Duhamel's book. Nonetheless, they contain fewer fruit varieties[9] than Le Berriays's treatise-catalogue. The final source is Louis Noisette's nursery catalogue, which appeared after the first edition of his *Jardin fruitier* (1821) and contains a greater number of fruit varieties than that book.

COUNTING VEGETABLE VARIETIES

The question of the stability of a plant variety becomes acute when turning to vegetables, a food category that forms a far more diverse group than fruits. What Europeans considered as "fruit" corresponded, with relatively few exceptions, to the botanical definition of fruit (the result of a pollinated ovary) that has grown on a woody plant. A vegetable, on the other hand, can be a fruit, leaf, root, or any part thereof, generally of an herbaceous or non-woody plant. Additionally, most of these herbaceous food plants are reproduced from seed. Because of this sexual reproduction, which combines genetic material from different plants, vegetables are generally in a state of flux from one generation to the next. While descriptions of fruit varieties were available in the sixteenth century and rapidly became more accurate during the following era, the first reliable descriptions in France of vegetables at a varietal level only appeared in the middle of the eighteenth century. Before that date, there were some published vegetable variety names as well as some scattered descriptive information, but the systematic description of basic morphological characteristics that allowed botanists and horticulturalists to distinguish varieties within the same species was lacking. **TABLE 6.2** illustrates the situation between the mid-eighteenth century and the beginning of the nineteenth century.

	La Quintinie, 1690	Pitton de Tournefort, 1700	De Combles, 1749	Andrieux et Vilmorin, 1778	Le Berriays, 1785	Vilmorin-Andrieux, 1856
CABBAGE (including cauliflower)	9+ (1)	26 (1)	25+ (3)	28+ (6)	28 (3+)	146+ (18)
BEANS	1+	12	16+	8+	100+	73
LETTUCE	15	15	41	32+	37	134
TOTALS	25	53	82	68	165	353

Table 6.2 Numbers of some vegetable varieties listed in selected French horticultural texts, 1690–1856

Three species are included here. Cabbage was and remains one of the most important French food vegetables. Moreover, the plant is allogamous; the pollen of a different individual is necessary for seed production. Since the variety does not automatically reproduce to type, a certain amount of variation is immediately evident from one generation to the next. Careful isolation of the seed-bearing plants can limit this variation, but cannot eliminate it. Beans were also significant food plants in France. Counted here are two of the many New World beans (*Phaseolus vulgaris* L. and *P. coccineus* L., both named by Linnaeus). These beans are autogamous plants; that is, the pollen from a flower can pollinate that same flower. Varieties of autogamous plants are therefore far more easily stabilized and maintained, though care is still needed and breeding "accidents" do sometimes occur. Lettuce, another allogamous plant, is included because it was the vegetable species with the longest list of known varietal names at the end of the seventeenth century.

Compared to the previous table on fruit, this table contains a much smaller number of varieties per species. A plus sign (+) indicates that the author of the source named a number of varieties and then added that others exist, but did not provide any additional information. Comparing the numbers within the table, it is remarkable that the royal botanist Pitton de Tournefort seemed more interested in vegetable varieties than the royal gardener La Quintinie. Tournefort counted many more cabbage and bean varieties than La Quintinie; the opposite was true for fruit varieties. This is an inversion of the typical difference between gardeners, who are concerned with varieties, and botanists, who are generally interested in species, but not variations within species. Almost fifty years later, writing in his *École du jardin potager* (1749), De Combles did not radically change the number of vegetable varieties he listed. But where his predecessors offered only lists of names, De Combles often proposed a full paragraph of description for each variety. His section on beans also contains what may be the first mention in France of a collection of vegetable varieties: an individual who had amassed seventy-three different varieties of beans.[10] Collections of citrus fruit or pear varieties had been known in France since the sixteenth or early seventeenth centuries,[11] but not collections of vegetables. The remaining three sources for Table 6.2 are seed catalogues. Other treatises or catalogues existed between 1785 and 1856, but before 1856, no individual source seems to go beyond what Le Berriays announced as available in 1785 from Vilmorin-Andrieux. Table 6.2 demonstrates the complexity of the world of vegetables compared to fruits. It also, however, corroborates what has been observed concerning fruit: a change in the number of varieties described during the second half of the eighteenth century and, in particular, at the beginning of the nineteenth century.[12]

COUNTING NURSERIES

Nursery catalogues represent a different economic approach than did agronomic or horticultural treatises. A history of these catalogues confirms the growing interest in fruit and vegetable varieties during the period, as well as the difficulty of counting vegetable varieties. The first plant catalogues in France, which date from the middle of the seventeenth century, are for flowers.[13] The first mention I have found of a French commercial fruit tree catalogue dates from the late 1720s,[14] and the first dated commercial seed catalogue is from 1760.[15] This progression of dates can be understood in terms of the reliability of the plants provided. Flowers were considered inherently variable and as long as they were beautiful, a producer could hope to satisfy a client. Fruit could be reproduced identically, although, as many authors pointed out, one must be careful not to mix up the labels. But it was not until the 1760s that a French seed merchant dared to place his or her name on a supply of seeds. In addition, the names generally remained generic, such as "gros haricots blancs" (large white beans).[16] In the following years, nursery catalogues became somewhat more common. Seed catalogues also flourished during the French Revolution and the early nineteenth century. Although the Vilmorin-Andrieux seed company (formed after the 1774 marriage of Philippe-Victoire Lévêque de Vilmorin to Adélaïde d'Andrieux) apparently did not publish its own catalogue between 1783 and 1856, the company seems to have actively collaborated with the *Bon Jardinier* almanac, a popular annual gardening publication, to compile its lists of recommended varieties. With the diffusion of knowledge about how plant sexuality functioned and improved growing practices, elite seed producers were perhaps better able to increase the stability of vegetable varieties, even if only minimally.

The growing market for a diversified selection of fruit and vegetable varieties posed an economic dilemma. The commercial fruit or vegetable producer would have preferred to be the exclusive possessor of an exceptional variety. That variety could allow him or her to command a higher market price and, ideally, to do so year after year. The commercial seed merchant also had the same difficulty. Once clients had bought a variety, why would they return to buy it again? Although the agricultural and horticultural treatises of the eighteenth and early nineteenth centuries often mentioned how to cultivate a plant for seed, relatively few details were provided. Among the most notable examples were two garden treatises of the 1840s. J. G. Moreau and J. J. Daverne (1845), two Parisian market gardeners, and Courtois-Gérard (1844), a Parisian seed merchant, avoided giving any detailed information concerning specific varieties in their books.[17] Furthermore, the first general handbook in French concerning the production of seeds for sowing was not published until 1859.[18] Successfully reproducing varieties of fruit, and especially vegetables, gave nursery operators a significant economic advantage; little wonder that they did not wish to share their expertise.

Fig. 6.1

Nargeot (engraver), Portrait of Antoine-Nicolas Duchesne, undated. Bibliothèque municipale de Versailles

SOW, SOW, SOW

Three brief case studies of "gardeners" will open a window on the scholarly work still needed to understand the relationships between the scientific and socioeconomic contexts of the era, particularly in connection with prevalent notions of plant sexuality and heredity. The plant selection work of Antoine-Nicolas Duchesne, Jean-Baptiste Lelieur, and Antoine Poiteau represents the diversity of social origins within the horticultural milieu. In addition, through their work on plant selection by sowing, they collectively exemplify the differing perceptions and practical consequences of the discovery of plant sexuality.

In his article on plant improvement at the Muséum d'Histoire naturelle in the nineteenth century, Jean Gayon argued that André Thouin, the famous gardener and first holder of the *Chaire de culture* ("culture" professorship) at the Muséum, was a partisan of what would later be called "the heredity of acquired characteristics." Gayon added that the "doctrine of the amelioration of plants by sowing" was the very basis and justification for the *Chaire de culture*.[19] Yet, while Thouin seemed to be interested in improving varieties, he did not appear to mention or search for specific methods of obtaining new varieties. Duchesne, Lelieur, and Poiteau were all particularly interested in that very question.

CASE STUDY 1: ANTOINE-NICOLAS DUCHESNE, BRILLIANT SCIENTIST-GARDENER

The son of a provost of buildings at the Château de Versailles, Antoine-Nicolas Duchesne (**FIG. 6.1**) is well known for his work with strawberries in the 1760s and squash in the 1770s.[20] After the French Revolution, Duchesne apparently ceased actively experimenting with plants. Although he did not practice artificial cross-pollination (introducing the pollen from one plant onto the pistil of another), he would purposely place one plant next to another to enable crosses to occur.

In 1772, in his *Jardinier Prévoyant* or "Provident Gardener," an almanac that appeared between 1770 and 1779 or 1781, Duchesne added a brief section on the "improvement of races."[21] He did not use the word "hybrid", but he did link those two pages specifically to a discussion of plant sexuality. Duchesne wrote of "crossing Races with discernment so as to gain *Métis* [mixes] that would be better in certain respects than their fathers or mothers, while reuniting their good qualities." He added that cultivators who thought in terms of profitability did not follow this practice; only rich amateurs could spend the time to cultivate thousands of defective individuals before gaining a better one.[22]

Duchesne perhaps considered himself one of those wealthy amateurs. In 1771, he collaborated with the Andrieux seed company. He was not only the author of the vegetable variety descriptions; his strawberry collection was also featured in the commercial catalogue.[23] Duchesne's work on crossing squash did not receive the same treatment in the catalogue. Squash were undoubtedly not as popular as strawberries, but a more likely reason could be that while Duchesne was able to demonstrate differences among squash species, he apparently did not succeed in stabilizing ("fixing") a new variety.

Duchesne also participated in a series of cross-breeding experiments with potato varieties. During the French Revolution and afterwards, from 1798 to 1804, a botanical garden was established within the Potager du Roi at Versailles. Duchesne became its director and the first secretary of the Société d'Agriculture de Seine-et-Oise, which reported on the garden's experimental activities. In 1803, among the twenty-six potato varieties cultivated, fourteen were planted two by two (seven couples) in an isolated manner: "the flowers of each variety were brought close to the flowers of the other and the seeds carefully harvested separately before being sown."[24] In France, this could be one of the first accounts of the deliberate sexual crossing of a major food plant with the explicit aim of obtaining a new cultivar. The results were not published, as the botanical garden was closed in 1804–1805 and the Potager du Roi was annexed by the new imperial administration in 1806.

CASE STUDY 2: COMTE JEAN-BAPTISTE LELIEUR, IMPASSIONED ARISTOCRATIC GARDENER

Jean-Baptiste-Louis, Comte Lelieur de Ville-sur-Arce (**FIG. 6.2**), was named *intendant général* (supervisor) of all imperial gardens and parks in 1804. Louis XVIII removed him from his functions in 1818, forcing him to retire. He lived the rest of his days in a house and garden in Versailles, continuing to write and experiment with plants and to regret his eviction. Lelieur's adventures with plant selection and breeding began in 1792, however, when he abandoned his military profession and immigrated to the United States. He lived near Philadelphia and married Elisabeth Frazer, a woman from Princeton, New Jersey.[25] By 1801, when he returned to Europe, he had become a promoter of American plants, particularly corn, sweet potatoes, and dahlias.

Lelieur was immediately sensitive to questions of variety. His first publication, an essay on the cultivation of corn and sweet potatoes dating from 1807, included details about how to keep different varieties pure.[26] In 1811, in a treatise on rose cultivation, Lelieur offered a justification for plant breeding and a glimpse of his American fruit experiments. Lelieur dedicated his book to Empress Josephine, declaring "Madame, the reception that the flowers

from your gardens receive from your Majesty, make it my duty to find means
of creating new varieties, so as to multiply my praise."[27]

Lelieur noted how to conserve a spontaneous mutation and to multiply it by grafting, even using several pages in his rose book to describe his
experiments with white- and red-fruited peach varieties.[28] He admitted that
the seeds of a grafted fruit tree would yield new plants that were predomi-
nantly like that of the grafted tree, but he recalled that old agricultural texts
claimed that the root stock would transmit some of its characteristics to the
seeds. Although Lelieur enthusiastically embraced the possibility that cross-
pollination would create new varieties,[29] he insisted that grafting was just as
useful. In his effort to create new rose varieties, Lelieur constructed a chart
describing all the different possible crosses between pollen and grafts. Noting
that double-flowered roses no longer possessed stamens and therefore could
not be pollinators, he hoped that when those varieties were used as rootstock,
they would communicate some of their characteristics to the seeds of other
types of roses grafted onto them.[30]

Today's rose or dahlia collectors remember Lelieur as one of the first
breeders of their favorite plants. Surprisingly, though, he also had success
with an apple variety. When Lelieur returned from the United States, he
brought a series of grape, peach, and apple varieties. He declared that he
lost the peach varieties during the crossing and gave seventeen apple trees
to Christophe Hervy at the Luxembourg nursery in Paris.[31] Some of these
trees were included in Hervy's 1809 imperial *Catalogue*. Antoine Poiteau
included two of these apple varieties in his and Turpin's completely revised
edition of Duhamel's *Traité des arbres fruitiers* (1807–1835): the "Joséphine"
and "Lelieur" apples.[32] Today, the former is known as "Belle Joséphine"
and is considered a traditional apple of the eastern Parisian region (**FIGS. 6.3**
and **6.4**).

CASE STUDY 3: ANTOINE POITEAU, MULTITALENTED
HORTICULTURAL PUBLICIST OF MODEST ORIGIN

In the early 1800s, Antoine Poiteau (**FIG. 6.5**) recounted the story of the
first half of his life in a letter to Antoine-Laurent de Jussieu.[33] The illiterate
agricultural laborer from a small village to the northeast of Paris, near
Soissons, became a gardener at the Jardin du Roi in Paris and taught himself
to read using Linnaeus, among other authors. He was chosen to establish a

Pomme Joséphine.

Fig. 6.3 *Joséphine* apple variety. Engraving by H. Legrand
after a drawing by A. Poiteau, printed by Langlois. A. Poiteau,
*Pomologie française, recueil des plus beaux fruits cultivés
en France; ouvrage orné de gravures coloriées avec un
texte explicatif et usuel* (Paris and Strasbourg, 1838–46).
Bibliothèque municipale d'Avranches

ANTOINE JACOBSOHN

Fig. 6.4

Joséphine apple variety
today. Living fruit collection,
Potager du Roi, Versailles.
Photograph by Henri Fourey

garden in Dordogne but ended up travelling to Santo Domingo in the West
Indies on the recommendation of André Thouin. When he returned to France
in 1801 or 1802, he had collected some six hundred packets of seeds and twelve
hundred prepared plant specimens. Antoine Poiteau became a botanical artist,
a fruit specialist, and the editor of several periodicals. He combined minute
botanical description with an immense interest in economically important
cultivated plants, particularly fruit. Poiteau's dilemma concerning the stability
of varieties is particularly relevant to this discussion.

From 1826 to 1842, Poiteau was one of two principal editors of the *Bon
Jardinier* almanac, which began publication in 1755 and went through 153
editions. His name even remained on the cover until 1865, some ten years after
his death. With others in 1829 he created the regular periodical *Revue horticole*
as a complement to the *Bon Jardinier*. He apparently remained active at that
publication until at least 1851. For several years in the 1830s and early 1840s, he
was also the mainstay author of the *Annales de la Société centrale d'horticulture*.
Through these major publications, Poiteau was one of the principal agents
for the diffusion of novel plants and new horticultural trends and ideas.

In 1830, among other activities, Poiteau taught a class in horticulture
at the Institut royal horticole de Fromont, created, financed, and directed
by Soulange Bodin (who was also *secretaire général* of the Société centrale
d'horticulture). Poiteau's thirteenth lesson was devoted to varieties. In 1848,
Poiteau republished those lectures in two volumes, which gave him an opportunity to rework his convictions and bring them up to date. In this particular
case, the text seems to be unchanged. He wrote: "varieties are not children
of nature as are natural species" and listed four principal causes for variation:
change in place, change in the nature of the soil, cross-fertilization, and
methods of cultivation. He also remarked that the word "variety" had different
meanings for different people. Poiteau ended his lesson by declaring that both
natural species and varieties degenerate over time, although natural species
do so far more slowly.[34]

In the sixteenth lesson, Poiteau presented Belgian botanist Jean-
Baptiste Van Mons's theory about obtaining new and better fruit varieties
through sowing. The seeds of a fruit variety (pears or apples in particular)
almost never yield the same or even a similar variety as the known (maternal)

Fig. 6.5

Portrait of Antoine Poiteau.
Engraving. Académie
d'agriculture de France

parent, instead tending toward the wild or non-domesticated characters of
the species. Van Mons posited that it is possible to obtain new, larger, rapidly
setting fruit varieties through a re-sowing of successive generations of seed.
In other words, if one sows the seed of a variety, then sows the seed of the
new plant, and then sows the seed of that new plant, and so forth, the end
result would be new and interesting fruit varieties. This principle is almost the
same as the one defended by André Thouin, although here it is specific to fruit
trees whereas Thouin applied his theory of sowing especially to herbaceous
annual plants.[35] Poiteau was the most vocal of Van Mons's French defenders
during the 1830s,[36] collaborating with nurseryman and writer Louis Noisette to
create an experimental nursery for testing the Belgian's ideas. In 1836 Noisette
acquired a piece of land in Montrouge, south of Paris, to establish a new nursery. In 1837, Vibert reported that Poiteau and Noisette had collected more than
twelve hundred pear varieties or accessions.[37] Noisette was soon required to
move the nursery and it appears that the experiments were discontinued.
Finally, although Poiteau was well aware of plant sexuality, he did not mention
it when discussing Van Mons's theory. After a presentation of his arguments
against "naturalization," the idea that the manipulation of plant sexuality
could become a method for selecting new plants appears only in Poiteau's
course lectures.[38] It was a tentative and experimental suggestion, a tantalizing
possibility only, not part of the normal mode of functioning.

ANTOINE JACOBSOHN

This essay is exploratory. An immense number of sources from the eighteenth and early nineteenth centuries concerning how, why, and when French gardeners and scientists attempted to breed plants remains to be explored and questioned. Here, I have juxtaposed the discovery of plant sexuality with the understanding of that discovery's consequences. In the late 1760s and early 1770s, Duchesne already comprehended the possibilities of plant sexuality on both the commercial and scientific levels. Lelieur prefigured some characteristics of modern plant breeding in the early 1800s, but did not abandon his beliefs about the transfer of characteristics from the rootstock to the seeds of the grafted plant. From Linnaeus, Poiteau inherited the idea of stability and perfection of species. When confronted with the instability of sexual reproduction, however, he remained a gardener and a botanist, never entirely becoming a breeder. The study of other gardeners and experimenters in the same period, such as Jacques-Louis Descemet, Auguste Sageret, and Philippe-André de Vilmorin, could greatly add to our understanding of the growing comprehension of the notion of heredity: what information is passed from one generation of living beings to the next and how this transfer occurs.

I have evoked different contexts in this essay: an ever-increasing exchange between the many spaces and locations of food cultivation; the creation of learned societies and the diffusion of their discussions or debates; the opposition between those who perceived stability and those who perceived flux in plants; the influence of market demand for new products, but also the divergent interest between an elite market (seeking the exceptional specimen) and the mass market (aimed at feeding the population, stability of production, and reproducibility). With the overview of changes in the number of "ordinary" fruit and vegetable varieties, as well as the three individual examples of initial empirical confrontation with plant cultivation, it is apparent how processes formerly considered divine and mysterious became understandable, even malleable to a certain degree.

APPENDIX: PRIMARY SOURCES FOR TABLES 6.1 AND 6.2

Andrieux and Philippe-Victoire Lévêque de Vilmorin, *Catalogue des plantes, arbres, arbrisseaux et arbustes dont on trouve des graines, des bulbes et du plant, chez les Sieurs Andrieux et Vilmorin* (Paris: Chez Andrieux et Vilmorin, 1778).

De Combles, *École du jardin potager*, 2 vols. (Paris: Ant. Boudet et P. A. Le Prieur, 1749).

Henri-Louis Duhamel Du Monceau, *Traité des arbres fruitiers*, 2 vols. (Paris: Saillant, 1768).

Henri-Louis Duhamel Du Monceau, *Nouveau traité des arbres fruitiers de Duhamel Du Monceau: Nouvelle édition . . . par MM. Veillard, Jaume Saint-Hilaire, Mirbel, Poiret et Loiseleur-Deslongchamps* (Paris: Roret, 1850).

Jean-Baptiste de La Quintinie, *Instructions pour les jardins fruitiers et potagers* (Paris: Barbin, 1690).

René Le Berriays, *Traité des jardins, ou le nouveau La Quintinie*, 2 vols. (Paris: P.-F. Didot jeune, 1775); and 4 vols. (Caen: Manoury; Paris: Belin, 1785–88).

Louis Noisette, *Catalogue méthodique des arbres fruitiers, cultivés dans les jardins et pépinières de L. Noisette* (Paris: Rousselon, 1825).

Joseph Pitton de Tournefort, *Institutiones Rei Herbariae* (Paris: Etypographia Regia, 1700).

Vilmorin-Andrieux et Cie., *Description des plantes potagères* (Paris: Chez Vilmorin-Andrieux et à la Librairie agricole, 1856).

1   H. F. Roberts, *Plant Hybrid-
    ization Before Mendel*
    (Princeton, N.J.: Princeton
    University Press, 1929);
    Conway Zirkle, *The
    Beginnings of Plant Hybrid-
    ization* (Philadelphia:
    University of Pennsylvania
    Press, 1935).

2   Zirkle, *Beginnings of Plant
    Hybridization*, 107–8.

3   Marc J. Ratcliff, "Duchesne's
    Strawberries: Between
    Grower's Practices and
    Academic Knowledge," in
    *Conference: A Cultural
    History of Heredity I: 17th and
    18th Centuries*, Preprint 222,
    ed. Hans-Jörg Rheinberger,
    Peter McLaughlin, and
    Staffan Müller-Wille (Berlin:
    Max-Planck-Institute for
    the History of Science,
    2002), 53.

4   See Michel-Christophe
    Hervy, *Catalogue méthodique
    et classique de tous les arbres,
    arbustes fruitiers et des
    vignes formant la collection
    de l'École impériale établie
    près le Luxembourg* (Paris:
    Imprimerie Impériale,
    1809), 5.

5   For a different interpreta-
    tion, see Philippe Marchenay,
    "Ethnobotanique et conserva-
    tion génétique: L'exemple
    des arbres fruitiers," *Journal
    d'agriculture traditionnelle
    et de botanique appliquée*
    28:2 (1981): 85–158; or
    Florent Quellier, *Des fruits
    et des hommes: L'arboriculture
    fruitière en Île-de-France
    (vers 1600–vers 1800)*
    (Rennes: Presses universi-
    taires de Rennes, 2003),
    63–69.

6   Antoine Jacobsohn, "De
    l'accroissement des variétés,
    ou 'sortes,' de fruits au 16e
    et 17e siècles," *Le patrimoine
    fruitier: Hier, aujourd'hui,
    demain; Actes du colloque de
    La Ferté-Bernard (Sarthe),
    16–17 octobre 1998*, ed. Michel
    Chauvet (Paris: AFCEV,
    1999), 109–110.

7   For a history of Duhamel's
    book, see Antoine Jacobsohn,
    "Cent ans de pomologie et
    d'arboriculture fruitière: Les
    choix variétaux et culturaux
    des trois principales éditions
    du *Traité des arbres fruitiers*,
    du milieu du XVIIIe au
    milieu du XIXe siècle," in
    Jacobsohn, *Fruits du savoir:

    Duhamel Du Monceau et
    la pomologie française*
    (Versailles: École nationale
    supérieure du paysage;
    Saint-Épain: Lume, 2007),
    84–101 (catalogue for an
    exhibition at the Potager
    du Roi at Versailles, 2007).

8   René Le Berriays, *Traité des
    jardins; ou, le nouveau La
    Quintinie*, 2nd ed. (Paris,
    1785), n.p. (opposite title
    page). The first edition had
    appeared in 1775; there were
    also other editions.

9   Quellier, *Des fruits et des
    hommes*, 65.

10 De Combles (first name
    unknown), *École du jardin
    potager* (Paris: Ant. Boudet
    et P. A. Le Prieur, 1749),
    2:71.

11 Antoine Schnapper, *Histoire
    et histoire naturelle: Le géant,
    la licorne et la tulipe*, vol. 1 of
    *Collections et collectionneurs
    dans la France du XVIIe
    siècle* (Paris: Flammarion,
    1988), 214ff.

12 For changes concerning
    another plant group, flowers,
    see, among others, Hélène
    Denis, "Flore, imaginaire
    et quotidien à Paris:
    Bruyères et roses écossaises
    1800–1848," *Dix-Neuf:
    Journal of the Society of
    Dix-Neuviémistes*, no. 4
    (April 2005): 6–20.

13 Pierre Morin, *Catalogue de
    quelques plantes à fleurs,
    qui sont présent au jardin
    de Pierre Morin le jeune, dit
    troisième, fleuriste* (Paris,
    1651, 1655).

14 It would have been sent
    from Orléans, south of Paris,
    to England, according to
    Richard Bradeley in *A
    Philosophical Account of the
    Works of Nature* (London:
    W. Mears, 1721), 186.

15 Pierre Andrieux, *Catalogue
    de toutes sortes de graines,
    fleurs, oignons de fleurs … qui
    se trouvent chez le sr Andrieux*
    (Paris, 1760). An undated
    seed catalogue, *Catalogue de
    toutes sortes de graines, tant
    potagères, que légumes …
    graines de fleurs et oignons
    de fleurs, qui sont … chez le
    sieur Le Febvre* could be by
    Andrieux's precursor and
    father-in-law.

16 Andrieux, *Catalogue*,
    1760, 37.

17 J. G. Moreau and J. J.
    Daverne, *Manuel pratique
    de la culture maraîchère de
    Paris* (Paris: Chez Mme
    Veuve Bouchard-Huzard,
    1845) 315–16; Courtois-
    Gérard, *Manuel pratique de
    culture maraîchère* (Paris:
    Librairie horticole de H.
    Cousin et chez l'auteur,
    marchand grainier,
    horticulteur, 1844).

18 Pierre Joigneaux, *L'art de
    produire des bonnes graines*
    (Bruxelles: E. Tarlier, 1859).

19 Jean Gayon, "Le Muséum
    national d'Histoire naturelle
    et l'amélioration des plantes
    au XIXe siècle," in *Le
    Muséum au premier siècle de
    son histoire*, ed. Claude
    Blanckaert, Claudine Cohen,
    Pietro Corsi, and Jean-Louis
    Fischer (Paris: Éditions du
    Muséum national d'Histoire
    naturelle, 1997), 387, 388.

20 Ratcliff, "Duchesne's Straw-
    berries," 43–65; Günter
    Staudt, *Les dessins d'Antoine
    Nicolas Duchesne pour son
    "Histoire naturelle des
    fraisiers"* (Paris: Publications
    scientifiques du Muséum
    national d'Histoire naturelle,
    2003); Harry S. Paris, *Les
    dessins d'Antoine Nicolas
    Duchesne pour son "Histoire
    naturelle des courges"* (Paris:
    Publications scientifiques du
    Muséum national d'histoire
    naturelle, 2007).

21 Antoine-Nicolas Duchesne,
    Le Jardinier prévoyant
    (Paris: Didot jeune, 1772),
    45-73.

22 "Chercher en croisant les
    Races avec discernement, à
    gagner des Métis qui soient
    préférables par quelques
    endroit à leurs pères et à
    leurs mères, en réunissant
    leurs bonnes qualités. Cette
    pratique toute contraire à
    la précédente, n'est pas le
    fait des cultivateurs qui
    tirent au profit: c'est à des
    amateurs aisés qu'on
    l'indique, comme un moyen
    très efficace de parvenir au
    but où leur générosité les
    fait viser. Ils savent qu'en
    semant des plantes, dont
    on propagent ordinaire-
    ment par bourgeons les individus
    élités par leurs dévanciers,
    ils sont exposés à élever des
    milliers d'individus
    défectueux, avant d'en
    gagner un qui les

    récompense de leur
    courage." Ibid., 71–72.

23 Baron A. F. de Silvestre,
    "Notice biographique sur
    M. Antoine-Nicolas
    Duchesne," *Mémoires de la
    Société d'agriculture* (1827),
    10; Andrieux, *Catalogue
    raisonné des plantes, arbres
    et arbustes dont on trouve
    des graines, des bulbes et du
    plant chez le Sieur Andrieux,
    marchand grainier fleuriste et
    botaniste du Roi* (Paris: Chez
    Andrieux, successeur du
    Sieur Lefebre, 1771), 11–12.

24 "Le rapprochement des
    fleurs a été soigné
    assidument; la récolte des
    graines s'est faite avec
    exactitude, et les différens
    produits viennent d'être
    semés ce printemps,
    séparément." "Rapport à
    la Société d'agriculture du
    département de Seine-et-
    Oise par sa Commission
    d'expériences sur celles
    faites en l'an 12, Séance du
    25 pluviose an 13," *Journal
    de la Société d'agriculture
    du département de Seine-et-
    Oise* (1804–1805), 18.

25 See Arthur Chuquet, *Études
    d'histoire: Troisième série*
    (Paris: Fontemoing, 1910),
    207–26; and Archives
    départementales des Hauts-
    de-Seine, 5 MI 3 and 4.
    Many thanks to Gabriela
    Lamy, gardener and histo-
    rian, for this archival ref-
    erence with the name and
    origin of Lelieur's first wife.

26 Jean-Baptiste Lelieur,
    *Essais sur la culture du maïs
    et de la patate douce* (Paris:
    Imprimerie de P. Didot
    l'aîné, 1807), 12.

27 "Madame, l'accueil
    qu'éprouvent de Votre
    Majesté les fleurs qui
    lui parviennent de ses
    jardins, m'a fait un devoir
    de m'occuper des moyens
    d'en créer de nouvelles
    variétés, afin de pouvoir
    multiplier mes hommages."
    Jean-Baptiste Lelieur, *De
    la culture du rosier avec
    quelques vues sur d'autres
    arbres et arbustes* (Paris:
    De l'imprimerie de P. Didot
    l'aîné, 1811), n.p. Napoleon
    allowed Josephine to retain
    her title of *impératrice*
    (empress) after their 1810
    divorce.

ANTOINE JACOBSOHN

28 Ibid., 49, 64–74.

29 Ibid., 69.

30 Ibid., 75ff.

31 Ibid., 73–74. The historic fruit orchard at the Jardin du Luxembourg still flourishes today.

32 Antoine Poiteau and Pierre Jean François Turpin, *Traité des arbres fruitiers de Duhamel Du Monceau: Nouvelle édition augmentée d'un grand nombre d'espèces de fruits obtenus des progrès de la culture,* 6 vols. (Paris and Strasbourg: Levrault, 1807–1835).

33 See Jean Louis Marie Poiret, "Voyages, voyageurs," in Jean-Baptiste Lamarck and J. L. M. Poiret, *Encyclopédie méthodique: Botanique* (Paris: H. Agasse, 1808), 8:750–52.

34 "Des variétés. Les variétés ne sont pas des enfants de la nature comme les espèces naturelles; ce sont des végétaux qui, ou par une cause inconnue ou par l'industrie humaine, ont modifié plus ou moins leurs caractères naturels ou en ont contracté d'autres que la nature ne reconnaît pas, et que, par conséquent, elle ne se charge pas de perpétuer. On signale quatre causes qui peuvent contribuer à faire varier les végétaux: 1. le changement de localité; 2. les diverses natures de terre et leurs divers degrés de fertilité; 3. les fécondations croisées; 4. la culture. On accorde à la culture, surtout, une grande puissance pour forcer les espèces naturelles à varier . . . Quoiqu'il en soit, le mot variété, en horti-culture, n'a pas un sens bien déterminé; les uns voient un grand nombre de variétés parmi les Ormes de nos grandes routes; il n'y voient que des différences indi-viduelles, telles que celles qu'on observe entre les individus de l'espèce homme et entre les individus de l'espèce cheval ou bœuf. Au reste, la règle établie par Linné pour distinguer les espèces des variétés n'a plus de valeur depuis que l'horticulture montre journellement que plusieurs variétés se reproduisent semblables à elles-mêmes par le semis." Antoine Poiteau, *Cours d'horticulture* (Paris: Imprimerie et librairie de Mme Vve Bouchard-Huzard, 1848), 1:191–95, 13ᵉ leçon.

35 Gayon, "Le Muséum et l'amélioration des plantes," 384.

36 See Antoine Poiteau, *Théorie Van Mons; ou, Notice historique sur les moyens qu'on emploie M. Van Mons pour obtenir d'excellens fruits de semis* (Paris: Madame Huzard, 1834).

37 Vibert, "Rapport sur la pépinière d'expériences de MM. Noisette et Poiteau, fait à la Société royale d'Horticulture de Paris, le 6 décembre 1837, par une Commission composée de MM. Sageret, Godefroy, Camuzet, Pépin et Vibert, rapporteur," *Annales de la Société royale d'horticulture de Paris,* 20 (1837): 312.

38 Poiteau, *Cours d'horticulture,* 1:212.

ABOUT GARDENS AND GARDENING

THE GOLDEN AGE OF FRENCH NATURAL SCIENCE, FROM 1790 TO 1830, TOOK PLACE IN AN ERA OF DISCOVERY AND EXPLORATION. It was governed by the encyclopedic impulse of the Enlightenment—the desire to inventory, to classify, to order, hence to control and civilize. Advances in the scientific knowledge of plants and horticulture coupled with the great influx of exotic plants and animals from all over the world contributed to the economic, social, and aesthetic appeal of gardens and gardening at this time. As the essays in this session make clear, the interest in gardens and gardening under Napoleon was propelled by and echoed the growth and glory of the Empire. Agricultural renewal was promoted as key to the prosperity and well-being of society. The epicenter of this efflorescence in the post-revolutionary decades was divided between two locations, the Muséum d'Histoire naturelle in Paris with its public garden (Jardin des Plantes) and the pleasure garden of the Empress Josephine at Malmaison, seven miles west of the city.

The Muséum d'Histoire naturelle was formerly called the Jardin du Roi (King's Garden). The name change occurred in 1790, motivated by the revolutionary desire to rid the institution of its royal association. A decade later, Josephine's devotion to plants and horticulture established her place within a long tradition of royal garden patronage. She capitalized on her royal status in the development of her garden at Malmaison, using it strategically as a means to acquire plants and as a way to legitimize her royal identity. At the same time, Malmaison, as a prosperous ornamental farm with gardens and agriculture, emerged as a model of bourgeois landownership.

Bernard Chevallier and Susan Taylor-Leduc's essays focus on Malmaison and the many facets of Josephine's passion for the natural sciences, affirming that Josephine's pursuit of her interests at Malmaison was more than a royal indulgence. Clearly, her knowledge of and devotion to the natural sciences approximated that of a trained specialist. Chevallier shows that during the fifteen years of her residence at Malmaison, from 1799, when the property was purchased, to 1814, the year of her death,

Josephine engaged the leading artists, architects, landscape gardeners, and botanists to assist her in transforming the estate into a pleasure garden of botanical and zoological richness rivaled only by the Muséum d'Histoire naturelle. It was her desire that Malmaison become the garden of the Empire, a distribution point for plants in gardens throughout the country. To record and develop her botanical collections, Josephine employed prominent botanists. To illustrate their scientific descriptions, she engaged artists, most notably Pierre-Joseph Redouté. This patronage resulted in the production of spectacular books of botanical illustration, making this particular moment one of the high points in the history of this art form. As Chevallier also details, Malmaison was known for its celebrated menagerie with its many rare and exotic animals, including kangaroos, llamas, emus, and the famous black swans. Taylor-Leduc focuses specifically on the merino sheep farm and Josephine's identity as shepherdess at Malmaison. She discusses Josephine's interest in estate management in the context of changing attitudes towards landownership, and she argues that in transforming Malmaison into a pleasure garden as well as an agriculturally productive ornamental farm, the empress was providing a model for a new class of landowners. Indeed, through Malmaison, Josephine demonstrated that agricultural productivity and its various rewards were available to many. She became a symbol of the abundance of the realm. The cornucopia, one of many allegorical emblems adopted during the Empire, was specifically associated with the iconography of the empress.[1] Symbolizing abundance, prosperity, good fortune, peace and good government, the cornucopia appeared as an attribute of Josephine in imperial emblems designed by Charles Percier and Pierre François Léonard Fontaine and in contemporary prints. Fashioned into the form of an initial "J" filled with flowers, it was used as a decorative monogram on all manner of objects: furniture, porcelain, books, and so forth.

By shining light on Josephine's contributions to the fields of botany, horticulture, zoology, and agriculture, Chevallier and Taylor-Leduc do much to dispel the myth of the "frivolous Josephine." Formerly distinguished for her love of fashion, her ability to spend money and accumulate debts, and her promiscuous behavior, Josephine has been the subject of considerable historical reassessment in recent years. The victim of a double bias in the construction of her narrative, Josephine's importance was previously understated in the literature due to the patriarchal dominance of Napoleon, under whose reign most figures, but especially women, were diminished in significance. She was also subject to gender bias in history writing, which resulted in an overemphasis on the more superficial and stereotypical aspects of her identity. In 1977, the Napoleonic scholar Jean Tulard dismissively admitted "how little is known of her political role."[2] Given more serious critical attention in recent scholarship, Josephine is now regarded as a figure of significant authority with influence in the cultural, scientific, and political life of her times.

Shifting attention to the activities of the Muséum d'Histoire naturelle, the remaining essays in this session continue the focus on the promotion of agriculture as essential to the economic and moral renewal of the nation. Paula Young Lee's essay concerns the ways the institution, which was historically rooted in botanical science, was reorganized with an increased emphasis on agricultural commerce. In addition,

Lee brings to light the little-known, aborted architectural design by Claude Nicolas Ledoux for a four-level circular "Musaéum [sic]" on the grounds of the existing Muséum. In the final essay, Antoine Jacobsohn examines patterns of collecting, breeding, and selling new varieties of fruits and vegetables near Paris around the turn of the nineteenth century through the comparative analysis of a variety of sources (plant and seed catalogues as well as botanical and horticultural treatises). The author seeks to expose the prevailing knowledge of plant sexuality, a discovery which took place a century earlier, and the impact of that knowledge on the practice of botanists and gardeners.

The essays in this session highlight the central role of the Empress Josephine and the contributions of numerous botanists, landscape gardeners, botanical illustrators, and others in illuminating a major moment in French horticulture and garden history. Malmaison and the Muséum d'Histoire naturelle operated in a spirit of lively competition, cooperation, and exchange in the early years of the nineteenth century.

1 On the cornucopia and other emblems associated with the empress, see Carol Solomon Kiefer, *The Empress Josephine: Art and Royal Identity* (Amherst, Mass.: Mead Art Museum, Amherst College, 2005), 12–15.

2 Jean Tulard, *Napoleon, The Myth of the Saviour*, trans. Teresa Waugh (London: Weidenfeld and Nicolson, 1984), 363.

PART II

ABOUT GARDENS AND GARDENING

SYMPOSIUM DISCUSSIONS

INDIVIDUAL PAPERS

3. EMPRESS JOSEPHINE AND THE NATURAL SCIENCES

Bernard Chevallier (BC)

Question: I wanted to ask you about how patronage functioned in all of this, what kind of role Josephine played as a patron of scientists and explorers. What did they seek to gain by giving her all these plants and animals?

BC: It was really not a role; it was a passion for Josephine. She knew the names of the plants in French and in Latin, and the professors of the Muséum d'Histoire naturelle considered Josephine to be like one of themselves. They wrote each other letters. It's not really the role of a sovereign; it was a passion for her.

4. JOSEPHINE AS SHEPHERDESS: ESTATE MANAGEMENT AT MALMAISON

Susan Taylor-Leduc (STL)

Question: You portrayed Josephine as an entrepreneur for her estate. Did she have any link with the physiocratic movement in France, which was extremely important, and whose main idea was that wealth would come through agriculture and breeding?

STL: She certainly could have known about the physiocratic writings; she certainly was aware of Rambouillet as an experiment and knew about the importance of agronomics. But I have a feeling that since she was brought up on Martinique, her real experience of husbandry and production came from her plantation background, rather than through a direct knowledge of French physiocratics, or the work of Turgot. Although I decided not to really involve myself with the dialogue between

Marie-Antoinette and Josephine, I do think that the latter's investments at the merino farm were much different from anything going on at the Hameau. Both women were really involved more with an idea of seigneurial virtue than with real physiocracy per se.

Question: I'm really interested in this connection between Josephine's experience in Martinique and her experience in France. One of the things I have found with plantation owners is their sense of self as managers of land and managers of people. Did she actually involve herself in the labor relations there—the people physically taking care of the sheep, taking care of the land—as well as with the land itself?

STL: Josephine was very well known for her incredible generosity and her helpfulness and aid to many people. And she did take quite an interest in all aspects of her collections, including her farm. I was really inspired by Jill Casid's work, *Sowing Empire* (2005). Casid doesn't speak of Josephine, since she writes about the eighteenth century, but I was inspired by the timing here. During the French Revolution, Josephine fled to Martinique, experienced the slave uprisings in the revolution there, and then came back and influenced Napoleon in the decision to reinstate slavery on Martinique and Guadeloupe. So her assumption of this role as a nice, pastoral, generous shepherdess effaced that background quite intentionally.

5. OF CABBAGES AND KINGS: THE POLITICS OF PLANTING VEGETABLES AT THE REVOLUTIONARY JARDIN DES PLANTES

Paula Young Lee (PYL)

Question: Could you talk a little bit more about the relationship between the Committee for Public

Health in the French Revolution and the desire for farm products? I was also wondering about Rousseau and his lectures and role at the Jardin des Plantes at this time.

PYL: What's extraordinary is the degree to which the revolutionary committees were actively involved in shaping the Muséum. There are literally boxes and boxes of documentation regarding their desire to turn all the land into farms and I have seen explicit orders to carry out this program. But the crucial factor they didn't fully appreciate was the resistance from the people who actually lived there. Pretty much the whole Latin Quarter would have disappeared, replaced by an enormous garden; there are plans and drawings for that. Part of the difficulty was that they didn't know exactly what they were going to do with the space once they had the land. Also, the people who lived there resisted, since they didn't think it was fair or right that the government could come in and just take their property without proper compensation. Then Napoleon came in and everything changed.

But the Committee on Public Health (the Comité de salubrité, also called the Comité de santé) was extraordinarily active. They were in fact actively promulgating a physiocratic vision, in which they truly saw agriculture as the salvation of the nation. At the height of Year II (1793–94), it got to the point where all foreign trees were being pulled up and castigated as terrorists. There was a lot of political intensity being directed towards agriculture as the solution to everything.

Rousseau was an extraordinarily important component in these developments. He was constantly being invoked for alternate education and the correct rearing of youth. This was closely tied to a program of public education and literacy particularly aimed at farmers and the rural poor, who were largely illiterate—85 percent of the French were illiterate at this time. They really wanted to try to tie those two together.

So the pastoral ideal, combined with the practical realities of agriculture, were being promoted simultaneously. It isn't a complete picture; the picture is rather complex. And there were sheep there too, running around quite happily, and lots of crossbreeding was going on. People were very interested in the domestic commercial potential of exotics, and sheep were the primary target.

6. SEED ORIGINS: NEW VARIETIES OF FRUITS AND VEGETABLES AROUND PARIS AT THE TURN OF THE NINETEENTH CENTURY
Antoine Jacobsohn (AJ)

Question: Because of those thoughts on the degeneracy of plants once they come into cultivation, was there a feeling that new plants perpetually needed to be coming in? Would that provide an increased role for the botanist, for the explorer, for the collector, because of the perception that you always needed new things to revive the cultivars?

AJ: It's clear that everyone was continually cultivating, and with certain species they knew how to do certain things, and with others they didn't. But also, how did things change? The collectors were going to bring in new varieties because they were always trying to have new kinds of plants. When Chaptal defended the creation of the collection of grape varieties at the Luxembourg during the Revolution, he justified it on economic grounds. The producers only brought in new varieties when they lost other ones. So again, it depends on whom we're talking about. I'm sure the collectors were worried about degeneration and wanted to add new varieties, and I'm sure that cultivators didn't worry as long as they succeeded in maintaining what they already had.

Question: You mentioned that all of these people had contact with the Potager du Roi (King's Kitchen Garden), so were they all living in Versailles, and were they competing with the Jardin des Plantes? Were they working as a separate scholarly and productive community?

AJ: They all lived in Versailles at one time or another. Duchesne was from Versailles, and essentially lived there his entire life. Lelieur came to Versailles in 1804 and spent quite a bit of time in Saint-Cloud before really settling in Versailles around 1810, and then stayed until he died around 1848 or 1852, so he lived most of the second part of his life there. Poiteau only spent two to three years in Versailles but regularly visited the Potager du Roi. Duchesne was a student of Jussieu, and the botanical garden established at the Potager du Roi in the 1790s was begun following Thouin's recommendation. Lelieur wasn't interested in botanical collections. He was remarkable in terms of his practical attitude, but most people who worked with him hated him. He wrote the first unique treatise on tree diseases, *Mémoire sur les maladies des arbres fruitiers* (1811).

The Potager du Roi had its ups and downs. There was a time where research was being done there, but during the Revolution there was a kind of opposition in the relationship with the Jardin des Plantes in Paris. The Potager du Roi was basically a center of production; it wasn't really a place where plants were studied. It participated, it exchanged, but most of the time it wasn't a place of botany or of fundamental research.

Question: Thank you for this interesting contrast between stability and variety. You know that Antoine Chaptal was the minister of the interior in the early nineteenth century. He was also a chemist, and as a chemist he was extremely concerned with stability. There were many efforts from chemists to obtain stabilized and standardized products, and they designed many tests for standardization. In the case of chemical products, their first concern was risk, since chemicals are dangerous. There were also tests because of patenting; the first patent in France was for Nicolas Leblanc's process for making soda ash from salt. But how can you account for the concern for stability with plants in agricultural commerce? Why did consumers require stable products rather than ever-changing, new products? Because there were no patents for seeds there was no risk, so why was this a desire for stability rather than a desire for variety?

AJ: I think most people look for stability, but whether they want it or not is another question. Again, that goes back to my two contrasts: between popular and elite culture, between peasant and bourgeois culture. We are talking about a society that is still afraid of not eating, where most people go through periods of time without enough to eat. So seeking stability is a search for abundance. What we want is a plant that produces regularly; if it's good, *tant mieux* (all the better), if it's not, too bad. And that's how I would link it.

   With your question, I'm interested in the search for stability in chemistry, and what that has to do with the understanding of how natural phenomena function. Because in French, that term *l'ensemencement* (sowing or seeding) works both in chemistry and in plants, in terms of how you can make crystallization occur; maybe it's just wordplay, but I think there's more to it than that. For plants, the discovery of plant sexuality had a real influence, with people suddenly realizing that they could control breeding (not necessarily that they succeeded, but that they could try). In the 1720s Duhamel Du Monceau wrote about pear grafting, but also about wild species being stable while cultivated species were not, and what could be done about it. And it's all linked to Sébastian Vaillant and his pollination research. During the entire eighteenth century, people continue to explore how to deal with plant breeding and how to produce regularly from an economic point of view.

Question: Lamarck was a botanist before he was a zoologist and a transformist. Related to what you just said about natural and cultivated species, I think I recall Lamarck saying at one point, "we

botanists, we really study the natural species, and whatever a horticulturalist develops in terms of a beautiful rose or something, that's very interesting, but that's not what we do." Yet Duchesne, as a disciple both of Jussieu and of Thouin, as you say, seems to be following a new path. And then you finally get to Poiteau when he's talking about degeneration of a type. Does his work ever get related back to, let's say, the scientists who are looking at natural species? Do they take an interest in it? Or, can you start with Duchesne, and then talk about the relation between some of your later people and maybe somebody like Lamarck who was saying that the real scientist, the real botanist, was not playing with these kinds of developments that come through the horticulturalist?

AJ: I don't remember Lamarck saying that, but I'm happy to hear it because you usually only hear about Linnaeus saying, "I don't want to hear about varieties, it just doesn't interest me. The only thing that interests me is the species." That was the whole basis for his binomial system. That's what Duchesne is interested in. There's a debate among some people about his choice of strawberries and squash. Duchesne basically wants to be able to distinguish between a species and a variety. He wants to know what's what: "Am I supposed to give the strawberry from Montreuil a new name in Linnaeus's system, or am I supposed to call it *fragaria* like I think I should? What do I do?"

   It's confusing that he stops suddenly; Lamarck published his work on squash in *L'Encyclopedie méthodique: Botanique* in the 1790s. I haven't worked enough on Poiteau to answer you, but I want to understand why Poiteau has this ambivalent relationship to what he does. On the one hand, he has a botanist's attitude, and on the other, he's totally immersed in the fashion of new plants, so I don't know what to do with him yet.

END-OF-SESSION DISCUSSION

Carol Solomon (CS): We've traveled quite a distance in these talks about the late eighteenth and early nineteenth centuries, going between the poles of pleasure and utility, utopian visions and more practical realities, and concepts of nature and culture. I'd like to consider the whole context and the correspondences between these different poles.

   The talks and the wide range of objects in the exhibition evoke the amazing experience of visiting Malmaison, where you would have encountered such a variety of new and exciting things. You would taste fresh milk at the dairy and you would see the merino sheep and witness the production of wool. When you wandered through the grounds, you might see kangaroos bounding about and the spectacle of the black swans in the pond. If you were invited into the château, the entryway would be full of caged birds singing, and perhaps a curtseying orangutan would greet you at the door. And Josephine herself might take you on a tour of the art collection. Who was invited to visit Malmaison? What did access entail, and how did contemporary visitors talk about this place?

It's clear that the conception of Josephine has changed drastically. Up until the last twenty years, there was a myth of the frivolous Josephine, whose interests and identity were pretty much defined by her passion for clothing, her interest in spending money and accumulating debts, and her promiscuous behavior. This myth can now be considered passé. It's largely through the work of Bernard Chevallier and others that this changing conception of Josephine has taken place. These talks and the current literature are raising a new way of addressing the question of her political role and her motivations in all of these pursuits, many of which certainly went beyond pure pleasure.

I'd also like to ask Paula to talk about the idea of the museum, which at this moment was germinating in a number of contexts. There are many new and competing conceptions of the historical museum and the encyclopedic museum (with people marching through time at Alexandre Lenoir's Musée des Monuments français, for instance). Finally, for Antoine, I am curious about what goes on at the Potager du Roi and what you do there.

BC: You asked me about the gardens of Malmaison. They were not really open to the public, but people interested in the natural sciences could visit the garden and the greenhouse. There is a letter from Josephine to Prince Eugène, her son, in which she says "now I see many people walking in my gardens," but she didn't know who was walking in the garden, though it was really open to the scientists.

Natural sciences were not Josephine's only interest. She was very interested in the arts, in painting, sculpture, antiques. She protected young artists; she decided that the great names like David, Gérard, Gros, had commissions from the government and she preferred to protect young artists. What we call troubadour painting (anecdotal paintings relating the history of the Middle Ages and the Renaissance) and the taste for the Middle Ages started in this time, with the patronage of Josephine, as early as 1802 or 1803. It's the same with sculpture. She wanted to have most of the works of Canova, the most important sculptor of the period. But of course she could

only have five sculptures by him, which are now at the Hermitage at St. Petersburg.

She was really an intelligent woman and when she wanted something she went to the source. Of course, she must have been intelligent because Napoleon kept her as his wife for a very long time. When he divorced her, he said to the court, "she embellished fifteen years of my life." This is not what people usually say when they get divorced. She really was a remarkable woman.

STL: I would address this notion of the frivolous female patron. I do think that in the last fifteen years or so we've all learned to debunk that myth; however, with Josephine it is important to remember that no matter how much she invested—in merinos, for instance—it really was minimal in relation to what she spent. It made no dent in her debt. She might have been committed to this investment and understood it and wanted to set an example, and I think she understood the importance of her role and the image that she could promote, but I think on a personal side you have to understand that the economics didn't quite add up.

PYL: I'm glad you pointed out that the economics of her farm did not add up. I think with the ornamental farm in the aggregate, the pastoral ideal in particular, there is a sense that somehow these sheep make money. And in reality if you had tried to actually run a self-sustaining farm, it's exceptionally expensive. Those sheep eat a lot, so you need a huge amount of land. So yes, you lose money on a farm unless you're very lucky or very gifted.

For me, discovering this rather remarkable several years of the Muséum's history is interesting because it's taking an externalist view of the museum as an institution as opposed to an internalist one. I wrote a paper about the Museum of Alexandria because people used to ask me all the time why the museum of natural history is called a "muséum," as opposed to a "musée." It's become a standard reference now in museum history, because everybody wants to know the answer to this question, and one word affects the entire legacy.

You can actually see some of that legacy in Ledoux's museum plan. He had a residential area for scholars, somewhat evoking a monastic ideal, with separate work cubicles for each individual that would be layered together with living quarters as well as housing for animals. Including the housing for animals is of course very different—actively condensing the farm, the barn, the storage unit, as well as the library and the museum as we now understand it today, and making it all into a temple to the muses. When you look at that in its totality it's rather shocking, because we can't really fit it into any kind of museum model that we hold today. It's remained utterly unanalyzed; no architectural historian has ever addressed it and it is virtually forgotten.

I would also like to mention the work of Dominique Poulot, a very good museum historian. He has published exclusively in French and unfortunately his work is not translated. His work provides background for mine in terms of the politicization of the museum ideal during the Revolution. He speaks articulately about the remarkable factions that contributed to the discourse surrounding the creation of the Muséum at the height of the Terror. What most people also aren't aware of is that the Muséum d'Histoire naturelle was the first to be created, preceding the Louvre, and it set the dominant model until Napoleon took over and remade the museum into the model we understand today.

So what I'm focusing on is these lost years for the museum when it was vague, incredibly amorphous, but intensely politicized to a degree that I think is very difficult for us to fully grasp today. Blood was spilled over the nature of the museum. And again, the project for the Muséum d'Histoire naturelle was to raze the Latin Quarter in order to foster these national gardens that would regenerate all of France. The sacrifice would have been simply astonishing, but that was the museum ideal directly linked to a utopian garden, as well as to a particular political vision. So it's tied into this notion of what a museum should be or should not be and the realization that agriculture played such an enormous role for this rather narrow window, such that today we could be thinking that museums are about seeds. If it had followed that trajectory, that would have been the case, and museums of art would have been the exception rather than the norm.

AJ: We have a debate about genetically modified organisms (GMOs) and biodiversity, but in terms of the Potager du Roi, as soon as I say I buy seeds, people think it's because we can't reproduce them. It doesn't work that way. For example, with cabbage, we have about twenty-five different varieties of cabbage growing in the garden. If we try to plant the seeds from those cabbages, since most of them flower at more or less the same time, we don't have any of the cabbages turning out how they looked initially. So we buy them from seed producers, who have in turn contracted out to seed producers who live in different parts of France, far away from other seed producers or even from producers of that species in their neighborhood.

That's how it functions, and that's why keeping a variety true to type is so difficult and

why there are so few varieties described up until a certain understanding of plant sexuality took place. The first real conscious crossbreeding of plants was in the 1760s and 1770s, with Joseph Gottlieb Kölreuter in Germany in particular. It became rather popular everywhere and led to Gregor Mendel's experiments in the 1860s. If you have grown vegetable varieties in your garden, you know that beans are easy, peas are easy, but cabbage is very difficult.

Question: I have a three-part question about Josephine. First of all, do we know how much formal education she had before she crossed the ocean? Second, given her investment of time and money in Malmaison, how much of what was going on there, the sort of laboratory it became, was that partly nostalgia for the other world, for Martinique, or was it really intellectual and scientific curiosity? And you named a few scientists who worked at Malmaison and did all kinds of experiments. Was there one in particular who was her mentor?

BC: Josephine came from the convent in Fort-Royal (now Fort-de-France) on Martinique, where she learned what the young ladies of the nobility learned at the time: to sing and to sew, that was all. No foreign languages, nothing. But she was intelligent and she learned a lot when she was in France, especially from her father-in-law, the Marquis de Beauharnais, who lived in Fontainebleau near the court. She read a lot of books, and I think that she educated herself after she crossed the ocean, not before.

Then at Malmaison she spent a lot of money of course, but you have to know that Josephine was born in 1763, that is to say, only eight years after Queen Marie-Antoinette; they were almost of the same generation. She was a lady of the eighteenth century, educated in the anción regime. When she met Napoleon she was thirty-five, and had lived more than half of her life. She bridged the old and new societies. And of course she spent a lot of money because she was rooted in the old society. Napoleon was very bourgeois about money—he always reduced the bills—but Josephine never did, she didn't know what money meant. That's why it was always expensive. When she divorced, Napoleon gave her three million francs per year to live on—those days, a worker at Malmaison earned only 600 francs a year. So with three million, she could live. But in three years she already had four million francs in debt.

Regarding her mentor, Napoleon used to say that it was Étienne Soulange-Bodin, but we are not sure at all, because Soulange-Bodin was very fond of the botanist Fromont, established near Paris. But before Josephine bought Malmaison we have no idea if she loved botany or not. We are accustomed to saying that she brought this idea from Martinique and wanted to acclimate in Malmaison the plants that she knew when she was young, but we don't know for certain. It was just like an explosion after she had the means to plant and to enlarge the estate; it was quite small when she bought it, and when she died it covered more than two thousand acres.

Question: There was always music in the courts in the eighteenth century and earlier, and you mention that Josephine was interested in so many things, but I don't hear anything about music. I know Malmaison was not a court actually, more of a residence, but was she interested in music at all and were there concerts at Malmaison?

BC: They had a small theater of two to three hundred seats at Malmaison, and Josephine was very interested in music; we still have all the music books that she had marked with her intial "J." A lot of the music came from the eighteenth century, such as works dedicated to Madame Élisabeth, the sister of Louis XVI, or to the Comtesse d'Artois, wife of the grandson of Louis XV. Josephine's harp is still at Malmaison. She didn't play herself, because she considered that she was the empress, so she didn't play on the stage like Marie-Antoinette. Her daughter Hortense was the star of the troupe of the young people around Bonaparte. They used to act *L'Avare* (The Miser) by Molière and so forth, but Josephine herself did not act.

Nonetheless, she understood that she had a role like the queen's. Marie-Antoinette had asked Gluck to come from Austria to Paris to renovate the French Opéra, and Josephine did the same. She asked Gaspare Spontini, an Italian musician, to come to Paris. He dedicated *La Vestale* to the empress in 1806. This is the first instance of what we call the *grand opéra* (great opera), the ancestor of the operas of Berlioz and even of Gounod. This is the *opéra à la française*, and Josephine patronized Spontini at that time. And there were concerts at Malmaison, of course, in the great gallery.

CS: Also, I don't know if many are aware that Hortense de Beauharnais, Josephine's daughter, was a musician and composer herself who composed many pieces.

BC: Hortense composed a lot of songs, more than four hundred. One of the most famous ones was "Partant pour la Syrie" with lyrics by Alexandre de Laborde, which became a sort of national anthem

under Napoleon III. The poor emperor couldn't go anywhere without hearing "Partant pour la Syrie."

Question: Antoine, what was the influence of the people that you were talking about on scientists at the Muséum, and at Josephine's? You talked about it rather separately, but I'm curious to know what impact it had on either the scientific community or on the people who were actually the gardeners in the big gardens.

AJ: It's a long story. Duchesne was clearly in regular contact with the Muséum, with Thouin, Jussieu, and Adanson. At the Hunt Institute for Botanical Documentation in Pittsburgh, there's a whole series of annotations by Adanson of Duchesne's "Essai sur l'histoire naturelle des fraisiers," and on the *courges* (squash), in terms of the different systems of classification. What's interesting about Duchesne is that he really is a *systematicien* (systematizer or taxonomist). He's a botanist, but he's only interested in how he can regroup things, not in describing plants as such.

Lelieur is a real enigma. Everyone who worked with him hated him, and he's constantly self-serving in what he wrote, but there's no real scientific link. He put himself forward; he wrote for different magazines and journals, but he's really a politically isolated figure, a kind of misanthropic count in a little house in Versailles who said, "My roses are nicer, and I did corn and you should have too." He made some major exaggerations, such as saying there were more sweet potatoes in Philadelphia than potatoes. He had a thing about moving sweet potatoes from the south to the north, so he was trying to justify himself. It's not easy to know where he was going.

Poiteau began as a son of a peasant, worked in a convent as a gardener, and really discovered botany at the Jardin des Plantes where he initially got a job as a simple gardener and then went up the ladder rather quickly. He became *le préparateur* for Daubenton, preparing the plants for Daubenton's classes. During the Revolution, he was sent to the southwest of France; then, through a series of strange events, he ended up in the Caribbean. Throughout this whole circuit, he was regularly in contact with the Muséum. That's why I'm so curious about the relationship between the *Revue horticole*, the *Bon Jardinier*, and scientific research at the beginning of the nineteenth century, because I'm interested in the relationship between research and producers in the market feeding people. What were the positive pragmatic aspects of places like the Muséum, the Potager du Roi, and Malmaison, and how did they function with the rest? There are links, but they're not easy to make.

Question: It used to be said that the establishment of the Muséum d'Histoire naturelle in 1793 was almost a stroke of luck. Other academies were about to be abolished, and the fact that this was the old garden of the king was a lucky chance that got the Muséum refurbished and in much better shape than it had been before, while the Académie des sciences was disappearing. From what Paula says, it would have actually been much bigger had it not been for the dangers with respect to the working people. One of the old stories was that Daubenton becoming one of the professors of the Jardin du Roi was a great advantage; he was a sheep breeder as well as an anatomist. This relates to what Susan said about Josephine getting extra credit, as it were; her utility as a raiser of sheep helped remove some of that view of her as just an elite person. Could you comment on whether Daubenton's image really was critical, or is that something that just makes the story easier to tell about that transition point?

PYL: This is the introductory chapter to a book I'm working on—this is effectively the historiographical distinction. There are three separate threads, one of which argues that the Jardin du Roi was saved when other institutions were being razed because it was so prestigious, and its legacy as an institution of natural history was so important, that you could not possibly touch it. I don't personally find that very convincing. Another reason says that the revolutionaries got tired, so effectively, they couldn't be bothered. There were those high gates around the Jardin that Buffon had already installed to keep the peasants out, so to break down those barriers would have been a lot of work and effort when they had just taken down the Bastille. The third possibility is that Daubenton was already held in such esteem by the people. He had already established a sheepfold on the grounds, and had started trying to breed merino sheep there, so he was so beloved by the people that to attack his institution would be to attack the man himself, therefore nobody touched it.

The fourth version of the story, the one that I'm arguing, is because the Jardin was going to be situated as an agricultural institution. The political narratives were so deeply involved in narrating it as a place where France would find its food, its financing, and it would be restructured all through agriculture—so to attack those plants and trees, and eventually animals, would be to attack the very soul of France. It was also communicated to the peasantry in a very direct way, a way of understanding the work that was going on there that made a lot of sense to the common man, and therefore it was simply not attacked. I would argue this based upon the work of another French scholar who is not translated, Yvonne Letouzey, who wrote a really good, archivally-based biography of André Thouin.

From what I understand, when I read all the different documents, especially the political ones of the various committees, Thouin was truly instrumental in making sure that the institution stayed safe. Daubenton indeed had prestige and stature and was greatly beloved, but because of the Société d'Agriculture and its tremendous influence at the time, and ultimately through Thouin's extraordinarily intimate relationship with Grégoire, there are reams of documentation that go back and forth. When you quote Grégoire on agriculture, you are quoting Thouin every time. I found the corresponding documents where there is no question that he is taking his ideas directly from Thouin. And that would also ensure the institution's survival, if not necessarily its success, because of his enormous prestige at the time.

But considering that the Jardin du Roi was the only institution to receive funding during the Terror and it was the only institution during the Revolution that got a new building, it was a pretty special place in multiple regards. Even if you just take away the fact that it wasn't razed, simply surviving was great at the time. It's an extraordinary conflation of different agendas, but my particular research interest has been the political one, and on the ways the political dialogues ultimately saved it long enough for it to become what it is today.

STL: The only thing I would add is that even at the Hameau they didn't destroy the sheep, even at Versailles. They kept the *potager* around the Hameau, they kept that part of the structure that recalled the importance of agriculture.

PYL: I read a lot of police documents to find out about vandalism at the Muséum precisely during the Terror, because there was such anxiety from the professors about, "Oh, they're going to steal trees." There was virtually none. Considering how much food insecurity there was during the Revolution and how much of the narrative is about how there's no bread, "let them eat cake," I only found one instance where people stole a sheep, presumably for the purposes of eating it. It's surprising how little pilfering there was of the tasty chickens, the yummy swans, all these things. They really didn't touch them, and that is surprising considering the easy availability of food that these animals also represented. People were starving to death, but they were not going after those camels, they were not going after the rams, and the emus and things like that, which were all quite tasty.

PART III

CULTIVATING USEFUL KNOWLEDGE

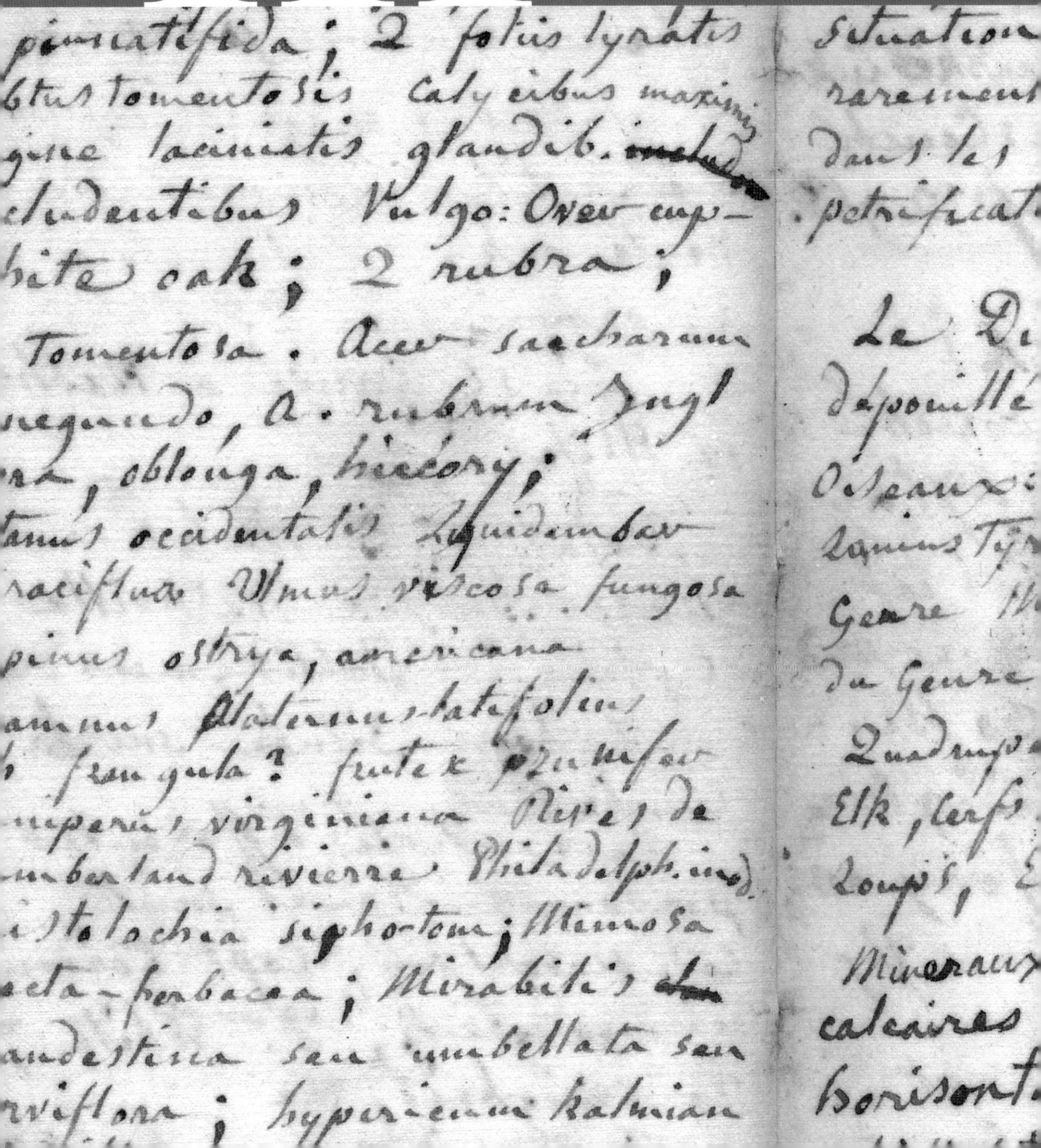

PART III

CULTIVATING USEFUL KNOWLEDGE

Previous page and detail, left André Michaux,
Botanical Journal in North America, vol. 8, 1793–95,
pamphlet-bound manuscript notebook (detail). APS
(see Fig. 7.4)

ANDRÉ MICHAUX AND FRENCH BOTANICAL DIPLOMACY IN THE CULTURAL CONSTRUCTION OF NATURAL HISTORY IN THE ATLANTIC WORLD

ELIZABETH HYDE

ON NOVEMBER 13, 1785, André Michaux arrived in New York City to begin his botanical exploration of North America on behalf of France. The mission: to collect North American trees that might be sent back to France where they would find a "culture heureuse" (happy culture) and, once acclimatized, repopulate French forests and ultimately contribute to the building of a French navy.[1] The history of Michaux's expeditions is well-known: his exploration of the mid-Atlantic, his founding of gardens in New Jersey and South Carolina to serve as nurseries for the gathering and study of North American specimens before their shipment to France, and his exploration of the Appalachians and the American South. His contributions to North American botany, recorded in his *Histoire des chênes de l'Amérique* in 1801 and the *Flora Boreali-Americana*, published posthumously in 1803, are duly celebrated (FIG. 7.1).[2] Michaux built his botanical legacy, however, in a complex but particular diplomatic, political, and economic context that gives contour to his work. An examination of this work—the methods and means by which he gathered and shared knowledge—reveals that Michaux was particularly adept in the deployment of his cosmopolitan and scientific identity on the American frontier and in its centers of power. His mission and its outcomes spoke simultaneously to universal botanists and to French and American nationalists.

James E. McClellan, among others, correctly reminds us that Michaux's mission must be situated in the context of French colonial botanical endeavors. He demonstrates that in the seventeenth and eighteenth centuries, the French government sought to grow botanical wealth from its colonies. The government implemented a system of botanical gardens, stretching from Mauritius off the eastern coast of Africa to Saint Domingue (Santo Domingo) in the Caribbean, which were not only connected to botanical gardens on coastal France but also to each other. Such gardens had both political and commercial purposes: the development of commercial-grade spice plants for distribution to colonists and to other botanical gardens, with the intent that the French increase the value of their colonies and their share in the spice trade.[3] Since Michaux's mission involved the gathering of botanical specimens and the generation of botanical knowledge about foreign lands to benefit France, it must be considered within this French system of colonial botanizing.

Fig. 7.1

White Oak from André Michaux, *Histoire des chênes de l'Amérique*, 1801. © Dumbarton Oaks Research Library and Collection, Rare Books Collection, Washington, D.C.

QUERCUS alba

But Michaux's mission also differed in important respects. For the United States, however young and unsteady when Michaux arrived in 1786, was *not* a French colony. This altered the context within which both the French and the Americans operated. French botanists necessarily engaged with American citizens and the fledgling American government as they sought to explore North America. It was not, therefore, French merchants or farmers who initiated botanical exchanges, but rather the French diplomatic corps. The French had only haphazardly attempted to learn about North American plants while in possession of Canadian colonies. It was only after the loss of Canada to Great Britain in the Seven Years' War that the French sought to gather systematically botanical knowledge of the continent.[4] Michaux's mission, however, was the culmination of a marked escalation of French botanical reconnaissance of North America dating from French involvement in the American Revolution. The Americans, newly independent from Britain, were uncertain of their future relationship with the French, and at the same time conscious of the superiority of French scientific institutions and botanical wealth. But the nature of scientific and, in particular, botanical inquiry and plant collecting in Europe and Great Britain allowed the colonials a stronger position than they had in strictly economic and other cultural endeavors. European botanists, gardeners, and collectors valued American specimens that were exotic and rare in Europe. Thus, as Susan Scott Parish has observed in context of the scientific and cultural relationship

90

between colonial Americans and Britons, "empiricism and the pastoral could then turn the center-periphery hierarchy on its head," for "colonials were hungry for institutional connections, for print matters and scientific equipment, and in certain ways for publicity, whereas Londoners needed the stuff of nature and connections with people reliable enough to send steady shipments and accurate descriptions of that matter."[5] In their dealings with the French, the Americans revealed themselves to be quite aware of what the French sought and what Americans could both offer and stand to gain.

As early as 1779, Conrad Gérard, French envoy to the American Congress, sought American plants and duly made contact with the Bartrams, Philadelphia physician Thomas Bond, and nurseryman and botanical gardener Humphry Marshall.[6] In writing about Gérard's mission to Marshall on August 7, 1779, Bond suggested that the relationship with Gérard could benefit both parties: "It is in his power—it is his wish, to improve the useful productions of this new world. He wants our curiosities and novelties: we want his valuable collections from all other parts of the world." He asked Marshall to fill the order from his gardens.[7] Bond highlighted the potential for botanical reciprocity; and indeed, botanical, intellectual, and diplomatic reciprocity would inform subsequent French-American exchanges.

The job of obtaining seeds desired by the French fell not to Gérard, but to François Barbé-Marbois, who served under consul general Anne-César, Chevalier de la Luzerne, the French minister to the United States. In 1780, Marbois circulated his (now famous) questionnaire to each of the thirteen American states. Marbois requested information about each state, including its population, towns, and economy (domestic and foreign). He inquired about the geography of each state, and requested information about "trees plants fruits & other natural riches."[8] Seemingly, Marbois desired a natural, political, and economic history of each state, a challenge that prompted Thomas Jefferson to write his *Notes on the State of Virginia* (first published in 1785). But Marbois also wanted specimens. In October 1780, Bond wrote to Marshall, "Since my last, no intelligence from Mr. Gerard: but Mr. MarBois, has apply'd to me in behalf of the Marshal Noailles, and the Royal Garden at Paris, to enter into a commerce of exchange of such trees, plants, &c, as would be a mutual advantage and improvement, in the natural productions of Europe and America."[9] But Bond clarified French demands in terms that anticipated Michaux's mission. "They do not," he explained, "desire botanical curiosities; but such things only as would enrich France,—such as *Pines, Oaks, Hickories, Poplars, Persimmons, Magnolias,* &c, and wish to have a parcel of the *nuts* sent as soon as possible—for planting next spring."[10]

These early epistolary exchanges between Gérard, Marbois, Bond, and Marshall were accompanied by the exchange of seeds meant to demonstrate both botanical and diplomatic goodwill. Marshall furnished Bond with a selection of specimens intended for the French. Bond wrote, "the collection, though small, is valuable and curious. I wish to keep up a correspondency in Europe, on a small scale, and solely with a view of furnishing each country, reciprocally, with such things as may be useful." The initial seeds were a gift, but Bond made clear that Marshall should be paid for fulfillment of Marbois's list."[11] Gérard subsequently also sent two boxes of French seeds, from which, Bond reported in August 1781, several plants had grown.[12]

It is not clear if such exchanges whetted French appetites for more American specimens, or if difficulties surrounding the transactions necessitated a simpler but more robust means to facilitate the exchange of plants and knowledge. But it is clear that the French raised the botanical stakes by proposing more substantial partnerships. In 1783, J. Hector St. John de Crèvecoeur, having just published his *Letters from an American Farmer*, wrote in his new capacity as consul of France to the governors of the states of New York, New Jersey, and Connecticut. He had a formal proposal: should said state establish a botanical garden, the French would share specimens from their collections in exchange for American plants. William Livingston, governor of New Jersey, responded by submitting the French proposal to the State Assembly. He reported to Crèvecoeur that the Assembly expressed thanks and "to assure him that whenever this state hath formed an Establishment of a Botanical Garden, His Most Christian Majesty's offer will be gratefully accepted."[13] If New Jersey built a garden, the French could contribute specimens. No garden was built in New Jersey, though Crèvecoeur's proposal in Connecticut did result in the founding of a garden by a medical society in New Haven.[14]

None of the proposals resulted in the scale of botanical exchange sought by the French. So the task next fell upon Louis-Guillaume Otto, the French diplomat who first served as secretary to La Luzerne in Philadelphia, and then as *chargé d'affaires* in New York from 1785 until 1791. Otto corresponded directly with Charles-Claude de la Billarderie, Comte d'Angiviller, the director of the Bâtiments du Roi. Their correspondence is revealing. On October 27, 1785, Otto wrote, "I have followed your instructions in addressing the large landowners in making them the offer to send at our expense all the fruit trees and other objects of which they desire from France." D'Angiviller's suggestion reveals French assumptions that American men of property, like their French counterparts, could be expected to expend time and effort on the improvement of their estates through the building of gardens. Otto assured d'Angiviller that he was trying this approach: "I have written, among others, to W. Livingston, one of the more considerable proprietors." But Otto was skeptical that this approach would work. Gardening in America was in its infancy, as the attention of Americans was primarily occupied, he wrote, with the production of a few bad fruits and vegetables.[15] Otto therefore purchased American seeds and plants from Boston and Philadelphia sources, warning d'Angiviller that "these shipments will not come from botanists, that is to say they come from the same people who have for a long time exhausted the patience of M. l'Abbé Nolin." The Americans, he suggested, were not scientifically rigorous enough for Nolin. And, he added, they charged exorbitant prices.[16]

Otto therefore proposed an alternative: "I think I cannot insist too much, Monsieur le Comte, that [you should] send a French botanist to this country. Traveling to the different states would allow him certainly to make a number of interesting discoveries in natural history." If the French were serious about acquiring better botanical knowledge of North America, they should send their own man. Otto acknowledged that other European botanists had begun the work, but plenty of information remained to be gathered: "Kalm, Carver et Katesby[17] [sic] have . . . left their successors a vast field in which to employ their talents."[18]

Importantly, Otto also revealed a new urgency to the project. He stated bluntly, "The Emperor is already ahead of us in this measure, for around two years ago, he sent to America a botanist charged with gathering all the specimens cultivated in the United States and sending to his court the seeds and plants of different trees that they found there."[19] The emperor was Joseph II, Holy Roman Emperor and Archduke of Austria, Hapsburg brother of Marie-Antoinette. In 1783, Joseph II, interested in agriculture and botany, had indeed sent an expedition to explore the southeastern United States and the Caribbean for the purposes of bringing specimens back for the imperial collection housed in the gardens and greenhouses at Schönbrunn Palace.[20] For Otto, the expedition represented an imperial challenge to French botanical and scientific supremacy that the French needed to meet.

As Otto wrote to d'Angiviller, André Michaux was already crossing the Atlantic and headed for New York; Otto had been preaching to the converted. But Otto's letter, together with the efforts of Gérard, Marbois, and Crèvecoeur and their American respondents, reveals a broader diplomatic, political, economic, and scientific context from which to view Michaux's mission: a French need for trees to compete with the English in creation of a navy, a continued need to compete with other European powers in the race to generate knowledge of the natural history of North America that served utilitarian needs of state (military and economy), and a mutual French and American desire to build economically and culturally upon the new French alliance with the United States.

How did Michaux see his place in this nexus? Through Michaux's journals, letters, and publications, it is possible to tease out aspects of his scientific and professional persona. That persona suggests he conducted his work with the knowledge of the unique scientific and diplomatic position he occupied. Once in America, André Michaux presented himself as an accomplished and curious botanist. When he petitioned the New Jersey state assembly for permission to purchase land, he presented himself as botanist to the king and touted his botanical experience with specific reference to his Persian expedition, the most exotic of destinations in the imagination of eighteenth-century Europeans. His scientific curiosity and discrimination is apparent in his journals. For example, while traveling from Danville towards Louisville, Kentucky, in 1793, he recorded that he "recognized many Plants not found elsewhere" adding "the neighborhood would be very interesting for a Botanist [himself, presumably] to visit."[21] Just a day later he noted, "the country between Beardstown and Louisville possesses no interest for a Botanist."[22] Historians of science have noted a tendency among early scientists to depersonalize their writing to enhance the perception of authority.[23] Yet Michaux used the personal to accentuate his authority. Michaux cited his experience in the field observing and studying American oaks in every stage of their development on the ground in America itself. The materiality of his work—trekking across the American frontier, gathering specimens, and carefully shipping them back to France—is apparent in the dried and pressed specimens he prepared and in the packets of acorns sent back to France and still extant in their original packaging (**FIGS. 7.2** and **7.3**). The lack of similar experience in others, Michaux asserted, rendered them incapable of producing accurate depictions of their structures and shapes. In his *Histoire des chênes de l'Amérique*, he wrote, "American oaks that are cultivated in Europe are not always exact because their growth has been retarded by a temperature that is less favorable than in their birth country, and because of this they maintain longer variations in foliation characteristic of their adolescent."[24] Indeed, Michaux did not shy away from calling out other botanists who had been led astray. In a footnote to the passage just cited, he wrote, "Many figures given by Du Roi and Plucknet represent oaks that have not yet reached maturity."[25]

But he did engage with fellow botanists: his *Histoire des chênes de l'Amérique* includes a bibliography of the botanical and natural history texts he consulted.[26] His comments about these sources create dialogues with their authors. Of the water oak, he wrote, "This is probably the variety that BARTRAM named Quercus dentate (narrow leaved winter green oak)," referring his reader to pages in William Bartram's *Travels Through North & South Carolina, Georgia, East & West Florida* of 1791.[27] In discussing the upland willow oak (*Quercus cinerea*), he cited Linnaeus's use of Mark Catesby's *Natural History of Carolina, Florida and the Bahama Islands* (1731–43).[28] Michaux used both his field experience and bookishness to establish his botanical authority.

If Michaux's scholarly personality seems somewhat testy, we do know that he was a savvy observer of society. In a letter he wrote to his then adolescent son François-André from Persia in 1783, Michaux expressed concern over his son's character. In advising him to take care in the choice of models to emulate, he advised him to be aware of the qualities of the *homme hônnete*, an honest or honorable man, and the *hônnete homme*, an "honorable gentleman" noted more for his display of learning, wit, and manners than for his character.[29] Michaux's distinction between the two types demonstrates

Fig. 7.2

White Oak (*Quercus abietum*, "Quercus alba virginiana"), collected by André Michaux in United States, 1786–96, herbarium sheet. © MNHN-Patrick Lafaite

Fig. 7.3

Acorns of Scarlet Oak (*Quercus coccinea*), collected by André Michaux in United States, 1786–96. © MNHN-Patrick Lafaite

ELIZABETH HYDE

a keen social awareness that served him well as he negotiated the broad range of peoples—Americans, French Americans, Native Americans, farmers, thinkers, and political leaders—he encountered in North America. Michaux noted his encounters with fellow Frenchmen in the American frontier, as well as men who distinguished themselves by their wit and education. But he also met and shared French seeds with botanically curious men of property such as George Washington and Thomas Jefferson.[30] With these men, he practiced the required reciprocity of the cosmopolitan world of botanical exchange on both sides of the Atlantic—by exchanging seeds.

Michaux's work also reveals him to be conscious of the political, economic, and environmental context in which he worked and the purpose of his mission. His journal is a natural history: it reads as though he, himself, were completing Marbois's questionnaire (**FIG. 7.4**). The 1795 entry on Nashville, Tennessee, is representative:

> *Soile of Nashville clayey, rocky, limestone Rocks somewhat similar to the Kentuckey formation, position of the Rocks horizontal, occasionally Quartz Veins in the Rocks, abounding in marine petrifications.*

> *Sunday 21st of June 1795, killed and skinned some birds.*

> *Birds: Robin, Cardinal, Tetrao (grouse), Lanius Tyrannus rare, Quantities of the Genus Muscicopa; few species of the Genus Picus: Wild Turkeys. Quadrupeds: Musk-rat, Beaver, Elk, dwarf Deer, Bears, Buffalos, Wolves, small grey Squirrels.*[31]

In Pittsburgh, previously claimed by the French and the British, he noted rich coal deposits and what had become of the French Fort Duquesne and the English Fort Pitt as the Americans built a city numbering 250 houses and their own fortress.[32] Significantly, he also described economic activity related to the natural resources he observed, recording, for example, iron works he encountered: in 1795, he visited "the Iron works called Hill's Iron Works operated by Colonel Hill."[33] Days later he passed another iron works, and two miles beyond that, found "a Rock of mineral, pieces whereof on being crushed and reduced to powder dye cotton red; this mineral is boiled etc."[34] Similarly, he recorded in 1795 that, "being obliged to stay, watched the Process of manufacturing Salt,"[35] which he then described.

If Michaux's journal is natural history, his books, as discussed above, are botanical studies. Yet even within *Histoire des chênes de l'Amérique*, he addressed matters of French and American political economy, noting the economic impact of specific trees. Of the red oak (**FIG. 7.5**), he wrote, "this tree is one that would be most advantageous to grow in Europe. The wood, though of lesser quality than the White Oak, is used in building and by wheelwrights. Its bark is preferred to that of all other species for tanning. European tanners settled in the United States found it contained a much more active quality than European oaks used for the same purpose."[36] About the downy black oak (**FIG. 7.6**), he stated, "the wood of this tree is used for zigzag fences," and added that the overconsumption of the wood contributed both to deforestation and forest fires."[37] Here, the Frenchman offered the Americans a lesson in the environmental circumstances that made his mission necessary for France.

In her analysis of early American natural history writing, Joyce Chaplin observed a tension between the universal and the national.[38] Plumbing this tension in the context of Michaux, a Frenchman exploring the United States as "botaniste du roi," then as citizen of the republic of France, and as scientist serving the universal field of botany, one sees the complexities of his position and his skill in navigating them. Michaux's official mission was a utilitarian charge intended to address French needs at the intersection of French military, economic, and imperial ambitions. American officials understood it as such. When William Livingston received a copy of Marbois's questionnaire from John Witherspoon, president of Princeton University, he replied, "I have received Mr. Marbois's Queries, with your Letter that accompanied them. Whether it be from a groundless jealousy or a laudable caution, but I frankly confess *entre nos* [sic] that with respect to many of them I do not feel myself disposed to furnish him or any other foreigner with the solution."[39] "Some of them [the questions]," he continued, "indeed seem to be mere matters of innocent Curiosity & every friend to Science will think himself happy in lending his assistance to disseminate useful knowledge through the

universe. Whether these are inserted for their own sakes, or for the sake of recommending by their harmless company the political ones I know not." Livingston eventually responded to Marbois, but wrote that he was hesitant to hand over information of a more sensitive nature.[40] Marbois thanked Livingston for the information with a packet of seeds from the king's garden, which he planted at his estate called Liberty Hall.[41]

Fundamental French and American differences were highlighted again when Otto appealed to Governor Livingston for help in allowing Michaux to purchase land for a French garden in New Jersey. Livingston wrote, "so useful an establishment, Sir, cannot but be universally applauded. The improvement of the vegetable kingdom ought to be a darling object with America, and for their skill in that science, the French are justly celebrated." But Livingston then politely reminded the Frenchman that as governor, he was no monarch free to operate above the law: "Were it only to gratify his majesty's wishes; I cannot think that Mr. Michau [sic] will meet with any obstacles in the execution of his commission. It is not however in the power of the Governors of any of these states to because what the Laws do not permit. As the interposition of the

Legislature is necessary to facilitate the designs of Mr. Michau, I cannot doubt it will be obtained at their next sitting which will be in February."[42]

The tension between French and American perspectives came to a head in 1793. Michaux, facing uncertain financial support from the increasingly unstable French republican government, had nearly secured permission and funding to "explore the interior country of North America, from the Missisipy along the Missoury, and Westwardly to the Pacific Ocean" on behalf of the American Philosophical Society, then headed by Thomas Jefferson (FIG. 7.7). That mission fell apart, however, with the arrival of Edmond Charles (or "Citizen") Genet, the new envoy to the United States on behalf of the French Republic. Michaux unfortunately became embroiled in Genet's plot to challenge Spanish control of the Mississippi with military means. American suspicion of Genet's motives—his hopes of inciting Kentuckians to fight the Spaniards—together with George Washington's declaration of American neutrality in the wars being fought in Europe (over the French Revolution) led to Genet being recalled and Michaux having lost an opportunity to explore the American West.[43] The two failed ventures importantly expose both French and American awareness that the rest of the continent was a colonial territory ripe for imperial picking.

In 1793, the French republican government took stock of existing botanical missions. Michaux's new superiors determined that while the Charleston garden offered access to "pretty plants" from the American South that were suitable for "botanical gardens and for the progress of Science," the New Jersey garden produced "less curious objects" but objects of "greater utility."[44] The new government decided in favor of the utilitarian:

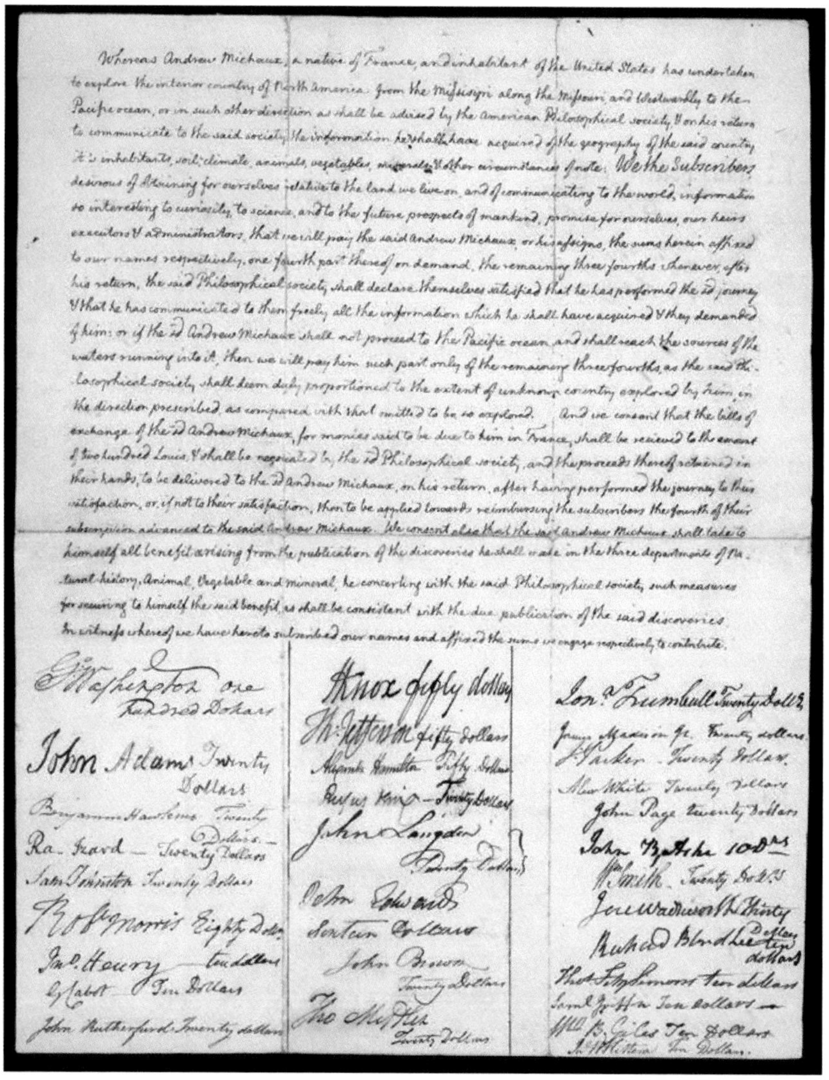

Fig. 7.7

Thomas Jefferson, Manuscript Subscription List Put Forward by Jefferson to Support a Proposed Scientific Expedition under André Michaux, 1793, ink on paper. APS

the Charleston garden would be sold and Michaux would return to France. Back in France, he would focus his energy on the writing and publication of his histories of American oaks and North American flora. His *Histoire des Chênes de l'Amérique* demonstrates Michaux's understanding of the place he occupied: a scientist inextricably caught (though perhaps fruitfully so) between the imperial and scientific goals of both countries he served.

---

1 "Instruction au Sieur André Michaux, Botaniste du Roi," Archives nationales de France, Série O¹2113, "Pépinière d'Amérique: Mission Michaux"; reproduced and catalogued as "Documents on his [André Michaux's] botanizing in the United States, 1785–1807," American Philosophical Society, microfilm, Mss. Film.330 (hereafter AN Série O¹2113 at APS).

2 See André Michaux, *Histoire des chênes de l'Amérique; ou, Descriptions et figures de toutes les espèces et variétés de chênes de l'Amérique septentrionale* (Paris: Crapelet, 1801); and André Michaux, *Flora Boreali-Americana, sistens caracteres plantarum quas in America septentrionali collegit et detexit* (Paris: Crapelet; Paris and Strasbourg: Levrault, 1805).

3 James E. McClellan III, "André Michaux and French Botanical Networks at the End of the Old Regime," *Castanea: Occasional Papers in Eastern Botany* 2 (December 2004): 69–97. See also James E. McClellan III and François Regourd, *The Colonial Machine: French Science and Overseas Expansion in the Old Regime* (Turnhout: Brepols, 2012), 361–76.

4 Gilbert Chinard, "André and François-André Michaux and Their Predecessors: An Essay on Early Botanical Exchanges between America and France," *Proceedings of the American Philosophical Society* 101, no. 4 (1957): 344–61.

5 Susan Scott Parrish, *American Curiosity: Cultures of Natural History in the Colonial British Atlantic World* (Chapel Hill: University of North Carolina Press, 2006), 106.

6 Gilbert Chinard, "André and François-André

Michaux," 350. Bond was a Philadelphia physician who was co-founder of the Pennsylvania Hospital, lecturer in medicine at the University of Pennsylvania, and friend and intellectual compatriot of Benjamin Franklin. Humphry Marshall, cousin to John and William Bartram, was a farmer, naturalist, and nurseryman whose botanical garden would serve as a source of American plants to Britons. In 1785, he would publish his *Arbustrum Americanum: The American Grove, or, An Alphabetical Catalogue of Forest Trees and Shrubs, Natives of the American United States, arranged according to the Linnaean System* (Philadelphia: Joseph Crukshank, 1785).

7 Thomas Bond to Humphry Marshall, 7 August 1779, in William Darlington and Peter Collinson, *Memorials of John Bartram and Humphry Marshall with Notices of their Botanical Contemporaries* (Philadelphia: Lindsay and Blakiston, 1849), 536–37. He continued, "This is, therefore, to request you would come forth with me, to make an offer of mutual good offices; and to furnish me with a list of such seeds, vegetables, plants, trees, &c, as this country wants, and what we could give him."

8 William Livingston, "Articles on which M. de Marbois desires some details," William Livingston Papers (microform; Ann Arbor, Mich.: University Microfilms International, [1986]), reel 18.

9 Bond to Marshall, 26 October 1780, in Darlington and Collinson, *Memorials*, 538.

10 Ibid. Bond continued, "The proposal is public-spirited, and worth our notice,—and if it will not be too much trouble to you, I should be glad to accept it."

11 Bond to Marshall, 2 December 1780, in ibid., 539. "As the other [formal request made by Marbois] is a very large affair, and will cost you [Humphry Marshall] much trouble, you ought to be well paid for it."

12 Bond to Marshall, 24 August 1781, Philadelphia, in ibid., 540.

13 Livingston to Crèvecoeur, December 11, 1783, Trenton, N.J., William Livingston Papers (microfilm).

14 Crèvecoeur made similar suggestions to Pennsylvania and Connecticut. See Julia Post Mitchell, *St. John de Crèvecoeur* (New York: Columbia University Press, 1916), 106–7.

15 "J'ai suivre vos instructions en m'adressant à de grands possessieurs de terre et en leur faisant l'offre de leur faire parvenir aux depens du choix tous les arbres fruitiers et autres objets quils pouvroient desirer de France." Otto continued, "J'en ai ecrit entre autres à W. Livingston, un des proprietaires les plus considerables. . . . Le jardinage est ici [in the United States] dans son enfance, ou est très indifferent pour toutes les ameliorations de ce genre et les devreér conumerables absorbent tellement toute l'attention des Americains qu'ils ne s'occupaient de leurs jardins que pour avoir quelques mauvais fruits et des legumes." Otto to d'Angiviller, 27 October 1785, New York, AN Série O¹2113 at APS.

16 " . . . mais ces envois ne seront encore faits que par des Botanistes, c'est à dire par les mêmes gens qui ont depuis se longtemps lassé la patience de M. l'Abbé Nolin. . . . Les Botanistes Americaines sont d'une chereté exorbitante. Le Sr Prince qui se trouve à environ 16 miles de New Yorck [sic] est très exigeant

et ne peut neanmoins me fournir qu'une très petite partie de ce que je lui démande." Ibid.

17 See Peter (Pehr) Kalm, *Travels into North America: Containing its Natural History, and a Circumstantial Account of its Plantations and Agriculture in General* (1770); Mark Catesby, *The Natural History of Carolina, Florida, and the Bahama Islands* (London, 1729); Jonathan Carver, *Travels Through The Interior Parts of North America, in the Years 1766, 1767, and 1768* (London, 1781).

18 Otto to d'Angiviller, New York, 27 October 1785. Otto wrote, "Je pense que vous ne saurier trop insister, Monsieur le Comte, sur l'envoi d'un Botaniste françois dans ce pays ci. En voyageant dans les differens Etats il servit certainement quantitie de decouvertes interessantes pour l'histoire naturelle." Otto continued, "n'ont encore qu'effleuré cette matiere et ont laissé à leurs successeurs un vaste champs pour deployer leur talens." The letter continues, "Quant aux depenses que celle Commission pourroit [*illeg.*], elles se trouveroient presque comprensées par la bonté et le bon marché des envois. . . . M. de Crevecoeur qui est actuellement en France avoit forme pendant plus de 20 années de sejour des liasons qui lui faciletoient beaucoup les commission de ce genre; mais je trouve chés toutes les personnes à qui je m'adresse une indifference qui une fait mal augerer du [*illeg.*] de mes demanders." Otto's citations of Kalm, Carver, and Catesby were references, of course, to Peter (or Pehr) Kalm, Jonathan Carver, and Mark Catesby, Swedish, American, and English naturalists, respectively, who had already explored

and published on North American natural history.

19 "L'Empereur nous a deja devancé dans cette mesure, il y a environ deux ans qu'il envoya en Amerique un botaniste chargé de parcourir toutes les partiens cultivées des Etats unis et de faire passer à sa Cour les graines et les plantes des differens arbres qu'ils y trouveroit." Otto to d'Angiviller, 27 October 1785, New York, AN Série O¹2113 at APS.

20 The contents of the imperial collection were published in Nikolaus Joseph von Jacquin, *Plantarum rariorum horti cæsarei schoenbrunnensis descriptiones et icones* (Vienna: C. F. Wappler, 1797–1804).

21 André Michaux, journal entry, 15 September 1793, in "André Michaux's Travels into Kentucky, 1793–96," in *Early Western Travels, 1748–1846*, vol. 3, ed. Reuben Gold Thwaites (Cleveland, Ohio: A. H. Clark, 1904), 41. The above is translated from "Portions of the Journal of André Michaux, Botanist, written during his Travels in the United States and Canada, 1785 to 1796," ed. C. S. Sargent, in *Proceedings of the American Philosophical Society* 26, no. 129 (January–July 1889): 1–145.

22 André Michaux, journal entry, 15 September 1793, "André Michaux's Travels," 3:41.

23 For a discussion of this point in the context of empire and science, see James Delbourgo and Nicholas Dew, "Introduction: The Far Side of the Ocean," in *Science and Empire in the Atlantic World*, ed. Delbourgo and Dew (New York: Routledge, 2008), 13–15.

24 "Chênes d'Amérique que l'on cultive en Europe, ne sont pas toujours exactes, parce que leur accroissement y est retardé par une temperature qui leur est moins favorable que celle de leur pays natal, et parce qu'ils y conservent plus longtemps les varieties de foliation qui caractérisent leur adolescence." Michaux, *Histoire des chênes de l'Amérique*, 5.

25 "Plusieurs figures données par Du Roi, et celle de Plucknet, pl. LVI, fig. 5, représentent des Chênes qui n'avaient point acquis l'état de perfection que donne l'âge adulte." Ibid., 6.

26 Michaux's "Table des auteurs" cites twenty-two works. Among them are William Aiton, *Hortus Kewensis* (1789); John Banister, *Catalogus Plantarum in Virginia observatorum* (1686); William Bartram, *Travels through North and South Carolina, Georgia, East and West Florida* (1791); Luigi Castiglione, *Viaggio negli Stati Uniti dell'America settentrioale* (1790); Mark Catesby, *The Natural History of Carolina, Florida, and the Bahamas* (1751); P. F. X. de Charlevoix, *Histoire et description générale de la Nouvelle-France* (1744); Carolus Clusius, *Rariorum Plantarum historia* (1601); and Johann Philipp DuRoi, *Die Harbkesche wilde Baumzucht* (1771). Ibid., n.p.

27 "C'est probablement cette variété que BARTRAM a nommée Quercus dentate (Narrow leaved winter green oak)." Ibid., "Water Oak," n.p.

28 "Linnaeus a rapporté à cette espèce la description et la figure de Catesby; mais cette figure est si peu exacte, qu'j'en ai supprimé la citation dans les cynonymes [sic]." Ibid., "Upland Willow Oak," n.p.

29 André Michaux to [François-André] Michaux, 15 May 1783, "André Michaux Letters and Papers, 1783–1890," Mss. B. M58, document 1, American Philosophical Society.

30 Michaux's meeting with George Washington is recorded in Washington's diary and reproduced in Henry Savage, Jr., and Elizabeth J. Savage, *André and François-André Michaux* (Charlottesville: University of Virginia Press, 1986), 50–51.

31 Michaux, journal entry, 21 June 1795, "André Michaux's Travels," 63.

32 Ibid., 6 August 1793 through 13 August 1793, 32.

33 Ibid., 26 April 1795, 54.

34 Ibid., 22 May 1795, 58.

35 Ibid., 20 July 1795, 65.

36 "Cet arbre est un de ceux qu'il serait le plus avantageux de cultiver dans toute l'Europe. Son bois, quoiqu'inférieur en qualité à celui du Chêne blanc, est cependant très-employé pour la charpente et le charronnage. Son écorce est préférée à celle de toutes les autres espèces pour le tannage. Les Tanneurs Européens établis dans les états-Unis, ont observé qu'elle contenait un principe beaucoup plus actif que celle des Chênes d'Europe employée au même usage." Michaux, *Histoire des Chênes de l'Amérique*, "Red Oak," 20.

37 "Le bois de cet arbre est employé pour les clôtures en zigzag. . . . La grande consommation de bois qui résulte de cette mauvaise manière d'enclore les terres, ne contribue pas moins à la destruction des forêts, que les incendies annuels." Ibid., "Downy Black Oak," 14.

38 Chaplin explores this tension in, among other places, "Nature and Nation: Natural History in Context," in *Stuffing Birds, Pressing Plants, Shaping Knowledge: Natural History in North America, 1730–1860*, ed. Sue Ann Prince (Philadelphia: American Philosophical Society, 2003), 75–77.

39 William Livingston to John Witherspoon, 17 December 1781, Trenton, William Livingston Papers.

40 Ibid. My thanks to Dr. Christopher Bellitto for directing me to the Biblical reference.

41 His estate, Liberty Hall (now Liberty Hall Museum), is located in Union, New Jersey, on the campus of Kean University; it is open to the public.

42 Livingston to Otto, 3 January 1786, Elizabeth Town, N.J., William Livingston Papers.

43 On the Genet Affair, see Charlie Williams, "Explorer, Botanist, Courier, or Spy? André Michaux and the Genet Affair of 1793," in *Castanea: Occasional Papers in Eastern Botany*, 2 (December 2004): 98–106; and Savage and Savage, *André and François-André Michaux*, 124–61.

44 Anonymous, 1 floréal [1793], AN Série O¹2113 at APS. They wrote that while the Charleston garden offered access to "belles plantes" from the American South that were suitable for "les jardins botaniques et pour les progrès de la Science," the New Jersey garden produced "objets moins curieux" but of "plus grande utilité."

THE "ELEPHANT IN THE ROOM": THE IMPACT OF THE FRENCH SEIZURE OF THE DUTCH STADHOLDER'S COLLECTION ON RELATIONS BETWEEN DUTCH AND FRENCH NATURALISTS

ELISE LIPKOWITZ

OF ELEPHANTS & ROSES, the exhibition that inspired this symposium, opened with the singular story of a musical-cum-scientific experiment conducted on the Muséum national d'Histoire naturelle's two live elephants, Hans and Parkie (**FIG. 8.1**). On the afternoon of May 29, 1798, musicians from the Conservatoire de musique serenaded the elephants with fourteen tunes in a range of rhythms, tempos, and keys. This unusual concert aimed to ascertain how the elephants would respond to different kinds of music.[1] The Muséum's head librarian, who recorded the elephants' responses, concluded that they were stirred into the greatest frenzy by the revolutionary tune "Ça ira" when played in D-major with both orchestral and vocal accompaniment. The French public, who had eagerly followed the elephants' acquisition as war booty and their arrival in Paris in the spring of 1798, celebrated the elephants' preference for France's revolutionary anthem.[2]

Hans and Parkie were the weightiest of the live animals and the tens of thousands of natural history objects entering the Paris Muséum's collections as a result of French conquests in Continental Europe during the 1790s. While much could be said about Hans and Parkie, who hailed from the menagerie of the deposed Dutch head of state, the Stadholder William V, this essay addresses the metaphorical "elephant in the room" created by revolutionary-era French naturalists' expropriation and removal of live animals and natural history collections from the cabinets, museums, and menageries of fellow Europeans. The French seizure of natural history collections within Europe during the 1790s departed from the prior wartime practices of the early modern European powers and from European savants' longstanding understanding that it was inappropriate to seize collections from fellow Europeans.[3] Inspired by a new ideology that linked natural history to moral reform and political regeneration, prominent revolutionary-era French naturalists, under the aegis of the government-sponsored Commission temporaire des arts, revived the ancient practice of seizing natural history objects as war booty.[4] Pierre-Yves Lacour has estimated that 21 percent of the birds and mammals that entered the Muséum between 1793 and 1809 did so through confiscations, suggesting that the spoils of French conquest contributed significantly to the Muséum's fourfold expansion during the French Revolution and the Napoleonic Wars.[5] Three

Fig. 8.1

J. P. Hoüel, *Du caractère dans les phisionomies des Eléphants*. From J. P. Hoüel, *Histoire naturelle des deux éléphans, male et femelle, du Muséum de Paris* (Paris, 1803), plate IV. The Academy of Natural Sciences of Drexel University, Ewell Sale Stewart Library

aspects of the French seizures have previously received substantial scholarly treatment: the French naturalists' participation in the confiscations; the process of seizing and transporting specimens and live animals to Paris; and the Dutch, German, Belgian and Italian efforts to reclaim their confiscated collections at the conclusion of the Napoleonic Wars.[6] Minimal attention, however, has been devoted to the consequences of France's seizure of European natural history collections for relations among Europe's naturalists, for the subsequent development of natural history, or for the character of transnational science in the revolutionary era.[7]

This paper explores the changing relationship between French and Dutch naturalists through the lens of the seizure of the Dutch Stadholder's collection. Whereas French and Dutch naturalists had been peers and rivals in the pre-war era, the seizure of the Stadholder's collection recast French

ELISE LIPKOWITZ

PL. IV.

Fig. 2.

E

A
A

nomies des Éléphants.
le mâle et la femelle
nourrissent

naturalists as both the expropriators of a celebrated Dutch natural history collection and, ironically, as the patrons and protectors of Dutch savants. As the geopolitical dynamic of conqueror and vanquished became manifest within the scientific realm, French naturalists sought to normalize transnational scientific relations by minimizing their role in the seizure of the Stadholder's collection, by distancing their extractive activities on the Commission's behalf from their scientific identity, and by serving as protectors of Dutch savants. Such efforts, though, could not disguise that French naturalists' participation in the activities of the Commission temporaire des arts obscured the line between science and state and helped propagate a French imperial vision of transnational science. This nationalist vision co-opted and distorted the ideals and practices of the pre-war scientific Republic of Letters, a cosmopolitan scholarly community characterized by actual networks and

THE "ELEPHANT IN THE ROOM"

institutions linking savants throughout Europe and beyond, and by a commitment to such governing ideals as neutrality, merit, community, and apolitical character. The transport of the Netherlands' most prized specimens to Paris ultimately inaugurated a period of unrivaled French leadership in natural history and of increased Dutch dependence on France for such knowledge.

To appreciate the profound effects of the seizure of the Stadholder's collection on French-Dutch scientific relations, one must acknowledge the preeminence of eighteenth-century Dutch natural history. Amsterdam's role as Europe's premier entrepôt for the sale and distribution of natural history specimens, along with the pioneering work of naturalists such as Albertus Seba, Peter Pallas, Jean Allamand, and Aernout Vosmaer, had made the Netherlands a primary locus for Europe's aspiring naturalists.[8] In particular, the Dutch were known to possess the rarest and best-preserved natural history specimens, many of which had originated in their colonies. Strict limits on other Europeans' access to Dutch colonial treasures coupled with Dutch naturalists' judicious use of the collections had enabled Dutch savants to be the first to describe many exotic species.[9] Indeed, the Dutch naturalists easily rivaled, if not surpassed, their French counterparts by producing some of the eighteenth century's finest works on natural history.

By the 1770s, many of the Netherlands' natural history riches were aggregated in the collection and menagerie of the Dutch Stadholder William V, where they were utilized by Dutch naturalists. However, the French conquest, which overthrew the Stadholder's government and precipitated his flight to England in January 1795, left the Stadholder's abandoned collections at The Hague and the menagerie at Apeldoorn in French hands.[10] The French naturalists of the Commission immediately recognized their good fortune in acquiring this collection. As the botanist André Thouin wrote, "I estimate that two-thirds of the objects composing [the Stadholder's collection] will enter the Muséum's galleries either by filling in for a missing component, or by replacing objects of inferior preservation or beauty. The national collection will become, by these additions, the most magnificent in the world and the most useful for the progress of the natural sciences."[11]

Thouin's jubilation at the acquisition of this exquisite collection, which would augment the Muséum's holdings and promote the revolutionary program of public instruction, was tempered by his recognition that seizure of this collection jeopardized relations with Dutch savants. For although the laws of war entitled a victorious France to seize the defeated Stadholder's property, French savants' participation in its expropriation violated the transnational scientific community's longstanding practices governing the circulation of specimens, its notions of gentlemanly comportment and trust, as well as its claim to science's apolitical character.[12] Faced with conflicting allegiances to France and to the transnational scientific community, Thouin and his fellow Commissioner, the geologist Barthélemy Faujas de Saint-Fond, undertook the transfer of the collection and menagerie to Paris while attempting to minimize the detrimental effects of its seizure on their relationship with Dutch savants.[13]

The contrasting rhetoric of Faujas and Thouin in writing to French and Dutch audiences suggests the fraught nature and the political complexities of the collection's seizure. In correspondence with French officials and French naturalists, Faujas and Thouin employed the rhetoric of military victory, spoils, imperial might, and national aggrandizement as they presented the collection's acquisition as a boon to French science. In writing to the Comité d'instruction publique, they stated, "Holland will open soon to our research and will provide us with ample harvests in all genres. We will follow our armies as they progress and we will not neglect anything that could contribute to the glory and above all the welfare of the nation."[14] In a letter to the Muséum's naturalists, Thouin emphasized that the future of the nation depended on garnering the specimens and scientific knowledge of conquered peoples. He wrote, "if as exemplified by the conquerors of China we instruct ourselves in the art of vanquished nations, it will be the means for us to make the most of our victories."[15] Nevertheless, when communicating with Dutch savants, Thouin and Faujas muted such sentiments while attempting to normalize their activities within the framework of the pre-war scientific Republic of Letters. Generally eschewing reference to the Stadholder's collection, they emphasized a more innocuous aspect of their mission: their mandate to observe Dutch agriculture, industry, and customs. Although this directive was motivated by the same scientific-political vision as the seizure of the Stadholder's collection, Thouin and Faujas used the framework of the scientific voyage to depoliticize their activities and make them seem routine. For example, in a letter to the Haarlem-based natural philosopher Martin van Marum, Faujas stated that he had been "traveling" (an accurate, albeit euphemistic statement), and that he wished to share his portfolio of observations and drawings with Van Marum and to exchange publications.[16] Such references to the routine activities and practices of the pre-war Republic of Letters ironically served to reinforce the notion of neutral, apolitical science at the very moment when Faujas's involvement in the activities of the Commission temporaire des arts challenged the notion of scientific neutrality.

While the rhetoric of the "scientific voyage" may have been plausible to their Dutch correspondents residing outside The Hague, Faujas and Thouin were unable to minimize the seizure of the Stadholder's collection with Aernout Vosmaer and Sebald Brugmans, the Dutch savants who aided the Frenchmen as they catalogued and packed the Stadholder's collection for shipment. Although the historical record is frustratingly silent about this encounter, the savants' biographies and the history of the collection's dispersal suggest it was an awkward meeting. All these savants had known one another by reputation. Moreover, Thouin and Brugmans had been correspondents in the pre-war period. All parties would have recognized that the seizure and transport of scientific objects as war booty was at variance with practices governing specimens and scientific collections in prior early modern European wars. In a period when natural history scholarship depended on access to and observation of specimens, all present would have understood the ramifications of the forced removal of the Netherlands' finest collection to France.

The French and Dutch savants' contrasting political allegiances would have further augmented the disjuncture between the ideals of the pre-war Republic of Letters and the new dynamic of the conqueror and the conquered. Faujas and Thouin's writings suggest that they eagerly supported the Revolution, embraced participation in the Commission, and were more committed to the advancement of French science than to the credo of the scientific Republic of Letters. By contrast, Vosmaer was a committed royalist who had loyally served the Stadholder for over thirty years. Indeed, Marinus Boeseman has suggested that Vosmaer demonstrated his loyalty to the Stadholder by hiding some of the collection's most valuable specimens from the French naturalists— eventually transmitting them to the Stadholder's son.[17]

Thouin and Faujas may well have approached this fraught interaction with Dutch savants at The Hague by adopting the "technocratic pose," a term that Ken Alder defined in his work on French engineers.[18] This technocratic pose enabled Faujas and Thouin to cast themselves as doing the bidding of French officials under compulsion. This approach had the virtue of denying their interest in the seized collections and their eager participation in the Commission's activities in order to maintain the useful fiction that they were fundamentally apolitical naturalists. By suggesting that they, like the Dutch savants, were ultimately victims of their respective nations' geopolitical circumstances, the French naturalists created the possibility for the preservation of a modicum of Franco-Dutch scientific amity. Given that Thouin and Faujas used the rhetoric of "duty" and "obligation" in the few letters to Dutch naturalists in which they acknowledged their activities at The Hague, it is possible that they employed similar rhetoric when interacting with Brugmans and Vosmaer.

Indeed, Thouin and Faujas, adhering to their directive from Paris to cultivate relations with Dutch savants, showed their Dutch colleagues some consideration. A letter exchanged between Faujas and Van Marum suggests that the two Commissioners played a role in exempting their Dutch counterparts from the mandated billeting of French soldiers in Dutch homes.[19] It has also been suggested that Thouin may have played a vital role in limiting the seizures of Dutch scientific collections to that of the Stadholder.[20] Additionally, French savants and officials permitted Vosmaer, Brugmans, and other Dutch savants to retain several specimens from the Stadholder's collection as a public gesture of French respect for the Dutch scientific community.[21]

These favors extended to Dutch savants should not be confused with the persistence of the values and practices of pre-war scientific cosmopolitanism. On the contrary, Faujas and Thouin's actions illustrate the French naturalists' role in crafting a new nationalist vision of transnational science, which I refer to as "French scientific universalism." This nationalist vision co-opted the values and mores of the pre-war scientific Republic of Letters.[22] In practice, the gifting of a few items from the Stadholder's collection to Dutch savants effectively made those savants party to the French nationalist agenda of appropriating the vast majority of the collection. When the Dutch sought to reclaim the Stadholder's collection in 1815, the Muséum's savants used their distribution of specimens to Dutch savants in 1795 to their advantage. Similarly, the French savants' ability to negotiate with officials to exempt Dutch savants from billeting troops revealed not so much the persistence of scientific amity as a new power dynamic in which French savants became the patrons and protectors of Dutch savants.

For the remainder of the French Revolution and the Napoleonic Wars, the framework of an imperial and nationalist French science profoundly shaped natural history practice in the Netherlands. Patronage flowed from Paris, as did attempts to reform the Dutch universities and scientific societies. Many Dutch naturalists concluded that collaboration with Batavian Republic officials and French savants was the lesser of two evils, since it provided them with a toehold in the transnational scientific community. Although they exchanged letters and made visits to Paris, Dutch naturalists exhibited concern that the French policy toward the remaining collections might be altered at any moment. Such concern was warranted given the Commission's previous wide-scale confiscations in Belgium and the German lands as well as its subsequent ones in Italy. Relations among Dutch and French naturalists also became increasingly lopsided. Much like the Stadholder's collection itself, the French naturalists treated their Dutch counterparts as resources to be mined rather than as genuine co-equals.

The extended correspondence between Georges Cuvier and Adriaan Gilles Camper from 1800 to 1811 provides a window onto the state of French-Dutch naturalists' relations in the wake of the expropriation of the Stadholder's collection. Camper was the son of the comparative anatomist Peter (or Petrus) Camper, whose work on elephant anatomy had made him one of Europe's early practitioners of that discipline. After 1800, the French anatomist Cuvier became the dominant figure in comparative anatomy, in part because of his access to the confiscated collections. Indeed, Cuvier's post-mortem dissection of the elephant Hans in Paris in January 1802 built upon the work of the late Peter Camper and enhanced Cuvier's status as a comparative anatomist. Two aspects of the correspondence between Cuvier and the younger Camper are salient. First is Camper's sense that his relationship with Cuvier was a unilateral one. Camper repeatedly lamented that while he responded swiftly to Cuvier's information requests, he received little information and correspondence in return. Indeed, Bert Theunissen has noted that Camper's complaint is borne out by the trajectory of the correspondence of the two savants. Their correspondence diminished in frequency once Cuvier had obtained the drawings and relevant information that Camper's late father had generated regarding the elephants.[23] Second, the expropriation of the Stadholder's collection remained a source of contention. In a letter to Cuvier in 1801, Camper described France as "the capital of the scientific world enriched by the spoils of all of Europe," contrasting it to a scientifically moribund Holland.[24] In yet another letter to Cuvier, Camper commented on the exiled Stadholder's son's 1802 visit to the Paris Muséum. Camper wrote, "He [the Stadholder's son] needed much philosophy and a great desire for instruction when he decided to visit the Muséum enriched by the spoils of his own father and of a nation that has become immiserated by your [France's] conquests."[25]

The seizure and transport of the Stadholder's collection played a vital role in shifting the epicenter of European natural history from the Netherlands to France. Items from the Stadholder's collection enhanced the Paris Muséum's collections of quadrupeds, insects, shells, and fish, as well as its menagerie. Study of these specimens and live animals enabled the Muséum's naturalists to attain breakthroughs in the fields of zoology and comparative anatomy. As Richard W. Burkhardt has noted, specimens from the Stadholder's collection formed the basis for Cuvier's work on living and fossil species of elephants, Cuvier's and Étienne Geoffroy Saint-Hilaire's study of orangutans, and Jean-Baptiste Lamarck's study of the features of the squid, cuttlefish, and octopus.[26] Similarly, the skull of the "Maastricht animal," which Florence Pieters has stated was illegally confiscated from the Netherlands, became the subject of Faujas' *Histoire naturelle de la Montagne de Saint-Pierre de Maestricht*.[27] Moreover, the French Commissioners' vision of using the collections to force other nations' savants to pay tribute to France, both politically and intellectually, was achieved. The Dutch naturalists turned to French savants for patronage, protection, and the latest developments in natural history.[28] The effects of the collection's seizure endured even beyond the end of the Napoleonic Wars. Deputized by the Dutch government, Brugmans went to Paris in 1815 to reclaim the Stadholder's collection for the Netherlands. However, Thouin and the other French naturalists thwarted Brugmans' efforts, arguing that the retention of this collection at the Muséum conformed to "the interest of our Establishment, which as you know, is also the interest of science and all who love and cultivate it."[29] After the French naturalists erected a series of impediments to the collection's return, Brugmans ultimately accepted an inferior, substitute collection consisting of doubles from French navigator Nicholas Baudin's voyage to the Pacific.[30]

This essay has shown that specimens and live animals (including Hans and Parkie) obtained as war booty from fellow Europeans contributed significantly to the vitality of the Paris Muséum and the preeminence of French natural history between 1790 and 1830. Unlike specimens that arrived at the Muséum via gifting, exchange, or sale, specimens entering as the spoils of war posed profound challenges to the relations between French savants and Dutch savants. Such specimens pitted a new vision of French scientific universalism against pre-war notions of the circulation of specimens and of the ideal of science as an apolitical domain. Both parties sought to preserve the illusion of the persistence of scientific cosmopolitanism amid the geopolitical circumstances. This is apparent in the French naturalists' double discourse, in which they used contrasting rhetoric with officials and savants in Paris and with Dutch savants, and by the Dutch savants' outward cooperation with the Commissioners despite their displeasure and even covert resistance to the collection's expropriation. However, the nods that both parties made in the direction of the ideals of pre-war scientific cosmopolitanism could not ultimately mask the "elephant in the room"—namely, the extent to which Dutch scientists had been dispossessed to the benefit of the Muséum and French natural science.

1   For additional details on the concert, see Richard W. Burkhardt, Jr., "Constructing the Zoo: Science, Society, and Animal Nature at the Paris Menagerie, 1794–1838," in *Animals in Human Histories: The Mirror of Nature and Culture*, ed. Mary Henninger-Voss (Rochester, N.Y.: University of Rochester Press, 2002), 239–41.

2   The saga of Hans and Parkie's transport to Paris as well as the story of their early days at the Paris Ménagerie were featured in French magazines including the *Décade philosophique* and the *Magasin encyclopédique*.

3   Although books and artwork had been seized as war booty in previous early modern European wars, natural history collections in Europe proper were respected until the French Revolution. There appears to have been a consensus prior to the French Revolution that scientific collections within Europe were to move via purchase, exchange, or gift. Europeans' respect for the property rights associated with the collections of fellow Europeans contrasts with their evident lack of concern about the property rights of the non-European peoples from whom many of the specimens were originally seized.

4   For discussion of the political resonance of revolutionary-era French natural history, see E. C. Spary, *Utopia's Garden: French Natural History from Old Regime to Revolution* (Chicago: University of Chicago Press, 2000), and Richard W. Burkhardt's essay in this volume.

5   Pierre-Yves Lacour, "La place des colonies dans les collections d'histoire naturelle, 1789–1804," in *Les mondes coloniaux à Paris au XVIIIème siècle: Circulation et enchevêtrement des savoirs*, ed. Anja Bandau, Marcel Dorigny, and Rebekka von Mallinckrodt (Paris: Karthala, 2010), 49–73.

6   On the origins of the collection, see Florence Pieters, "Notes on the Menagerie and Zoological Cabinet of the Stadholder William V of Holland, Directed by Aernout Vosmaer," *Journal of the Society for the Bibliography of Natural History* 9 (1980): 539–63; and Florence Pieters, "De menagerie van stadhouder Willem V op Het Kleine Loo te Voorburg/La ménagerie du stathouder Guillaume V dans le domaine Het Kleine Loo à Voorburg," in *Een vorstelijke dierentuin: De menagerie van Willem V/Le zoo du prince: La ménagerie du stathouder Guillaume V*, ed. Bert Sliggers and A. A. Wertheim (Zutphen: Walburg Institute, 1994), 39–59. On the process of seizing, packing, and sending the collection to France, see Ferdinand Boyer, "Le transfert à Paris des collections du Stathouder (1795)," *Annales historiques de la Révolution française* 43 (1971): 394; Pierre-Yves Lacour, "Les amours de Mars et Flore aux cabinets: Les confiscations naturalistes en Europe septentrionale," *Annales historique de la Révolution française* 4 (2009): 71–92; and Teunis Willem van Heiningen, "Le vol et la restitution des objets d'histoire naturelle du Stathouder Guillaume V ou Les péripéties des collections du Stathouder Guillaume V entre 1795 et 1815," *Archives internationales d'Histoire des sciences*, 56 (2006): 21–42. For discussion of the rhetoric among the French savants around the seized collections see Elise Lipkowitz, "Seized Natural History Collections and the Redefinition of Scientific Cosmopolitanism in the Era of the French Revolution," *British Journal for the History of Science* (forthcoming); and Lacour, "Les amours de Mars et Flore." On the process of transferring the menagerie from Loo to Paris, see Roger Saban and Michel Lemire, "Les éléphants de la ménagerie du stathouder Guillaume V d'Orange au Muséum d'Histoire naturelle, sous la Convention nationale et le Directoire," *Scientifiques et sociétés pendant la Révolution et l'Empire: Actes du 114e Congrès national des sociétés savantes, Paris 3–9 avril 1989* (Paris: Éditions du Comité des travaux historiques et scientifiques, 1990), 275–300; and Michel Lemire, "Frankrijk en de verzmelingen van stadhoude Willem V van Oranje / La France et les collections du stathouder Guillaume V d'Orange," in Sliggers and Wertheim, *Een vorstelijke dierentuin/ Le zoo du prince*, 87–114. On the legal questions surrounding the collection see Lipkowitz, "Seized Natural History Collections." On the question of restitution of the collection at the end of the Napoleonic Wars, see Van Heiningen, "Le vol et la restitution," and Lipkowitz, "Seized Natural History Collections."

7   Pierre-Yves Lacour, "Les commissions pour la recherche des objets d'arts et de sciences en Belgique, Allemagne, Hollande et Italie; 1794–1797: Des voyages naturalistes?" in *Voyager en Europe de Humboldt à Stendhal: Contraintes nationales et tentations cosmopolites, 1790–1840*, ed. Nicolas Bourguinat and Sylvain Venayre (Paris: Nouveau Monde, 2012), 21–39.

8   These themes are treated in Dániel Margócsy's manuscript in preparation, titled *Commercial Visions: Science, Trade, and Visual Culture in the Dutch Golden Age.*

9   The naturalists Albertus Seba, Peter Pallas, and Aernout Vosmaer used the Dutch collections to pen works that rivaled the Comte de Buffon's *Histoire naturelle*. Indeed, Vosmaer's *Regnum animale* was viewed as having the best illustrations of any eighteenth-century natural history work. And several decades before Georges Cuvier became known in France for his work on comparative anatomy, the Dutch naturalist Peter (Petrus) Camper pioneered the field.

10 In addition to the live animals, the French obtained 10,000 mineral specimens, 3,872 botanical specimens, 5,000 insects, 9,800 shells, and 1,176 stuffed birds from the Stadholder's collection. Pieters, "Notes on the Menagerie and Zoological Cabinet of Stadholder William V," 542.

11 "J'estime que les deux tiers d'objets qui la compose entreront dans les galeries du Muséum, soit comme choses complémentaires qui manquent entièrement à sa composition, soit en remplacement d'individus inférieurs en conservation et en beauté. La Collection nationale deviendra par cette réunion, la plus magnifique qui existera dans le monde et la plus utile aux progrès des Sciences Naturelles." André Thouin to unknown correspondent, 4 ventôse an 3 [22 February 1795], F17A/1276/dossier 2, Archives nationales, Paris (hereafter AN).

12 This period predates the Hague Convention that, in its various iterations since 1899, has made the seizure of artistic and scientific objects as war booty a violation of international law.

13 La Commission des Relations extérieures to the Administrateurs du Muséum national d'Histoire naturelle, 14 nivôse an 3 [3 December 1794], AJ 15/578/dossier 4, AN.

14 "La Hollande s'ouvrira bientôt à nos recherches, et nous fournira d'amples moissons dans tous les genres. Nous y suivrons nos armées au fur et à mesure qu'elles y entreront, et nous tâcherons de ne rien négliger de tout ce qui peut contribuer à la gloire et surtout au Bonheur de la Nation." Les Commissaires des sciences et des arts dans les pays conquis par

les armées de la République to the Citoyens commissaires de l'instruction publique, 1 brumaire an 3 [1 October 1794], F17/1229/dossier 12 #246, AN.

15 "Ces récoltes sont intéressantes sans doute, mais si à l'exemple des vainqueurs de la Chine nous nous instruisons dans les arts des Peuples vaincus, c'est le moyen de tirer le plus grand avantage de nos victoires." Thouin to the Professeurs-Administrateurs du Muséum d'Histoire naturelle, 20 floréal an 3 [9 May 1795], AJ 15/836/ dossier 2, AN.

16 Faujas de Saint-Fond to Martin van Marum, pluviôse an 3 [January/ February 1795], Faujas folder, Series 529, Box 16, Noord Hollands Archief, Haarlem (hereafter NHA).

17 For further discussion of Dutch naturalists' efforts to conceal certain specimens in the Stadholder's collection from the French, see Marinus Boeseman, "The Vicissitudes and Dispersal of Albertus Seba's Zoological Specimens," *Zoologische Mededelingen* 44, no. 13 (January 1970): 186; and Pieters, "The Menagerie and Zoological Cabinet of Stadholder William V," 541.

18 For further discussion of the notion of the technocratic pose, see Ken Alder, *Engineering the Revolution: Arms and Enlightenment in France, 1763–1815* (Princeton, N.J.: Princeton University Press, 1997), 292–318.

19 Faujas de Saint-Fond to Martin van Marum, 23 ventôse an 3 [13 March 1795], Faujas folder, Series 529, Box 16, NHA.

20 Yvonne Letouzey, *Le Jardin des Plantes à la croisée des chemins avec André Thouin, 1747–1824* (Paris: Éditions du Muséum nationale d'Histoire naturelle, 1989), 441.

21 The text of Alquier's decree of 11 March 1795 regarding the distribution of specimens to Dutch savants is cited in Boyer,

"Le transfert à Paris des collections du Stathouder," 394.

22 For an in-depth discussion of "French scientific universalism" and the contrasting French and British approaches to seized scientific collections in this era, see Lipkowitz, "Seized Natural History Collections."

23 Bert Theunissen, "De Briefwisseling Tussen A. G. Camper en G. Cuvier," *Tijdschrift voor de geschiedenis der Geneeskunde, Natuurwetenschappen, Wiskunde en Techniek* 3 (1980): 155–77.

24 Camper discusses a Frenchman in Holland who was "heureux de rejoindre sa patrie, la capitale du monde savant enrichie des dépouilles de l'Europe entière." Adriaan Gilles Camper to Georges Cuvier, brumaire an 10 [October/November 1801], Cuvier Papers, 3223:37, Bibliothèque de l'Institut de France (hereafter BI).

25 "Il lui a fallu beaucoup de philosophie et une grande envie pour l'instruction lorsqu'il s'est résolu à visiter le Musée enrichi des dépouilles de son propre Père et d'une nation devenue malheureuse par vos conquêtes." Adriaan Gilles Camper to Georges Cuvier, 19 germinal an 10 [19 April 1802], Cuvier Papers, 3224:31, BI.

26 Richard W. Burkhardt, Jr., *The Spirit of System: Lamarck and Evolutionary Biology* (Cambridge, Mass.: Harvard University Press, 1995), 119.

27 Florence Pieters, "Natural History Spoils in the Low Countries in 1794/ 1795: The Looting of the Fossil Mosasaurus from Maastricht and the Removal of the Cabinet and Menagerie of Stadholder William V" in *The Rise of National Museums in Europe, 1794– 1830*, ed. Ellinoor Bergvelt, Debora Meijers, Lieske Tibbe, and Elsa van Wezel (Berlin: G. and H. Verlag, 2009), 55–72.

28 In a letter to the Comité de salut public, Thouin offered this vision: "This tribute [the Stadholder's collection] by a vanquished power will contribute much to perpetuate the glory of the victors, and make the neighboring powers tributary of France by forcing their subjects to draw on France for useful knowledge" ("Ce tribut d'une puissance vaincue ne contribuera pas peu à perpetuer la gloire des vainqueurs et à rendre les puissances voisines tributaire de la France en portant leurs sujets à venir dans son sein puiser les connaissances utiles"). Thouin to the Comité de salut public, 20 floréal an 3 [9 May 1795], F17/1277/ dossier 1 #60, AN.

29 "Nous avons quelques idées, qui nous paraissent concilier à les droits de S.M. Le Roi des Pays Bas, avec l'intérêt de notre établissement, qui, vous le savez est aussi l'intérêt de la science, et de tous ceux qui l'aiment et le cultivent." Professeur-Administrateurs du Muséum d'Histoire naturelle to Brugmans, 22 September 1815, AJ 15/611, dossier "Séance des Professeurs-Administrateurs du Muséum d'Histoire naturelle du vendredi 22– dimanche 24 septembre, 1815," AN.

30 Ibid.

PART III

CULTIVATING USEFUL KNOWLEDGE

SYMPOSIUM COMMENTARY

SARA S. GRONIM

———

I
T WAS A PLEASURE TO BE ASKED TO
COMMENT ON THESE TWO FINE ESSAYS THAT SITUATE NATURAL HISTORY IN
AN EXPLICITLY TRANSNATIONAL FRAME. Both authors' historical subjects act on behalf of
France, for all of them are driven by French desires for material things: oak trees for the navy, fruits and
vegetables to boost agricultural production, animal corpses to elevate French scientific renown. Elizabeth
Hyde points out quite specifically that André Michaux can only be understood within a "French system
of colonial botanizing." We are all now quite familiar with the vibrant literature of natural history as a *colonizing* enterprise, a set of practices that took advantage of the subordinated places Europeans developed
around the world.[1] Yet in these two essays we have one example of the French moving off the European
continent to a space that was no longer open to colonization, and one example of the French moving within
Europe and yet acting as colonizers. It is particularly interesting that both historians situate their studies
during a period in which the polities themselves are in flux: the crisis of the monarchy, the Revolution, and
then Napoleon in France, the United States shifting from one national configuration under the Articles of
Confederation to another under the Constitution, while in the Netherlands the Batavian Republic replaced
the Dutch Republic by force of French arms. In this context, each nation was being constructed and reconstructed at the same time, creating complex and fascinating transnational relationships.

In this context, it struck me that the title
of this panel, "Cultivating Useful Knowledge,"
doesn't quite mean what historians of science
usually mean by the term. We all recognize that
natural history in this period concerned itself
simultaneously with the abstract (the dissociation
of the specimen from its place via taxonomies
and the encyclopedia) and the useful (finding
new medicines or dyes or minerals).[2] But there
is a more interesting sense of "useful" at work
here: useful knowledge in the sense of *politically*
useful. Sometimes the knowledge discussed in
these papers is indeed knowledge about natural
objects: transplanting a tree, dissecting a specimen. But mostly, *social* knowledge is critical
here: how to coax (in Hyde's work) or compel
(in Lipkowitz's) cooperation across national
borders. In both cases, this knowledge is political because it is about drawing people into
relationships intended to facilitate the flow of

goods, to mobilize them in ways that work to the
advantage of particular people.

That said, I suggest perhaps paying a bit
more attention to politics. In her essay, for example, Elizabeth Hyde is justly attentive to diplomatic relations. In her study, exchanges of botanical
specimens are the materialization of a political
relationship between equals; she describes an
impressive range of French diplomatic initiatives
focused on access to natural products. And,
indeed, if the outcome of Americans' political and
military struggles against Britain made André
Michaux's travels possible, the crisis in the relationship precipitated by Edmond Charles Genêt's
efforts on behalf of France rendered them impossible. One might think that transnational diplomatic relationships, which the French cultivated
so carefully as a partnership of equals, would
have facilitated the ideals of open exchange of
specimens among natural historians. But Hyde's

Frenchmen often found constructing mutual natural history relationships difficult. Michaux found many people to talk to in his travels and certainly received support from the American Philosophical Society, but Hyde also describes the complaints of the French consul in New York about Americans' reluctance to cooperate. She also cites the skepticism of William Livingston, the governor of New Jersey, about the provision of natural history information being as innocent as it seemed. What explains this uneven pattern of cooperation? Do the struggles over competing visions for the United States that coalesced in the Federalist and Republican parties help illuminate this issue? Alternatively, perhaps the *lack* of national identity among some people meant they were open to conversations about their local natural phenomena because they saw nothing "political" about them.[3] Perhaps not—Hyde's evidence may simply reflect a range of Americans' interest in natural history, rather than any political stake in sharing information and specimens. But I think it is a question worth asking.

If Hyde might do more to explain the reluctance to cooperate, then Elise Lipkowitz might do the opposite, explaining collaboration in the presence of French military victory. Lipkowitz, with her delightful opening story of Hans and Parkie listening to "Ça ira," sets her analysis within an entirely different international relationship. Here she argues that French conquests altered natural historians' relationships from egalitarian international norms to the asymmetry of victor and vanquished. Lipkowitz's work opens up fascinating connections that show what the best transnational work can do, for here are the classic disparities of power in Hyde's "French system of colonial botanizing." I myself had never considered the ways in which wars between Europeans had affinities with colonialism, a very fruitful line of thought. Nonetheless, I can see a place for more attention to national politics. After all, when the French invaded the Netherlands in the 1790s, they entered a space with its own political dynamics. For some ten years, a faction of Netherlanders had been struggling against an oligarchy headed by the Stadholder William V. Indeed, Lipkowitz can identify one of the cooperating Dutch naturalists as a "committed royalist." But I wonder if any of the consciously apolitical rhetoric André Thouin and Barthélemy Faujas de Saint-Fond

deployed in their communications with Dutch naturalists resonated with the explicitly political ideas circulating in the Dutch milieu (for example, ideas about what constituted progress or reason or liberty). Could such an analysis explain the cooperation that the French experienced? Or was it simply a case of the Dutch making the best of a done deal?

If both essays share this concern with the constraints and opportunities that political developments offered to natural history, they also share a concern with the construction of the persona of the scientist as the instrument of such relationships. In the context of Franco-American relationships, Hyde says that Michaux did not disguise himself behind a depersonalized façade, but rather was personally present in his writings. She implies that this was distinctive, understanding the *erasure* of self as normative for a naturalist. By contrast, Lipkowitz describes the "technocratic pose" adopted by Faujas and Thouin as a façade consciously deployed to display selflessness in order to disguise the raw exercise of power. The foil here for both historians is a Republic of Letters that expected the decorum of a performance of selflessness.[4] It strikes me that our construction of the selfless participant in the Republic of Letters is akin to our construction of "objectivity" in the history of science more generally. Much of the rich historiography of the last thirty years has shown how embedded scientific practice has been in its social and cultural context; this is now a familiar concept. In this literature, "objectivity," whatever practitioners may have claimed or believed, takes on the quality of an ever-receding horizon rather than something one can point to and say, "aha—there's where it was achieved." The selflessness of the participant in the early modern Republic of Letters has this same quality: endlessly invoked but actually hard to nail down. But nonetheless, this ideal is not irrelevant. Faujas and Thouin's use of it is ample testimony to its power, whatever tensions existed between the ideal and acts of self-promotion and competitive advantage.

And this brings us back to politics. Historians of the French and American revolutionary eras have tried to determine when and how individuals began to *feel* an attachment to the nation, often through looking at print culture and festivals.[5] Lipkowitz is explicitly concerned with "a new nationalist vision of transnational science," while Hyde refers to Michaux and "both countries he served." Thouin and Faujas seem to have introjected national identity into their personal senses of self; Michaux seems not to have done so. These two excellent essays suggest, then, that the scientist's shifting historical sense of self might be not only a relevant question in the history of science, but also a fruitful avenue to explore for political history.

1   The literature on this subject is huge. One starting point is James Delbourgo and Nicholas Dew, eds., *Science and Empire in the Atlantic World* (New York: Routledge, 2008).

2   The subject of the simultaneous projects of abstraction and utility in the history of science is another vibrant area of scholarship. An entry point into this scholarship is John V. Pickstone, *Ways of Knowing: A New History of Science, Technology, and Medicine* (Chicago: University of Chicago Press, 2001).

3   Historians of natural history in the early American republic have been particularly interested in the question of links between national identity and ideas about the natural world. For recent examples, see Andrew J. Lewis, *A Democracy of Facts: Natural History in the Early Republic* (Philadelphia: University of Pennsylvania Press, 2011); and Richard W. Judd, *The Untilled Garden: Natural History and the Spirit of Conservation in America, 1740–1840* (Cambridge: Cambridge University Press, 2009).

4   Lorraine Daston made this point cogently in "The Ideal and the Reality of the Republic of Letters," *Science in Context* 2 (1991): 367–86. By contrast, for the visible self in Romantic science, see Laura Dassow Walls, *The Passage to Cosmos: Alexander von Humboldt and the Shaping of America* (Chicago: University of Chicago Press, 2009).

5   For the French Revolution, see Lynn Hunt, *The Family Romance of the French Revolution* (Berkeley and Los Angeles: University of California Press, 1992). For the American Revolution, see David Waldstreicher, *In the Midst of Perpetual Fetes: The Making of American Nationalism, 1776–1820* (Chapel Hill: University of North Carolina Press, 1997).

SARA S. GRONIM

CULTIVATING USEFUL KNOWLEDGE

END-OF-SESSION DISCUSSIONS

Elizabeth Hyde (EH): As Sara Gronim noted in her commentary, nationalism is a very interesting topic. One of the things about William Livingston, for example, that I didn't mention, is that in the last years of his legal career in New York, he was agitating (often anonymously) in New York newspapers for the revolutionary cause. For many years, then, he was generating this sentiment, and was responsible, I think, for helping to push New Jersey opinion towards the Revolution, so he was someone who had thought about these issues a great deal.

I'd like to explore the responses that André Michaux got when he went around the country and find more examples of how he was received. There are other examples, such as the French beginning to think, "All right, this reciprocity is nice and we finally found some people" when they encountered Americans who were willing to say, "Oh yes! I can get you specimens!" However, there were Americans who said, "That's great! I'll take you all over the countryside to get everything that you want to find in Virginia, and here's the list of everything I want from Versailles and from the Jardin des Plantes." And one gentleman submitted a letter that was perceived as being a little too long and there were letters back and forth as they tried to figure out what to do about this man who exceeded the bounds of reciprocity—and yet they still wanted the help he could offer. So these questions of reception, the instances where you can see both sides of the debate, are absolutely fascinating and if I can find more of those examples, that would be crucial.

Elise Lipkowitz (EL): On the issue of nationalism, one of the goals of my larger project is to make the case that the revolutionary and Napoleonic wars were very different from the wars that generally occurred in the seventeenth and eighteenth centuries, particularly in their implications for

science. These were truly the first profoundly ideological wars. In France, it was the first war with mass mobilization and conscription into the army. It was also a war in which scientists were very explicitly mobilized, which had a profound impact on scientific relations more broadly throughout Europe.

To speculate about this sort of nationalist trend: while it really flowered in the Revolution in terms of impact on the scientific community, it's already there starting in the 1760s and 1770s, certainly in the competition over many of the voyages to the Pacific that we've talked about in the last couple of days. And as natural history became the "big science" (as Kapil Raj puts it) of the late eighteenth century, it definitely opened spaces for nationalist competition and nationalist claims.

Comment: Thank you for pointing out the kind of French imperialism in science that went hand in hand with the military imperialism of Napoleon. I think it is important to recontextualize this claim of France as a universalist country. In the late eighteenth-century context, French was the language of science, as English is today. Secondly, in the late decades of the eighteenth century, French chemists imposed a new nomenclature, a new language for chemistry, and it was accepted all over Europe except for England (where Joseph Priestley came from, here to the American Philosophical Society in Philadelphia). And the metric system, which really imposed the view of Paris as the center of the world, was a similar case.

It wasn't just France, it was Paris. The provincial cities that were extremely active in the eighteenth century were totally emptied of their activities and money and collections and everything moved to Paris. On the occasion of the bicentennial of the French Revolution, we realized that the history of European science, which had been a decentralized community in the pre-revolutionary period, became centralized around Paris after the Revolution. This was a strange side effect of the convergence between the French Revolution and all the scientific revolutions that occurred in this period.

Question: Within this context of 1783 until 1790, what about the changing perception of the American debt following the end of the American war and leading to the political situation of the French Revolution? Because this question of the American debt—was it going to be played out in this overlong list for plants? Was this one way of getting payback?

EH: That's a very good question, and I haven't found explicit references to that. But seen in the context of these larger colonial ventures, what they're trying to do about introducing spices around their colonies, and trying to grow the wealth of those territories, I have to think that the end result was prosperity within France. It wasn't just about the navy—we have to repopulate the forest so we can build all kinds of things with those trees. That process took decades and was obviously very different than sharing different cinnamon plants, for example, across colonies. I haven't found any references in the correspondence I've looked at that acknowledges the botanical chronology involved, but it seems that they are carrying out these efforts in larger economic, commercial, and colonial contexts.

Question: This is a question for Elise. I was very persuaded by your presentation of looking forward, of the new organization of science and the mode in which internationalism took place afterwards. It resonates with a lot of things that happened in the nineteenth century with the expositions and different international institutions, the spaces where people got together, agreed about standards, and exchanged findings, but which were also spaces for intense competition.

I'd like to hear more about what was novel here—how was this new, as opposed to what went before? Because you're using the idea—a quite idealized idea—of a Republic of Letters, and I'm not sure to what extent that is more than just rhetoric before this time. There were many instances of different kingdoms and nations speaking in that language but nevertheless holding on

to their knowledge very closely, not exchanging it freely, undergoing reciprocity in ways that were somewhat deceptive, speaking in double languages (much like Thouin did), and of course state secrets existed long before this period. So how novel was this form? How was it different from what went before?

And another thought: the French were very cagey in the cases you mentioned about not talking about the elephant in the room, the fact that these were specimens seized during conquest. But that leaves us to believe that those specimens naturally belonged to the Dutch. Of course there's an earlier case of expropriation that this is all founded on, which is the original seizing of those materials, usually from the colonies. So is that elephant in the room ever brought up?

EL: I'm going to start with the second question. No, the second elephant in the room really wasn't brought up, because most late eighteenth-century Europeans didn't spend a lot of time thinking about the property rights of peoples in the Pacific or the Americas, where these items came from. And this was in keeping with all the racial hierarchies we've been talking about this morning. And I explicitly focused on the Netherlands as opposed to Egypt, because even Egypt entered into that realm of something that's unproblematic legally and culturally, from a European perspective. It's a very important point, that all of these collections are starting out in places where Europeans really aren't acknowledging what they've done in getting these from local people.

You also bring up a key point about the Republic of Letters, that throughout the history of this ideal it was matched by an infrastructure of correspondence and publications. I think it's fair to say that over the course of the second half of the eighteenth century, to about 1792 to 1793, with the outbreak of international war (which I see as the pivotal year, much more so than 1789 for these international networks), one can make a case that the exchanges among European scientists are growing in intensity, the networks are denser and broader, and they include Philadelphia and the Atlantic world. So yes, while there were political demands and hidden agendas, it was not entirely rhetoric. There was genuinely a much higher volume of transnational interaction that occurred between 1750 and 1792 and became disrupted.

MAKING ART,
COMMUNICATING
SCIENCE

PART IV

PART IV

MAKING ART, COMMUNICATING SCIENCE

Previous page and detail, left François Gérard, *Psyche
and Amor*, 1798, oil on canvas. Musée du Louvre, Paris.
Scala/ Art Resource, N.Y. (see Fig. 11.4)

09

PICTURING NATURE IN A NATURAL HISTORY MUSEUM: THE ENGRAVINGS OF THE *ANNALES DU MUSÉUM D'HISTOIRE NATURELLE*, 1802–13

PIERRE-YVES LACOUR

DURING THE AGE OF ENLIGHTENMENT, the natural history image sometimes referred to a specimen, chosen as an example that served as a referent. But more often, the natural history image produced an ideal type from constant traits, those shared by all individuals of the same species. In all cases, the drawing was supposed to be created "after nature," despite possible borrowings from graphic or literary tradition, which were viewed with scorn during the eighteenth century. The drawing defined the "type" of the species; the form produced a norm. Thus, around 1800, as Lorraine Daston and Peter Galison have shown, the plate in a natural history book, following the "truth-to-nature" approach, represented an ideal image of the species and not an isolated specimen.[1]

Speaking of the engravings in Buffon's *Histoire naturelle*, Thierry Hoquet remarked that they permit "the stabilization of the species and the constitution of a body of homogeneous references," avoiding the multiplication of names, misunderstandings and confusions.[2] By necessity, the engraving represented a precise species, even when the accompanying article dealt with a broader category (the genus, for example). The type, as produced by the image, also defined the unity of the species from the multiplicity of individuals provided by experience. It was located on the level of Michel Foucault's "epistemological threshold . . . from which scientific knowledge can begin."[3] Below this threshold, there was no science recognized as such, but only the knowledge of jewelers or florists who valued individual exceptions or remarkable varieties.

This play of three terms among names, images, and things was quite new, or at least very different from standard practices of the late Renaissance, when no consensus existed on what the image should represent (specimen, variety, or species) and when the printer could reuse the same engraving to represent different species, as Sachiko Kusukawa has shown.[4] The early modern period also saw a shift in the uses of natural history engraving. During the Renaissance, because of engraving (and reuses), the same single image could represent different species under different names. The print was at the root of these confusions; it could even, as John Ray put it, cause a "multiplication of species" that recalled the biblical chaos of languages.[5] In the Age of Enlightenment, thanks to engraving (and its diffusion), one image accompanied by a

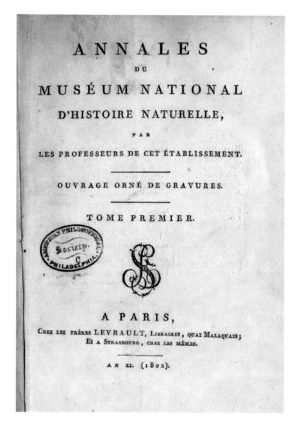

Fig. 9.1

Title page of the first
volume of the *Annales du
Muséum* (1802). APS

name could no longer designate more than a single
species, and representations were required to be
entirely new. From then on, engraving assured a
tight bond between the species name and its image.

In 1802, the Muséum d'Histoire naturelle
in Paris, at the time the preeminent natural history
institution in Europe, launched its own periodical. The *Annales du Muséum national d'Histoire
naturelle* immediately became the most important
journal in the field of natural history in the early
nineteenth century (**FIG. 9.1**). As the Muséum's
historiographer Joseph-Philippe-François Deleuze
wrote, "everything was thriving" that year. The
collections were finally arranged, "work was
accomplished with surprising activity," and "the
amphitheater was often filled."[6] Deleuze interpreted
the launch of the *Annales* as a mark of this new
prosperity. The periodical was purely a creation
of the Muséum; the professors wrote most of its
articles and the foreign memoirs accepted
for publication earned official recognition for their
authors. The birth of the periodical was a sign of
the Muséum's institutional autonomy and its professors appeared as new patrons of natural history.
The *Annales* soon replaced a series of encyclopedic
periodicals that had previously published natural
history articles, as can be seen in Georges Cuvier's
list of publications after 1802.[7]

THE GOOD IMAGE

Around 1800, lacking individual specimens at their
disposal, naturalists turned to what Martin Rudwick
called "specimens of substitution."[8] These could
be descriptions, drawings, or even casts of fossils.
Thus, at the Muséum, the vellums had to fill "the
gaps existing in the series of living plants."[9] All
these substitutes were more or less valued. In his
article on the ibis of Egypt (see **FIG. 2.3**), Cuvier
proposed a hierarchy of "positive proofs," in which
the mummified remains of the bird were worth
more than "the exact figures" of the ancients, which
in their turn had more value than their "excellent
descriptions."[10] Usually, naturalists preferred
engravings to written descriptions, which were
always judged to be too long. For example, Buffon
wrote that "it is up to the figures to supply all these
little traits, and the discussion should be reserved
for the large ones; from a single glance at the figure,
one will learn more than from a similar description, which sometimes becomes less clear as it
becomes more minute."[11] Unlike images, descriptions did not need to be complete. Emphasizing the
most remarkable traits of the species would suffice.

During the French Revolution, the librarian
Jean-Baptiste Lefebvre de Villebrune and the assistant naturalist Joseph-Philippe-François Deleuze
defined the good natural history image by its concern for "truth," for close resemblance to its objects.

In 1795, the Muséum's professors asked for new drawings of the plants from the Bibliothèque nationale in order to complete the collection of vellums. Lefebvre de Villebrune reacted sharply to this request. His argument was based on a distinction between two uses of the drawings and on an opposition between two qualities of images. The "beauty" of certain images made them preferable for the "arts," where they would provide "models for fabric manufacturers." The "truth" of others destined them instead for botanists to "study science." The first group would stay in the Cabinet des Estampes (the national engraving and drawing collection), while the second could join the collection of vellums.[12] A few years later, in 1803, in the death notice of artist Nicolas Maréchal, Deleuze distinguished natural history illustration from history painting. In its need for exactitude, "drawing applied to sciences" was close to technical drawing, requiring "at the same time the talents of the painter and the knowledge of the naturalist."[13]

Such a discourse on the necessary transparency of the scientific image should not be surprising. Michel Adanson, in his 1763 book *Familles de plantes*, offered precise recommendations on the "method of rendering the most useful figures." He described six of these methods: uniting figures with descriptions because "they cannot function without each other"(1);[14] using engraving instead of painting, because colors are nonessential and traits etched in copper are sharper and more detailed (2); engraving plants without shadows, since shadows make the outlines less clear (3); showing all the plants' details from root to seed (4); depicting plants in their natural form, whether creeping, prostrate or twisted (5); and using a medium-sized quarto format with an indication of scale (6).[15] At the end of the eighteenth century, Adanson's principles, though seldom stated, defined the norm of what a good image in natural history was supposed to look like.

THE DRAWING WORKSHOP

The collection of vellums was the entry point for the engravings in the *Annales*.[16] In 1630, Gaston d'Orléans began forming the collection, which contained representations in watercolor on fine parchment of more or less regular dimensions. At first, the collection was not connected with the Jardin du Roi, but under Louis XIV's reign and then for the entire eighteenth century, the ties between the vellums and the Jardin became increasingly strong. In the 1660s, the collection of vellums was bequeathed to the new king, and his painter Nicolas Robert received the title of "Peintre ordinaire du roi pour la miniature." Robert took his models from the Jardin du Roi and the menagerie of Versailles, while the naturalists of the Jardin oversaw the accuracy of his paintings. At the end of the seventeenth century, the Academicians planned a history of plants.[17] In 1667, Claude Perrault proposed to continue the collection by adding missing parts (roots and vignettes of leaves, fruits, seeds, and so forth) to the existing vellums.[18] The project of complementing the vellums was quickly abandoned, along with the planned history of plants. Perrault's idea of transforming an artistic collection into a working scientific collection was yet to be realized.

In the eighteenth century, painters were at first housed in the Jardin, then placed under the authority of the superintendent of the Jardin and paid from his budget. During the French Revolution, the collection of vellums saw two major evolutions. First, in 1793, the decree of the refounding of the Muséum ordered the transfer of the collection "of plants and animals painted after nature" from the Bibliothèque nationale to the Muséum's library.[19] In August of 1793, the collection was transported from the Cabinet des Estampes to the Muséum. The total then stood at sixty-four portfolios of natural history images, principally showing plants. In December, the professors' assembly chose Nicolas Maréchal and the two Redouté brothers, Pierre-Joseph and Henri-Joseph, to carry on with the enterprise.[20] Secondly, in October of 1804, the Muséum's professors asked Sébastien Gérardin to collaborate with

POLYPTÉRE BICHIR

them in compiling a catalogue of the vellums. The vellums would be arranged methodically, each linked to an independent card and listed in a register of six columns indicating the order number, the name of the painter, the name of the species depicted, its common name, and above all a "judgment on its merit in relation to art and on the parts that must be added so the drawing can be complete relative to science."[21] The botany vellums were finally classified in this way in 1807.

The decree of June 10, 1793, also established a chair of iconography of natural history, which was immediately assigned to Gerard van Spaendonck. He gave daily iconography classes in the library with the collection of vellums within reach. The "school objective was the perfection of natural history by reuniting representations of described objects with their descriptions."[22] This school also responded to an old request, brought forward by the Académie des sciences in the mid-eighteenth century; young draftsmen, rather than previously trained ones, were required because they were still malleable, unmannered, and devoid of artistic personality.[23] These classes were also exceptional at the Muséum because they welcomed many young ladies,[24] who were rare in Lamarck's classes and not admitted in Cuvier's because their "sensibility was easily affected," as Jean-Baptiste Pujoulx wrote.[25] Their sensibility seemed to destine them for painting plants, but certainly not for attending anatomy sessions where they might feel ill. By March 1806, the collection contained more than five thousand pieces. During the revolutionary period, their number had increased significantly (though the exact proportions are unknown), and above all, the contents were diversified.[26] Before the Revolution, the collection primarily contained plants and birds, as well as several butterflies. With the Revolution, the collection was enriched with drawings of reptiles, fishes, shells, mammals, and depictions of animal anatomy, a completely new category.

Fig. 9.2

"Polyptére Bichir"
(*Polypterus bichir*).
Annales du Muséum
1 (1802), pl. v. APS

At the very beginning of the nineteenth century, the links between the vellums and the *Annales du Muséum* appeared in different ways. Some older plates, like those of Aubriet drawn during the early eighteenth century, were engraved for Desfontaines' articles at the beginning of the following century.[27] The collection of vellums also included most of the drawings published in the *Annales* to illustrate the professors' articles, as the professors did not own the original drawings. The image in the original drawing and the image in the engraving were never exactly the same. Thus, Henri-Joseph Redouté's watercolor of a fish from the Nile River (*Polypterus bichir*), kept in the vellums and printed in the *Annales*, was not only reversed by the engraving process, but also partly cropped and accompanied by numbers for the legend (**FIG. 9.2**).[28]

Between 1802 and 1813, the engravings published in the first twenty volumes of the *Annales* totaled about one thousand plates. The arrangement on the plate, which was more particularly standardized in botany, gives an impression of homogeneity. Most plates included one or several drawings with the species name at the bottom of the image, the volume number on the upper left, the plate number on the upper right, the drafts-man's name on the lower left, and the engraver's name on the lower right. Some artists were

Fig. 9.3

The symmetry of engravings. *Annales du Muséum* 6 (1805), pl. xlvi. APS

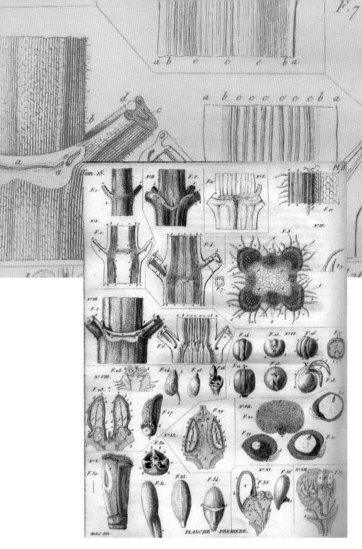

Fig. 9.4

A case of accumulation.
Annales du Muséum 15
(1810), pl. xiii. APS

professors, such as the mineralogist René Just Haüy and above all, Cuvier. Others were contemporary illustrators, such as Sophie de Luigné or Pierre-Joseph Redouté.[29] The engravers are less well-known, though several names are recorded.[30] Various species were often depicted on the same plate. Nearly always, the figures were related to the same article describing a genus or a natural family, which made it possible to compare species traits.

Surprisingly, in the illustrations for his articles on shells, Jean-Baptiste Lamarck played with symmetry. Both sides of the same shell species were represented not next to each other, but separated by two more representations of another species (**FIG. 9.3**). In these plates, Lamarck adapted for his own purposes a manner of organizing conchology plates from earlier naturalists such as Albertus Seba or Antoine-Joseph Dezallier d'Argenville. Furthermore, to limit printing costs, a single plate would sometimes crowd together many figures from one article (**FIG. 9.4**), or even, very occasionally, combine figures from different articles.

THE STYLE OF THE ENGRAVINGS

In the iconic representation of plants and animals (mineralogy was the poor relative in these engravings, appearing in relatively few plates), the text was reduced to a caption at the bottom of the drawing. The engraving simply bore the species name and very infrequently an indication of scale, whereas the long caption was always included at the end of the article (**FIG. 9.5**). The natural history plate was not only stripped of textual indications; the image was also shorn of anything that could hinder the reading of the species represented. With only a few exceptions, backgrounds are absent from nearly all the plates. Shadows were also reduced, but rarely completely so, as recommended by Adanson. The plates that accompany some of Augustin Pyramus de Candolle's articles pursue the process further, only representing the most marked contours of the plant in the form of line drawings (**FIG. 9.6**).

At the same time, drawing was privileged over color. Nearly all the plates are in *grisaille* (tones of gray). The underlying motive was obviously an economical one, as colored plates were costly and reserved only for luxury publications. But there was also a deeper epistemological motive. In botany, Linnaeus required naturalists to ignore the color of flowers, since color permitted only the characterization of plant varieties.[31] In mineralogy, Haüy grouped the ruby and the topaz under a single species of the genus of quartz, despite their differences in color.[32] In zoology, Cuvier said that the colors of animals "owed much to the light" and "that superficial traits are the most variable."[33] With colors, it was possible to distinguish varieties but not species. Color did not concern naturalists, but it did matter to those who traded in appearances, such as jewelers, bird sellers, or florists. In a sense, the colored plate was seen as a poor scientific image precisely because it represented a

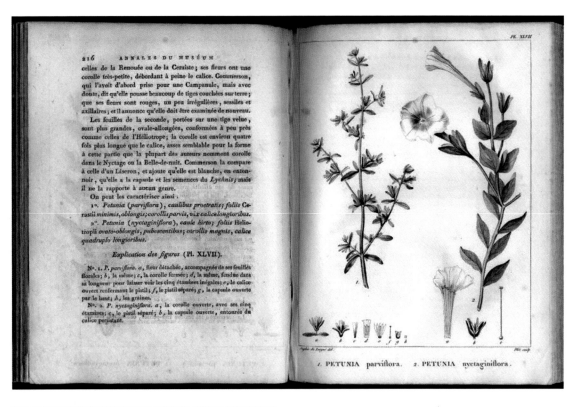

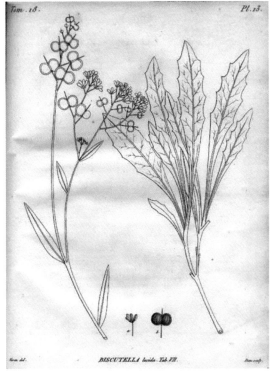

Fig. 9.6 (left)

Marked contours. *Annales du Muséum* 18 (1811), pl. xiii. APS

Fig. 9.5 (above)

Page spread showing typical plate with caption on opposite page (petunias). *Annales du Muséum* 2 (1803), pl. xlvii. APS

variety rather than a species and showed variable traits, instead of the constant characters essential for the determination of the species.

The main feature of these engravings was an economy of representation; everything needed to be represented.[34] Leonhard Fuchs wanted to render plants *"absolutissima,"* that is in all their parts, including roots, seeds, and fruits.[35] Adanson proposed several images of the same shells "to show the back and the front or the opening at the same time," and did the same for the animals in the shells.[36] The vellums of the Muséum also obeyed the principle of displaying specific traits in a comprehensive manner.[37] All the *Annales'* engravings followed this ancient principle of highlighting all the parts of the plant or animal, but they valued the essential traits of the species above all.[38] In botany, the plates illustrating Desfontaines' texts and other botanical articles often neglected the roots of plants, whereas small vignettes described their sexual organs (essential for fixing the species) with great accuracy (as in **FIG. 9.5**). In zoology, drawings privileged the profile view for the body or the three-quarter view for the head. For the same reasons, snakes were represented in "unnatural" contortions, simultaneously showing their bellies and their backs (**FIG. 9.7**). In all these examples, the natural history image seemed to obey a general principle of economy, offering the spectator a maximum of specific information with the fewest possible views. Moreover, in zoology, in the case of sexual dimorphism, the same species of bird is sometimes represented by two images (**FIG. 9.8**). This choice, which avoids the male and female

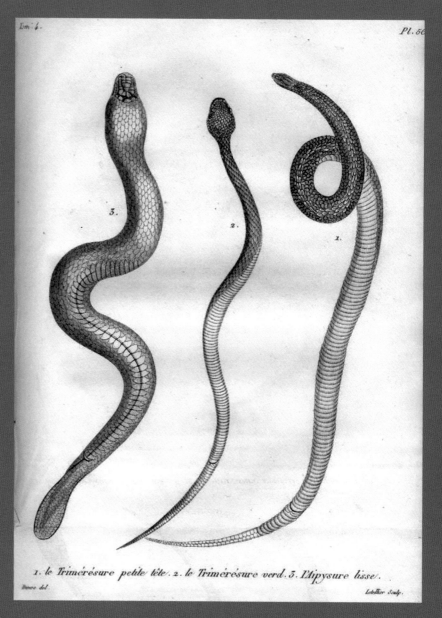

Fig. 9.7

The economy of the image. *Annales du Muséum* 4 (1804), pl. lvi. APS

1. le Trimérésure petite tête. 2. le Trimérésure verd. 3. L'hipysure lisse.

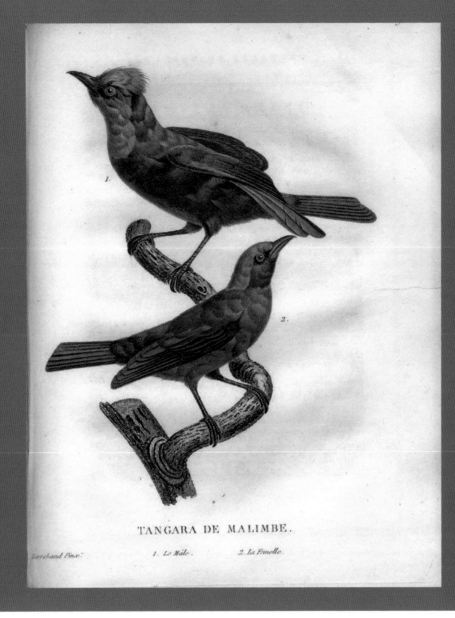

TANGARA DE MALIMBE.

Barraband Pinx.   *1. Le Mâle.*   *2. La Femelle.*

being taken for two different species, was an additional method of stabilizing
the species as a conceptual category.

The style of the *Annales'* engravings might be described as "severe" in
opposition to the "pleasant" manner of the *Ménagerie du Museum* (published
1802–3), in which animals were represented in settings such as a cell in the
menagerie for the lion or antique ruins for the Egyptian goose.[39] The difference
between the style of the *Annales* and that of the *Ménagerie* was not due to the
authors of the notices (in both cases, they were professors of the Muséum), nor
to the artist (Maréchal drew for both publications), nor to the different origin
of the plates (some of the zoology vellums also appeared as engravings in the
Ménagerie), but to the intended public of the two publications. The *Ménagerie*
was aimed at the general public, including children, whereas the *Annales*
were intended for the naturalists of Europe. The plates of the *Annales* provide
only a glimpse of the immense pictorial production of natural history at the
beginning of the nineteenth century. But the periodical's reputation, along
with the Muséum's support, earned recognition for the articles and for the
plates that were published. These engravings were considered as "legitimate"
images in the natural history world in the early nineteenth century.

1   Lorraine Daston and Peter Galison, *Objectivity* (New York: Zone Books, 2007), 55–113.

2   "... la stabilisation de l'espèce et la constitution d'un corpus de références homogènes." Thierry Hoquet, *Buffon: Histoire naturelle et philosophie* (Paris: Honoré Champion, 2005), 273–76.

3   "... seuil épistémologique ... à partir duquel la connaissance scientifique peut commencer." Michel Foucault, "La situation de Cuvier dans l'histoire de la biologie," *Revue d'histoire des sciences et de leurs applications* 23, no. 1 (1970): 63–72.

4   Sachiko Kusukawa, "The Uses of Pictures in the Formation of Learned Knowledge: The Case of Leonhard Fuchs and Andreas Vesalius," in *Transmitting Knowledge: Words, Images, and Instruments in Early Modern Europe*, ed. Sachiko Kusukawa and Ian MacLean (Oxford: Oxford University Press, 2006), 74.

5   Quoted in ibid., 96.

6   "... tout prospérait ... les travaux se faisaient avec une activité surprenante... l'amphithéâtre était souvent rempli." Joseph-Philippe-François Deleuze, *Histoire et description du Muséum royal d'Histoire naturelle* (Paris: A. Royer, 1823), 1:98–100.

7   Henri Daudin, *Cuvier et Lamarck: Les classes zoologiques et l'idée de série animale, 1790–1830* (1926; repr., Paris: Éditions des archives contemporaines, 1983), 2:285–93.

8   Martin J. S. Rudwick, "Recherches sur les ossements fossiles: Georges Cuvier et la collecte d'alliés internationaux," in *Le Muséum au premier siècle de son histoire*, ed. Claude Blanckaert, Claudine Cohen, Pietro Corsi, and Jean-Louis Fischer (Paris: Éditions du Muséum national d'Histoire naturelle, 1997), 591–606.

9   "[Le Muséum] a disposé dans un ordre méthodique correspondant à celui du jardin les plantes peintes dans la collection des vélins déposés dans la bibliothèque. Au moyen de cette disposition les élèves peuvent avec leur livre [sic] élémentaire parcourir de suite cette collection et le professeur a la facilité chaque jour de leçon de placer sous des cadres les dessins correspondants à la leçon et de remplir par ce moyen les lacunes existantes dans la série des plantes vivantes." Professors of the Muséum national d'Histoire naturelle to the Comité d'instruction publique, May 13, 1795, F/17/3979, Archives nationales, Paris (hereafter AN).

10 "Aucun autre animal n'auroit dû être aussi facile à reconnoître que celui-là, car il n'en est aucun autre dont les anciens nous aient laissé à la fois, comme de l'ibis, d'excellentes descriptions, des figures exactes et même coloriées, et le corps lui-même soigneusement conservé avec ses plumes" (117); "Les preuves positives, telles que des descriptions, des figures et des momies" (132); "Les anciens, dira-t-on, n'en parlent point dans leurs descriptions, et leurs figures ne les expriment pas; mais j'ai beaucoup mieux à cet égard qu'un témoignage écrit ou qu'une image tracée. J'ai trouvé précisément les mêmes plumes dans l'une des momies de Saccara" (133). Georges Cuvier, "Mémoire sur l'Ibis des anciens Égyptiens," *Annales du Muséum national d'Historie naturelle* 4 (1804): 116–35.

11 "... c'est aux figures à suppléer à tous ce petits caractères, et le discours doit être réservé pour les grands: un seul coup d'œil sur une figure en apprendrait plus qu'une pareille description, qui devient parfois moins claire qu'elle est plus minutieuse." Quoted in Hoquet, *Buffon*, 276.

12 "Ces dessins de plantes avoient été faits pour fournir des modèles aux manufactures d'étoffe en soie et autres qu'Henri IV et Louis XIII avoient fait établir à Paris. Depuis cette époque, ils avoient fourni la plus grande ressource aux artistes qui venoient les copier; et Buffon nous avoit assuré qu'elle ne seroit jamais enlevée du cabinet des Estampes, dépôt bien plus commode pour nous que le Muséum où il faut aller les chercher.... Rabel étoit un peintre d'histoire qui ne fit ces dessins que par contrainte et pour ne pas désobliger le Prince qui la collection lui demandait. Si la beauté s'y montre quelquefois avec tous ses charmes, rarement la vérité l'accompagne. On ne se doutait pas même alors que la botanique devînt jamais une science systématique. Aussi n'y voit-on ni classes, ni genres, ni divisions d'espèces. Tout y paraît jetté au hazard. L'auteur y a dessiné ce qu'il trouvait, et souvent très imparfaitement quant à la botanique. Or ce n'est pas avec de pareils modèles qu'on peut étudier la science.... La collection de Roussel, dessinée par les frères Prévôt, ne présente que des sujets qu'il faut tous retoucher ou refaire en totalité si l'on veut qu'il servent à la botanique. Le port des plantes est de la plus grande incorrection, les couleurs fausses pour la plupart ou sans âme. C'est une nature presque toujours dégradée. La collection se prête non plus à aucun système complet; elle fournit cependant aux artistes des idées des dessins qu'ils peuvent varier, orner, embellir à leur gré: c'est ce que demandent les manufactures." Villebrune to the Comité d'instruction publique, July 21, 1795, F/17/3979, AN; see also Professors of the Muséum national d'Histoire naturelle to the Comité d'instruction publique, May 13, 1795.

13 "Mais le dessin appliqué aux sciences ou aux arts mécaniques, est une sorte de langue qui parle seulement à la raison, et qui a besoin d'être très-exacte pour ne pas nous jeter dans l'erreur.... Ce genre de dessin exige donc à la fois les talens du peintre et les connoissances du naturaliste, et ses difficultés sont sur-tout très-grandes lorsqu'on l'applique à la zoologie." Joseph-Philippe-François Deleuze, "Notice sur le citoyen Maréchal," *Annales du Muséum national d'Histoire naturelle*, 2 (1803): 66.

14 "... moyen de rendre les figures plus utiles.... il faut nécessairement allier les descriptions aux figures, & réciproquement les figures aux descriptions, parce qu'elles se prêtent un secours mutuel & qu'elles ne peuvent marcher les unes sans les autres." Michel Adanson, *Familles des plantes* (Paris: Vincent, 1763), clxxxiii, clxxxiv–v (revised spelling).

15 Ibid., clxxxiv.

16 See Léon Bultingaire, "Les peintres du Muséum à l'époque de Lamarck," *Archives du Muséum*, série 6 (1930): 49–58; Bultingaire, *Les Vélins du Muséum d'Histoire naturelle de Paris: Fleurs exotiques* (Paris: Librairie des Arts décoratifs, 1927); and Yves Laissus, *Les Vélins du Muséum* (Paris: Palais de la Découverte, 1967).

17 Yves Laissus, "Les plantes du Roi: Note sur un grand ouvrage de botanique préparé au XVIIᵉ siècle par l'Académie royale des Sciences," *Revue d'histoire des sciences et de leurs applications* 22, no. 3 (1969): 193–236.

18 Annie Chassagne, *La Bibliothèque de l'Académie royale des sciences au XVIIIᵉ siècle* (Paris: Éditions du Comité des travaux historiques et scientifiques, 2007), 142.

19 "... des plantes & animaux peints d'après nature." *Décret de la Convention nationale relatif à*

l'organisation du Jardin national des Plantes & du Cabinet d'Histoire naturelle, sous le nom du Muséum d'histoire naturelle, Séance du 10 juin 1793, title III, article 4.

20 Laissus, *Les Vélins du Muséum,* 9–12.

21 "Ce registre était divisé en six colonnes, destinées à recevoir respectivement pour chaque vélin un numéro d'ordre, le nom du peintre, le nom de l'objet porté sur le vélin, le nom actuel de l'espèce et enfin deux jugements dont l'un sur la valeur artistique du vélin et l'autre sur sa valeur scientifique. . . . [le] jugement sur le mérite relatif à l'art et sur les parties qu'il faudrait ajouter pour que le dessin fût complet relativement à la science." Quoted in Bultingaire, "Les peintres du Muséum à l'époque de Lamarck," 52.

22 "Cette école a pour but la perfection de l'histoire naturelle en réunissant aux descriptions la représentation même des objets décrits." *Décade philosophique,* no. 10 (June–August 1796): 546–52; quotation on 549.

23 Chassagne, *La Bibliothèque de l'Académie royale des sciences,* 134.

24 There were many women among natural history painters: Madeleine Basseporte (following Aubriet), Marie-Thérèse Vien (for Adanson), Hélène du Moustier de Marsigli (for Réaumur), Geneviève Regnault (for Nicolas François Regnault), Mademoiselle B. Michel Adam (for Fusée-Aublet), and Mademoiselle Blazac and Adèle Riché (students of Van Spaendonck).

25 ". . . j'ai voulu aussi faire sentir qu'il serait imprudent d'y conduire soit les dames étrangères à ce genre d'études, dont la sensibilité s'affecte aisément, et dont l'imagination peut recevoir des impressions fortes et dangereuses à l'aspect de certaines monstruosités, soit des jeunes gens qui ne sont pas préparés à ce genre d'études." Jean-Baptiste

Pujoulx, *Promenades au Jardin des plantes* (Paris: Librairie économique, 1803), 1:73.

26 Bultingaire, "Les peintres du Muséum à l'époque de Lamarck," 54–58. The butterflies painted before the revolutionary period were by Aubriet and the shells by Basseporte. After 1793, plants were painted by P. J. Redouté in particular; mammals and birds by Maréchal, de Wailly, and Nicolas Huet; shells by Maréchal, Oudinot, and Huet; and anatomy by Maréchal, Werner, Formant, Chazal, and Huet.

27 René Louiche Desfontaines, *Choix de plantes du Corollaire des Instituts de Tournefort publiées d'après son herbier, et gravées sur les dessins originaux d'Aubriet* (Paris: Levrault, 1808), 2.

28 For the watercolor, see Jean-Marc Drouin, "Calculs et circonstances: Portée et limites de l'œuvre des savants," in *Il y a 200 ans: Les savants en Égypte,* ed. Yves Laissus (Paris: Nathan and Muséum national d'Histoire naturelle, 1998), 86.

29 Among the draftsmen, there were also: Pierre-Antoine Poiteau, F. B. de Balzac, Jean François Turpin, and L. B. Freret (botany); Haüy (mineralogy); Henri-Joseph Redouté, de Wailly, Mounier, and Oudinot (zoology); Cuvier, Maréchal, De Wailly, Devillliers, and Charles-Léopold Laurillard (comparative anatomy).

30 There were several engravers who were also called "sculptors". Jourdan, Massole, and Jacques Chailly (zoology); Sellier, L'Espine, Canu, Plée, Cloquet, and T. T. Droüet (botany); Lambert, Miger, Milsan, and Couet (comparative anatomy).

31 Foucault, "La situation de Cuvier," 64–65; and Lorraine Daston, "Type Specimens and Scientific Memory," *Critical Inquiry* 31, no. 1 (Autumn 2004): 167.

32 René-Just Haüy, *Traité de minéralogie* (Paris: Louis, 1801), 2:480–90. See also Pujoulx, *Promenades au Jardin des plantes,* 1:235–36.

33 ". . . tient beaucoup à la lumière. . . . Ainsi les caractères les superficiels sont les plus variables." Georges Cuvier, *Recherches sur les ossemens fossiles de quadrupèdes* (Paris: Deterville, 1812), 79.

34 On this concept, see Brian W. Ogilvie, *The Science of Describing: Natural History in Renaissance Europe* (Chicago: University of Chicago Press, 2006), 196.

35 Kusukawa, "The Uses of Pictures in the Formation of Learned Knowledge," 77–79.

36 ". . . afin d'en faire paroître en même temps le dos et le devant ou l'ouverture." Quoted in Chassagne, *La Bibliothèque de l'Académie royale des sciences,* 120.

37 Laissus, *Les Vélins du Muséum,* 15.

38 See Chassagne, *La Bibliothèque de l'Académie royale des sciences,* 117. Tournefort recommended emphasizing the flowers and fruits of plants; Mathurin Brisson echoed this advice for the legs and bills of birds.

39 Georges Cuvier, Bernard-Germain-Étienne Lacepède, and Étienne Geoffroy Saint-Hilaire, *La Ménagerie du Muséum national d'histoire naturelle* (Paris: Miger, 1803–4), 1:24–25.

10

REPRESENTING ANIMALS WITH EMPATHY, 1793–1810

MADELEINE PINAULT SØRENSEN

AT THE END OF THE EIGHTEENTH CENTURY, following the publication of literary and philosophical texts that definitively rejected the "machine-animal" of René Descartes, scientists and artists began studying both the moral and physical aspects of animals. In fact, they evolved toward more empathy regarding animals; in rare cases among artists, this empathy had existed for a long time, but it became more common in this period.

As Georges-Louis Leclerc, Comte de Buffon, and Louis-Jean-Marie Daubenton reasoned, however, to better understand animals, it was necessary to study living ones. They had studied some animals without ever seeing them—only using stuffed specimens, skins, skeletons, drawings, paintings, and sculptures—and they dreamed of creating a menagerie in Paris.

THE CREATION OF THE MÉNAGERIE AND ITS INFLUENCE

To support the creation of a menagerie as desired by scientists, Jacques Henri Bernardin de Saint-Pierre, the last superintendent of the Jardin du Roi, wrote a *Mémoire sur la nécessité de joindre une ménagerie au Jardin national des plantes de Paris*. His purpose was clear: "The state of nature is the basis of all human knowledge."[1] For him, if a menagerie were to be useful for the study of nature, it would also be useful for the liberal arts. As examples, he mentioned all the artists who came every day to draw exotic plants at the Jardin des Plantes when they needed to represent subjects set in faraway places. Bernardin affirmed that animals from those regions would be useful to artists, who could then study their forms, behaviors, and emotions. He rejected the copying of plaster models and criticized the lion sculpted by Pierre Puget in his group of *Milon de Crotone* (Milo of Croton).[2] He continued by chastising artists who always copied and extolling those who worked from reality, recommending that they seek models only in nature. Bernardin considered that the only possible study of an animal was made from a living specimen, since the dead animal lost all its physical and psychological characteristics. Even the best-prepared specimen had "no warmth, no movement, no feeling, no voice, no instinct" and "presented nothing but a stuffed skin, a skeleton, an anatomy. The principal part is lacking: the life that classified it in the animal kingdom."[3] Bernardin posed the essential question from the viewpoint of scientists and artists: What was the use of knowing a dead animal, if you did not know it living? For him, nature needed to aid human knowledge and underline the associations between animals and humanity.

After multiple discussions in government circles, circumstances permitted the establishment of the Ménagerie of the Muséum national d'Histoire naturelle in 1794, where artists and scientists could study living animals, primarily wild ones, from then on.

The establishment of a course in natural iconography beginning in 1793 was a crucial step in the representation of living animals. The painter Gérard Van Spaendonck, named as the professor of this subject, wanted to give art a leading role in society, continuing efforts already made in the second half of the eighteenth century by many provincial academies that had created drawing schools intended to educate young people. Under his direction, students learned to render truthfully the features of animals, plants, and minerals.

The decision to resume the enrichment of the collection of the Vélins du Roi, the royal vellums (natural history illustrations on fine parchment) was also important. Because the artists chosen to continue the project, Van Spaendonck's student Nicolas Maréchal, Henri-Joseph Redouté, and Nicolas Huet II, had solid artistic educations, their paintings were simultaneously works of art and works of science. To avoid misleading scientists and the public, they were required to represent animals in the most faithful manner possible.

The artists continued the tradition of the royal vellums, most often painting animals seen in profile, but sometimes with the head facing front. Maréchal, the most talented of all these artists, was interested in the animals' moral and physical dimensions and showed true empathy toward them. He placed them in landscapes that recalled their natural environment, as Jacques de Sève, Buffon's draftsman, had done previously. He painted a Chienne Levrette (female greyhound) as the ideal type of her race, standing upright on her fine paws, with prominent muscles, pointed muzzle, and pink ears, and placed her in an equally elegant landscape.[4]

Maréchal went far in researching the personality of his models. His *Magot* (Barbary ape) looks at herself in a mirror with an attitude that shifts between pleasure in her own reflection and questioning of a face that is hers, but which she does not know.[5] Maréchal perfectly captured an expression in the monkey that could be human.

As for the scientists, Georges Cuvier, Étienne de Lacépède, and Étienne Geoffroy Saint-Hilaire published *La Ménagerie du Muséum national d'Histoire naturelle* beginning in 1800.[6] This book played an important role in the evolution of the scientific outlook on animals. The authors, thanks to their study of live specimens in the Ménagerie, took account of the physical aspect of animals and their behavior. In his introduction to the work, Lacépède underlined the importance of living animals and insisted on the role of the menagerie as a service to science and public instruction. The institution needed to support the study of animals and animal behavior and give them a certain degree of freedom "without the grievous burden of chains."[7] Lacépède recommended using talented artists to paint the animals in the Ménagerie, believing that with their assistance, the science of animal physiognomy could be created—a less complicated study than human physiognomy because it was simpler, and a stronger and truer one because it was never distorted by disguise.

The text of the *Ménagerie du Muséum national d'Histoire naturelle* is of great importance regarding animal behavior. Indeed, with only a few exceptions, the forty-one plates that illustrate the book, engraved by Simon-Charles Miger from vellums executed "after nature" by Maréchal, De Wailly, and Huet, represent the Ménagerie's animals in a somewhat cold manner. Two such animals were the *Tigre* (Tiger),[8] depicted with perfect precision but lacking life, by De Wailly, who was named painter of the Muséum after

Maréchal's death; and the *Ichneumon* (ichneumon or mongoose)[9] from Egypt painted by Maréchal, who showed it devouring a crocodile in front of the Pyramids.

If the plates of *La Ménagerie* belonged to the tradition of scientific illustration that privileged the physical appearance of animals, other works were marked by the artist's empathy toward his models.

LIONS AND ELEPHANTS AS EXAMPLES

Three works devoted to lions show different approaches to this animal with a reputation for natural ferocity, but all ended up portraying the opposite, a humanized lion, while elephants were presented as friends of humans.

The first lion, named Woira, was quite famous, thanks to the article "Histoire du lion de la Ménagerie du Muséum national d'Histoire naturelle et de son chien" by Georges Toscan, which appeared in the *Décade philosophique, littéraire et politique* in 1794.[10] Captured in Senegal at the age of six months and raised freely with other animals at the home of the director of the Compagnie des Indes in Senegal, the lion became the inseparable friend of a dog that was the same age. Offered to Louis XVI, the two animals arrived at Versailles in 1788. When the Versailles menagerie was closed down, the lion and the dog were taken to the Ménagerie of the Muséum. They became symbols of a love beyond differences. The dog died quickly in 1796, the victim of severe mange. The lion died soon afterward in complete distress, poisoned by tainted horse-meat given to him for lack of money.

To illustrate Toscan's text, Maréchal, full of empathy towards the two animals, drew the lion and his dog "after nature" in the Year II (1794–95; **FIG. 10.1**).[11] The artist's training as a history painter explains his method of depicting the animals in an architectural setting. His drawing showed the emotional ties that united the two animals, which Toscan underlined by insisting on the fact that society, without detracting anything from the lion's courage, gave him the possibility of knowing affections that he would not have experienced while free. His ties with the dog, reinforced by captivity, led him to give it signs of tenderness, as Maréchal's drawing clearly demonstrated.

Fig. 10.1

Nicolas Maréchal, *Le lion Woira et son chien*, 1794–95. © Christie's Images Limited

At the same time, Dominique Vivant Denon also provided an eyewitness account of the lion. Ordered to draw the animal for a planned engraving, he spoke of him as a friend in a letter to his lady friend Isabella Teotochi Albrizzi, whom he called Bettine. He gained a "great esteem for his character," and judged him to be as sensitive as he was noble.[12] Denon was impressed by the fact that the lion's strength did not stop him from being full of tenderness for the dog. Woira was also very gentle with those, like Denon, who approached him in a friendly manner; the artist raged against people who treated the lion badly.

The second example concerns animal-human relations. Jean-Baptiste Huet, father of Nicolas Huet, drew the male and female lion along with their keeper, Félix Cassal. The lions, named Marc and Constantine in honor of their origin in Constantine (in present-day Algeria), had arrived at the Ménagerie in April 1798. The drawing, known by the engraving by Jean-Baptiste-Chatelain,[13] shows the three with the lion cubs Marengo, Fleurus, and Jemmapes (named for French military victories), born during the night of November 9–10, 1800. Contemporary eyewitness accounts testify to Cassal's affectionate relationship with the wild animals. He even held one of the cubs in his arms without the parents trying to reclaim it.

This same empathy of artists toward lions is also found in a third example, which is the direct consequence of the two previous instances, although it is very different from them. In the Salon of 1801, Nicolas André Monsiau presented a painting that achieved great success (**FIG. 10.2**).[14] The painting is known by two titles: *Le Lion de Florence*[15] and *Trait sublime de maternité du siècle dernier, arrivé à Florence.*[16] The scene depicts a lion that had escaped from the menagerie of the Grand Duke of Florence in the seventeenth century. In fleeing from the animal, a woman dropped her child, and the lion seized him in his jaws. The lion has a gentle expression closely resembling that of Woira, showing that he had no desire to hurt the child. Horrified, the mother cried out and gestured in a pantomime fashion. The lion placed the child back on the ground without having harmed him and backed away. Reviews of the Salon basically emphasized the mother's heroism, with the exception of Ducray-Dumenil, who thought that the "sublime trait" came more from the lion than from the mother.[17] The reasons that impelled the artist to paint such a peculiar subject are unknown, but there may be a link to the lions of the Ménagerie, in whom observers noted the part of animality found in humans and the part of humanity found in animals. This was a long-debated topic over the course of the second half of the eighteenth century, notably regarding the relations of monkeys with humans.

For his part, the painter and draftsman Jean Hoüel showed all the empathy an artist could have towards animals by publishing his *Histoire naturelle des deux éléphans, mâle et femelle, du Muséum de Paris, venus de Hollande en France en l'an VI* in 1803 (see **FIGS. 2.5, 8.1, 10.4,** and **10.5**).[18] The work relates the history of the two elephants of the Stadtholder of Holland, which had arrived in France in March of 1798. Hoüel worked as an artist who wanted to understand nature, observing the animals daily and drawing many pencil sketches of them from life. He presented plates devoted to the physical features of the elephants, to their physiognomy, and to principles of drawing intended to represent correctly the features of the head seen in various positions and proportions, in keeping with arts of imitation such as drawing, painting, and sculpture. This approach brings Hoüel's work close to research on physiognomy done by Giambattista della Porta and Charles Le Brun in the seventeenth century and by Peter Camper in the eighteenth century.

Hoüel gave much attention to the elephants' daily life and the events of their existence. His good relations with the Muséum's scientists and the animals' keepers gave him the opportunity to approach the elephants closely. He could thus study the pachyderms' sleep, becoming the first to affirm that

they lay down at full length and rose only the following day. He also observed that they were sometimes agitated during their sleep, deducing that they dreamed as humans do.[19]

Houël observed the intelligence and "good manners" of the elephants, attributing human passions to them such as unhappiness, joy, calmness, or anger. He felt they could attain hatred and friendship and that they were capable of revenge and magnanimity. In some circumstances, it seemed to make them react according to human feelings.[20]

ANIMAL PRISONERS

Artists had always represented animals imprisoned in menageries, in private homes, or exhibited at fairs, chained or unchained. They hardly ever showed the bars that held the animals back. Thus, the appalling conditions in which animals were kept were not depicted. Some scientists and artists emphasized the fate of animal prisoners and supported their liberty, as Houël had done with the elephants. Bernardin de Saint-Pierre devoted several lines of his *Mémoire* to this question, remarking that solitude strengthens the character of all beings, human or animal, but that captivity embitters them. He added that the Ménagerie's lion was a proof of the influence of society on the most savage character, noting that he was much more cheerful than a solitary lion.[21] For his part, Toscan wrote that one must search in the history of the species for what the lion has lost in captivity or what he has acquired by the influence of society and its benefits, but he also remarked that the lion's long captivity had not altered his nobility.[22]

Maréchal painted a vellum to celebrate the motherhood of the female lion Constantine and the first lion cubs born in captivity[23] on 18 Brumaire, Year IX (November 9, 1800). In this vellum, engraved in Lacépède's *La Ménagerie*, Maréchal presented two images. In the first, he showed the lion's motherhood in a manner similar to Jean Baptiste Oudry's *Lice et ses petits* (Lice and Her Young).[24] Here, the animals are not prisoners, but rather are sheltered in a stable opening onto trees. In 1739, Oudry also painted a *Léopard agacé par des dogues* (Leopard Attacked by Mastiffs).[25] Seen through the bars of its cage, this is a rare representation of a truly imprisoned animal, but there appears to be no claim of freedom for animals in this work.

The second image in Maréchal's vellum (**FIG. 10.3**) shows the state of the imprisoned mother lion, confined in her cell and surrounded by reed

Fig. 10.3

Nicolas Maréchal, *La lionne Constantine et ses trois lionceaux*. Bibliothèque centrale du MNHN, collection des Vélins. © MNHN, Dist. RMN / image du MNHN, Bibliothèque centrale

screens to give her a little privacy. The lion does not look after her young, but turns her head and her sad gaze toward the blue sky, symbol of liberty, that she sees between the bars and toward the keeper blocking the barred gateway. This work, intended to celebrate the Ménagerie where a lion had just given birth in captivity for the first time, instead denounces her lack of liberty and the future of her cubs, also destined to be prisoners. Contemporary with the Revolution that was supposed to bring liberty to humanity, this work shows that animals had not yet acquired freedom.

Hoüel was concerned to give animals, which he called "my friends," a status that enabled them to be respected as living beings. In the explanation for Plate XII of his work (**FIG. 10.4**), devoted to some occurrences in the elephants' lives as observed in Holland, he wrote that the elephants did not enjoy any freedom at the Muséum. Thus, he depicted them in a setting that bore little resemblance to the cages that contained them. He continued by clearly affirming his position with respect to the captive elephants, refusing to represent the animals in their "cell" because that situation would have degraded those "noble children of nature."[26] Instead, he preferred to present the illusion of freedom by placing them in a landscape showing the Dutch forest they came from. He showed them in their free state and their domestic condition, preferring this view to that of the animals in their cages. Hoüel again used this same concept of an imaginary place in the last plate of his work, devoted to the "Éléphans couchés et dormant" (Elephants lying down and sleeping) in a rocky setting (Plate XX; **FIG. 10.5**). He explained that he had transformed their "wretched prison" into a cave and that he had given the animals an appearance of freedom, appropriate during their sleep at least.[27]

Fig. 10.4 J. P. Hoüel, *Quelques circonstances de la vie des Eléphants observée* [*sic*] *en Hollande*, from J. P. Hoüel, *Histoire naturelle des deux éléphans, mâle et femelle, du Muséum de Paris* (Paris, 1803), plate XII. Fondation Custodia, Collection Frits Lugt, Paris

Fig. 10.5 J. P. Hoüel, *Les éléphants couchés et dormants*, from J. P. Hoüel, *Histoire naturelle des deux éléphans, mâle et femelle, du Muséum de Paris* (Paris, 1803), plate XX. Fondation Custodia, Collection Frits Lugt, Paris

MADELEINE PINAULT SØRENSEN

CONCLUSION

Thus, over twenty years, artists transformed their methods of seeing and representing animals. In giving animals their own lives, they prepared artists of the romantic generation who would release the chains and bars, no longer seeing wild animals as free beings dominated by their passions. In denouncing the living conditions of animals in menageries, artists announced the nineteenth-century struggles for their rights.

Translated from the French by Jane E. Boyd

Acknowledgments

For their help, I wish to express my gratitude to Ketty Gottardo, Gabriel Naughton, Mariska de Jonge, Ger Luijten, Bent Sørensen, and a private collector who prefers to remain anonymous, as well as to Sue Ann Prince, Sarah G. Sonner, Catherine L. Skeen, Tara Miller, and Jane E. Boyd, all at the American Philosophical Society.

1   "L'état de la nature est la base de toutes les connaissances humaines." Jacques Henri Bernardin de Saint-Pierre, *Mémoire sur la nécessité de joindre une ménagerie au Jardin national des plantes de Paris* (Paris: P.-F. Didot, 1792), 1.

2   Musée du Louvre, Paris, Département des Sculptures, inv. MR 2075.

3   "L'animal perd par la mort encore plus que le végétal, parce qu'il avait reçu une plus forte portion de vie. Ses principaux caractères s'évanouissent: ses yeux sont fermés, ses prunelles ternies, ses membres roides; il est sans chaleur, sans mouvement, sans sentiment, sans voix, sans instinct. . . . L'animal mort le mieux préparé, ne présente qu'une peau rembourrée, un squelette, une anatomie. La partie principale y manque; la vie qui le classait dans le règne animal." Bernardin de Saint-Pierre, *Mémoire*, 33.

4   Bibliothèque centrale du Muséum national d'Histoire naturelle (hereafter MNHN), Paris, Collection des Vélins, vol. LXXXI, no. 13; published by Madeleine Pinault Sørensen in "L'animal entre art et science," in Emmanuelle Héran, *Beauté animale, de Dürer à Jeff Koons* (Paris: Réunion des musées nationaux–Grand Palais, 2012), 38, fig. 21.

5   Bibliothèque centrale du MNHN, Paris, Collection des Vélins, vol. LXIX, no. 31; published in Luc Vézin, *Les artistes au Jardin des Plantes* ([Paris]: Herscher, 1990), 47.

6   Georges Cuvier, Étienne de Lacépède, and Étienne Geoffroy Saint-Hilaire, *La Ménagerie du Muséum national d'Histoire naturelle, ou Description et histoire des animaux qui y vivent ou qui ont vécu* (Paris: Miger, Patris, Grandcher, Dentu, 1800–5).

7   ". . . mettre en action les tableaux des habitudes des animaux, et les portraits des espèces, que les Pline, les Linné et les Buffon nous ont transmis; de substituer aux attitudes de la contrainte, les mouvements d'une sorte d'indépendance, aux privations de la réclusion, quelques jouissances de la liberté, aux poids douloureux des fers, l'heureuse absence de toute entrave." Ibid., 7.

8   Bibliothèque centrale du MNHN, Paris, Collection des Vélins, vol. LXXI, no. 50; published by Pinault Sørensen in "L'animal entre art et science," 40, fig. 22.

9   Bibliothèque centrale du MNHN, Paris, collection des Vélins, vol. LXXI, no. 32; published in Madeleine Pinault, *Le peintre et l'Histoire naturelle* (Paris: Flammarion, 1990), 175.

10 *Décade philosophique, littéraire et politique*, no. 8 (30 vendémiaire an 3, 1795–6): 129–38; and no. 19 (10 brumaire an 3): 193–99; see also *L'Ami de la nature, ou Choix d'Observations sur divers objets de la Nature et de l'Art*, with a Supplement (Paris: Cuchet, an 3), 15–47.

11 Private collection; an engraving after the drawing is reprinted in Yves Laissus and Jean Jacques Petter, *Les animaux du Muséum: 1793–1993* (Paris: Muséum national d'Histoire naturelle and Imprimerie nationale, 1993), 88.

12 "J'ai passé ma matinée avec un lion qui appartient à la Nation, que l'on veut faire graver et que l'on me fait dessiner. Depuis deux jours que j'ai fait sa connaissance, j'ai pris une grande estime pour son caractère. Il est aussi sensible que noble, il a un grand attachement pour un chien qui est allé lui demander secours dans un moment de détresse. Ils ne peuvent plus vivre l'un sans l'autre et rien n'est plus curieux que de voir la force se rapprocher de la délicatesse et lui céder toujours par un sentiment intérieur de sa supériorité. Cet animal me met en fureur contre ceux qui le rudoient et est de la douceur d'un chien pour ceux qui prennent avec lui le ton de l'amitié." Denon to Bettine (Isabella Teotochi Albrizzi), 20 messidor an 2 [July 6, 1794]; reprinted in Dominique Vivant Denon, *Lettres à Bettine*, ed. Fausta Garavani (Arles: Actes Sud, 1999), 325.

13 Bibliothèque centrale du MNHN, Paris, IC 2769 GF; reprinted in Laissus and Petter, *Les animaux du Muséum*, 95.

14 Musée du Louvre, Département des Peintures, Paris, inv. R.F. 1983–104; on deposit at the Musée des Beaux-Arts, Chambéry.

15 Charles Paul Landon, *Annales du Musée* (Paris, 1804), 15, plate 4; and 2nd edition (Paris, 1833), 66, plate 36.

16 Paris, Salon booklet, 1801, no. 250.

17 François Guillaume Ducray-Dumenil, "Salon de Paris," *Petites affiches de Paris*, 1801 (Copie manuscrite, Bibliothèque nationale de France, Département des Estampes, Collection Deloynes, t. XXVII, 312–360, pièce 704).

18 J. P. Hoüel, *Histoire naturelle des deux éléphans, mâle et femelle, du Muséum de Paris, venus de Hollande en France en l'an VI* (Paris: L'Auteur, 1803).

19 Ibid., 115–16.

20 "Je les ai vus susceptibles de nos sentiments, de nos passions, passant de la tristesse à la joie, du contentement à la peine, de la tranquillité à la colère, accessibles à la haine comme à l'amitié; capables de vengeance et de magnanimité." Ibid., 16; see also 115.

21 Bernardin de Saint-Pierre, *Mémoire*, 18.

22 Georges Toscan, *Mémoire*, 23–24.

23 Bibliothèque centrale du Muséum national d'Histoire naturelle, Paris, collection des Vélins, vol. LXXI, no. 46; reprinted in Laissus and Petter, *Les animaux du Muséum*, 98–99.

24 Paris, Salon of 1753, no. 22; Musée de la Chasse et de la Nature, Paris, inv. 71.2.1.

25 Nationalmuseum, Stockholm, inv. no. 863.

26 "Ayant annoncé que je décrirois spécialement les figures des Eléphans du Muséum, où ils ne jouissent point de leur liberté, il paroîtra peut-être, à l'aspect de la planche XIII, que je m'écarte de mon plan, puisque je représente ces animaux libres, et dans un lieu qui n'aucun rapport aux cages dans lesquelles ils sont renfermés. . . . En exprimant dans mes dessins les murs et les barreaux énormes qui les renferment, j'aurois avili ces nobles enfans de la nature." Hoüel, *Histoire naturelle des deux éléphans*, 85.

27 "J'ai métamorphosé en grotte leur ignoble prison, et j'ai donné à ces animaux un air de liberté qui leur convenoit au moins pendant leur sommeil." Ibid., 115.

BOTANY AND THE PAINTING OF FLOWERS: INTERSECTIONS OF THE NATURAL SCIENCES AND THE VISUAL ARTS IN LATE EIGHTEENTH- AND EARLY NINETEENTH-CENTURY FRANCE

DOROTHY JOHNSON

LATE EIGHTEENTH- and early nineteenth-century France witnessed an efflorescence of interest in the life, beauty, and spectacular diversity of plants and flowers that were brought together and cultivated in exotic botanical gardens such as those at the Jardin des Plantes and at Malmaison. These public gardens inspired the private gardens that enjoyed a pan-European popularity around 1800 and beyond. World travel to record and represent as well as secure and transport exotic specimens back to Paris characterized this period, during which botanical writings, illustrated flower and botanical books, poetry dedicated to flowers and their biodiversity, and literature in which flowers and gardens played a central role flourished in France and throughout Europe.[1]

This late eighteenth-century botanical movement in France, manifested in the love of gardens and flowers of all types, was given impetus by the writings of the great naturalist and taxonomist Linnaeus, who gave the gift of modern nomenclature to the species of the vegetal world.[2] Botany as a mode of exploring the natural world for enlightened amateurs had been popularized in France by Jean-Jacques Rousseau. An avid amateur botanist, Rousseau had written *Letters on Botany*, published posthumously in 1805 and illustrated by one of the great flower painters of his age, Pierre-Joseph Redouté.[3] Erasmus Darwin's poem, *The Loves of the Plants*, published in 1789, had an enormous impact on ideas concerning the sexual life of plants.[4] In addition, Ovid's *Metamorphoses*, with its numerous tales of human-to-plant transformation, was one of the most popular and frequently re-edited and reprinted illustrated books of the era. Ovid's narratives were depicted in many paintings and sculptures of the period, as well as in prints and book illustrations.[5]

In this essay, using specific examples as case studies, I will explore the flourishing of French botanical representations of flowers and plants around 1800, as seen in the art of botanical illustration, still-life painting, and mythological painting. Artists working in these different genres visualized and made manifest the widespread passion of the period for botany and flowers, part of the fascination with the exciting discoveries being made in the natural sciences overall. The beauty, variety, and diversity of plants and

P. J. Redouté.

Alstrœmeria Pelegrina.

flowers as incarnations of nature's creative profusion and vitality captivated the imagination of painters and their public, who were enthralled by beauty and by concepts of the secret life and language of flowers.

Redouté was a central figure in this movement. In his botanical illustrations and prints, as well as his floral still lifes, he united what was seen as careful scientific or objective description and observation with the dazzling beauty of art. Redouté diverged from the more typical illustrations seen in botanical books of the period.[6] The intensity and brilliance of color of his flower specimens and their diversity and variety of forms endow them with tangibility and life. Redouté gave his flowers real presence rather than the look of a specimen on a page (**FIG. 11.1**). His botanical illustrations follow the prevailing model of representing a plant or flower removed from its native soil or habitat and shown against a white ground, a format intended

Fig. 11.1

Pierre-Joseph Redouté, *Alstrœmeria Pelegrina* (Peruvian Lily), color stipple engraving from *Choix des plus belles fleurs* by Redouté (Paris, 1827), plate 23. The LuEsther T. Mertz Library, The New York Botanical Garden / Art Resource, N.Y.

to provide precise observations of the flower's parts and characteristics. But Redouté also emphasized their unique appearance and ways of holding themselves, the hardness or softness of their forms—petals, stems, leaves, and so forth; he conveyed their fragility and apparent strength as well as their singular floral personalities. His depictions of flowers transcend the principal objectives of botanical illustrations of the period, namely the accurate rendering or transcription of nature. The viewer has the vivid impression that Redouté has created portraits of individual flowers. The brilliancy of his descriptive prowess and his intense visualizations in these floral portraits embody prevailing Enlightenment ideas in France about the centrality of precise description in the domain of botany and the natural sciences.[7]

Artists of the time realized the aesthetic and cultural importance of flowers and how difficult it was to paint them in a tangible, naturalistic manner. The history painter and art writer Jean-Joseph Taillasson, for example, wrote eloquently in 1807:

> If painting did not owe its origin to love, she would owe it to flowers. Oh, who, in effect, can see them softly balancing on their stems, who can experience intimately the harmony of their brilliant colors and the grace of their forms without desiring to paint them? Nature creates them only in joy; what tender soul can ever look at them without emotion! They bring to mind a thousand dear memories; images of the fragility of all that shines, they blend a type of bitterness with the pleasure they create, which gives them an even greater interest. Source of the sweetest perfumes, the touching richness of springtime, ornament of all celebrations, they are the gifts of friendship and of love. We bring them to the graves of those we cherished. . . . That which pleases us and touches us the most, a friend, children, a spouse whom one loves, strews the path of life with flowers.[8]

Taillasson also wrote about the great difficulty of painting flowers convincingly, since the models are never still, but are in continual movement until they reach a point of perfection and then very quickly fade and die.[9]

Redouté had the gift of making individual flowers come to life at the apex of their life's perfection before they begin to fade. His brilliant ability to capture this evanescent moment and make it tangible helps to explain why his botanical illustrations were so highly esteemed then, as now, by naturalists, artists, art lovers and connoisseurs. Redouté catapulted the genre of botanical illustration into the realm of high art. He became known as the "Raphael of Flowers" for good reason.[10]

Fig. 11.2

Pierre-Joseph Redouté, *Amaryllis Josephinae,* color stipple engraving from *Les Liliacées* by Redouté, vol. 7 (Paris, 1813), plates 370–71. The LuEsther T. Mertz Library, The New York Botanical Garden / Art Resource, N.Y.

DOROTHY JOHNSON

When Redouté, a Belgian painter born in the Ardennes, arrived in Paris in 1782, he was already an accomplished painter of flowers. He quickly gravitated to the Jardin des Plantes, studying with the amateur botanist Charles Louis L'Héritier de Brutelle, who taught him flower dissection and whose works he would illustrate. He also studied with the famous botanical flower and still-life painter Gérard van Spaendonck, who had perfected the technique of illustrating flowers in watercolor on vellum.[11] Redouté would eventually replace his teacher as professor of flower painting at the Jardin des Plantes. He would take the watercolor technique to new heights in depictions of flowers from Josephine's gardens at Malmaison (he was named flower painter to the empress in 1805).[12] We can see Redouté at the height of his powers in his magnificent depiction of Josephine's March lily (*Amaryllis Josephinae*) painted in watercolor on vellum between 1802 and 1805 and later published as a stipple engraving (**FIG. 11.2**; see also **FIG. 3.4**). Josephine had acquired the March lily, a native plant of South Africa, from Holland where it had made its first appearance in Europe in 1789. Redouté named the plant in his patron's honor, most likely because he wanted to accentuate the many characteristics she had in common with this plant. It is exotic, sensual, complex, and beautiful, and seems to be vibrating with a remarkable intensity and vitality. It reaches out in many directions and is filled with multiple flowers and blooms. Unusual and exotic herself, Josephine hailed from Martinique and was famed for her striking appearance and strength of character that captivated Napoleon and many other suitors. She was also known for her keen aesthetic sense and her love of beauty, shown in her patronage of the arts and in her cultivation of flowers at Malmaison. She shared in a European passion of the period for exotic botanical gardens, a key aspect of the Enlightenment's embrace of the natural sciences.[13]

Redouté imbued his floral paintings with multiple layers of associations and meanings. Like other flower painters of the period, he was aware of the rich language of flowers, which included religious, imperial, mythological, and medical meanings as well as those of courtly love. In addition to his watercolor botanicals, during this period he produced thousands of botanical illustrations for a wide variety of publications (including the 1805 edition of Rousseau's *Botanical Letters* mentioned earlier). He also became a master engraver, proud of innovations he made in the domain of stipple and color engraving of flowers. He is perhaps best known for two florilegia associated with Josephine's cultivation at Malmaison— *Les Liliacées* of 1802–16 and *Les Roses* of 1817–24 (see **FIG. 3.3**). Roses, of course, were Josephine's special flower, and Redouté had been painting her roses since 1802.[14] Throughout his long and remarkable career, Redouté worked for the ruling classes and served many successive regimes, to be honored by them all. His remarkably prolific and successful career attest to the extent to which botany and the natural sciences in general were esteemed during this period.

Redouté achieved the remarkable distinction of being esteemed not only by the ruling classes, and the naturalists and aficionados of flowers, but also by some of the greatest French painters of the period, including Jacques-Louis David, François Gérard, Anne-Louis Girodet and Jean Baptiste Isabey, among many others. Heir to the floral still-life tradition exemplified in the works of eighteenth-century Dutch painter Jan van Huysum (an artist he greatly admired whose legacy extended to Van Spaendonck, his own teacher), Redouté excelled in this genre. His luminous floral still life exhibited at the Salon of 1796 depicts in great detail sumptuous and sensuously rendered flowers that seem to be in dialogue with one another.[15] The artist created a rich narrative based on the syntax of the floral grouping in which the types of flowers, their references and associations in the language of flowers, their placement in relation to each other, their contrasting colors and other qualities, collectively express a complex nexus of meanings.

Fig. 11.3

François Gérard, *P. J. Redouté, Peintre de Fleurs*, 1811, engraving by C. S. Pradier from *Les Roses* by Redouté, vol. 1 (Paris, 1817). Print Collection, Miriam and Ira D. Wallach Division of Art, Prints and Photographs, The New York Public Library

P. J. REDOUTÉ,
Peintre de Fleurs

In the 1790s Redouté had the great privilege of living and working in the Louvre side by side with history painters such as David. In addition to a separate portrait in 1798, the famous genre painter Louis-Léopold Boilly included Redouté in his representation of the *Atelier of Isabey*, where he is depicted as an equal among the great artists of the period.[16] In 1799 Redouté was appointed member of a jury that awarded prizes to artists who had shown works in the previous Salon. This was an honor reserved for the painters of the period held in the greatest esteem. The members of this jury included the renowned history painters David, Gérard, Charles Meynier, and François Vincent, among others. Gérard, who collected Redouté's floral watercolors, also painted his portrait, a work that was disseminated through prints (**FIG. 11.3**).[17]

Gérard, one of the history painters of the period fascinated by flowers, associated with botanical painters at the Jardin des Plantes, a site frequented by many artists. In 1797 he painted a portrait of *La Revellière Lépaux, Member of the Directory*, seated in his garden, holding a bunch of forget-me-nots.[18] Louis-Marie de La Revellière Lépaux was an amateur botanist. I contend that Gérard wanted the flowers to be as botanically accurate as possible in order to honor the sitter. He thus asked Van Spaendonck, then professor of flower painting at the Jardin des Plantes, to paint in the flowers. This collaboration between a history painter and a botanical painter is remarkable but should not be surprising, given the status of botany and flowers in French culture of the period.

The following year, 1798, Gérard exhibited *Psyche and Amor* at the Salon to great acclaim (**FIG. 11.4**).[19] He lavished attention on the springtime flowers in the lovely meadow that provides the setting for the adolescent, mythological lovers. The flowers play an important metaphorical role in the narrative, for they correspond to the delicate and youthful beauty of Psyche. She is about to receive a first kiss from the god of love himself, Amor, shown here as a chaste and hesitant lover. Their love in this morning springtime meadow is about to blossom. In this painting beloved by its first viewers, Gérard revealed his interest in the variety of meadow flowers, which he depicts in descriptive detail. I propose that the botanical painters of the period, such as Redouté whom Gérard so admired, directly influenced this work. Amor, as shown in the detail (**FIG. 11.5**), is about to crush a daisy underfoot. Daisies symbolized innocence and purity.[20] This

DOROTHY JOHNSON

Fig. 11.4

François Gérard, *Psyche and Amor*, 1798, oil on canvas. Musée du Louvre, Paris. Scala/ Art Resource, N.Y.

Fig. 11.5

Detail of flowers from Gérard, *Psyche and Amor* (Fig. 11.4)

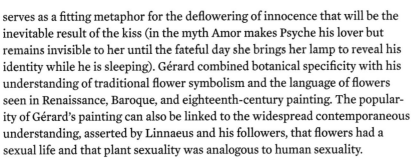

serves as a fitting metaphor for the deflowering of innocence that will be the inevitable result of the kiss (in the myth Amor makes Psyche his lover but remains invisible to her until the fateful day she brings her lamp to reveal his identity while he is sleeping). Gérard combined botanical specificity with his understanding of traditional flower symbolism and the language of flowers seen in Renaissance, Baroque, and eighteenth-century painting. The popularity of Gérard's painting can also be linked to the widespread contemporaneous understanding, asserted by Linnaeus and his followers, that flowers had a sexual life and that plant sexuality was analogous to human sexuality.

Similar ideas were developed in some of the late eighteenth-century mythological paintings of Gérard's friend, Girodet, a literary and learned artist who was profoundly engaged with several domains of the natural sciences, including anatomy, medicine, physiology, meteorology, astronomy, and botany.[21] Girodet, an amateur botanist, combined his empirical observation

Fig. 11.6 (above)

Anne-Louis Girodet, *Sleep of Endymion*, 1791, oil on canvas. Musée du Louvre, Paris. RMN / Art Resource, N.Y.

Fig. 11.7

Detail of flowers from Girodet, *Sleep of Endymion* (Fig. 11.6)

of flowers and plants with his study of botany in several paintings. I believe that these works also embody Linnaean ideas about the sexual life of plants and the symbolic and metaphorical language of flowers.

In his famous painting, *The Sleep of Endymion* of 1791 (**FIG. 11.6**), recognized as a tour de force at its first appearance at the Salon in Paris in 1793, Girodet conveyed ideas of mythology as an allegory of Nature expressed through mystical revelation, using his love and knowledge of botany and flowers to help convey the meaning.[22] Vegetal imagery plays a vital role in this painting. Endymion, the shepherd and hunter, sleeps eternally in a lush bower on Mount Latmos (punishment for his amorous interest in his father's wife, Juno). The goddess of the moon, Diana, a huntress herself, spies him in this vulnerable state, falls hopelessly in love, and visits him nightly, in some versions giving birth to fifty children as a result.[23] Girodet has depicted the goddess of the moon in the form of moonbeams that enter the bower, kiss the lips, and caress the side of the sensual Endymion, who appears to be enjoying this mystical visitation in his dreams.[24] Endymion leans against the trunk of a mighty oak tree (the tree sacred to his father, Jupiter). The mantle and leopard skin on which he reclines soften the rough bark. Girodet's original title for the painting was *Endymion, effet de lune* (effect of moonlight), thereby placing the painting in the landscape tradition of mysterious moonlit scenes beloved by romantic painters.

Nature, in fact, is the medium for the message of the painting. Girodet studied landscape painting and had made many landscapes while in Italy. He also wrote, "landscape painting is the universal genre to which all others are subordinated because they are all contained within it."[25] For Girodet, nature, the earth and sky, terrestrial and celestial realms, circumscribed all of life and was therefore the supreme subject in art. The moonlight enters the bower because Amor pulls aside the laurel branches, revealing the beautiful sleeping figure to the goddess of the moon and allowing her to mystically enter the bower as moonlight. Amor is disguised as Zephyr, the west wind who with his gentle spring-time breezes helps inseminate the earth with plants and flowers. Girodet was very proud of this original conceit, which he described in his letters.[26] Amor holds a garland of myrtle and white ribbon (myrtle stood for purity and also for marriage) and looks lovingly at Endymion. Girodet represented the myrtle and laurel in great detail. Laurel was the evergreen associated in antiquity with victory and also with eternal life, enjoyed by both Endymion and Diana. And the artist also precisely painted the beautiful and rare trumpet-shaped evening glory (**FIG. 11.7**), the flower that blossoms in moonlight for just one night and is replaced the next night by new blooms: a brilliant floral metaphor for the relationship between the moon goddess and the lover whose beauty blossoms at night in her moonlight.

Girodet's emphasis on vegetal life in nature should not be surprising. Endymion participates in this world, for in his eternal slumber he is rooted to one spot, becoming a permanent part of the terrestrial world of trees and plants. Girodet, whose library contained several botanical volumes, shared in the pan-European fascination for botany and understood it as a new way of penetrating the mysteries of nature.[27] Like his contemporaries he owed this fascination to famed naturalist and taxonomist Linnaeus, who had been enthralled by the great diversity of plant life and particularly the sexual life of plants, which he wrote about in great detail. Rousseau had helped to popularize Linnaeus's ideas, promoting botany as an important activity for all citizens. As with so many late Enlightenment philosophers and intellectuals, Linnaeus inspired Rousseau to become an amateur botanist. The philosopher collected specimens for his herbaria and recommended the study of botany as the best way to learn about nature firsthand. Many took this advice, including Girodet.[28]

Linnaeus's *Fundamentals of Botany* of 1736 and *Philosophy of Botany* of 1751 profoundly influenced Erasmus Darwin. The grandfather of Charles Darwin wrote about the sexual life of plants in his popular poem, *The Loves of the Plants* of 1789, a work that was almost immediately translated into French. By 1800 in France, England, Germany, and throughout Europe, botanical ideas about vegetal life on earth and its importance to human life, including analogies between plant and human sexuality, had arisen and had entered popular culture.[29] Earlier, the French *philosophe* Julien Offray de la Mettrie (author of *L'homme machine*, or *Man a Machine*) had explored Linnaeus's concepts of plant sexuality and its human analogies in a fascinating book entitled *L'homme plante* (*Man a Plant*) of 1748. In this work, La Mettrie drew astonishing physical, anatomical and physiological comparisons between human beings and plants. Here, he made analogies between plant and human sexuality:

One can regard the womb of a virgin or rather of a woman not yet preg-
nant, or, if you wish, the ovary as an unfertilized seed. The stylus in a
woman is the vagina. The vulva or mount of Venus and the odor that
exhales from the glands of these parts correspond to the stigma. The
uterus, vagina, and vulva together form the pistil, which is what modern
botanists call the female parts of plants. . . . For us men . . . sons of Priapus,
spermatic animals, our stamen is rolled into a cylindrical tube, the rod.
And the sperm is our fertilizing pollen. . . . Plants are male and female and
in coitus they squirm about like a man and a woman.[30]

Ideas about the sexual life of plants, the fertility and diversity of nature's
vegetal life seen in trees, bushes and exotic flowers, inspired Girodet to create
the resplendent vegetal setting for the sleeping Endymion. These concepts
also inspired another nocturnal mythological painting, this time lit by starlight,
Danae from 1798 (**FIG. 11.8**). Girodet again introduced flowers as a central element of the mythic narrative. In his highly original interpretation of the theme,
he invented an episode not found in
literary or visual sources.[31] He portrayed
Danae as moved from her room in the
tower where she had been imprisoned
by her father to the rooftop on a warm
summer night replete with shimmering
stars. (Her father, King Acrisius, feared
the oracle that foretold he would be
slain by his grandson, a prediction

Fig. 11.8 (left)

Anne-Louis Girodet,
Danae, 1798, oil on
canvas. Museum der
Bildenden Künste,
Leipzig. Erich Lessing /
Art Resource, N.Y.

Fig. 11.9 (above)

Detail of flowers
from Girodet, *Danae*
(Fig. 11.8)

fulfilled when Jupiter visited her as a shower of gold and impregnated her with Perseus.) Instead of gold coins, Girodet imagined the seduction taking place with flowers, a reference to the sexual life and propagation of plants and their analogies to human sexuality. Thanks to the poppies that appear next to them, the guards have fallen asleep. Thus, they miss the mystical moment when Jupiter announces his presence with a magnificent profusion of flowers of many different types and colors from around the world, a reminder of the era's passion for exotic botanical gardens. Girodet depicted the flowers with such precise descriptive detail (**FIG. 11.9**) that they rival their inspiration, Redouté's remarkable botanical and still-life paintings. The gift of flowers, with their heady perfume, beauty, and sensual grace that complements her own, make Danae susceptible to this seduction by the king of the gods.

Many other categories of painting of the period reveal how botany and the painting of flowers informed artistic decisions and the multiple meanings of art. A concluding example comes from the realm of imperial portraiture: Pierre-Paul Prud'hon's captivating painting of *The King of Rome Sleeping* from 1811

(**FIG. 11.10**). The work revels in the lush landscape and precise painting of flowers that shelter the baby king and also help to tell his story. Napoleon's long-awaited heir, illuminated by the early morning glow of the sun, is embraced and surrounded by a nurturing nature. Two imperial crown flowers (**FIG. 11.11**) that lean over him

Fig. 11.11 (left)

Detail of flowers from Prud'hon,
The King of Rome Sleeping (Fig. 11.10)

Fig. 11.10 (right)

Pierre-Paul Prud'hon,
*The King of Rome
Sleeping*, 1811, oil
on canvas. Musée du
Louvre, Paris. RMN /
Art Resource, N.Y.

Fig. 11.12

Pierre-Joseph Redouté, *Fritillaire Impériale* (Crown Imperial Fritillaria), color stipple engraving from P. J. Redouté, *Choix des plus belles fleurs* (Paris, 1827), plate 38. The LuEsther T. Mertz Library, The New York Botanical Garden / Art Resource, N.Y.

DOROTHY JOHNSON

refer to his parents, Napoleon and his Austrian queen Marie-Louise. In their botanical accuracy, the flowers resemble Redouté's magnificent *Fritillaire Impériale* (**FIG. 11.12**).[32] All the plants and flowers in Prud'hon's work convey meanings; for instance, the myrtle bespeaks purity and the laurel signifies victory and eternal life. Through the language of vegetal life in the landscape, the artist revealed the child's position in the world and the hope for his glorious future. Once again, the life of flowers and the life of man merge and fructify in the work of art.

1   See Carolyn R. Rebbert, "Excursions into Botany with Redouté," in *The Floral Art of Redouté*, ed. Marianne Roland Michel (Greenwich, Conn.: Bruce Museum of Arts and Science, 2002), 27–33; Wilfrid Blunt and William T. Stearn, *The Art of Botanical Illustration*, rev. ed. (London: Antique Collectors' Club, 1994), 173–82; Madeleine Pinault Sørensen, *Le livre de botanique: XVIIᵉ et XVIIIᵉ siècles* (Paris: Bibliothèque nationale de France, 2008); Georges Mauguin, "Une Impératrice botaniste," *Revue des études napoléoniennes*, 20ᵉ année, vol. 37 (October–November 1933): 234–37; and Roger L. Williams, *Botanophilia in Eighteenth-Century France: The Spirit of Enlightenment*, Archives internationales d'histoire des idées, 179 (Dordrecht: Kluwer, 2001).

2   Though botanists Augustin Pyramus de Candolle and Antoine-Laurent de Jussieu would famously contest Linnaeus's ideas, his nomenclature would be retained. James L. Larson, *Reason and Experience: The Representation of Natural Order in the Work of Carl von Linné* (Berkeley and Los Angeles: University of California Press, 1971); Frans A. Stafleu, *Linnaeus and the Linnaeans: The Spreading of their Ideas in Systematic Botany, 1735–1789*, Regnum Vegetabile, 79 (Utrecht: International Association for Plant

Taxonomy, 1971); Henri Daudin, *De Linné à Jussieu: Méthodes de classification et idée de série en botanique et en zoologie (1740-1790)* (Paris: Félix Alcan, 1926–7); Jean-Marc Drouin, *Réinventer la nature: L'écologie et son histoire* (Paris: Flammarion, 1993).

3   Jean-Jacques Rousseau, *Lettres sur la botanique*, in *Œuvres complètes*, vol. 4, ed. Bernard Gagnebin and Marcel Raymond (Paris: Gallimard, 1969), 1149–97.

4   See Janet Browne, "Botany for Gentlemen: Erasmus Darwin and 'The Loves of the Plants,'" *Isis* 80, no. 4 (December 1989): 592–621.

5   See Frank E. Manuel, *The Eighteenth Century Confronts the Gods* (Cambridge, Mass.: Harvard University Press, 1959); and recently, Dorothy Johnson, *David to Delacroix: The Rise of Romantic Mythology* (Chapel Hill: University of North Carolina Press, 2011), 63–64, 146–48.

6   For typical examples, see Pinault Sørensen, *Le Livre de Botanique*.

7   See Joanna Stalnaker, *The Unfinished Enlightenment: Description in the Age of the Encyclopedia* (Ithaca, N.Y.: Cornell University Press, 2010), 68–96; and Cynthia Wall, *The Prose of Things: Transformations of Description in the Eighteenth Century* (Chicago: University of Chicago Press, 2006).

See also Lorraine Daston and Peter Galison, *Objectivity* (New York: Zone Books, 2007).

8   "Si la peinture ne devoit pas sa naissance à l'amour, elle la devroit aux fleurs: eh! qui peut, en effet, les voir se balancer mollement sur leurs tiges, qui peut bien sentir l'harmonie de leurs teintes brillantes et la grâce de leurs formes, sans désirer de pouvoir les peindre? La nature ne les forme que dans sa joie: quelle âme tendre les voit jamais sans émotion! Elles rappellent mille souvenirs chers; images de la fragilité de tout ce qui brille, elles mêlent au plaisir qu'elles nous font une sorte d'amertume qui leur donne encore un nouvel intérêt. Source des plus doux parfums, richesse touchante de toutes les fêtes, elles sont les dons de l'amitié, de l'amour; on les porte sur les tombeaux de ceux qu'on a chéris. . . . Ce qui plaît, ce qui touche le plus, un ami, des enfans, une épouse qu'on aime, sèment de fleurs le chemin de la vie." Jean-Joseph Taillasson, *Observations sur quelques grands peintres* (Paris: Dumenil-Lesueur, 1807), 199–200.

9   "Le premier est le mouvement continuel des fleurs; beautés mobiles et fugitives, elles s'agitent sans cesse pour arriver à la perfection de leurs formes; à peine

y sont-elles parvenues, qu'elles vont avec rapidité à leur destruction." Ibid., 197–98.

10 Marianne Roland Michel, "La botanique est-elle un art? Is botany an art?," in *The Floral Art of Redouté*, ed. Marianne Roland Michel, 13–26; Claudia Salvi, *Pierre-Joseph Redouté, le Prince des fleurs* (Tournai: Renaissance du Livre, 1999).

11 Peter C. Sutton, "Redouté and Northern Flower Painting," in Michel, *The Floral Art of Redouté*, 10–11.

12 Michel, "La botanique est-elle un art?," 17.

13 Ibid.

14 Ibid., 15, 18–19.

15 Ibid., 15–17; illustrated on p. 47.

16 Ibid., 16, fig. 15.

17 Ibid., fig. 1.

18 Geneviève Lacambre, "Portrait of Larevellière-Lépaux, Member of the Directory," in *French Painting, 1774–1830: The Age of Revolution*, ed. Frederick J. Cummings, Pierre Rosenberg, and Robert Rosenblum (Detroit: Detroit Institute of Arts; New York: Metropolitan Museum of Art, 1975), 432–34.

19 See most recently, Johnson, *David to Delacroix*, 81–88.

20 See Beverly Seaton, *The Language of Flowers: A History* (Charlottesville:

University Press of Virginia, 1995).

21 Sylvain Bellenger, *Girodet, 1767–1824* (Paris: Éditions Gallimard / Musée du Louvre, 2005), 21–23.

22 Ibid., 206–15. See Johnson, *David to Delacroix*, 40–52.

23 Discussed by Thomas Crow in *Emulation: Making Artists for Revolutionary France* (New Haven, Conn.: Yale University Press, 1995).

24 See Barbara Stafford, "Endymion's Moonbath: Art and Science in Girodet's Early Masterpiece," *Leonardo* 15, no. 3 (1982): 193–98.

25 Pierre Alexandre Coupin, *Œuvres posthumes de Girodet-Trioson* (Paris: Paul Renouard, 1829), 2:431. Discussed by Dorothy Johnson in "Rousseau and Landscape Painting in France," in *The Nature of Rousseau's Rêveries: Physical, Human, Aesthetic*, ed. J. C. O'Neal, Studies on Voltaire and the Eighteenth Century, 3 (Oxford: Voltaire Foundation, 2008), 53.

26 Johnson, *David to Delacroix*, 49.

27 See Valerie Bajou and Sidonie Lemeux-Fraitot, *Inventaires après décès de Gros et de Girodet* (Paris: Bajou/Lemeux-Fraitor, 2003).

28 Alexandra Cook, "The 'Septième promenade' of the *Rêveries*: A Peculiar Account of Rousseau's Botany?" in O'Neal, *The Nature of Rousseau's Rêveries*, 9–36.

29 Martin Kemp, "*The Temple of Flora*: Robert Thornton, Plant Sexuality and Romantic Science," in *Natura-Cultura: L'interpretazione del mondo fisico nei testi et nelle immagini*, ed. Giuseppe Olmi, Lucia Tongiorgi Tomasi, and Attillio Zanca (Florence: Leo S. Olschki, 2000), 15–28.

30 Julien Offray de la Mettrie, *Man a Machine and Man a Plant*, trans. Richard A. Watson and Maya Rybalka (Indianapolis and Cambridge, Mass.: Hackett Publishing, 1994), 79–80. "On peut regarder la matrice vierge ou plutôt non grosse, ou, si l'on veut, l'ovaire, comme un germe qui n'est point encore fécondé. Le stylus de la femme est le vagin; la vulve, le mont de Vénus avec l'odeur qu'exalent les glandes de ces parties, répondent au stigma: et ces choses: la matrice, le vagin et la vulve forment le pistil, nom que les botanistes modernes donnent à toutes les parties femelles des plantes. . . . Pour nous autres hommes, sur lesquels un coup d'œil suffit, fils de Priape, animaux spermatiques, notre étamine est comme roulée en tube cylindrique, c'est la verge; et notre sperme est notre poudre fécondante. . . . Les plantes sont mâles et femelles et se secouent comme l'homme dans le congrès." Francis L. Rougier, *Offray de la Mettrie: L'Homme-Plante* (New York: Institute of French Studies, Columbia University, 1936), 124–25, 126–27. See also Arum Vartanian, "La Mettrie, Diderot, and Sexology in the Enlightenment," in *Essays in the Age of Enlightenment in Honor of Ira O. Wade*, ed. Jean Macray (Geneva: Droz, 1977), 347–67.

31 Johnson, *David to Delacroix*, 58–60.

32 Sylvain Laveissière, *Pierre-Paul Prud'hon* (New York: Metropolitan Museum of Art and Harry N. Abrams, 1998), 208–9.

THE GIRAFFE'S KEEPERS AND THE (DIS)PLAY OF DIFFERENCE

DANIEL HARKETT

IN 1829 AN INTRIGUING IMAGE APPEARED IN PARIS: a lithograph depicting a beached whale at Ostend in the Netherlands surrounded by other famous curiosities that occupied public attention in the 1820s (**FIG. 12.1**).[1] They include an elephant, six Native Americans from the Osage tribe, four Chinese Jesuit missionaries, and the giraffe sent to France as a gift from the Egyptian pasha Muhammad Ali, accompanied by its two keepers.[2] In the print, by Jacquemain, the keepers are shown performing their duties: one leads the giraffe with a halter while the other watches attentively, ready to assist if necessary (**FIG. 12.2**, detail).[3] Yet, dressed in turbans and baggy trousers, these figures exceed their caretaking role; they are as much a part of the exotic spectacle as the giraffe. The keepers' gestures map their two positions: the figure on the right appears absorbed in his task, while the figure on the left is pictured making an open-armed gesture of self-display.

As Jacquemain's print suggests, the giraffe exhibition was not just a display of an exotic animal but a display of humans too, one of many such exhibitions in this period.[4] It is slightly unusual, however, in the way that its human dimension is only half acknowledged. Despite attracting the spectator's eye, the keepers in Jacquemain's lithograph are subsumed by the animal in the print's title, which mentions only "la giraffe [sic]." In other images and texts produced during the giraffe craze, the keepers flicker in and out of view, occupying a place on the margins yet performing important work for the producers and consumers of such material. Placing the peripheral at the center of analysis, the present essay explores the shifting roles of the keepers in representations that circulated in the 1820s. It argues that the keepers connected the giraffe to ethnographic discourse and also invited Parisian spectators to engage in limited forms of identificatory play.

From letters written by the French consul general in Egypt, Bernardino Drovetti—the middleman who handled the logistics of the gift of the giraffe from Muhammad Ali to Charles X—we know that the giraffe was accompanied from Egypt to Marseille by four attendants.[5] Two seem to have returned immediately to Egypt while the remaining pair accompanied the giraffe to Paris. The primary keeper was Hassan el Berberi, a man of Bedouin origin who had been Drovetti's animal keeper in Egypt, while the second-in-command was a Sudanese man named Atir. In expense accounts the two

La Baleine d'Ostende,
Visitée par l'Éléphant, la Giraffe les Osages et les Chinois.

Déposé à la direction.

chez Valani, Éditeur rue de Castiglione, N.º 6.

Fig. 12.1 (above)

Jacquemain, *La Baleine
d'Ostende, Visitée par
l'Eléphant, la Giraffe, les
Osages et les Chinois*,
1829. Lithograph. BnF

Fig. 12.2 (right)

Detail of Jacquemain,
La Baleine d'Ostende
(Fig. 12.1)

keepers are referred to as the "l'arabe conducteur"
and "le nègre son aide," which indicates that within French bureaucratic discourse Hassan and
Atir performed specific ethnic and racial identities in order for their labor to be rendered visible
and their place in an administrative hierarchy
established. Hassan remained in Paris until late
1827, when he returned to Egypt in poor health.[6]
Atir stayed much longer, finally traveling back
to Egypt in 1838.[7]

　　If the expense accounts attempt to fix the
keepers using ethnic and racial categories, two
other figures who played roles in caring for the
giraffe called such fixity into question. One of
these men, Youssef or Joseph Ebed, was a translator hired to facilitate communication with
Hassan and Atir and to assist with the giraffe's
passage overland from Marseille to Paris.[8]
Recruited from the Franco-Arab community in
Marseille, Ebed stood as an embodied sign of more
fluid identities than those linked to Hassan and
Atir in the expense accounts.[9] Also hired to help
with the journey to Paris was a white man from
Marseille named Barthélemy Chouquet.[10] Some
Parisian press accounts of the giraffe refer to the
attendants—Barthélemy presumably among

DANIEL HARKETT

Fig. 12.3

G. Renou, *La Girafe*, 1827. Lithograph from *Dernière notice sur la girafe* (Paris, 1827). BnF

them—as the "quatre nègres," indicating that the term "nègre" itself was unstable.[11] It was capable of expanding to include figures proximate to signs of otherness, as well as signaling a racial category organized by vision.

In the descriptive pamphlets that accompanied and sustained the frenzy of interest in the giraffe in Paris in the 1820s, the keepers come and go. Unsurprisingly, given the importance of visual difference in the giraffe's reception, many of the pamphlets include an image. In some of these images, such as the lithograph by G. Renou accompanying the *Dernière notice sur la girafe* (1827), the giraffe appears alone, isolated against a blank background (**FIG. 12.3**). Even here, however, we find an allusion to human presence through the inclusion of a halter. Whether signaling anxiety about the potential for the exotic to escape its defined boundaries or underlining the status of the giraffe as a mediating object between humans— the halter suggests something controlled and in transition between two places—this piece of equipment ties nature to culture.[12] In other pamphlet images (such as **FIG. 12.4A**), a single attendant is pictured with the giraffe. Never named, these figures do not perform the individuating function of a portrait; we don't know whether to read them as Hassan, Atir or Youssef/Joseph, or even whether to try to do so. The figures are nevertheless called upon to operate as relatively stable frames of reference for viewers by establishing a scale that brings the animal into a human-centered schema even if, in a further twist, the scaling is sometimes distorted.[13]

Figs. 12.4a, b

Frontispiece and title page from L. D. Ferlus, *Nouvelle notice sur la girafe* (Paris, 1827). BnF

Visite à la Giraffe

Fig. 12.5 (top left)

La Giraffe, from *Œuvres complètes de Buffon avec les supplémens, augmentées de la classification de G. Cuvier* (Paris, 1835), vol. 6, plate 102. Paired with a copy of Geoffroy Saint-Hilaire's *Sur la girafe* (Paris, 1827) at the Bibliothèque nationale, Paris. BnF

Fig. 12.6 (top right)

A. Prévost, *Giraffe femelle*, 1827, colored lithograph. MNHN. RMN / Art Resource, N.Y.

Fig. 12.7 (bottom)

François Houiste, *Visite à la Giraffe*. Musée Carnavalet, Paris. © Musée Carnavalet / Roger-Viollet

The inconsistent presence of the human figure in the pictures accompanying the descriptive texts resonates with the mixed nature of their contents, which bring together natural history and cultural commentary. The notice by Étienne Geoffroy Saint-Hilaire—the zoologist charged with supervising the giraffe's journey from Marseille to Paris—is a good example of this type of hybrid writing.[14] Although the pamphlet was not illustrated at the time of its publication in 1827, a copy at the Bibliothèque nationale was subsequently paired with a print of the giraffe and an attendant (**FIG. 12.5**). In the pamphlet, Geoffroy provides an account of the gift of the giraffe, describes aspects of the animal's appearance and anatomy, offers a history of its nomenclature, and explores relationships between giraffes and various African cultures. When discussing the capture of Charles X's giraffe and its passage to France, Geoffroy sketches a relationship between "the arabs" and the giraffe that intertwines notions of mastery and affinity, just as many images of the keepers do. The giraffe's "first masters," he says, were able to educate it in "domesticity" by offering the animal milk and some grain they had prepared for their camels.[15] Later, after asking "what use is the giraffe?" Geoffroy suggests that for "black Africans" the giraffe is a type of game, an equivalent to the deer found in European forests.[16] In so doing, he constructs the giraffe as a cultural object—that is, knowable through its relations with humans—as well as an object of natural history. The presence of a human figure in many of the pamphlet pictures reinforces this tendency, tethering the giraffe to forms of ethnographic discourse.

Stepping back from the descriptive pamphlets to take in a wider range of giraffe-related imagery from the 1820s reveals that representations of the giraffe's keepers are frequent yet variable in their ethnic and racial inflections. We can find apparent attempts to produce the kind of differentiation featured in the expense accounts. A. Prévost's print of the giraffe (**FIG. 12.6**), for example, carefully distinguishes one keeper from the other by differences in skin tone. Elsewhere the emphasis is on a generalized, uninflected Egyptian or Ottoman identity, signaled by the figures' attire: turbans, vests, and baggy pants; or turbans and long robes. At times the figures look like doubles of one another, with the repetition suggesting the infinite reproducibility of an Orientalized type (**FIG. 12.7**). In another group of representations, the keeper or keepers are constructed as non-Ottoman black figures, as in a shaving bowl (**FIG. 12.8**).

Fig. 12.8

Plat à barbe, décor à la giraffe (Shaving bowl with giraffe and attendant), ca. 1827, earthenware. © MNHN, Bibliothèque centrale

In this variability we are likely seeing a negotiation between an older paradigm for representing a human context for the giraffe and a newer account based on the display in Paris. Earlier French representations of giraffes, such as the illustration in the Comte de Buffon's *Histoire naturelle* (1776), often include figures that look like the one on the shaving bowl: small, dark-skinned, and wearing a loincloth.[17] One might imagine, then, that direct observation of the giraffe's keepers yielded a different figure, and indeed Renou's representation of the giraffe with a turbaned attendant is labeled "drawn from nature" (see FIG. 12.4A). But to interpret the difference between these two types of figures as a conflict between the conventional and the observed masks the conventionality of the "Ottoman" representations and misses the broader implications of the shifting visual identification of the giraffe's keepers. Instead we might read the simultaneous presence of these two figure types in the Parisian public sphere as an equivalent to the ongoing attempts by writers in the 1820s to find appropriate human frames for the giraffe. Many of the pamphlets, including Geoffroy's, oscillate between characterizing the giraffe's human context as "arab" on the one hand and "black" or "Hottentot" on the other.[18] That oscillation suggests that we are witnessing the effects of an interpretive process through which French audiences attempted to read the giraffe as a trace of a mysterious African interior. Many descriptive accounts of the giraffe dwell on the animal's origins deep within Africa, far from the coasts understood and mapped by Europeans. They speculate about this environment, considering both its physical geography and its human presence. The inconsistency of the representations of the giraffe's keepers suggests an analogous visual form of speculation about origins.

The variability in the representation of the giraffe's keepers can also be seen as evidence that the giraffe and its keepers were being assimilated to a generalized category of otherness. The print of the beached whale at Ostend represents a paradigmatic vision of this category. It features great variety: we see a whale, an elephant, and a giraffe as well as human representatives from China, North America, and Africa. But, the print suggests, underlying this variety is a form of sameness: all of the curiosities share the quality of being a curiosity, of being the opposing term in a relation of difference with the European spectator. By virtue of sharing this quality, the various animals and humans can be substituted for one another in the viewer's imagination.

In August 1827, the logic of substitution that knits together this category of otherness was activated when another attraction arrived in Paris: a group of six Native Americans from the Osage tribe—the group represented in the Jacquemain print.[19] Organized for commercial gain by a Frenchman living in St. Louis, the visit of the Osages was treated, like the giraffe's presence, as a parody of official diplomacy.[20] The visit of the Osages included open-top carriage rides, frequent trips to sites of public spectacle such as theaters and the Jardin du Roi, and, like the giraffe, an audience with Charles X. As they performed the role of official visitors, the Osages were the focus of relentless public attention as crowds bought tickets to see them, newspaper articles were written about them, and visual representations of them were put into circulation. Present in Paris at the same time, the Osages and the giraffe were brought together in texts and images.

In one example the giraffe and the Osages are shown occupying the same space in the Jardin du Roi (FIG. 12.9). They are supposedly engaged in conversation, with the Osages making the punning request for the giraffe to be their "tall mother" or their "grandma." This fantasy of communicative possibility—the idea that the giraffe and the Osages might be able to speak to one another—was picked up elsewhere at this time in various pamphlets.[21] The fantasy establishes an affinity between the giraffe and the Osages, joining them together through their shared difference. The print does not portray the giraffe's keepers, but in other images they are shown occupying

Ah! soyez notre grand maman... Belle Girafe.

Fig. 12.9

Langlumé, *Ah! soyez notre grand maman... Belle Girafe*, 1827, lithograph. Musée Carnavalet, Paris. © Musée Carnavalet / Roger-Viollet

the same space.[22] The Osages have thus taken the keepers' place and are performing their role, extending the range of potential substitutions for them beyond Africa.

If the position of keeper is open to substitution, how might we interpret the relationship between the giraffe's keepers and Parisian spectators? Many of the images produced during the period of public excitement about the giraffe include representations of the animal and its keepers being viewed by a Parisian crowd. In many cases, the keepers mark a boundary between the exotic creature and its viewers. In a view of the Jardin du Roi in the collection of the Musée Carnavalet, the keepers represent the last in a series of framing structures for the giraffe, after the buildings and the trees.[23] In a lithograph by H. D. Plattel representing a crowd of spectators at the Jardin du Roi, the keepers are just, but crucially, visible (see **FIG. 17.1**). Their heads are aligned with the row of spectators' heads but theirs are inside the enclosure rather than outside. They come between the giraffe and the Parisian crowd.

At the same time as marking a boundary, the keepers offer a bridge over it: they mediate between the giraffe and Parisian viewers. Their mediating role is frequently expressed in the images through formal parallels between the keepers and the spectators. In *Visite à la Giraffe* (see **FIG. 12.7**), French women mirror the two keepers: two make hand gestures that mimic that of a keeper, while another wears a turban that is similar to the keepers' turbans. In connecting the headgear of the keepers and the female spectator, the print reaffirms the wearing of turbans, already a fashionable practice, as an Orientalist performance.[24] If some prints could join the keepers to French femininity, other representations suggest a different type of identification, one that links men to the keepers and women to the giraffe. In a print titled *Giraffe* (**FIG. 12.10**), the couple in the background—she tall, seen in profile with a long neck and a lorgnette that mimics the giraffe's muzzle; he shorter and facing the viewer—echo the giraffe and keeper in the foreground. Like

Fig. 12.10

Unidentified artist,
published by Pillot, *Giraffe,
âgée de 2 ans haute de
12 pieds*, 1827, etching.
Musée Carnavalet, Paris.
© Musée Carnavalet /
Roger-Viollet

the variability in the ethnic and racial coding of
the keepers, these acts of satirical identification
between keepers and Parisian spectators suggest
a certain fluidity. The giraffe and its keepers
become unstable sites of identificatory play.

Such play was an important element of
an actual theatrical production, *La Girafe, ou Une
journée au Jardin du Roi*, which ran at the Théâtre
du Vaudeville in July 1827.[25] Set at the Jardin du
Roi, the play follows Madame Bétophile (a pun for
beast-lover) and her two nieces Claire and Cécile
as they seek out the giraffe. The nieces have also
arranged to meet their lovers Durand and Vincent
at the Jardin du Roi. In order to approach Claire
and Cécile without being detected by a bailiff who
is pursuing them for unpaid debts, Durand and
Vincent disguise themselves as visiting Egyptians
(or Turks; the terms are used interchangeably).[26]
Although Durand and Vincent do not refer
explicitly to themselves as "keepers," they perform
ethnic identities associated with the keepers in
the space of the Jardin du Roi. Within the context
of the play, this space functions as a site of permeability that allows for boundary crossing and ethnic
performance of a type seen in the prints. The notion of the Jardin du Roi as a venue for shifting identities is reinforced by the
event that takes place at the end of the play, when the giraffe briefly escapes
from its keepers and ascends to the Belvedere, a notable decorative structure
in the Jardin located at the top of a small hill. There the giraffe momentarily
occupies a space associated with visual power before being recaptured.[27]

Just as the giraffe is recaptured at the end of the play, so the play puts
limits on the boundary-crossing it authorizes with regard to ethnic performance. Dressed as "Egyptians," Durand and Vincent quickly run into difficulties when they encounter some "real Egyptians"—quite plausible because
Muhammad Ali had established a school for Egyptian students in Paris the
previous year.[28] The "real Egyptians" attempt to converse with Durand and
Vincent and, in an important contrast to the fantasy of communicability
sustained in representations of the giraffe and the Osages, the result is mutual incomprehension.[29] Desperate to preserve their disguise, Durand and
Vincent make the rather shortsighted decision to proclaim themselves Greek,
prompting the Egyptians to draw their daggers and threaten violence. Saving
themselves by hiding behind Claire and Cécile, who are now on the scene,
Durand and Vincent must explain their disguises, which they describe as a
"ruse de l'amour."[30] At the end of the play, of course, all is resolved: Durand
and Vincent's "true" identities are revealed to all; an uncle pays their debts,
and they are free to marry the two young women. The play has thus opened
a space in which Parisians could imagine adopting the subject position of the
giraffe's keepers, only to close down that very possibility. Durand and Vincent's
failure to perform their roles effectively tells us that in the end, the logic of
substitution allowing representatives of otherness to exchange places does
not apply to white French spectators.

One of the authors of *La Girafe*, Emmanuel Théaulon, was also the
coauthor of a play inspired by an earlier Parisian display of otherness, the
exhibition of the Hottentot Venus. The play ran at the Théâtre du Vaudeville
in 1814, more than a decade earlier. [31] In 1827 the memory of the Hottentot
Venus haunted the exhibition of the giraffe and its keepers in many ways.
Like the figure of Sarah (Saartjie) Baartman, the giraffe operates as a sign
of African difference, with difference located in a body perceived to be
grossly exaggerated. Both Baartman and the giraffe were scrutinized by

DANIEL HARKETT

naturalists at the Jardin du Roi—in some instances the same ones—and both were redisplayed publically after death.[32] In 1827 pamphlets and newspaper articles on the giraffe put the term "Hottentot" into circulation to describe the human context for the giraffe in Africa.[33] And in the giraffe vaudeville, one of the "real" Egyptians sings a song to a tune named the "Hottentot Venus," extending the identification with the Hottentot Venus beyond the giraffe to include the keepers and associated figures.[34]

Théaulon's earlier play organizes its spectators in a similar way to the giraffe vaudeville. As Denean Sharpley-Whiting has argued, *La Vénus hottentote* creates a space for projective fantasy and represents a call to order.[35] Here, a female character, Amélie, is keen to attract the attention of Adolphe, a man who, frustrated by some previous marital experiences, has resolved to marry a non-French woman. In order to woo him, Amélie impersonates the Hottentot Venus and succeeds in entrancing Adolphe. Upon the arrival of the "real Hottentot Venus," in the form of a portrait, however, the "ruse de l'amour" is revealed, the Hottentot Venus is shown to be grotesque, and Amélie and Adolphe are left free to marry as representatives of the same race and culture.[36]

Thinking about the Hottentot Venus in relation to the display of the giraffe and its keepers allows us to see the field of potential substitutions extending backwards historically and across different exhibitions at the same moment. Although in 1827 commentators were quick to suggest that the giraffe and then the Osages were passing out of favor, the reference to the Hottentot Venus in Théaulon's play shows us that memories of encounters with difference persisted in Parisian exhibition culture, remaining available to frame new experiences.[37] Such experiences were, as I have argued, constructed in complex ways in period texts and images. Although many representations ultimately reinforce boundaries separating white French spectators from the exoticized objects of their gaze, they also mark encounters with difference as moments of play, characterized by freewheeling speculation and fantasies of substitution.

Acknowledgments

I would like to thank Tanya Sheehan for her comments on this essay.

1   Fishermen discovered the whale floating dead in the North Sea in November 1827. It was subsequently towed towards the port of Ostend, then part of the kingdom of the Netherlands, but the towline broke and the whale came to rest on a beach nearby. An immediate focus of public curiosity, the whale was subsequently dissected and its skeleton put on display in various European towns and cities. For an account of the discovery and reception of the whale, see Mathieu Benoît Félix Bernaert, *Notice sur la baleine échouée près d'Ostende, le 5 novembre 1827 et sur les fêtes données par H. Kessels à l'occasion de la prise de possession, au nom de S. M. le roi des Pays-Bas, du squelette de ce cétacé* (Paris, 1829). The print and Bernaert's text were published in Paris
when the whale's skeleton was exhibited in the French capital in 1829. The print was likely inspired by a lithograph by Jobard after a drawing by Van Cuyck showing the whale being viewed on the beach, by Bernaert's description of public festivities organized to mark the gift of the whale to the king of the Netherlands, and by this verse from a poem delivered during a banquet that formed part of those festivities: "On vit le public incertain / Entre l'éléphant, les Osages, / Et la girafe au port hautain; / Ils se partageaient les suffrages. / Mais abaissez vos pavillons, / Eléphant et girafe vaine: / Vous n'êtes que des mirmidons / Auprès de la Baleine" (quoted in ibid., 55).

2   On the giraffe, see (in addition to the essays in this volume): Michael Allin, *Zarafa: A Giraffe's True Story, from Deep in Africa to the Heart of Paris* (New York: Delta, 1998); Ian
Coller, *Arab France: Islam and the Making of Modern Europe, 1798–1831* (Berkeley and Los Angeles: University of California Press, 2011), 176–81; Gabriel Dardaud, *Une girafe pour le roi* (Bordeaux: Elytis, 2007); Olivier Lebleu, *Les Avatars de Zarafa: Première girafe de France: Chronique d'une girafomania, 1826–1845* (Paris: Arléa, 2006); and Michele Majer, "La Mode à la girafe: Fashion, Culture, and Politics in Bourbon Restoration France," *Studies in the Decorative Arts* 17, no. 1 (Fall–Winter 2009–10): 123–61.

3   Although the text on the print only includes the names Langlumé (likely the printer in this case) and Valant (the publisher), the relevant entry in the *Bibliographie de la France* (13 June 1829, 416) states that the work was "lithographié" by Jacquemain. Jacquemain is presumably the "L. P. Jacquemain" listed in the Bibliothèque nationale's
Inventaire du fonds français après 1800 as a lithographer working on genre and landscape scenes during the Restoration. Jean Adhémar, Jacques Lethève and Françoise Gardey, *Inventaire du fonds français après 1800*, vol. 11, *Humboldt–Jyg* (Paris: Bibliothèque nationale de France, 1960), 135–37.

4   For recent discussions of the history of human display in the nineteenth century, see Pascal Blanchard, ed., *Human Zoos: Science and Spectacle in the Age of Colonial Empires*, trans. Teresa Bridgeman (Liverpool: Liverpool University Press, 2008); and Sadiah Qureshi, *Peoples on Parade: Exhibitions, Empire, and Anthropology in Nineteenth-Century Britain* (Chicago: University of Chicago Press, 2011).

5   Cited in Lebleu, *Les Avatars de Zarafa*, 62–64.

6   Ibid., 160–62.

7   Ibid, 173.

8 Ibid., 90–92.

9 For further discussion of the complexities of early nineteenth-century "Arab France," see Coller, *Arab France.*

10 Allin, *Zarafa,* 140; Lebleu, *Les Avatars de Zarafa,* 87–88, 94.

11 See, for example, *Petit Courrier des Dames,* June 20, 1827, 270–71.

12 See *La Gazette de France,* July 6, 1827, 3, for an article on the giraffe that expresses anxiety about the giraffe's potential for resisting containment. "Bien que la girafe nous parût fort douce… et qu'elle ne semblât disposée à aucun mouvement désordonné, on la promène maintenue par quatre longes, deux desquelles se rattachent à un collier sur le garrot, et les deux autres à un licol comme celui des chameaux. . . . Le motif de ces précautions nous a été expliqué par un mouvement assez brusque, comme celui d'un cheval qui se cabre, que fit l'animal à l'instant où on le rentrait dans la vaste orangerie qui lui sert provisoirement de demeure."

13 For a discussion of an earlier European image in which the presence of animal keepers asserts that "the natural was … an extension of the social," see Alex Potts, "Natural Order and the Call of the Wild: The Politics of Animal Picturing," *Oxford Art Journal* 13, no. 1 (1990): 14–15. The picture in question is George Stubbs, *Cheetah and Stag with Two Indians* (ca. 1765, Manchester Art Gallery, England). Potts (31n9) suggests a comparison between Stubbs's picture and Jacques-Laurent Agasse's painting of the giraffe sent by Muhammad Ali to King George IV of the United Kingdom in 1827 (*The Nubian Giraffe,* 1827, Royal Collection, England).

14 Étienne Geoffroy Saint-Hilaire, *Sur la girafe* (Paris, 1827).

15 Ibid., 5.

16 Ibid., 11.

17 Georges-Louis Leclerc, Comte de Buffon, *Histoire naturelle, générale et particulière: Servant de suite à l'histoire des animaux quadrupèdes,* supplément, vol. 3 (Paris, 1776), 330, plate 64.

18 In his *Nouvelle notice sur la girafe* (Paris, 1827), L. D. Ferlus notes that the giraffe was captured near Sennar in Sudan, but he emphasizes links between the animal and the peoples of southern Africa. Like Geoffroy Saint-Hilaire, Ferlus represents such links in terms of claims about hunting and eating, writing for example that the "Hottentots" find the bone marrow of the giraffe to be "exquise" (exquisite) (11). For a general discussion of the representation of the San in nineteenth-century European texts and exhibitions, see Qureshi, *Peoples on Parade,* 173–75.

19 On this visit by members of the Osage tribe to France, see Alain Lescart's essay in this volume and Tracy N. Leavelle, "The Osage in Europe: Romanticism, the Vanishing Indian, and French Civilization during the Restoration," in *National Stereotypes in Perspective: Americans in France, Frenchmen in America,* ed. William L. Chew III (Amsterdam and Atlanta, Ga.: Rodopi, 2001), 89–112.

20 Although the gift of the giraffe was an official diplomatic initiative by Muhammad Ali, it was often represented in parodic terms in France.

21 See, for example, the *Discours de la girafe aux chef des six Osages* (Paris, 1827).

22 See, for example, Nicolas Hüet's *Study of the Giraffe Given to Charles X by the Viceroy of Egypt* (1827; Morgan Library and Museum, New York). The substitution of the Osages for the giraffe's keepers is also hinted at in G. Renou's *La Girafe et les Osages* (1827), a lithograph that illustrates the pamphlet of the same name published by Paul Ledoux. In Renou's print, the giraffe's halter extends towards the outstretched hand of one of the Osages, while the Osages' pipe rhymes visually with representations of the sticks used by the giraffe's keepers.

23 *La Girafe au Jardin du Roi.* Reproduced in Lebleu, *Les Avatars de Zarafa,* 144.

24 The signification of turbans when worn by French women at this time was open: they were capable of suggesting Orientalist fantasy and could also signal adherence to the intellectual legacy of Madame de Staël. For an acknowledgement of this openness and a discussion of various meanings attached to turbans in this period, see two articles that appeared in the *Petit Courrier des Dames* in 1824: "Modes. Les Turbans et les chapeaux," *Petit Courrier des Dames,* February 15, 1824, 65–68; and "Modes. Les Turbans et les chapeaux. Suite," *Petit Courrier des Dames,* February 20, 1824, 73–75. On the relationship between the French fashion for wearing turbans and the Napoleonic expedition to Egypt, see Majer, "La Mode à la girafe," 126; and Aileen Ribeiro, *Fashion in the French Revolution* (New York: Holmes and Meier, 1988), 131–32.

25 Emmanuel Théaulon, Théodore Anne, and Jean-Baptiste Gondelier, *La Girafe, ou Une journée au Jardin du Roi* (Paris, 1827). For additional interpretations of this play, see Alain Lescart's essay in this volume, and Majer, "La Mode à la girafe," 150–52.

26 Théaulon et al., *La Girafe,* 13–15.

27 Ibid., 35.

28 On the École Égyptienne, see Coller, *Arab France,* 168–69, and Majer, "La Mode à la girafe," 126.

29 Théaulon et al., *La Girafe,* 17–20.

30 Ibid., 20.

31 Emmanuel Théaulon, Nicolas Brazier, and Armand d'Artois, *La Vénus hottentote, ou Haine aux françaises* (Paris, 1814). Recent discussions of the Hottentot Venus include: Janell Hobson, *Venus in the Dark: Blackness and Beauty in Popular Culture* (New York: Routledge, 2005), 1–86; Sadiah Qureshi, "Displaying Sara Baartman, the 'Hottentot Venus,'" *History of Science* 42 (2004): 233–57; and Deborah Willis, ed., *Black Venus 2010: They Called Her "Hottentot"* (Philadelphia: Temple University Press, 2010).

32 Sarah (Saartjie) Baartman was subjected to examination at the Jardin du Roi over three days in March 1815. Among those in attendance was Geoffroy Saint-Hilaire (Hobson, *Venus in the Dark,* 45–6). After her death in late 1815, Baartman was dissected by Georges Cuvier. Her brain, genitalia, and skeleton were subsequently put on display in Paris and remained on view until the late twentieth century (ibid., 46). The giraffe died in 1845, was then stuffed, and eventually entered the collection of the Muséum d'histoire naturelle de La Rochelle (Lebleu, *Les Avatars de Zarafa,* 178–84; Allin, *Zarafa,* 195–97).

33 Ferlus, *Nouvelle notice sur la girafe,* 11; *Dernière notice sur la girafe, contenant la relation de son voyage à Saint-Cloud* (Paris, 1827), 8; "Nouvelle notice sur la girafe. Par M. L. D. Ferlus," *Le Corsaire,* July 7, 1827, 3.

34 Théaulon et al., *La Girafe,* 18.

35 T. Denean Sharpley-Whiting, "Representing Sarah—Same Difference or No Difference at All? *La Vénus hottentote, ou haine aux Françaises,*" in *Black Venus: Sexualized Savages, Primal Fears, and Primitive Narratives in French* (Durham, N.C.: Duke University Press, 1999), 32–41.

36 Ibid., 41.

37 "On ne parle plus du célèbre animal que la générosité du pacha d'Egypte a envoyé sur nos bords … les Osages voient déjà le devant de leur hôtel désert." "Modes," *Petit Courrier des Dames,* September 5, 1827, 97–98.

THE VISUAL TERMS OF CULTURAL ENCOUNTERS: PETIT AND CUVIER'S AUSTRALIAN EXPERIMENT

ANNE LAFONT

THIS SYMPOSIUM ON FRENCH NATURAL HISTORY at the end of the eighteenth century and beginning of the nineteenth is a special occasion to revisit an altogether exceptional group of drawings: the immense collection (nearly eight thousand drawings and manuscripts) of naturalist and artist Charles-Alexandre Lesueur, held at the Muséum d'histoire naturelle in Le Havre. The collection includes a set of drawings by Nicolas-Martin Petit, a little-known student of famed painter Jacques-Louis David. Petit participated in Captain Nicolas Baudin's expedition to Australia (1800–1804), during which he was charged with portraying Aboriginals.

Since my first work on this collection in 2005 and the partial publication of my research in a 2010 article,[1] two fascinating exhibitions have highlighted this gold mine for the researcher and enthusiast interested in these curiosities and documents—drawings that had artistic value and scientific merit for the brand-new anthropological ambitions of the Idéologue moment of post-revolutionary France.[2] A 2009 exhibition dedicated to Lesueur related the exceptional life of this explorer-artist, originally from Le Havre in Normandy, who traveled to Australia and the United States. I have chosen, however, to concentrate on Petit's production in relation to the Australian expedition, especially since this material has been partly published thanks to another exhibition, *L'Autre: Les Naturels vus par l'Occident (1800–1804)*, mounted in 2008.[3]

Relying on these publications, which restore the documentary aspects of this scientific enterprise, I will briefly summarize the most important elements in order to understand the issues at stake in this body of images for a present-day art historian who investigates how the perception, representation, and restitution of the Other is mediated in various ways; and especially important, how the recipients of the "portraits"—whether politicians, anthropologists, or dilettante consumers of illustrated travel accounts—also have agency in mediating the image of the Other because of their own potential time-bound interpretive stance.

I will attempt to show that this Australian adventure of 1800, when viewed in the light of Lorraine Daston and Peter Galison's work on images in scientific atlases, was undoubtedly one of the definitive stages in a passage from a scientific community that demanded documents faithful to nature (the visual regime of "truth-to-nature" in Daston and Galison's book on the history of objectivity) to a scientific community in search of visual productions that could be used to establish scientific proof. Even if such proofs were not "objective" (it seems that subjectivity was not even imaginable at that time), they were at least theorized and systematized, before becoming mechanized in the second half of the nineteenth century thanks to the advent of photography. This scientific system, which inaugurated new theoretical and practical procedures for collecting visual testimony, was codified to a point where agreed-upon principles could be established and repeated under the same conditions and in all circumstances. Consequently, the graphic production coming out of this new mode of operation nurtured comparison—the foundation of modern science as Cuvier had envisioned it.

In other words, the insistence with which this brief Australian experiment inserted itself, through the voices of its actors, into a system of new scientific procedures, reveals how scientists disqualified the "truth-to-nature" image, regardless of the modes used previously (synthetic, generic, or specific), in favor of an image that could become a material object both constitutive of and exploitable by science.

For this study, it is essential to understand what mediation these drawings and engravings embodied, all the more so because the chosen body of works, still almost unknown, will serve to represent remarkably well the epistemological inquiries raised by the status of the image in natural science around 1800. I will thus examine how the demands of the supporters of a new science affected the form and the outcome of naturalist drawing at the beginning of the nineteenth century and revealed that what these images provided was not what the explorers actually saw. I will also consider, in a more general manner, the contribution of the tools of art history to the history of science, including natural history.

The first French anthropological society, the Société des observateurs de l'homme, was founded in Paris in 1799. It was modeled after the concepts of the Idéologues, who were numerous among its founding members. In fact, sensing the failure of the naturalist approach to the global comprehension of humanity—and still more the difficulty of precisely defining the Aboriginal—they attempted to understand humans simultaneously as social beings and as anatomical specimens. At the same time, Nicolas Baudin, an explorer enthusiastic about the natural sciences, imagined a round-the-world voyage. He submitted his project to the Institut de France, which decided to support this initiative but confined its ambition, restricting him to the exploration of Australia, then poorly known. In March of 1800, Bonaparte set the project in motion. The same year on October 19, Baudin's flotilla of two ships, *Le Géographe* and *Le Naturaliste*, set sail from Le Havre carrying sailors, artists including Lesueur and Petit, and scientists such as zoologist François Péron, a student of Cuvier and a partisan of the brand-new science of anthropology.

As Claude Blanckaert has reminded us in many works, there was no real rupture between eighteenth- and nineteenth-century representations of native peoples. The encyclopedic era of the naturalist Buffon and the philosopher Rousseau could not rid itself of a difficult paradox: Aboriginals represented a golden age of pre-civilization, before the corruption of customs observable in European cities.[4] Philosopher and theorist of education Joseph-Marie Gérando, member of the Société des observateurs de l'homme, echoed this idea at the very end of the century, writing that "the philosophical traveler who navigates towards the extremities of the earth in fact goes through the course of the ages; he travels in the past and crosses a century with each step."[5]

Taking account of this fantasy, it is difficult to imagine that the same intellectuals had succeeded in reconciling this image with contemporary ideas that men of science had defended from Buffon to Julien-Joseph Virey. They had argued that "savages"—the term of the time—belonged more to the animal kingdom, because of their cruelty, sloth, and lack of participation in a teleological project activated by ambitions of progress, conquest, and ascension, whether economic, territorial, commercial, or technical.

The first years of the nineteenth century saw the apogee of this conflicted vision of new worlds. Among the challenges facing the first anthropological society was the obvious necessity of resolving this antagonism by applying rational and objective methods to the observation of "natural man." It was to be a science established on the collection of reliable sources, modeled on textual and visual testimonies, formalized by contract from the beginning.

In his introduction for "Considérations sur les diverses méthodes à suivre dans l'observation des peuples sauvages," Gérando specified that his instructions were "addressed to Captain Baudin, correspondent of the society, ready to depart on his expedition of discovery, and to the observers who accompany him; they are also addressed to Citizen Levaillant, who will undertake a third voyage to the center of Africa."[6]

This proves the programmatic and conceptual character of this charge, which endeavors to be an abstract method, ready to be developed in all circumstances of encounter, exploration, and anthropological observation. If the procedures were well conceptualized at the start, they would be the means of an empirical investigation with rigorous and strict methods that would guarantee its instructive effectiveness. Gérando continued: "As it is possible that all and sundry had occasion to encounter peoples who belong to very different degrees of civilization or barbarism, one has believed it necessary to foresee all hypotheses, and to generalize these considerations to such an extent that they could apply to all nations that differ from European nations in their moral and political forms."[7]

In other words, the Société des observateurs de l'homme needed to combat mythologies of the good savage, henceforth unsatisfactory following the many expeditions pursued in the second part of the eighteenth century, from Bougainville to La Pérouse via the tragic and fatal experiment of James Cook, who was assassinated during a battle with Hawaiian natives in 1779— proof of the violence arising in these allegedly paradisiacal regions. The Société developed procedures likely to supply it with facts, and founded a new science authorizing (both practically and morally) the discovery, but soon also the conquest, of these territories and their natural resources, extremely valuable in the process of building colonial empires. François Peron asserted this notion quite directly: "Would it not be glorious for the French nation to precede these other peoples in this new and important course of action?"[8]

The apparent incapacity of these "savages" was organic according to some, climatic according to others, or could be caused by both reasons combined, as Péron envisaged. Before his departure, he had set out to "determine the physical nature of the climate, [and to] research and define its influence on the organic constitution of the people that live in it, as well as [its influence] on the development of their moral and intellectual faculties."[9] Therefore, by supposedly proving the incapacity of these populations to deal with the finality of their own individual lives and the destiny of their communities (that is, their perceived inability to think differently than in the present mode of individual and collective choices), the philosophical scientists or the anthropologists—as they called themselves—cleared the way for colonial ambitions that continued until the late twentieth century. This first anthropological enterprise (very brief, as the Société des observateurs de l'homme was dissolved in 1804), based on a generally dual ideology, initiated the raciological science that animated the entire nineteenth century, the same science that supported the construction of colonial empires and technological conquests.

In this context, Lesueur and Petit embarked on their scientific expedition to Australia. They were placed under the patronage of Baudin, but still more, for the nature of their work as observers and draftsmen, under the supervision of Péron, passport and guarantor of the precepts elaborated by Cuvier, one of the founding members of the Société. Cuvier was also the author of a "Note instructive sur les recherches à faire relativement aux différences anatomiques des diverses races d'homme."[10] Gérando developed similar ideas at length, notably regarding deaf-mutes. He edited the publication cited above titled *Considérations sur les diverses méthodes à suivre dans l'observation des peuples sauvages*.[11] These two texts, both written in 1799, testify to the new methods that members of the Société attempted to perfect and to their expectations, also completely new. The philosophical scientists came willingly from diverse disciplinary origins (medicine, zoology, climatology, visual arts, geography, etc.), but all became *anthropologists* joined in this intellectual and experimental adventure, resting most of their hopes on the visual production to come after the voyage.

Cuvier was the prescriber most engaged in drafting instructions essential to effectively carrying out the collecting of images, even though Gérando was not indifferent to the methods of art, even recalling that its vocation was to imitate nature, the equivalent of the scientific project they had inaugurated.[12]

The latter, in a memoir much more complete than Cuvier's on the missions of the expedition, showed on one hand a marked interest for the social being, his language, his beliefs, his institutions, his modes of transmission; and on the other, an interest in the circumstantial modalities of investigation (learning the language of the Other or developing a language of gestural signs likely to support communication, adapting to the habits of the "Savages" to gain their confidence, and so forth).

Before entering into the details of Cuvier's meticulous recommendations, it is important to understand that the dominant prejudice of his work or his expectations—presupposing that he shared these with his time (for instance, see Pierre-Jean-Georges Cabanis, author of a contemporary treaty on physical and moral man from 1802[13])—came from his belief in a perfect correspondence between "the perfection of the spirit and the beauty of the face."[14] In other words, according to Cuvier, physical man is in close relation with moral man; the morality of an individual can therefore be a gauge of his physical nature and vice versa. But even more, he introduced an aesthetic dimension: the physical configuration of the Caucasian is normative, because it is a guarantor of the morality of the population to which it is closest, and the moral perfection of an individual can be estimated by the beauty of his face. Consequently, the observation of Aboriginals occurred through prisms. Initially, they were judged for the conformity of their physiques with those of Europeans; and in a second stage, their beauty was considered in relation to the Caucasian canon, that is, the antique.

These two tools proved to be the major milestones in Europeans' moral evaluation of Aboriginals, at the very time these modern observers wanted to develop methods of objective science from a humanistic perspective. Gérando had insisted on this point, defending the idea "of reestablishing the august ties of universal society, of rediscovering those ancient relatives separated by a long exile from the rest of the common family [and above all] to extend a hand to them so that they can raise themselves to a more happy state!"[15]

In this fundamentally biased perspective, Cuvier developed a detailed method that required artists to read the *Dissertation* of Peter Camper,[16] a prerequisite, he believed, to putting craniological science into practice. Cuvier also indicated the necessity of paying particular attention to the "protrusion of the snout," to the "width of the cheekbones," and to the "form of the orbits" of the eyes, because those were considered as ostensibly distinct from one race to another.[17]

In contrast, it was necessary to abandon the visual regime of Daston and Galison's truth-to-nature for another, more complex mode. In Nature, the artist needed to distinguish the elements that were useful for his comprehension

Fig. 13.1 (above)

Jacques-Gérard Milbert, Drawing of Mororé. Muséum d'histoire naturelle, Le Havre, France

Fig. 13.2 (left)

Nicolas-Martin Petit, Drawing of Mororé. Muséum d'histoire naturelle, Le Havre, France

from the parasitical elements that would obscure its intelligibility. Thus, Cuvier used the following terms for this project of reworking Nature to reveal its essence and studying it scientifically:

> *Specific studies are needed for the kind of portraits that we require; it must join to the merit of ordinary portraits the geometric precision that one cannot obtain except in certain positions of the head, but which must be rigorous. Thus, it is necessary that the pure profile be included with the portrait of the face. Take [portraits] of various ages, different sexes, and diverse conditions for each people. The costumes, the marks with which most of the savages disfigure themselves, and which ordinary travelers take such care in communicating to us, serve only to mask the true character of physiognomies. It would be important for the painter to represent all his heads with the same arrangement of hair, as simple as possible, and above all, that which hides the forehead least and which alters least the form of the skull. All the foreign ornaments, the rings, the pendants, the tattooing, must be eliminated.*[18]

For this reason, the two drawings seen here are particularly relevant (**FIGS. 13.1** and **13.2**). The one on the left was created by Petit on-site, that is, in New Holland (currently Australia), and portrays an Aboriginal named Mororé, as the inscriptions on the drawing show. The second, which presents the same individual, carries no inscription documenting the model, his identity or his territory of origin; instead, the signature of the artist, Jacques-Gérard Milbert, dominates. While Petit's drawing is rather nuanced in its coloration and apparently faithful to the scarring of its model and to the roughness of his skin, Milbert's drawing is somewhat on the neutralizing side. The bust is idealized and the bodily marks have disappeared, whereas in the other, his furrowed brow and the shadows of his somber face reinforce the fearsome aspect of the individual. It is also known, however, that Milbert never met Mororé, for the artist had deserted before the expedition's destination (on the Île de France, currently the island of Mauritius, that is, midway through the voyage in May 1801). His effective collaboration came later, in France, when he participated in the publication of the second *Atlas* joined to the *Voyages de découvertes aux terres australes* (Voyages of Discovery in the Southern Lands) that appeared in 1824, using the material accumulated *in situ* by Lesueur and Petit.

In other words, was he then thinking of Cuvier's recommendations, which enjoined the draftsman not to depict bodily markings because they impeded anatomical study, especially because by 1824, Cuvier had become the preeminent man of science in France? Otherwise, did the fact that the direct witnesses had all been long dead (Baudin in 1803, Petit in 1804, and Péron in 1810) or distant (Lesueur had been in the United States since 1815) incite Milbert to reinvent, by little touches, an appropriate "Aboriginal"? This reinvention corresponded to the implicit injunctions of the notable scientist and to the visual clichés already in fashion in Paris during the 1820s. Finally, did he seek to assure the commercial success of the publishing enterprise by supporting received ideas? Milbert, completely penniless at this time, was truly in search of money. These various arguments combined to justify his stylistic choices, which were not very faithful to Petit's image sources.[19]

Cuvier added that it was imperative to eliminate academic drawing practices in order to escape from earlier representations of Aboriginals, for "all the world [knows] that the greatest painters [had] very poorly captured the character of the Negro and [had] painted nothing but a White smeared with soot."[20] According to the scientist, the draftsmen of the expedition, often modest technically, would suffer even more from this scholarly imprint than

Girodet. The great painter in question was likely another pupil of David, who had just completed a portrait of Jean-Baptiste Belley (**FIG. 13.3**), a former slave from Santo Domingo, elected as a deputy to the Convention in 1794. Girodet exhibited this portrait at the Salon of 1797. Despite Cuvier's assertions, it seems instead that the artist sought to portray an individual even if the context (the abolition of slavery and the elevation of this new citizen to the rank of deputy) required him to use a costume and scenery (including the bust of Raynal, a supporter of the emancipation of blacks) to mark this new integration by the Republic of its *other* citizens, until then royal subjects of a second or third zone. There is no trace of smearing with soot, no carnival, no artistic weakness here, but rather a project of positive representation of France and its colonies in its revolutionary advances—an impulse of short duration, however, for Bonaparte reestablished slavery in 1802.

On the other hand, it is necessary to recognize that Petit, who endeavored to respect Cuvier's instructions in portraying Aboriginals of all ages, in profile or full-face, highlighting the morphology of the skull (**FIGS. 13.4** and **13.5**), on

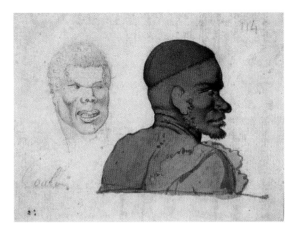

Fig. 13.4 (left)

Nicolas-Martin Petit, "Deux hommes de la terre de Diemen (Tasmanie)." Muséum d'histoire naturelle, Le Havre, France

Fig. 13.5 (left, below)

Nicolas-Martin Petit, Aboriginal woman with child. Muséum d'histoire naturelle, Le Havre, France

Fig. 13.6 (below)

Nicolas-Martin Petit, "Jeune femme de la tribu des Cam-Mer-Ray-Gal de Nouvelle Galles du Sud." Muséum d'histoire naturelle, Le Havre, France

Fig. 13.7 (bottom)

Nicolas-Martin Petit, "Bâtard hottentot." Muséum d'histoire naturelle, Le Havre, France

several occasions did not challenge academic teachings or at least the conventional schemas of representation belonging to tradition or to styles of Parisian fashions. There are images that demonstrate the point: a young woman with the same hairstyle Juliette Récamier wore in her famous portrait by David from 1800 (**FIG. 13.6**); an *Incroyable* (fop or dandy) whose animal-skin costume does not disguise the style of the Directory found in the portraits of Jean Baptiste Isabey (**FIG. 13.7**); or again, an image of a dark-skinned cavalier, which undoubtedly borrows from the Orientalist iconography of Antoine-Jean Gros and others (**FIG. 13.8**).

For this reason, we should perhaps abandon the idea that this schema was unconsciously activated in Petit's anthropological work. In that view, he would have appeared to be a passive subject of his education with David, unable to

Fig. 13.8

Nicolas-Martin Petit,
"Cavalier du Tomor
(Indonésie)." Muséum
d'histoire naturelle,
Le Havre, France

follow the advice of his patrons. Instead, one
can imagine that the draftsman, at one stage or
another in the reproduction of his discoveries,
chose to mediate a raw material that he may
have considered unacceptable for the Parisian
public, who were too unfamiliar with the foreign
worlds he, Petit, had experienced directly. This
public—more precisely, this Parisian readership—
needed to be guided in its reception, led to a form
of empathy (**FIG. 13.9**) that could not arise unless
this strangeness appeared embedded in familiar
visual codes.

Petit's pedagogical ambition could be
preferred to his victimization. The fact that
his images were destined to be published in a
travel account (in *Voyage de découvertes aux
terres australes,* 1807), and were no longer being
addressed exclusively to Cuvier and to the scientists of the Société des Observateurs, could have
led him to rework his drawings with an eye to
popularization. The drawings could also have
undergone market and political pressures via the
publisher, in this case the emperor, whose project
could not be perfectly in accord with the expectations of cranial science. Thus, the draftsman could
have "rounded" his brutal pictures, reintegrating
the conventions of pictorial tradition into his
images to facilitate their access to this second
level of subscribers and financers.

ANNE LAFONT

The production of an image, whether scientific, religious, or political, engages various mediating factors (individual, institutional, and potential recipients; conscious or unconscious ideologies; personal ambitions), which appear within the succession of choices that the maker operates. These layers intervene according to varied proportions and at different points in the realization of the image, but by questioning them, all the meanings of the image can be seen and understood. In his introduction to the catalog of a 2002 exhibition at Karlsruhe, Bruno Latour interrogated his readers and his visitors this way:

> *Thus, we can define an iconoclash as what happens when there is uncertainty about the exact role of the hand at work in the production of a mediator [in this case the image]. Is it a hand with a hammer ready to expose, to denounce, to debunk, to show up, to disappoint, to disenchant, to dispel one's illusions, to let the air out? Or is it, on the contrary, a cautious and careful hand, palm turned as if to catch, to elicit, to educe, to welcome, to generate, to entertain, to maintain, to collect truth and sanctity?* [21]

If the same questions are posed in front of Petit's images, the response could be that "the hand of the mediator" is all these at once at different moments of production, and thanks to the form of the visual arts themselves, simultaneously in the reception of the images. On the other hand, always following the argument of Latour, the reliability of supposedly objective scientific images depends on their number, on the multiplicity of perspectives translated into pictures. Better still, the production of images in series allows the viewer to perceive a form of reality.[22] The credibility of scientific images finally rests on a contract between producers and recipients, which stipulates tacitly that

Fig. 13.9

Nicolas-Martin Petit, "Enfant de Nouvelle Hollande (Australie)." Muséum d'histoire naturelle, Le Havre, France

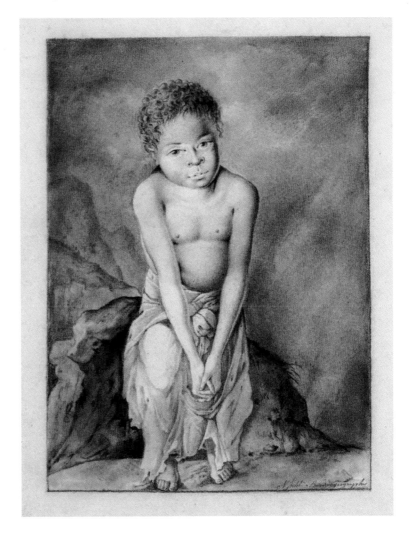

even the objectivity of images is a communal social construction,[23] a common language (such as academic painting to Petit?) from which one can build an exchange or knowledge, in this case about the Other—precisely the purpose of the collective enterprise of the Société des observateurs de l'homme and of the Baudin expedition in all its dimensions.

To conclude, I would like to underline the interest of studying images of scientific production. These images are credited, in natural history in particular, but certainly in the sciences in general, with a performativity that texts cannot equal. Cuvier expressed this idea well, emphasizing that "experience proves that in natural history, all absolute [verbal] description is vague."[24] Though the history of science has accepted that visuality is important in the elaboration of scholarly thought,[25] art historians have still all too rarely shown how valuable their approaches to visual worlds can be to their colleagues in the history of science. Following the work of German art historian Horst Bredekamp, notably his book on the role of Darwin's drawings in his elaboration of the theory of evolution,[26] it is obvious that intimate knowledge of images and of visual facts expressed historically, through time, is crucial. So too is an understanding of the wide variety in the status an image can hold, depending on the technique used in producing it, from drawing to engraving, printing to sculpture, daguerreotype to photographic print, or other media. These methodological approaches of art history and the history of images can participate in a refined comprehension of what is at play in all artistic and scholarly productions, including the history of science.

Translated from the French by Jane E. Boyd

1   Anne Lafont, "Etrange étrangeté: La science au cœur de la représentation de l'Africain," in *L'artiste savant à la conquête du monde moderne*, ed. Anne Lafont (Strasbourg: Presses universitaires de Strasbourg, 2010), 141–56.

2   See Jean-Luc Chappey, *La Société des observateurs de l'homme (1799–1804): Des anthropologues au temps de Bonaparte* (Paris: Société des études robespierristes, 2002). The Société des idéologues was a loose grouping of thinkers interested in the history of ideas, centered around Pierre-Jean-Georges Cabanis and Antoine-Louis-Claude, Comte Destutt de Tracy.

3   See the two exhibition catalogues: Gabrielle Baglione and Claude Blanckaert, *L'Autre: Les naturels vus par l'Occident (1800–1804)* (Le Havre: Éditions du Muséum d'histoire naturelle, 2008); and Gabrielle Baglione and Cédric Crémière, *Charles-Alexandre Lesueur, Peintre voyageur, un trésor oublié* (Paris, Éditions de Conti, 2009).

4   See especially Claude Blanckaert, "Code de la nature et loi de l'histoire: Les appropriations naturalistes du 'primitif contemporain' entre XVIIIᵉ et XIXᵉ siècles,"

in Baglione and Blanckaert, *L'Autre*, 10–15.

5   "...le voyageur philosophe qui navigue vers les extrémités de la terre, traverse en effet la suite des âges; il voyage dans le passé; chaque pas qu'il fait est un siècle qu'il franchit." Joseph-Marie, Baron de Gérando, "Considérations sur les diverses méthodes à suivre dans l'observation des peuples sauvages," manuscript, 1799, Bibliothèque centrale du Muséum national d'Histoire naturelle (hereafter MNHN), cote: M.M.6L; quoted in Jean Copans and Jean Jamin, *Aux origines de l'anthropologie française: Les mémoires de la Société des observateurs de l'homme en l'an VIII* (Paris: Jean-Michel Place, 1994), 76; and in Baglione and Blanckaert, *L'Autre*, 131.

6   "...adressées au capitaine Baudin, correspondant de la société, prêt à partir pour son expédition de découvertes, et aux observateurs qui l'accompagnent; elles sont adressées aussi au citoyen Levaillant, qui va tenter un troisième voyage dans le centre de l'Afrique." Ibid., quoted in Copans and Jamin, *Aux origines de l'anthropologie française*, 73–74; and in Baglione and Blanckaert, *L'Autre*, 130.

7   "Comme il est possible que les uns et les autres aient l'occasion de rencontrer des peuples qui appartiennent à des degrés très différents de civilisation ou de barbarie, on a cru qu'il fallait prévoir toutes les hypothèses, et généraliser tellement ces considérations, qu'elles pussent s'appliquer à toutes les nations qui diffèrent, par leurs formes morales et politiques, des nations de l'Europe." Ibid.

8   "Ne serait-il pas glorieux pour la Nation Française de devancer les autres peuples dans cette nouvelle et importante carrière?" François Péron, "Observations sur l'Anthropologie, ou l'Histoire naturelle de l'homme, la nécessité de s'occuper de l'avancement de cette science, et l'importance de l'admission sur la Flotte du capitaine Baudin d'un ou de plusieurs Naturalistes, spécialement chargés des Recherches à faire sur cet objet," manuscript written by Péron at the request of Georges Cuvier, 1799, Bibliothèque centrale du MNHN, cote: Y1.4186; quoted in Copans and Jamin, *Aux origines de l'anthropologie française*, 113; and in Baglione and Blanckaert, *L'Autre*, 123.

9 "...déterminer la nature physique du climat, [et à] rechercher et préciser son influence sur la constitution organique des peuples qui l'habitent, ainsi que sur le développement de leurs facultés morales et intellectuelles." Ibid.

10 Georges Cuvier's original 1799 memoir, "Note instructive sur les recherches à faire relativement aux différences anatomiques des diverses races d'homme," is lost, as are the archives of the Société des observateurs de l'homme. The text, however, is known thanks to its first publication in 1857, in Maurice Girard, *F. Péron, naturaliste, voyageur aux Terres australes* (Paris: Baillière, 1857), 261–69, and from its republications in Copans and Jamin, *Aux origines de l'anthropologie française*, 67–71, and in Baglione and Blanckaert, *L'Autre*, 128–29.

11 Gérando, "Considérations sur les diverses méthodes," reprinted in Copans and Jamin, *Aux origines de l'anthropologie française*, 75; and in Baglione and Blanckaert, *L'Autre*, 130.

12 Ibid., in Copans and Jamin, *Aux origines de l'anthropologie française*, 75; and in Baglione and Blanckaert, *L'Autre*, 130.

13 Pierre-Jean-Georges Cabanis, *Rapports du physique et du moral de l'homme* (Paris: Crapart, Caille et Ravier, 1802).

14 "...la perfection de l'esprit et la beauté de la figure." Cuvier, "Note instructive sur les recherches," in Copans and Jamin, *Aux origines de l'anthropologie française*, 69; and in Baglione and Blanckaert, *L'Autre*, 128.

15 "...de rétablir les augustes nœuds de la société universelle, de retrouver ces anciens parents séparés par un long exil du reste de la famille commune [et surtout] de leur tendre la main pour [qu'ils puissent] s'élever à un état plus heureux!" Gérando, "Considérations sur les diverses méthodes," in Copans and Jamin, *Aux origines de l'anthropologie française*, 76; and in Baglione and Blanckaert, *L'Autre*, 131.

16 Apparently the *Dissertation sur les variétés naturelles qui caractérisent la physionomie des hommes des divers climats et des différents âges, suivie de Réflexions sur la beauté; particulièrement sur celle de la tête, avec une manière de dessiner toute sorte de têtes avec la plus grande exactitude* (Paris, 1791), translated from the Dutch by Jansen (also the translator of Winckelmann).

17 "...la saillie du museau... la largeur des pommettes... la forme des orbites." Cuvier, "Note instructive sur les recherches," in Copans and Jamin, *Aux origines de l'anthropologie française*, 69; and in Baglione and Blanckaert, *L'Autre*, 128.

18 "Il faut des études particulières pour le genre de portraits que nous exigeons; il doit réunir au mérite des portraits ordinaires celui d'une précision géométrique qu'on ne peut obtenir que dans certaines positions de la tête, mais qui doit être rigoureuse. Ainsi, il faut toujours que le profil pur soit joint au portrait de face. Le prendre de divers âges, de divers sexes et de divers états dans chaque peuple. Les costumes, les marques par lesquelles la plupart des sauvages se défigurent, et que les voyageurs ordinaires ont tant de soin de nous transmettre, ne servent qu'à masquer le véritable caractère de la physionomie. Il serait important que le peintre représentât toutes ses têtes avec le même arrangement des cheveux, le plus simple possible, et surtout celui qui cacherait moins le front et qui altérerait moins la forme du crâne. Tous les ornemens étrangers, les bagues, les pendants, le tatouage, doivent être supprimés." Cuvier, "Note instructive sur les recherches," in Copans and Jamin, *Aux origines de l'anthropologie française*, 70; and in Baglione and Blanckaert, *L'Autre*, 129.

19 As Richard W. Burkhardt has kindly informed me, Milbert in fact returned to France in the fall of 1823 after spending seven years in the United States. In his correspondence with the museum all through 1824, he demonstrated his extreme material and financial deprivation. I also thank Professor Burkhardt for having given me the precise reference for Milbert's letter of April 6, 1824, in which he vows that he is about "to be reduced to his last *écu* [coin]" ("être réduit à son dernier écu"). See *Mémoires du Muséum d'Histoire naturelle* 12 (1825): 18–29.

20 "...tout le monde [savait] que les plus grands peintres [avaient] souvent mal saisi le caractère du Nègre et n'[avaient] peint qu'un Blanc barbouillé de suie." Cuvier, "Note instructive sur les recherches," in Copans and Jamin, *Aux origines de l'anthropologie française*, 69; and in Baglione and Blanckaert, *L'Autre*, 128.

21 Bruno Latour and Peter Weibel, eds., *Iconoclash: The Image Wars in Science, Religion, and Art* (Karlsruhe: ZKM; Cambridge, Mass.: MIT Press, 2002), 20.

22 Bruno Latour, *Sur le culte moderne des dieux faitiches suivi de Iconoclash* (Paris: La Découverte/Les Empêcheurs de penser en rond, 2009), 152, 186.

23 Ibid., 160.

24 "...l'expérience prouve qu'en histoire naturelle, toute description absolue est vague." Cuvier, "Note instructive sur les recherches," in Copans and Jamin, *Aux origines de l'anthropologie française*, 69; and in Baglione and Blanckaert, *L'Autre*, 128.

25 See the excellent article by Charlotte Bigg, "Les études visuelles des sciences: Regards croisés sur les images scientifiques," in *Histoire de l'art*, no. 70 (2012): 95–101, in an issue edited by Anne Lafont on visual approaches in art history.

26 Horst Bredekamp, *Darwins Korallen: Frühe Evolutionsmodelle und die Tradition der Naturgeschichte* (Berlin: Wagenbach Verlag, 2005).

MAKING ART, COMMUNICATING SCIENCE

SYMPOSIUM COMMENTARY

PAULA YOUNG LEE

A FAMOUS QUOTE ATTRIBUTED TO PABLO PICASSO READS: "ART IS A LIE THAT BRINGS US CLOSER TO THE TRUTH." Artists of all sorts may bristle at the word "lie," so laden with moral accusation and the corollary concept of deception. Yet those who have attempted to depict the visible world understand that image-making is a profound exercise in illusion. This has been particularly true since the Renaissance, with the invention of linear perspective and the accompanying humanist emphasis on the worldly observer replacing God's all-seeing eye. In particular, the scientific illustration offers the view of a questioner who sees the world through a measured gaze that carefully unveils nature's secrets.

Art historians such as Barbara Maria Stafford and Martin Kemp have explored the intersection between art and science.[1] The scientific illustration also inherits cultural conventions of the Renaissance or the "period eye" articulated by art historian Michael Baxandall, who argued that millers, drapers, and other merchants took literal measure of the material world based on an expert gaze.[2] Today we are all scientists of sorts, viewing the world through a mechanical lens called the television, the unlikely inheritor of the nineteenth-century obsession with the natural sciences, an obsession that Claudine Cohen and Göran Blix raise in their essays in this volume.

Extending and building on themes touched on throughout the symposium, the essays presented in this session vibrate inside that Boolean realm where artifice collides with nature and exposes the mutual fictions residing in the cultural construct called "the gaze." These essays raise discomfiting yet necessary questions regarding the active role played by scientific images in the construction of scientific knowledge. Considered casually, scientific illustrations are something more than passive agents in the construction of the known world, and yet somehow less than legitimate art because they were never made to be cultural representations fulfilling a mandate of display.

As Pierre-Yves Lacour's essay shows, some techniques of production claim mimetic authority, a point also raised differently by Anne Lafont. Both essays argue that the technical expertise manifested by the drawing itself confirmed the reality of specimens that often did not manifest as concrete objects before the public for years, even centuries. This circumstance invested the drawing with the power of agency while also (problematically) transforming it into a fetish. Daniel Harkett begins to explore this point in his essay, which reflects a particular fascination with figures on the sociohistorical margins. It is not the celebrated giraffe but their keepers that become the focus of his attention, their instability inside the visual field also implicating their cultural and semiotic instability. This fluxion reminded me of Antoine Jacobsohn's discussion of seeds and their cultivation. Seeds were either "types" to be conserved or propagates to be planted. Both practices gave the original seed an odd status; it was something precious yet nonexistent. As Jacobsohn comments, differing attitudes about the social usefulness of seeds can be understood as a reflection of class relations. Many of the same class distinctions resonate in the difference between prints and paintings. As examples of fine art and exponents of lasting cultural values, paintings are to be conserved. Prints, however, are to be disseminated, for printmaking is a popular medium reflective of bourgeois commercialism. For this reason, Dorothy Johnson's essay engages a different set of concerns than those raised by the other speakers in this session, since her analysis rests on juried paintings that inhabit the museums and salons. Subsequently, her well-argued essay shows precisely how the cultural appropriation of scientific ideas first occurred through history paintings, demonstrating how the beauty of living plants enhanced the aesthetic and philosophical appeal of major works of art.

By focusing our attention on the image as artifact, this group of essays as a whole helps us make the important distinction between the persuasive powers of the image and the stolid realities of the subject. The usual example of this split is the charcoal drawing by Albrecht Dürer of his mother at the age of sixty-three from 1514 (Kupferstichkabinett, Berlin). This is a gorgeous drawing of an unlovely woman, yet because Dürer's gaze was objective, in the manner articulated by Lorraine Daston and Peter Galison in their discussion of the visual tropes of scientific "objectivity,"[3] he frankly admitted her flaws, and thus her image is deeply, lovingly human. The sophistication of the drawing means that its mimetic accuracy is never doubted, even as this accuracy means that viewers readily forget that Dürer was an artist, not a passive recording device. He wielded his charcoal to find subtle, internal harmonies that create a satisfying and beautiful drawing. So objectivity is shown to have its limits, for what convinces us of the truth of Dürer's mother's existence is, ultimately, the exquisite skill he called upon to render this image.

Today, scientific illustrations no longer seem to be Renaissance windows, Enlightenment mirrors, or Modern screens. They function like Rorschach tests of the subconscious, sorting out the audience by hiding obscurities among the obvious. As Madeleine Pinault Sørensen notes in her essay in this session, the emergence of an empathetic stance towards captive animals also encouraged the pathetic conditions of their captivity to vanish from the visual narrative.

The bars of the cage disappear from the image, taking along with them our ability to remember that there were cages in the first place. What, then, is science's obligation to historical memory? Even as we submit visual documents to rigorous examination, is it legitimate to envision the context that is often omitted? Scientific drawings are routinely cast as pedagogical instruments, with the white space surrounding specimens working precisely to lift the body out of a temporal continuum. In the interest of critical inquiry, however, we might also consider these white spaces as the spaces of omission, here filled by the research of historians who provide text and context for the seductive illustration of science.

1   See, for instance, Barbara Maria Stafford, *Body Criticism: Imaging the Unseen in Enlightenment Art and Medicine* (Cambridge, Mass.: MIT Press, 1991); and Martin Kemp, *The Science of Art: Optical Themes in Western Art from Brunelleschi to Seurat* (New Haven, Conn.: Yale University Press, 1990).

2   Michael Baxandall, *Painting and Experience in Fifteenth-Century Italy: A Primer in the Social History of Pictorial Style* (Oxford: Clarendon Press, 1972).

3   Lorraine Daston and Peter Galison, *Objectivity* (New York: Zone Books, 2007).

MAKING ART, COMMUNICATING SCIENCE

SYMPOSIUM DISCUSSIONS

INDIVIDUAL PAPERS
9. PICTURING NATURE IN A NATURAL
HISTORY MUSEUM: THE ENGRAVINGS OF
THE *ANNALES DU MUSÉUM D'HISTOIRE
NATURELLE*, 1802–13
Pierre-Yves Lacour (PYLC)

Question: I was just wondering if you can explain
a little bit more about the transition in the vellums
from the seventeenth century to the eighteenth
century. What were the major criteria for the vellums from the seventeenth century? Were they
much more artistic?

PYLC: The main difference occurs because of
the splendid color plates. Also, at the end of the
Enlightenment, sexual characteristics of plants,
their sexual organs, were also shown in these
engravings. Before this time, a botanical image
mostly showed the general appearance of a
plant, not precisely the small vignettes with the
characteristics of the species.

10. REPRESENTING ANIMALS WITH EMPATHY,
1793–1810
Madeleine Pinault Sørensen (MPS)

Question: Were domesticated wild animals
used in the same way for thinking through
this problem of empathy, or was it solely these
exotic large ones?

MPS: At the end of the eighteenth century, the
animal had become more akin to what we call a
companion animal today, or a pet. So they were
not given the same kind of treatment, because
these were really exotic animals, already outside
the family norm.

11. BOTANY AND THE PAINTING OF FLOWERS:
INTERSECTIONS OF THE NATURAL SCIENCES
AND THE VISUAL ARTS IN LATE EIGHTEENTH-
AND EARLY NINETEENTH-CENTURY FRANCE
Dorothy Johnson (DJ)

Question: One of the things I find most interesting about these paintings and about a number
of images that you've shown is the fact that you
actually see flowers, vegetables, humans, in
context. You see in the eighteenth century in
language, you see harmonies or what we might
now consider even habitats or ecosystems in
some ways. And I find fascinating in this late
eighteenth-century painting, literature, natural
history, the fact that you have on the one hand
these abstracted, technical drawings of plants. At
the same time you also have an emerging discourse
in which you actually see the plants and humans
and animals and their interactions, not only their
affinities, not only their analogies, but actually
the ways in which they depend on each other. I'm
thinking in particular of one image of yours: the
Temple of Flora, where you have the birds, the
nests, the eggs, you see the pollination. Up to what
point are you actually seeing a habitat, harmonies,
or an ecosystem of some sort in these paintings?

DJ: That's a great question, because we always
associate the period of romanticism during the
first half of the nineteenth century with this
interest in representing animals in their native
habitats—and we've seen some of that earlier
in the symposium, this attempt to place animals
within their native soil. It actually starts in the
second half of the eighteenth century, with Buffon
and Bernardin de Saint-Pierre and these remarkable writings about nature, this fascination with
nature and artists combining this with their
mythological narratives, such as Ovid's *Metamorphoses*, and the interrelationship between man

and his products and buildings and nature. Man as a part of nature is what we see in these paintings; this is a small part of a larger study that I'm engaged with.

You also see this real attempt, in paintings and in scientific illustrations, to try and penetrate the secrets of nature through fossils, through the study of the earth, through plants, through primeval history and so forth, but you see it with the study of anatomy and the vitalist school in medicine trying to get to what makes up life. And of course, the question can never be answered. This was almost a comprehensive quest in literature and the arts and the sciences to understand the mysteries of nature and how they fit together. Thornton's *Temple of Flora* was criticized for its botanical inexactitude, for not being scientific enough, and of course he was trying to bring in the mythological realm. Some of the illustrations even have Cupid in them, aiming his bow at a flower to inseminate it. He was trying to achieve the whole fecundity of nature and its richness in this book, which he wanted to be a popular success, and which went through different editions. But it was an expression of the harmony of man in nature, right at a time when that was just being torn apart and would continue to be torn apart through the Industrial Revolution.

Comment: You mentioned exactitude, and it was my privilege a number of years ago to see the original vellums that Redouté painted for the *Sylva of North America* for François-André Michaux. The detail level in those very small paintings (approximately 4 by 7 inches) was just astonishing. I had a magnifying glass with me, and I could see that Redouté had painted the hairs on the stems, the hairs on the edge of the leaves. The exactitude of these people cannot be overstated. It's magnificent work, overlooked, but magnificent.

DJ: What's really stunning is that he did these in watercolor. And he would layer the watercolors, but they had to be done so rapidly, and part of the rapidity was because flowers are so ephemeral. As a friend of mine who is a flower painter said, "It's so frustrating to try and paint flowers because they're changing every minute, they're going through a life cycle so rapidly." She said it's very disconcerting to try to paint flowers; I was thinking about that in terms of Redouté's watercolors and the thousands that he produced, so the intensity and speed with which he worked was just incredible.

Question: I was wondering if you could also address Redouté, because his career is

phenomenal, from Marie-Antoinette to Charles X. And I'm wondering if the appreciation of his work has to do with not only his technique but also this larger issue about the importance of science, the importance of botany, or as you've just expressed in your response, this ability to try to penetrate the secrets of nature, because it's an amazing biography and success story.

DJ: I think it is completely amazing, and I've been trying to think about how he could succeed, because in spite of the portraits, the literary descriptions of him are of someone who's incredibly ugly and unpleasant to look at. But he had very good manners, and also he wasn't French, and I think that may have protected him. He was transplanted from the Ardennes—his brother worked as a set decorator in Paris, he came from a family of artists, and there was a huge respect for flower painters of the north in France, as we know, but that might have protected him somewhat.

I thought also maybe he was protected because he was in this natural sciences bubble (he seems not to have participated politically, except he was able to promote his career constantly), or because he was so highly esteemed for his remarkable talent, which led him to be accepted. I had come across his name and that of Van Spaendonck when I was a graduate student and I was studying the records and archives of pedagogy during the Revolution and the Directory, the reconstituting of the art school. I kept asking, how did Van Spaendonck and Redouté get on these juries that were judging history painters and portrait painters? Finally, when I was given the opportunity to give this talk, I could answer that question that I posed to myself all those years ago. And they were held in such esteem because somehow they were close to the secrets of nature and could replicate or express it in some way. I would love to analyze what I see as a very complex narrative in this painting that has to do with the flowers and the seasons—you see a little nest there.

Question: I'm interested in the continuities that I'm seeing from the seventeenth century, when flowers were absolutely used to articulate an understanding of the sexuality of human beings. Here, we seem to see human sexuality being used to help communicate something about the sexuality of plants. Could you elaborate on what you were saying, not just about the sexuality of plants, but about the essence of all living things— so is it all of them coming together to understand how life itself reproduces?

DJ: I think that's right. There was this remarkable investigation into the sexuality of human beings vis-à-vis plants, combined with the language of flowers and the mythology of flowers—the seventeenth-century tradition, the imperial tradition—so there are all these resonances. But I think people at the very end of the eighteenth century were excited about this rediscovery or popularization of Linnaeus's ideas through Erasmus Darwin. So in these poems—even with Goethe, in the *Metamorphosis of Plants*, which Erasmus Darwin also talks about—it's all in terms of wives and husbands, and monogamy and polygamy. So plant sexuality is really seen in terms of human sexuality or explained that way, in terms of marriage and courtship. There's also that long tradition of women being associated with flowers and different kinds of flowers.

12. THE GIRAFFE'S KEEPERS AND THE (DIS)PLAY OF DIFFERENCE
Daniel Harkett (DH)

Question: It's more an impression that I have, but in natural history drawings sometimes you have a natural object, and you have a scale. You have an object which represents the human scale to view the object. In some way, can we think of the giraffe in terms of urban spatiality? It is vertical, and its monstrosity is in its verticality. I wonder if there is something that can be thought of in terms of urban landscape and the importing of vertical objects like the obelisk from Egypt, for example, and the scale of humans. Cannot the humans be viewed as the scale for this immense object? And there would be something about the spatiality from the verticality in the urban space from the obelisk to the Eiffel Tower, which I think the giraffe resembles.

DH: I'm fascinated by the idea of scale, the idea of human scale of course is in a sense a joining of something to culture, and it's a way of seeing something in human terms. I'm interested in one of the first images I showed, where you have this figure that's being introduced, and one might argue that he's being introduced for scale; but of course, the effect for the giraffe, if we judge this figure as a scaling figure, is actually to accentuate the height even further. It's curious; the idea of reading this figure as a scaling figure, which one might do in a kind of scientific context, seems to produce the opposite effect of actually giving us knowledge about the likely true height of the giraffe in relation to human subjects. I'm interested in how the introduction of the figure then confounds the reason for which it was introduced, if one sees it in terms of scientific illustration.

13. THE VISUAL TERMS OF CULTURAL ENCOUNTERS: PETIT AND CUVIER'S AUSTRALIAN EXPERIMENT
Anne Lafont (AL)

Comment: The Société de l'ethnologie showed up in the early 1840s and was actually merging those two traditions. It continued racial science and craniometry (physiognomy was part of it as well), but also an interest in comparative religions and cultures. At the same time in that period you've got the development of Oriental studies and the study of languages, philology, which was meant to be a universal method. Much of the interest was for languages of the Orient, of India and China, but these were methods that provided the foundations for the cultural approach, and so in that interval both of those strands were developing but also encountering each other.

Richard W. Burkhardt, Jr. (RWB): When you mentioned the *construction Cuvier*, it also reminded me of what Pierre-Yves Lacour said earlier about Cuvier, in effect saying that colors are things that we don't want to see because they don't make any difference for species. Now that can't be true, and it certainly wasn't felt to be true by his brother Frédéric when he proceeded to put together the *Histoire naturelle des mammifères* with Geoffroy Saint-Hilaire. He said at the very beginning that you need colors often to distinguish species, and it's clearly better to have colors if you're thinking about sexual dimorphism too. It's not strange that Cuvier got away with lots of this, but in fact he seemed to be getting away with a good deal.

Lots of things got repressed by Cuvier. I'm thinking about his instructions, but he was also worried about the French sailors. He's worried when he has this notion that they shouldn't cause the deaths of any aborigines—but if there should be a skirmish in which some aborigines were killed, then it's important for the *équipe* to collect the bodies, and the sailors won't like it, but they need to boil them so that they can get the bones. Cuvier was above all a comparative anatomist and he loved bones after they've been bleached, so one can see why he was enthusiastic about craniometry—it's pretty close to bones. But in all sorts of respects Cuvier's role is very interesting because it doesn't necessarily fit what an average sailor would want to do, it doesn't necessarily fit what a zoologist interested in species might want to do, and I'm interested in what you can tell us about what he got Milbert to do. Did Milbert actually paint that image in 1824 when he was back from the United States?

AL: Milbert was in France, and all the participants in the Baudin expedition were dead or were elsewhere, like Lesueur who chose to be in United States. Milbert departed with the flotilla but deserted in the course of the expedition. As the other participants were not alive or not there, Milbert was asked twenty years afterwards to make another illustrated travel account working after Lesueur and Petit's drawings, but transforming them to have new images they would print.

RWB: So he must have done it in 1824, because from 1817 to 1823 he was in the United States collecting animals for the Ménagerie. It sounds like he did them very quickly under Cuvier's influence, as you suggest, which is extremely interesting.

END-OF-SESSION DISCUSSION

DJ: To address the issue of images and pedagogy, the tradition of imagery in the West from the Renaissance onwards (which becomes contested as we get to the end of the nineteenth century) was pedagogical in that images—not just scientific images but all kinds of imagery and art—were meant to delight as well as instruct. So I think that all the imagery that we looked at today did have a pedagogical or educational function. Something unifying these different talks that I found really interesting was the question of antecedents and the extent to which artists could not get away from earlier representations, even though they were supposedly looking at flowers or the giraffe or birds or the lion and the elephants, or the Aboriginal peoples—the extent to which those depended on images that the artist already had in their minds, because that's what they learned and that's what they knew.

I love the image of the huge beached whale—I'm very interested in the historical representations of whales and how much they diverge—and how much the conventions of representation diverge from the way we know that whales actually look from photographs, if not from actual experience, and the extent to which those drawings recalled eighteenth-century representations of Africans, and the same with animals, and with birds. So when you're drawing or representing from nature and all of those admonitions, what they were supposed to focus on—it's a very powerful influence of the paradigm. How can you get away from the paradigm and really represent something in a new way, or in a way that's more naturalistic?

Question: My question has been percolating in my head since Pierre-Yves's presentation about the

choice to abstract the specimen from its context. This style was typically used in the scientific drawings, where you would have just the flower without context or effort to show how it had grown, or in the case of animals, just the animal with no indication of its behavior, versus the other type of images, such as the lioness with the cubs or in the context of the cage, or in other situations. And this also connects to Paula's question of pedagogy. What was the rationale for this standard in scientific drawings, for the need to simply demonstrate the species as the scientists wanted to define it in its purest form, versus the desire to see the animal as much as possible in its natural habitat, versus perhaps the functionalist image of an animal or a plant species in its context?

PYLC: I think that natural history was probably concerned essentially with a description of plants and animals and so on. The habitats or the context were not really that important, especially at the end of the eighteenth century. All natural history was based on similar concerns of the *description des mœurs*, which was completely secondary compared to the description of the external characters.

I would like to come back to one of the plates from Redouté, because I think it was a marvelous example of something that could bridge art history and history of science. It is a wonderful image, but that's not really what's important for botanists. It's also a good image for science, because you have the whole flower, but in this case, the color is gone and you can see the pistil and the stamen. Redouté's plates are beautiful compositions, well painted, but at the same time they could support a scientific discourse. He created this conjunction between a good scientific image and a beautiful image by a flower painter.

DJ: And also, we're looking at these works out of context, of course, projected on a screen like this. Going back to your question, the destination and the function of the images is very important because the scientific images were meant for those who were studying the plant scientifically, the scientists and naturalists, whereas the paintings of course were appealing to a very different audience. Bringing that scientific knowledge into paintings, instructing the audience in that way, created other resonances that were not present in the botanical illustrations. But then, Redouté of course brought the aesthetics and conventions of the art of still-life painting into botanical images, which is a very interesting conjunction. But I do think the destination of the *Annales* and their scientific plates was a very different group that would look for certain things, rather than a broader audience and public for consuming art or images in a different way.

Question: In addition, there was the question earlier about the image that seemed to represent specimens in quite a different way, not as discrete items, but rather understandable as part of a system. And life is not limited to a single decontextualized object, but towards the end of the eighteenth century—particularly in Lamarck, with the concept of *milieu*—every entity exists as part of a wider ensemble. Did that start to show up in natural history representations into the nineteenth century, the idea of getting away from the specimen on a plate as somehow telling us about it in isolation, or was there an attempt to show it as part of a broader system?

And more specifically: Cuvier, whom we think of as introducing the concept of conditions of existence as very important for understanding discrete organisms, was still an anatomist and would rather show bones than animals in their environment. What about that apparent paradox?

To return to Anne Lafont's presentation, I think there is a tension between those two modes, in the comparison you showed between the two drawings. The artist was so attentive not simply to the physiognomy, but also to the cultural markings—so there's a history and society and symbolism that is crucial to that specimen, to that person. But then, as it's reproduced in Paris, those are removed because the image doesn't let us see what that painter thought was most important, that is, the body. This returns to the question of these two traditions of anthropology, one concerned with *les mœurs*, and the other concerned with bones and bodies.

AL: You explained it very well. I continue to think about what existed between the Société des observateurs de l'homme, and it's not clear for me, but I will do the research for that. And maybe I must also think about Milbert in 1823 and 1824, because those are the dates when he conceived the series of drawings after Petit, in this new context of how anthropology developed from the time of the Société des observateurs de l'homme to Pierre Paul Broca. So I need to research more to better contextualize this series of drawings of 1824 and the two trends of anthropology. In ten years I'll have a better explanation.

Claudine Cohen (CC): It's true that Cuvier was busy with bones, and his job was reconstructing these extinct animals, but he was really founding a discipline and he was at the start of the discipline. For example, plant paleontology was still to be born, and Brongniart would do the first book about

that, so I think the first issue for Cuvier was to reconstruct these animals. The environment, the milieu, the flora, were not yet known, so the next generation would do these *tableaux* of ancient life. And I think Cuvier was very careful not to go too far. For example, I showed these different animals with flesh, and De la Beche added some palm trees, to make them live a little more [see Chapter 14]. Cuvier didn't do such things, but I think he was a positivist (even if that is anachronistic) and he insisted on the scientific rigor of his research and not to extrapolate too much.

NATURAL HISTORY
AND FRENCH
CULTURE

PART V

PART V

NATURAL HISTORY AND FRENCH CULTURE

Previous page and detail, left One of the "ideal views"
illustrating Louis Figuier, *La Terre avant le déluge* (Paris,
1863): "L'Ichthyosaure et le Plésiosaure (période du lias
[Lower Jurassic])" (see Fig. 14.6)

THE QUEST FOR "LOST WORLDS": INTELLECTUAL REVOLUTIONS AND MUTATIONS OF THE IMAGINATION AT THE TURN OF THE NINETEENTH CENTURY

CLAUDINE COHEN

AFTER THE 1793 REORGANIZATION of the Jardin du Roi into the Muséum d'Histoire naturelle[1] and the old Académies into the Institut de France, the first decades of the nineteenth century saw the triumph of the natural sciences in France. These new institutions housed scientific collections unequalled in the whole world and also hosted the work and debates of highly eminent men of science such as Jean-Baptiste Lamarck, Georges Cuvier, and Étienne Geoffroy Saint-Hilaire.

In particular, these decades saw the birth of two major scientific disciplines: geology and paleontology. By the end of the eighteenth century, the word "geology" appeared in today's sense (different from speculative systems previously proposed as "theories of the earth"[2]) in the writings of Jean-André Deluc, a Swiss geologist and meteorologist. Scientists of a new kind now went to the field to produce knowledge about the earth and its history, relying on exploration and empirical observation of phenomena in order to identify permanent causes. In turn, Henri de Blainville coined the term "paleontology" in 1822. Up to that point, savants had used fossil remains mainly as stratigraphic markers because of their positions in the successive layers of the earth. Paleontology now became a separate scientific domain dealing with the history of the living world and the emergence and extinction of successive faunas and floras, considered not only in relationship to the geological history of the world, but also to those organisms' environments and geographic locations. The study of fossils imposed new research practices, new procedures of evidence, and particular kinds of scientific "laws," thus establishing its position among the recognized sciences.

Both disciplines brought about "a great and sudden revolution"[3] that opened the vertiginous dimension of "deep time," affecting even more profoundly the world vision and the imaginations of their contemporaries. At stake in this new notion of "deep time"—formed in the last decades of the eighteenth century, especially in the works of Scottish geologist John Hutton[4]— was a history of the globe and of living beings that largely encompassed the biblical chronology and surmised an immense length of time well beyond human existence and history. If, before the end of the nineteenth century, it

was still impossible to quantify this duration in its absolute value, the successive layers of the earth, the trace of impressive changes and great "revolutions," and the remains of unknown extinct animals and plants provided clues to the expanse of time that predated human existence.

As has often been noted,[5] the mid-nineteenth century saw the decline of the Paris Muséum d'Histoire naturelle and the French natural sciences, especially when compared to the dynamism of German, English, or American research and institutions. During the 1830s, Charles Lyell established the basis for scientific geology in his *Principles of Geology*.[6] The accumulation of empirical research provided evidence for the definition of successive geological stages (Cambrian, Silurian, Carboniferous, Jurassic, and so forth), through the works of English geologists such as Lyell, Adam Sedgwick, Henry Thomas De la Beche, and Charles Murchison. The great British paleontologist Richard Owen, whose scientific efforts aimed to reconcile Cuvier's and Geoffroy's theories,[7] created a new museum of paleontology in London in 1852 (now the famed Natural History Museum). Owen also supervised the construction of life-size models for the Great Exhibition at the Crystal Palace in 1851, giving a new dimension to the popular knowledge of extinct animals. The public could walk in geological landscapes and contemplate (almost) in bone and flesh the "great pachyderms" of the era then known as the Tertiary period and the newly discovered creatures *Megalodon* and *Iguanodon*.[8] In the United States, these decades saw the flourishing of existing institutions such as the American Philosophical Society and the creation of important research institutions and museums, including Louis Agassiz's Museum of Comparative Zoology at Harvard University and the Peale Museum in Baltimore.

In this paper, I will analyze some aspects of the impact of the paradigm shift resulting from the emergence of these sciences in France at the turn of the nineteenth century. I will insist in particular on the contradictions between the demands of scientific rationality in the age of positivism and the importance of imagination and irrationality in the visions engendered by the reconstruction and resurrection of extinct worlds.

THE RATIONAL BASIS OF A DISCIPLINE

Georges Cuvier, an authoritative and charismatic figure, dominated this period (**FIG. 14.1**). He established methods for studying fossils, demonstrated the existence of extinct species, and explained their extinctions, theorizing large disasters that repeatedly destroyed living fauna. His spectacular objects of study (the enormous "Pachyderms,"[9] the quadrupeds whose bones he exhumed from the gypsum quarry of Montmartre), his genius as a man of science, his style and talent as a writer, his international scientific connections, and his position as a public figure made him a leading light in the science, culture, and politics of his time.

Cuvier endeavored to base paleontology upon rational principles according to the "positivist"[10] canons of his time, making it a science equal in accuracy to Isaac Newton's physics. The constitution of paleontological

Fig. 14.1

Antoine Joseph Chollet, after Mme. Lizinska Aimée Zoé de Mirbel and Antoine-Cosme Giraud, Portrait of Georges Cuvier, n.d., colored etching and engraving. APS

CLAUDINE COHEN

evidence first required the establishment of stratigraphy to locate the place of fossils in the successive layers of the earth. Beginning in 1807, Cuvier explored the geology of the Paris Basin with chemist and mineralogist Alexandre Brongniart. Their study aimed to provide not only a geological framework for Cuvier's research, but more broadly to establish a methodological model for determining other sequences in stratigraphic paleontology (FIG. 14.2).

SCIENTIFIC "LAWS"

In the "Discours préliminaire" to his *Recherches sur les ossemens fossiles de quadrupèdes* of 1812,[11] Cuvier presented the physiological "laws" that he claimed would allow one to connect remains to their parent organism in a rigorous fashion. Two sets of structural laws enable this reconstruction of scattered bone fragments into an organized and finalized whole. In *Leçons d'anatomie comparée*, Cuvier had presented the famous principle of "correlation of characters" as a true scientific law with a value of predictability.[12] The principle, which relied on a functional dependence of the different parts of the vertebrate skeleton, was useful for describing the anatomical and physiological organization of living animals. The correlation of characters had a heuristic value for the paleontologist, providing him with a key for reconstructing extinct animals. As Cuvier wrote, "every organized being forms a whole, a single closed system in which all parts meet each other and contribute to the same definitive action by reciprocal reaction. None of these parts can change without triggering a change in the others. And therefore each of them taken separately indicates and gives the others."[13]

The second principle guiding Cuvier's anatomical reconstructions was the "subordination of functions." Cuvier established a hierarchy of physiological functions, with eating habits first. The adaptations of organs to these functions were "living conditions" or final causes. Ideally, within this conceptual framework, he could reconstruct fossil animals in a logical order. Correlation revealed the mechanical organization of the body; subordination confirmed the predominance of characteristic behaviors that adapted it to the environment; and comparison highlighted the similarities and differences among living and fossil species. All these procedures determined the place of the animal within a family and a genus and as a species. This meant the animal could finally be placed accurately, not only through its anatomy, but also by the precise knowledge of its original stratigraphic location at the moment of the find, within its geological environment and fauna. In principle, it would thus be possible to reconstruct a whole, previously unknown animal from a single tooth or bone. Spectacular applications of these "laws" led Cuvier to proclaim that through the practice of anatomical reconstruction, he had founded paleontology as an inductive and predictive science based on rationality and quantification (FIG. 14.3).[14]

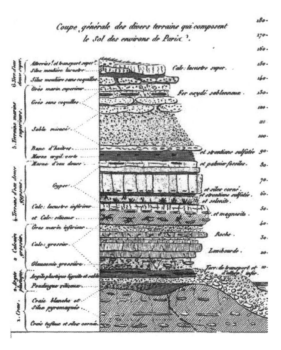

Fig. 14.2

Georges Cuvier and Alexandre Brongniart, Stratigraphy of the Paris Basin, from Cuvier, *Recherches sur les ossemens fossiles de quadrupèdes* (Paris, 1812), vol. 1.

Cuvier's reconstructions also provided a wealth of visual representations. In its form and spatial organization, an image embodies the power to highlight important features of the original specimen such as the sutures of a bone, the muscle attachments, or the facet joints of the spine. An image in itself can thus become an interpretation and even a scientific proof. The illustrations of Cuvier's *Recherches sur les ossemens fossiles de quadrupèdes* concentrated the different demonstrative powers of the image, showing a bone fragment either isolated or located as part of a whole. They also provided comparisons of structures in different animal species, emphasizing the similarities and dissimilarities among species. The image embodied a complex set of procedures and practices, especially when the paleontologist drew the entire skeleton of the animal with the various known bones in place, representing the missing structures with dotted lines. While these reconstructions offered new insight into the deep past, they also offered the possibility of visually representing extinct worlds. When disseminated to the larger public, these new and impressive images had a strong impact on the imagination and culture of the time.

Fig. 14.3

Comparison by Cuvier of the skulls, jaws and limb extremities of three species of elephants: two living (African and Asian elephant on the right) and one extinct (the "Russian mammoth" on the left). Cuvier's 1796 establishment of the existence of an extinct species of elephant can be considered as the "birth act" of vertebrate paleontology. Note that the mammoth skull was not drawn from nature, but was the reproduction of a drawing by Daniel Gottlieb Messerschmidt, an eighteeenth-century traveler-naturalist in Siberia. From Georges Cuvier, *Recherches sur les ossemens fossiles des quadrupèdes*, vol. 2 (Paris, 1812), plate II.

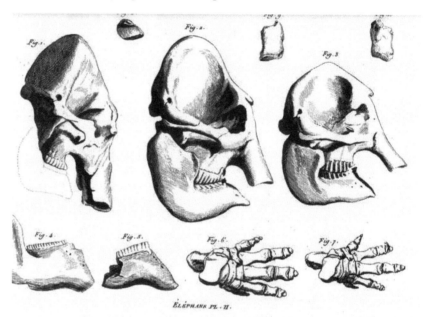

In the years 1830–1850, representations of the geological "eras" became a prolific and iconic genre. Scientific illustrators of the time produced sequences of engravings representing the succession of geological periods. First confined to the popularization of geological science, this type of illustration (which long maintained an ambiguous relationship with biblical imagery, as Martin Rudwick has shown[15]), started to establish itself as a truly scientific genre in the second third of the century. English geologist Henry Thomas De la Beche produced a series of watercolors in 1830,[16] including the famous *Duria Antiquior—A More Ancient Dorset* (**FIG. 14.4**). This image reconstructed the geological landscape and plants in the Jurassic era, along with the interactions between different animals (plesiosaurs, ichthyosaurs, and pterodactyls) whose fossil skeletons had been discovered in the region by Mary Anning[17] a few years earlier. Similarly, in the 1840s Austrian geologist Franz Unger painted a beautiful sequence of geological ages, chronologically organized as a series of landscapes whose vegetation and fauna encompassed available geological and paleontological knowledge. In France, some decades later, Louis Figuier, who specialized in the popularization of science through the explanation and illustration of current scientific discoveries, provided a series of "25 ideal views of the landscapes of the ancient world" in *La Terre avant le déluge of 1863* (**FIGS. 14.5 and 14.6**).[18]

Fig. 14.4 Henry Thomas De la Beche, *Duria Antiquior—A More Ancient Dorset*, 1803. This famous watercolor was painted by the paleontologist and geologist Henry De la Beche to depict the different Jurassic fossil marine animals (including ichthyosaurs and plesiosaurs) whose remains had been found by collector Mary Anning in the cliffs of Dorset. Amgueddfa Cymru – National Museum Wales

SCIENTIFIC IMAGINATION AND THE CONSTRUCTION OF MYTHS

Imagination was not absent from science itself, from the act of reconstructing visually extinct beings and fauna, to the construction of discourse with its use of rhetorical figures, verbal invention, narrative, and fiction for the creation and presentation of knowledge. Tropes such as synecdoche (using a part to indicate the whole) illustrated Cuvier's own methods of investigation and reconstruction. Furthermore, the naming of "lost species" following the principles of Linnaeus's binominal nomenclature was an occasion for extraordinary verbal creativity. A whole language was being invented, with new words whose sounds were both evocative and terrifying (*Megatherium, Megalonyx*), opening multiple poetic resonances at the heart of the scientific discourse.

Cuvier's own choice of his scientific objects (the gigantic quadrupeds) and the story he told (the "revolutions of the earth's surface") contributed to the grandeur of the discourse. Though Cuvier restored order to the succession of beds and gravels that formed the layers of the earth, he also read dramas and cosmic tragedies there: "the piles of debris and boulders, occurring in many places between the solid layers, testify to the strength of the movements that these commotions excite in the expanse of water." And he concluded with tragic emphasis, "life has often been disrupted on this earth by terrible events. . . . Innumerable living beings have been victims of these disasters; some have been destroyed by floods, others have been dried up when the seabed suddenly rose; their races themselves have ended forever, leaving nothing in the world but some debris barely recognizable to the naturalist."[19] The tragic and hyperbolic vocabulary was meant to capture the reader, to make the naturalist into a new hero, and to transform natural history into a new kind of epic.

Scientific development in these areas still included references to antique or biblical myths. Thus, the themes associated with the deep past of the earth and of the living world (giant and monstrous animals, great

Fig. 42. Vue idéale de la terre pendant la période devonienne.

Figs. 14.5 and 14.6

Two of the "ideal views" illustrating Louis Figuier, *La Terre avant le déluge* (Paris, 1863):
"la terre pendant la période dévonienne" and "L'Ichthyosaure et le Plésiosaure
(période du lias [Lower Jurassic])."

Fig. 130. L'Ichthyosaure et le Plésiosaure (période du lias).

CLAUDINE COHEN

cataclysms) were associated with a deluge more or less clearly identified with the biblical Flood. The ambiguous concept of *Diluvium*, coined by geologists, was long used to name the last stratigraphic levels before the advent of man.

Cuvier may well have been, as Balzac had said, "the greatest poet of [his] century."[20] The themes of his scientific work recapitulate biblical and antique mythologies, but also create secular myths. Cuvier, the positive scientist who wanted to equal Newton, also created a fantastic world full of powerful images that endure today in scientific representations as well as in popularized science. Through the dramatic presentation of his findings, he also constructed his own enduring image as a hero in the scientific pantheon. From Cuvier's works and writings emerges the myth of the paleontologist reviving extinct beings, as on the day of resurrection, making them rise to the call of the trumpet of judgment.

POETIC USES OF KNOWLEDGE

Cuvier's "catastrophic" construction echoed the post-Revolution and post-Empire vision of "worlds in ruins." The first decades of the century saw the expansion of a whole imagery of ruins and cataclysms, storms, floods, and abolished worlds, from the writings of François-René de Chateaubriand to Alfred de Musset's *Confession d'un enfant du siècle* of 1836 and Jules Michelet's and François Guizot's narratives of the French Revolution.[21] Images of disasters and floods haunted romantic dreams, and an indulgence in the macabre, such as ruins and tombs, is also reflected in "Gothic" literature.

The poetic use of geological and paleontological knowledge inspired a number of literary endeavors in France. Abbé Jacques Delille composed a long didactic poem, *Les Trois règnes de la nature*, published in 1809,[22] for which Cuvier agreed to write scientific annotations. Pierre Boitard used paleontological discoveries extensively in *Paris avant l'histoire*, a narrative of his imaginary travels into different ages of the prehistoric past with descriptions of the extinct geological and faunal landscapes.

Louis Bouilhet's *Les fossiles* exemplifies the genre of scientific poetry dedicated to geology and paleontology. Written between 1852 and 1854, this long poem narrates the successive appearance of flora, fauna, and man through geological time. Bouilhet's work is remarkable for its effort to incorporate scientific knowledge into a lyrical and epic form, rich in evocative images. He presented the successive episodes of the history of life on earth in a colorful vocabulary, sprinkled with brilliant metaphors and uncommon words. Alternations of silence and noise, violence and calm, light and darkness punctuate the poem. Each section was arranged according to a similar pattern: a landscape, initially immobile, suddenly becomes animated to feature the movement of life in the making, driven by expressive gestures, and presented each time as a development of a spectacular scene. These rich literary depictions allow the reader to "see" successive episodes in the development of life.

While Bouilhet's poem owed much to Cuvier's paleontology, it also relied upon his deep knowledge of classical literature: the works of Ovid and Lucretius were obvious sources. It also reflects a "Parnassian" aesthetic close to Charles-Marie Leconte de Lisle's[23] and a conception of writing similar to Gustave Flaubert's "art for art's sake." The writing of this poem, dedicated specifically to Flaubert, had been the subject of intense discussions, correspondence, and critical exchanges between the two friends. Despite the importance Bouilhet himself accorded to his poem, however, and Flaubert's efforts to publicize the work,[24] *Les fossiles* sank into oblivion soon after its first publication. One reason may be that the poem came too late; its scientific information, especially regarding the emergence of humanity, was already obsolete at the time of its publication as a book in 1859, the year of Charles Darwin's *On the Origin of Species*.

Well into the 1860s, Cuvier's catastrophism remained highly prominent in France. His influence extended long past his death in 1832 and his disciples disseminated his teachings with some dogmatism. Scientific works such as *Le Système des montagnes* by Léonce Élie de Beaumont (1852), *Introduction à la géologie* by Omalius d'Halloy (1833), *L'Histoire des plantes fossiles* by Adolphe Brongniart (1828), and *Les Lettres sur les révolutions du globe* by Alexander Bertrand (1824) enriched and disseminated geological and paleontological knowledge while remaining true to Cuvierian thought. In the eight volumes of his *Cours élémentaire de géologie et de paléontologie* published between 1849 and 1852, Alcide d'Orbigny[25] gave a systematic and detailed account of paleontological stratigraphy. He supported the notion of a history of the globe with twenty-two successive episodes separated by great catastrophes, claiming that each new level and its fauna and flora corresponded to a new creation. Although this claim was probably implicit in Cuvier's thinking, he had never explained it overtly.

If universal tribute was paid to Cuvier, criticism of his scientific system had been growing in France even during his lifetime. Cuvier had strongly criticized and even ridiculed Lamarck's transformism; in fact, Lamarck's works were largely dismissed during the second third of the century. Nevertheless, extensive discussions about the transformation of the living world and the antiquity of man occurred in non-academic circles, especially in provincial learned societies, whose members were often amateurs or less prominent scientific figures. The famed 1830 debate at the Paris Académie des sciences over the "unity of composition" had seen Cuvier's victory over Étienne Geoffroy Saint-Hilaire. By the 1840s, however, Geoffroy's concepts, inherited from German *Naturphilosophie,* became useful for a number of scientific endeavors.[26] Moreover, the mystic and poetic dimension that unfolded in his vision of the natural world aligned with the romantic imagination, inspiring the works of great novelists of the first half of the century such as Victor Hugo, George Sand, and even Honoré de Balzac. In the *Comédie humaine,* Balzac paid homage to Cuvier's talent for reconstructing lost worlds, but even more spectacularly invoked Geoffroy's concept of "unity of composition" in the living realm to illustrate the novelist's own ambitious literary project.[27]

French natural science of the heroic first decades of the century, following the Revolution and the Empire, remained a model and a reference for many further productions in the sciences and the arts. It had established the basis for a rational understanding of the past of life, shaken the ancient representation of the world's history, and established a whole new vision, offering a fully revised account of the origin and fate of the world, a novel kind of history. It had opened the realm of imagination and provided enduring images that even now remain deeply rooted in our representations.

1   For a thorough study of the new organization of the Muséum d'Histoire naturelle in 1793, and its institutional and intellectual consequences, see *Le Muséum au premier siècle de son histoire,* ed. Claude Blanckaert, Claudine Cohen, Pietro Corsi, and Jean-Louis Fischer (Paris: Éditions du Muséum national d'Histoire naturelle, 1997).

2   Gottfried Wilhelm Leibniz, *Protogaea,* trans. and ed. Claudine Cohen and Andre Wakefield (Chicago: University of Chicago Press, 2008); and Claudine Cohen, *Science, libertinage et clandestinité à l'aube des Lumières: Le transformisme de Telliamed* (Paris: Presses Universitaires de France, 2011).

3   This phrase is taken from Cuvier's *Discours sur les révolutions de la surface du globe,* 6th French ed. (Paris: Edmond d'Ocagne, 1830), 290: "S'il y a quelque chose de constaté en géologie, c'est que la surface de notre globe a été victime d'une grande et subite révolution."

4   As early as 1788, and then in his *Theory of the Earth* (1795), John Hutton explained that he saw "no vestige of a beginning, no prospect of an end" in geological evidence. Hutton, "Theory of the Earth; or, An Investigation of the Laws Observable in the Composition, Dissolution, and Restoration of Land upon the Globe," *Transactions of the Royal Society of Edinburgh* 1, no. 2 (1788): 304. His friend, mathematician John Playfair, wrote after their shared visit to Siccar Point in June 1788 and their observation of an angular unconformity in the succession of stata, that "the mind seemed to grow giddy by looking so far into the abyss of time." John Playfair, "Biographical

Account of the Late Dr[.] James Hutton, F.R.S. Edin.," *Transactions of the Royal Society of Edinburgh* 5, no. 3 (1805): 73.

5 See Camille Limoges, "The Development of the Muséum d'Histoire naturelle of Paris, c. 1800–1914," in *The Organization of Science and Technology in France, 1808–1914*, ed. Robert Fox and George Weisz (Cambridge: Cambridge University Press, 1980).

6 Charles Lyell, *Principles of Geology: Being an Attempt to Explain the Former Changes of the Earth's Surface, by Reference to Causes Now in Operation*, 3 vols. (London: Murray, 1830–33). See Martin J. S. Rudwick, *Worlds Before Adam: The Reconstruction of Geological Time in the Age of Reform* (Chicago: University of Chicago Press, 2008).

7 On Owen, see Nicolaas A. Rupke, *Richard Owen: Victorian Naturalist* (New Haven, Conn.: Yale University Press, 1994).

8 On the life-size reconstructions of extinct animals at the Crystal Palace, see, for example, Steve McCarthy and Mick Gilbert, *The Crystal Palace Dinosaurs: The Story of the World's First Prehistoric Sculptures* (London: Crystal Palace Foundation, 1994); and Martin J. S. Rudwick, *Scenes from Deep Time: Early Pictorial Representations of the Prehistoric World* (Chicago: University of Chicago Press, 1992).

9 Cuvier created the order *Pachydermata* (etymologically, "animals with thick skin") in 1797–98 to name the huge mammals (extinct species of rhinoceros, elephants, mastodons) that peopled the earth before the last "catastrophe." See Cuvier, *Tableau élémentaire de l'histoire naturelle des animaux* (Paris: Baudouin, Imprimeur du Corps législatif et de l'Institut national, an VI [1797/98]), 150. The taxon, considered too wide and disparate, is obsolete today.

10 Auguste Comte developed positivism as a philosophical system between 1830 and 1845. The word is used here in a broader meaning, to describe the absolute

value assigned to science and scientific rationality. This ideal was already expressed in the works of eighteenth-century thinkers such as Jean Le Rond d'Alembert, Joseph Louis Lagrange, or Jean-Antoine-Nicolas de Caritat, the Marquis de Condorcet.

11 Georges Cuvier, "Discours préliminaire," in *Recherches sur les ossemens fossiles de quadrupèdes, où l'on rétablit les caractères de plusieurs espèces d'animaux que les révolutions du globe paroissent avoir détruites*, vol. 1 (Paris: Déterville, 1812), 58 *et seq.*

12 Georges Cuvier, *Leçons d'anatomie comparée* (Paris: Baudouin, 1800–5); Cuvier, *Le règne animal distribué d'après son organisation, pour servir de base à l'histoire naturelle des animaux et d'introduction à l'anatomie comparée*, 4 vols. (Paris: Déterville, 1817).

13 "Tout être organisé forme un ensemble, un système unique et clos, dont toutes les parties se correspondent mutuellement, et concourent à la même action définitive par une réaction réciproque. Aucune de ces parties ne peut changer sans que les autres changent aussi; et par conséquent chacune d'elles, prise séparément, indique et donne toutes les autres." Cuvier, "Discours préliminaire," *Recherches sur les ossemens fossiles*, 58.

14 On Cuvier's methods, on his claim for scientificity, and more generally on the question of "laws" in paleontology, see Claudine Cohen, *La Méthode de Zadig: La trace, le fossile, la preuve* (Paris: Éditions de Seuil, 2011).

15 Rudwick, *Scenes from Deep Time.*

16 See ibid.

17 Mary Anning was a local collector of fossils in Lyme Regis (Dorset) who provided important specimens to the principal geologists and paleontologists of the time, such as William Buckland, Henry Thomas De la Beche, Joseph Prestwich, and others. See Hugh Torrens, "Mary Anning (1799–1847) of Lyme: 'The Greatest Fossilist the World ever Knew,'" *British Journal for the History of Science* 28, no. 3 (1995): 257–84.

18 The title page announced "25 vues idéales de paysages de l'ancien monde, dessinées par Riou; 310 autres figures et 7 cartes géologiques coloriées." Louis Figuier, *La Terre avant le déluge* (Paris: L. Hachette, 1863).

19 "Les déchiremens, les bouleversemens de couches arrivés dans les catastrophes antérieures, montrent assez qu'elles étoient subites et violentes comme la dernière; et des amas de débris et de cailloux roulés, placés en plusieurs endroits entre les couches solides, attestent la force des mouvemens que ces bouleversemens excitoient dans la masse des eaux.... La vie a donc souvent été troublée sur cette terre par des événemens terribles; calamités qui, dans les commencemens, ont peut-être remué dans une grande épaisseur l'enveloppe entière de la planète, mais qui depuis sont toujours devenues moins profondes et moins générales. Des êtres vivans sans nombre ont été les victimes de ces catastrophes; les uns ont été détruits par des déluges, les autres ont été mis à sec avec le fond des mers subitement relevé; leurs races même ont fini pour jamais, et ne laissent dans le monde que quelques débris à peine reconnoissables pour le naturaliste." Cuvier, "Discours préliminaire," *Recherches sur les ossemens fossiles*, 11–12.

20 "Cuvier n'est-il pas le plus grand poète de notre siècle?" Honoré de Balzac, *La Peau de chagrin, roman philosophique* (Paris, 1831), chap. 1.

21 Jules Michelet, *Histoire de la Révolution française*, 7 vols. (Paris, 1847–53); François Guizot, *Histoire de la civilisation en France*, 5 vols. (Paris, 1829–32).

22 Jacques Delille, *Les Trois règnes de la nature*, 3 vols. (Paris, 1809).

23 Charles-Marie Leconte de Lisle was the author of three major collections of poems, *Poèmes antiques* (1852), *Poèmes barbares* (1862), and *Poèmes tragiques* (1883). Along with Théophile Gautier and Théodore de Banville, he was the founder of a French school of poetry

named "le Parnasse" that developed in the second half of the nineteenth century. In opposition to the Romantics of the previous generation, they refused the expression of personal feelings in poetry and declared for formal perfection and themes inspired by antique models and scientific knowledge.

24 See, for example, Flaubert's very eulogistic preface to *Les Fossiles* in the posthumous edition of Bouilhet's works, *Dernières chansons: Poésies posthumes de Louis Bouilhet* (Paris: Michel Lévy Frères, 1872).

25 Alcide d'Orbigny was the author of an authoritative three-volume synthesis of bio-stratigraphic knowledge of his time: *Cours élémentaire de paléontologie et de géologie stratigraphiques* (Paris, 1849–52).

26 See Claudine Cohen, "De la biologie au roman: Le modèle morphologique et ses variations," *Romantisme*, no. 138 (May 2007): 47–59.

27 See Honoré de Balzac, "Avant-propos," *La Comédie humaine* (Paris, 1842), and Göran Blix's essay in this volume.

SOCIAL SPECIES IN THE *COMÉDIE HUMAINE*: BALZAC'S USE OF NATURAL HISTORY

GÖRAN BLIX

THE GREAT FRENCH NOVELIST HONORÉ DE BALZAC famously based his study of contemporary society on the model of natural history, setting out to do in the *Comédie humaine* for humanity what the Comte de Buffon had done for the animal kingdom. His work would offer an exhaustive description of the various social species that peopled nineteenth-century France. This analogy, spelled out in the "Avant-propos" (foreword), suggests political implications that have often puzzled and exercised commentators, especially since Balzac referred at the same time to the famous quarrel that arose between naturalists Georges Cuvier and Étienne Geoffroy Saint-Hilaire in 1830 over the so-called "unity of composition." Balzac took Geoffroy's side in this controversy in contending that all animals shared a common structural blueprint and only became differentiated into distinct species through their encounter with different environments. Cuvier, on the contrary, discerned at least four irreducible classes, and treated species as static entities with clearly marked boundaries.[1] This quarrel has been read, rightly or wrongly, as a confrontation between fixism and transformism, and readers of Balzac have long wondered about its political implications for his notion of "social species."[2] Did the belief in fixed social types imply the vision of an organicist caste society, and did the endless mutability of species imply, on the contrary, abstract equality and social mobility? And if so, how could Balzac's choice of Geoffroy be reconciled with his reactionary stance, his lifelong homage to Cuvier, and his obvious mania for classifying the actors in his novels? By way of answer, I will argue, first, that Balzac's unwavering praise of Cuvier had nothing to do with fixism; secondly, that his concept of the "social species" in no way committed him to the organicist vision of a caste society; thirdly, that his mania for classifying did indeed imply a desire to impose order—but less on society itself than on his own ambitious and unwieldy project; and lastly, that Geoffroy's "unity of life" allowed Balzac to look beyond his love of classification in order to capture instead what he called the "infinite variety" of human characters—or what we might call the universal monstrosity of the human condition.[3]

It is not hard to find evidence that Balzac conceived of social species as rigid entities allowing little chance of passage from one social destiny to another. This could of course be dismissed as a superficial ideological veneer reflecting Balzac's reactionary outlook, since in practice his novels chart the reality of social mobility in post-revolutionary France. His protagonists, whether they succeed or not, are always on the move, socially speaking, and often enough owe the beginnings of their fortune to the turmoil of the revolutionary period. But it should be remembered that the parvenu's success is often only apparent. Though the enriched merchant Père Goriot, for instance, succeeds in marrying off his daughters above his own station, they retain ineffaceable traces of their modest origins; thus Delphine de Nucingen still "betrays the Goriot in all her movements."[4] Marriage across class lines is also often a recipe for disastrous disappointments, as when the noble painter in *La Maison du Chat-qui-pelote*, Théodore de Sommervieux, marries a textile merchant's daughter who reminds him of Raphael's Madonnas. This relationship quickly turns sour, however, when the social and intellectual mismatch dawns on Théodore. His vanity was offended when Augustine, "despite her vain efforts, revealed her ignorance, the impropriety of her language, and the narrowness of her ideas."[5] Social mobility may be real, then, but it is often mere theater or masquerade, powerless to efface the inherited stamp of vulgarity, which always threatens to reappear and unravel the parvenu's achievements.

Balzac's use of natural history often seems to confirm this reactionary social pessimism. He referred to social species as fixed entities that were also numbered, premeditated, and carefully distributed in the cosmic order. Balzac suggested as much in *Le Député d'Arcis* when he presented the character of Philéas Beauvisage: "had God wanted," he wrote, "to put a provincial bourgeois in that place to complete his Species, he could not with his own hands have created a better, more perfect type than Philéas Beauvisage."[6] Elsewhere he noted that "Society is another Nature" and claimed that "Social Nature [*la Nature Sociale*] arms each species with the qualities necessary for the services it expects," as if society purposely shaped and distributed its members according to a master plan.[7] Most explicitly, perhaps, in the novel *Béatrix*, which starts out in the western provincial town of Guérande, Balzac stated that "the bourgeoisie, the nobility, and the clergy" remain clearly distinct categories, and that "the character of immutability that nature has conferred on its zoological species is reproduced here among men." Likewise, the sailors, peasants, and *paludiers* (salt collectors) in Guérande remain as distinct as "castes [are] in India." However, despite these categorical claims, Balzac was careful to stress that Guérande is in fact a town apart, "fervently Catholic and essentially Breton, closed to new ideas," which has resisted the leveling impact of 1789 and 1830.[8] Balzac thus seems to have acknowledged, at least implicitly, that social species elsewhere, in places swept by the Revolution, no longer possessed this rigid character, and that "the immutability of zoological species" offered a very poor analogy for modern society.

Indeed, every time Balzac resorted to this analogy, which clearly seduced him and allowed him to freeze the human comedy briefly in an intelligible constellation, it began to break down. Even in the programmatic text of the "Avant-propos," which sets out to theorize explicitly the "comparison of Humanity and Animality," Balzac appeared to lose sight of his purpose quickly, listing so many qualifications, complications, and asymmetries that the analogy begins to seem pointless. He wrote, for instance, that "Nature has set out barriers for animal species that Society is not obliged to observe" and that "the Social State involves randomness that Nature does not permit." Moreover, while the behavior of any given animal species remains constant and predictable, human habits, clothes, speech, and dwellings clearly differ both between men and civilizations. "Society," he finally admitted, is not just Nature; it is in fact "Nature plus Society"—a definition that one would have to call recursive, or at any rate unhelpful for an understanding of the analogy.[9]

But if Balzac did not believe in fixed species and sided with Geoffroy in the zoological controversy, why then did he continue to invoke Cuvier as the "greatest poet of our century," as he wrote in *La Peau de chagrin*,[10] and cite his name far more frequently than Geoffroy's in the *Comédie humaine*? Cuvier's name, I contend, did not primarily mean fixism for Balzac—as it did in the context of the controversy—but something entirely different, a type of inspired gaze he hoped to emulate. His standard homage to Cuvier refers inevitably to the naturalist's ability to reconstruct an entire animal from a mere bone fragment, and this quasi-magical power is also what Cuvier's name connotes more generally in nineteenth-century letters, rather than classification and fixism. This skill fascinated Balzac because it paralleled his own method of invention; given a face, a portrait, or a figure glimpsed in the crowd, Balzac liked to think he could extrapolate the person's character, history, and hidden dramas. Cuvier's power of reconstructing a coherent picture from a handful of scattered clues made him the very model of genius. Thus nothing about Cuvier's zoological doctrines really affected the *Comédie humaine*, but his genius and method, on the other hand, had real applications both for the author himself and for the promethean characters who shared his genius. Thus the master-criminal Vautrin, for instance, "divined truly in the sphere of crime, just as Molière did in the sphere of dramatic poetry and Cuvier with his vanished creations."[11] By the same token, the clairvoyant judge Desplein penetrated the inmost conscience of criminals the way a surgeon cuts open a body: "he prepared a trial much like Cuvier excavated the soil of the globe. Like that great thinker, he went from deduction to deduction before concluding, and reproduced the past of the conscience just as Cuvier reconstructed an anoplotherium" (a fossilized mammal).[12] The examples are endless. Cuvier was essentially the name of a hermeneutic procedure, a type of intuitive gaze central to Balzac's creative process as well as to his most gifted heroes. It should be recalled that genius was less a specific gift for Balzac than a form of intellectual capital applicable almost everywhere. Cuvier just happened to be the most compelling emblem for this power, which Vautrin, Desplein, Napoleon, and Balzac each exhibited in his own sphere.

Balzac's romance with natural history clearly exceeded any reference to Cuvier's fixism. Beyond adhering to any particular doctrine, Balzac paid tribute to natural history itself as a sort of indispensable master science. The reader often receives the impression that the discipline is required knowledge for anyone who wants to grasp the social process from above—or at least to avoid becoming the victim of the reckless beings that possess such insight. César Birotteau, the unhappy perfume merchant who "did not know an iota of natural history," suffered a catastrophic bankruptcy.[13] Incompetent husbands who micromanage their wives, said Balzac in the *Physiologie du mariage*, "understand no more of life than a nitwit knows about natural history."[14] Natural history would seem to confer a sort of practical wisdom that made its possessor less naive and gullible, more circumspect, and better equipped to succeed in the social jungle—despite the fact that life in nature, as the "Avant-propos" acknowledged, appears to be a great deal simpler than in society. "Among animals, there are few dramas, and little confusion; they just pounce on each other, that's all. Men," Balzac hastened to add, "clearly also pounce on each other, but their varying degrees of intelligence make this struggle much more complicated."[15]

But above all, natural history armed the novelist with a larger perspective, giving him a sort of master template for mapping society. Sounding somewhat like Émile Zola, his naturalist heir, Balzac referred at one point to the "naturalists of the novel" who had the literary mission of finding uncharted social types and manners.[16] Thus, for instance, "the mother and daughter in search of a husband," Balzac stated, are two social types that have so far been neglected by the "naturalists [who have nonetheless] depicted the behavior of many [other] ferocious animals."[17] Balzac's ideal novelist thus resembled the natural historian—but how, in what way precisely? He certainly studied the behavior of social animals, charting their battles and their efforts to survive and prevail. But he also believed that the naturalist should ascribe a set of traits and behaviors to a particular species, and go on to group that species into a hierarchical system of genera, families, orders, and so on—an organized system that Balzac at one point called "the sacred nomenclature . . . of natural history."[18] Studying the animal kingdom was on some level inseparable from the labor of classifying it. It was above all this formidable machinery of classification that impressed Balzac, providing him with the logic that underpins the main division of the *Comédie humaine* into a series of studies of private, provincial, Parisian, political, military, and country life. I should also stress here that Balzac's love of classification appears to go far beyond his apparent obsession with identifying distinct social types. It even embraces any human phenomenon worthy of reflection; at one point, for instance, he suggested that there might be a "natural history of the heart" that could "name them, class them into genera, sub-genera, families, crustaceans, fossils, [and] saurians."[19] Elsewhere, he noted that the "ideas and feelings" of the "moral kingdom . . . can be as varied as the species of the vegetable kingdom."[20] This is a critical point, because it shows that Balzac's obsession with typology may not be centered on ordering society and assigning each type its proper station in life, but should perhaps rather be seen as an analytical move meant to reduce the dizzying complexity of the world.

Let us take a closer look at how Balzac used classification. Undoubtedly, the main feature Balzac borrowed from natural history was its power to classify. He insisted that the "physiologist"—as he called himself—had the right to "establish his genera and sub-genera" just like the naturalist.[21] Indeed, when Balzac presented the reader with a new and noteworthy social type, he generally made an effort to situate it in a larger grouping of cognate types. Such meta-groups may be geographically grounded, such as the Parisian, the Tourangeau, or the provincial more broadly; but their logic may also be social, professional, sexual, conjugal, moral, or intellectual. The bureaucrat, for instance, makes up one subfamily, as do the notary, merchant, artist, rentier, peasant, and so on; but as Balzac succumbed to his irrepressible urge to classify, his socio-professional typology often gave way to strange and seemingly arbitrary categories. Thus he distinguished not just the class of women generally, or Parisian women in particular, but specifically bad Parisian women, or husbands prone to infidelity, successful idiots, brainless writers, savages, dandies, *flâneurs*, superior men, journal editors, travelers, and envious people. Each of these bizarre categories constitutes, at least for a fleeting moment, a coherent group that Balzac could call a social species and then break down into further nuances or package directly as a literary type. The Parisian woman, for instance, was too general for his purposes, so he proposed to distinguish "several species of women [in Paris . . .]: the duchess, the financier's wife, the ambassador's wife, the consul's wife, the minister's wife and the ex-minister's wife, the *rive droite* woman and the *rive gauche* woman."[22]

Balzac quite clearly possessed the demon of classification, and he classified as a matter of course, spontaneously, for sheer pleasure, taking joy in the quintessential gesture of separating humanity into distinct groups. Thus there were the young men in Paris, Balzac told us, and then there were the young men everywhere else; the former "can be [further] divided into two classes: the young man who has something and the young man who has nothing; or the young man who thinks [*pense*] and the one who spends [*dépense*]."[23] What might have been a purely descriptive phrase for another writer—the simple presentation of a penniless young man in Paris— became for Balzac a rather arbitrary occasion to cook up some categories and plant his figures in a dubious intuitive spectrum. Classification also gave the author an obvious intellectual thrill and sense of mastery, promoting him to a superior being, a sort of entomologist of the human comedy, at once pitying and laughing at his human insects. Indeed, it can hardly be an accident that Balzac favored primitive life forms in his zoological analogies. He incessantly compared men to sponges, polyps, insects, snails, and so on, but his favorite trope was no doubt the mollusk. Thus he likened Poiret in *Le Père Goriot* to a "snail, an anthropomorphic mollusk to be classed among the *Casquettifères*,"[24] much like the *boule* players in *Ferragus* who belong "to the genera of mollusks . . . if it is permissible to assimilate Parisians to the different zoological classes."[25] Similarly, he described a gullible capitalist in *La Peau de chagrin* as a "species of sponge overlooked by the naturalists in the order of Polyps," not for any good scientific reason, obviously, but because a sponge—especially one flush with cash—begs to be squeezed.[26] Even when Balzac deigned to call someone a mammal, it was not necessarily a compliment. Consider the indolent bureaucrats in *Les Employés*, whom Balzac perniciously called "feathered mammals" (*mammifères à plumes*) belonging to the "*nation plumigère*."[27] Clearly, the entire zoological analogy, and the license to classify it gave the author, owed much of its appeal to the quasi-divine power it conferred.

Given Balzac's playful and mischievous ways of classifying, one might wonder how serious he was about becoming the Buffon of Society, and whether he truly thought his social species had any ontological solidity.[28] I believe that he was never really the dupe of the pseudoscientific program he adopted, not simply because his species so clearly overlap, bleed into each other, fail to form larger systems, and owe their existence to arbitrary criteria. But more fundamentally, Geoffroy's unitary hypothesis, which Balzac translated in the "Avant-propos" as the claim that "there is only one animal," radically undermined all classification by making all life consubstantial. "The oyster, the coral polyp, the lion, the zoophyte, the microscopic animal, and man [would] all be the same apparatus," the novelist wrote in his satirical fable about the Cuvier-Geoffroy controversy.[29] In this curious text, called "Guide-Âne," which took the form of a guidebook purporting to help "animals who wish to attain an honorable station," Balzac went so far as to suggest that all animal life is essentially driven by a single instinct. As the donkey in the fable put it, his master and he "very much liked to be busy doing nothing and living well. This penchant common to Donkeys and Men is called ambition." He gave the donkey a single overriding concern: "will I ever be an animal couched on the grass of the budget?"[30] Both happily attain this objective when the donkey's master, Marmus, alias Geoffroy, invents the new science of *Instinctologie*, which successfully overturns the dominant theory of Baron Cerceau, alias Cuvier, by positing a radical zoological unity based on a single universal instinct. Instead of morphology, as in Geoffroy's theory, here instinct takes distinct forms as species diverge, but the unitary principle remains identical. Indeed, for the human zoologist, one might speculate that instinct is simply a code word for passion. In this case, Balzac's interest in the unitary theory of life could be explained as a desire to posit something like a single human passion infinitely varied by circumstances.[31] Even if, in the human sphere, this quintessential instinct took no more uplifting form than the desire for "gold" and "pleasure"—as Balzac suggested at the outset of *La Fille aux yeux d'or*—it would be difficult to avoid the political implication that all social species are fundamentally equal. No wonder Marmus meets establishment resistance: "you will be slandered," he is told. "Look what happened to Jesus Christ who proclaimed the equality of souls as you wish to proclaim the unity of life."[32] Despite Balzac's reactionary stance, then, he was clearly conscious of the political implications of Geoffroy's thesis, and did nothing to distance himself from it.

The species-rhetoric that pervades the *Comédie humaine* should therefore not be taken too literally. Classification was, for Balzac, a literary method rather than an ideology. Its auxiliary status as a tool is obvious from his awareness of its dangers and limitations. Geoffroy's disciple in the "Guide-Âne," reacting to the "barriers" that Cuvier has placed between species, notes that "nomenclatures are good to give ourselves an account of differences," but they can no longer be considered—if all life is truly one—as genuine "science."[33] Rather, they are useful simplifications designed to deal with what the "Avant-propos" calls "the infinite variety of human nature."[34] Balzac never denied this infinite variety, this teeming multiplicity that makes humanity so difficult to map. He never let his own interpretive grid obscure the irreducible singularity of the individuals it was meant to capture. In *L'Interdiction*, he offered a telling comparison between the divine and the human perspective, noting that "a judge is not God, his duty is to adapt facts to principles, and to judge species that are infinitely varied using a fixed measure."[35] Thus the human observer, Balzac admitted, is unable to do justice to the infinite diversity of individuals, and has to resort to common measures that erase their differences. Alternatively, this observer must think in terms of social species, as Balzac himself did. For the author, the social type is an expedient, not a reality; it is a tool made necessary by his ambition to capture the totality of the social spectacle. In order to be written, the "infinite variety" of humanity had to be reduced to what Balzac called the "drama of three or four thousand characters which a Society presents."[36] Indeed, the type theorized by Balzac in the "Avant-propos" has no intrinsic reality: it is merely a hermeneutic fiction constructed by the "assembly of traits from multiple homogeneous characters."[37]

Little wonder, then, that Balzac's efforts to classify often sound rather tongue-in-cheek, as if they sought simultaneously to affirm and undercut the virtues of classification. The *Physiologie de l'employé*, for instance, begins by tackling the insoluble conundrum: "what is an *employé*? At what rank does the *employé* begin, and finish?"[38] If one followed the revolutionary principles of 1830, Balzac scoffed, this class would comprise everyone from the concierge to the king, so it is necessary to establish precise criteria that would exclude such figures as the soldier, the customs officer, the prefect, and the statesman. The arbitrariness of the procedure, however, led Balzac, apparently laughing at his own efforts, to fall back into his initial dilemma, exclaiming again: "where does *employé* end? A grave matter!"[39] His foray into the "subtle distinctions" of bureaucratic zoology reached an aporia when he found himself obliged to invent neutral, intermediary classes to prevent his sub-groups from collapsing: the customs-officer thus became a "neutral" between the soldier and the bureaucrat, while the prefect was a "neutral" between the statesman and the bureaucrat.[40] It is as if Balzac's satire of the bureaucracy had led him to imitate its own manic quest for distinctions, and as if the very attempt to classify the *employé* became a comical illustration of the figure's stupidity.

At his best, Balzac tended to perform the opposite gesture. Rather than classifying a character, he tried to grasp its hybrid, multiple, and idiosyncratic nature by destabilizing the reader's ready-made categories. Thus later in this same text the *employé* morphs into "something marvelous, common, and rare, something unique and ordinary, drawing at once on the plant, the animal, the mollusk and the bee."[41] The type paradoxically becomes a unique, unnatural, and unrepeatable phenomenon, an unstable encounter of disparate passions and forces, much like the Parisian "clerk" (*caissier*) whose praise Balzac sang in *Melmoth réconcilié*. The clerk, he said there, was "a hybrid species," impossible to imagine in any other setting, a "genuine anthropomorphic product, irrigated by religious ideas, held upright by the guillotine, pruned by vices, and which grows on the third floor between a respectable woman and troublesome children."[42]

As the clerk-figure suggests, the Balzacian type is thus more often a fragile hybrid produced by chance than a stable ideal. There is no doubt, of course, that Balzac wanted to create representative types that might serve as class emblems, but as often as not, these templates crack open to reveal an unclassifiable figure beneath—or are themselves exposed as ad hoc creations valid only for a brief moment. In the end, Balzac's sense of nuance and his fascination for the grotesque singularity overshadowed his urge to classify. The *Comédie humaine* is more a repertory of monsters than of neatly distinguishable species, more a cabinet of curiosities than a well-ordered museum of natural history. The opening of *Le Père Goriot* probably gives a better description of his literary program than the "Avant-propos" does: "Paris is a veritable ocean," he wrote there. "Throw in a sounding-line, you will never reach the bottom. Travel across it, describe it! However thoroughly you explore and describe . . . there will always be a wilderness, a hidden den, flowers, pearls, monsters, something incredible, forgotten by the divers of literature." Balzac then goes on to present the hostel of Madame Vauquer, not as a representative institution, but rather as "one of these curious monstrosities," and its motley crew of lodgers struck him much less as types than as impenetrable enigmas.[43]

1   For a useful summary of the debate, see Jean Piveteau, "Le débat entre Cuvier et Geoffroy Saint-Hilaire sur l'unité de plan et de composition," *Revue d'histoire des sciences et de leurs applications* 3, no. 4 (1950): 343–63.

2   The question of Balzac's relative debt to Cuvier and Geoffroy Saint-Hilaire (which is not my main concern here) has often been discussed. For an overview of these varied assessments, see Richard Somerset, "The Naturalist in Balzac: The Relative Influence of Cuvier and Geoffroy Saint-Hilaire," *French Forum* 27, no. 1 (Winter 2002): 81–111. See also Madeleine Fargeaud, *Balzac et la recherché de l'absolu* (Paris: Hachette, 1968), 182–92; and Françoise Gaillard, "La science: Modèle ou vérité; Réflexions sur *l'avant-propos* à La Comédie humaine" in *Balzac: L'invention du roman,* ed. Claude Duchet and Jacques Neefs (Paris: Pierre Belfond, 1982), 57–83.

3   "Quoique, pour ainsi dire, ébloui par la fécondité surprenante de Walter Scott, toujours semblable à lui-même et toujours original, je ne fus pas désespéré, car je trouvai la raison de ce talent dans l'infinie variété de la nature humaine." Balzac, "Avant-propos," *La Comédie humaine*, vol. 1 (Paris: Gallimard-Pléiade, 1976), 11.

4   "Le Goriot perce dans tous ses mouvements." Balzac, *Le Père Goriot* (Paris: Gallimard, 1971), 170.

5   "Elle commença par offenser la vanité de son mari, quand, malgré de vains efforts, elle laissa percer son ignorance, l'impropriété de son langage et l'étroitesse de ses idées." Balzac, *La Maison du Chat-qui-pelote* (Paris: Gallimard, 1970), 69. Balzac here uses the same word, *percer*, as he does for Goriot's daughter.

6   "Dieu, dans son paradis terrestre, aurait voulu, pour y compléter les Espèces, y mettre un bourgeois de province, il n'aurait pas fait de ses mains un type plus beau, plus complet que Philéas Beauvisage." Balzac, *Le Député d'Arcis* (Paris: Furne, 1854), 395.

7   "Décidément la Nature Sociale arme toutes ses Espèces des qualités nécessaires aux services qu'elle en attend! La société c'est une autre Nature!" Balzac, *Splendeurs et misères des courtisanes* (Paris: Furne, 1846), 460.

8   "Ces deux classes [les Paludiers et les Paysans] . . . sont aussi distinctes entre elles que les castes de l'Inde, et reconnaissent encore les distances qui séparent la bourgeoisie, la noblesse et le clergé. . . . Le caractère d'immuabilité que la nature a donné à ses espèces zoologiques se retrouve là chez les hommes. Enfin, même après la révolution de 1830, Guérande est encore une ville à part, essentiellement bretonne, catholique fervente, silencieuse, recueillie, où les idées nouvelles ont peu d'accès." Balzac, *Béatrix* (Paris: Gallimard, 1979), 29.

9   "Cette idée vint d'une comparaison entre l'Humanité et l'Animalité. . . . Mais la Nature a posé, pour les variétés animales, des bornes entre lesquelles la Société ne devait pas se tenir. . . . L'État Social a des hasards que ne se permet pas la Nature, car il est la Nature plus la Société." Balzac, "Avant-propos," 7–8.

10 "Cuvier n'est-il pas le plus grand poète de notre siècle?" Balzac, *La Peau de chagrin* (Paris: Gallimard, 1974), 47.

11 "Ainsi, cet homme prodigieux devinait vrai dans sa sphère de crime, comme Molière dans la sphère de la poésie dramatique, comme Cuvier avec les créations disparues." Balzac, *Splendeurs et misères des courtisanes* (Paris: Gallimard, 1973), 399.

12 "Il creusait un procès comme Cuvier fouillait l'humus du globe. Comme ce grand penseur, il allait de déductions en déductions avant de conclure, et reproduisait le passé de la conscience comme Cuvier reconstruisait un anoplothérium." Balzac, *L'Interdiction* (Paris: Furne, 1844), 133.

13 "Birotteau parfumeur ne savait pas un iota d'histoire naturelle ni de chimie." Balzac, *Histoire de la grandeur et de la décadence de César Birotteau* (Paris: Gallimard, 1975), 79.

14 "Nous voulons parler des hommes inquiets et tracassiers . . . qui n'entendent pas plus la vie que les hannetons ne connaissent l'histoire naturelle." Balzac, *Physiologie du mariage* (Paris: Gallimard, 1971), 79.

15 "Enfin, entre les animaux, il y a peu de drames, la confusion ne s'y met guère; ils courent sus les uns aux autres, voilà tout. Les hommes courent bien aussi les uns sur les autres; mais leur plus ou moins d'intelligence rend le combat autrement compliqué." Balzac, "Avant-propos," 9.

16 "[Il se trouve en France] des sauvages . . . dont les mœurs sont encore peu connues malgré les efforts des naturalistes du roman." Balzac, *Petites misères de la vie conjugale* (Paris: Furne, 1854), 107.

17 "Les naturalistes nous ont dépeint les mœurs de beaucoup d'animaux féroces; mais ils ont oublié la mère et la fille en quête d'un mari." Balzac, *Le Contrat de mariage* (Paris: Furne, 1842), 227.

18 "Ces sauvages [les voleurs] ne respectent ni la loi, ni la religion, rien, pas même l'histoire naturelle, dont la sainte nomenclature est, comme on le voit, parodiée par eux." Balzac, *Splendeurs et misères des courtisanes*, 515.

19 "Lorsque nous arriverons au degré de science qui nous permettra de faire une histoire naturelle des cœurs, de les nommer, de les classer en genres, en sous-genres, en familles, en crustacés, en fossiles, en sauriens, en microscopiques, en . . . que sais-je ? alors, mon bon ami, ce sera chose prouvée qu'il en existe de tendres, de délicats, comme des fleurs." Balzac, *La Peau de chagrin*, 112.

20 "Si la fraction n'existe pas dans l'Ordre Naturel, elle existe encore bien moins dans l'Ordre Moral, où les idées et les sentiments peuvent être varies comme les espèces de l'Ordre Végétal, mais sont toujours entiers." Balzac, *Séraphîta* (Paris: Furne, 1846), 296.

21 "Si les zoologistes ne voient en nous qu'un mammifère . . . le physiologiste doit avoir aussi le droit d'établir ses genres et ses sous-genres." Balzac, *Physiologie du mariage*, 42.

22 "A Paris, il existe plusieurs espèces de femmes; il y a la duchesse et la femme du financier, l'ambassadrice et la femme du consul, la femme du ministre et la femme de celui qui ne l'est plus; il y a la femme comme il faut de la rive droite et celle de la rive gauche de la Seine." Balzac, *La Muse du département* (Paris: Furne, 1842), 376.

23 "En effet, les jeunes gens de Paris ne ressemblent aux jeunes gens d'aucune autre ville. Ils se divisent en deux classes: le jeune homme qui a quelque chose, et le jeune homme qui n'a rien; ou le jeune homme qui pense et celui qui dépense." Balzac, *Histoire des Treize: La Fille aux yeux d'or* (Paris: Flammarion, 1988), 231.

24 "L'abus des plaisirs en faisait un colimaçon, un mollusque anthropomorphe à classer dans les *Casquettifères*." Balzac, *Le Père Goriot*, 55.

25 "Ces groupes, qui, s'il était permis d'assimiler les Parisiens aux différentes classes de la zoologie, appartiendrait au genre des mollusques." Balzac, *Histoire des Treize: Ferragus* (Paris: Flammarion, 1988), 205.

26 "N'est-ce pas une espèce d'éponge oubliée par les naturalistes dans l'ordre des polypiers, et qu'il s'agit de presser avec délicatesse, avant de la laisser sucer par des héritiers?" Balzac, *La Peau de chagrin*, 78.

27 "Il est difficiles de décider si ces mammifères à plumes se crétinisent à ce métier, ou s'ils ne font pas ce métier parce qu'ils sont un peu crétins de naissance." Balzac, *Les Employés* (Paris: Gallimard, 1985), 141. "Il est une nation plumigère . . . espèce de Groenland administratif." Balzac, *Le Père Goriot*, 221.

28 For a comparison of Balzac and Buffon's descriptive practices, see Pierre Lazlo, "Buffon et Balzac: Variations d'un modèle descriptif," *Romantisme* 58 (1987): 67–80.

29 "L'Huître, le Polype du corail, Le Lion, le Zoophyte, les Animalcules microscopiques et l'Homme étaient le même appareil modifié." Balzac, "Guide-Âne à l'usage des animaux qui veulent parvenir aux honneurs," in *Scènes de la vie privée et publique des animaux* (Paris: Marescq, 1852), 55.

30 "Nous aimions beaucoup à nous occupier à ne rien faire et à bien vivre. On appelle ambition cette tendance propre aux Ânes et aux Hommes. . . . Serai-je jamais un Animal couché sur l'herbe du budget?" Ibid., 53–54.

31 The crucial role that the milieu plays in the process of speciation, for both Geoffroy and Balzac, is an issue I purposely leave aside in this article. Social context is evidently an all-powerful shaping force for Balzac, but even if this idea supports a "transformist" Balzac, closer to Geoffroy than to Cuvier, it does not quite resolve the problem of fixed and fatal character molds. Social contexts may well homogenize their products as much as innate characteristics do (see the drones of *Les Employés*). My point is rather that classification *tout court*—whether based on innate or imposed traits—has limits that Balzac's practice (if not always his rhetoric) quite systematically exposes. For Balzac's contribution to the scientific notion of milieu, see Claudine Cohen, "Balzac et l'invention du concept de *milieu*," in *Balzac Géographe: Territoires*, ed. Philippe Dufour and Nicole Mozet (Paris: Christian Pirot, 2004), 25–32.

32 "Or, voyez ce qui est arrivé à Jésus-Christ qui a proclamé l'égalité des âmes comme vous voulez proclamer l'unité zoologique!" Balzac, "Guide-Âne," 55.

33 "—Dès lors, reprit le disciple, les nomenclatures sont bonnes pour nous rendre compte à nous-mêmes des différences, mais elles ne sont plus la science." Ibid.

34 See n3, above. Balzac, "Avant-propos," 11.

35 "Un juge n'est pas Dieu, son devoir est d'adapter les faits aux principes, de juger des espèces variées à l'infini, en se servant d'une mesure déterminée." Balzac, *L'Interdiction*, 133.

36 "Mais comment rendre intéressant le drame à trois ou quatre mille personnages que présente une Société ?" Balzac, "Avant-propos," 10.

37 "En dressant l'inventaire des vices et des vertus, en rassemblant les principaux faits des passions, en peignant les caractères, en choisissant les événements principaux de la Société, en composant des types par la réunion des traits de plusieurs caractères homogènes, peut-être pouvais-je arriver à écrire l'histoire oubliée par tant d'historiens, celle des mœurs." Ibid., 11.

38 "Qu'est-ce qu'un employé? À quel rang commence, où finit l'employé?" Balzac, *Physiologie de l'employé* (Paris: Le Castor Astral, 1994), 17.

39 "Où cesse l'employé? Question grave!" Ibid.

40 "Cependant il y a peu d'hommes d'État parmi les préfets. Concluons de ces subtiles distinctions que le préfet est un neutre de l'ordre supérieur. Il est entre l'homme d'État et l'employé, comme le douanier se trouve entre le civil et le militaire." Ibid., 19.

41 "Oui, quelque chose de merveilleux, de commun et de rare, de singulier et d'ordinaire qui tient de la plante et de l'animal, du mollusque et de l'abeille." Ibid., 39.

42 "Cet homme est un caissier, veritable produit anthropomorphe, arrosé par les idées religieuses, maintenu par la guillotine, ébranché par le vice, et qui pousse à un troisième étage entre une femme estimable et des enfants ennuyeux." Balzac, *Melmoth réconcilié* (Paris: Furne, 1846), 241.

43 "Mais Paris est un véritable océan. Jetez-y la sonde, vous n'en connaîtrez jamais la profondeur. Parcourez-le, décrivez-le! quelque soin que vous mettiez à le parcourir, à le décrire; quelque nombreux et intéressés que soient les explorateurs de cette mer, il s'y rencontrera toujours un lieu vierge, un antre inconnu, des fleurs, des perles, des monstres, quelque chose d'inouï, oublié par les plongeurs littéraires. La Maison Vauquer est une de ces monstruosités curieuses." Balzac, *Le Père Goriot*, 34.

THE ANIMAL SERIES AND
THE GENESIS OF SOCIALISM

JOHN TRESCH

FROM THEIR EARLIEST DAYS, the botanical and anatomical collections of the Muséum d'Histoire naturelle reflected shifting understandings of
French society. In the Jardin du Roi, collections of medicinal herbs included
both exotic and utilitarian plants as symbols and instruments of the king's
dominion. In the revolutionary period, the Muséum's specimens were models
for a new political order that took its cues from natural law. Well into the First
Empire, the acclimatization of foreign plants and animals was seen as a test
of the power of French institutions to shape a new mankind.[1]

In the Restoration and July Monarchy (1815–1848), the collections at
the Jardin des Plantes, the Muséum, and the Ménagerie continued to inspire
comparisons between animal and human worlds. This was the time of a rising
tide of scientific *vulgarisation* (popularization). Along with new reading rooms,
lecture halls like the Athenée, weekly coverage of debates in the Académie des
sciences in the *feuilleton scientifique* (a newspaper science column) and the
national expositions of industrial products, the Muséum was one of the central
sites for a growing popular interest in the sciences, spurring reflection on the
order of nature, the order of society, and the public role of science.[2]

This reflection was often rooted in the observation of the various
species of Parisians, as found in the popular literary satires of character types
called the *physiologies*, wherein the analysis of human species was modeled
on the study of animals. In the frontispiece to the collection *Scènes de la vie
privée et publique des animaux* (FIG. 16.1), in which the conventions of the
physiologies were used to depict animals enacting typical Parisian dramas, the
illustrator J. J. Grandville drew himself sketching the captured specimens who
wrote the text for the book, including the authors George Sand and Honoré de
Balzac. In his other works, such as *Un autre monde*, Grandville delighted in
showing the mirroring between the curious and frequently nthropomorphized
animals collected at the Muséum and the bestial humans who gathered to
observe them (FIG. 16.2).[3]

Similarities between human and animal worlds could serve the aims
of comedy. They were also frequently the basis for the emerging sciences
of society. The term "sociology" was coined in Paris in the 1830s by Auguste
Comte, one of several thinkers concerned with creating a new science to
make sense of recent political, economic, and industrial upheavals, and to

Fig. 16.1

J. J. Grandville sketching Balzac, Sand, and others at the Ménagerie of the Jardin des Plantes. Frontispiece of J. J. Grandville, *Scènes de la vie privée et publique des animaux* (Paris, 1840). Courtesy Rare Book and Manuscript Library, University of Pennsylvania.

Fig. 16.2

J. J. Grandville, *Le Perchoir*, from J. J. Grandville, *Un autre monde* (Paris, 1844). Courtesy Rare Book and Manuscript Library, University of Pennsylvania.

chart—as well as guide— the progress of humanity. The life sciences were
a major inspiration for these early social scientists. Organic metaphors
inspired analyses of the basis of social unity and the division of labor, as well
as factors involved in social "crises" and adaptations.[4] One term ubiquitous
among nineteenth-century social theorists in France was "series." Charles
Fourier's phalanstery, a Utopian community, would be organized according
to "passionate series," while the anarchist Pierre-Joseph Proudhon wrote
that "everything that can be thought by the mind or perceived by the senses
is necessarily a series."[5] Among its various sources, the term derived from life
sciences and the concept of the "animal series." This was the portion of "The
Great Chain of Being" that ranked all terrestrial creatures in a single line of
increasing perfection or complexity, from lichens and sponges up to humans.
The animal series had been central to Enlightenment natural history. It also
served as the backbone for Jean-Baptiste Lamarck's theories of transmutation.[6]

According to a much-repeated argument in the history of biology, the
concept of the animal series was outmoded by the early nineteenth century.
According to this account, Georges Cuvier brought down the curtain on
eighteenth-century natural history by shattering the "table of representations"
and the animal series along with it, replacing them with his four distinct
"embranchements" and his emphasis on the relation between organisms'
functions and their conditions of existence.[7] Even though Cuvier insisted on
the fixity of species, he has been portrayed as more modern than his rival,
the transformist Lamarck. Others who insisted on using the animal series
have been seen as atavistic and reactionary—for example, the American
craniologist and polygenist Samuel Morton, who used the notion of a natural
hierarchy among humans as a justification and naturalization of slavery.[8]

But in fact the concept of the animal series was still very much alive
in mid-nineteenth-century French natural history, and not only among
reactionaries. The anatomist Henri de Blainville (a major influence on the
philosopher Auguste Comte) updated the chain of being with recent advances in physiology, while the doctrine of "unity of composition" advanced by
Cuvier's most famous opponent, Étienne Geoffroy Saint-Hilaire, was closely
associated with the animal series.[9] Furthermore, the animal series was an
important term in the development of social science and movements of social
reform. It served as a basis for historical comparison and analysis of crucial
social functions and was also used to trace and predict the direction of social
progress. Its impact was clearest in the work of the prophet of industry,
Claude-Henri de Saint-Simon, and his followers, as well as those who broke
away from that movement, including Auguste Comte and Philippe-Joseph-
Benjamin Buchez. Another apostate, Pierre Leroux, is particularly interesting
in this regard. Not only was he one of the first social philosophers to use the
term "socialism," but he applied the animal series in a new way under the
influence of Cuvier's opponent Geoffroy. These thinkers' use of the animal
series shows one aspect of the central role the Muséum played in broader
formations of French cultural and political life in the early nineteenth century.
In particular, it suggests how discussions about the Muséum's specimens
contributed to the political thought that led to the worker's revolution of 1848.

PROPHETIC PHYSIOLOGICAL SERIES

Saint-Simon, entrepreneur, bon vivant, and social prophet, dreamed of a
society directed by the most talented and industrious in which a new religion
preached by scientists would bring about social unity. His "Mémoire sur la
science de l'homme" of 1813 grounded his predictions in historical comparison
and in the increasingly influential science of physiology. In this essay, Saint-
Simon merged the Marquis de Condorcet's notion of stages of intellectual and
social development with the concept of the animal series. Condorcet drew on
the idea of a progression from savagery to civilization used by Scottish stadial
theorists such as Adam Ferguson and Adam Smith, who saw human history

unfolding in fixed stages from hunting and agriculture to commerce. Saint-Simon's concept of the animal series derived from the comparative anatomy being taught in the 1790s by Félix Vicq d'Azyr, for whom the notion of a hierarchy of beings in order of increasing complexity was a fundamental principle of classification.

The result was Saint-Simon's "tableau" of the successive "physiological" states of society, which placed the distinct phases of human history in historical order. This temporal order was also a ranking according to the extent of the division of labor, the state of the sciences and the arts, the degree of technical mastery over nature, and the overall harmony of the "organized machine" (*machine organisée*) of society. The "series," beginning with humans in a state barely different from animals (he referred to the *enfant sauvage*, the "wild boy" of Aveyron), continued through the Greeks and the Romans to the Arabs and medieval Christianity, finally reaching the nineteenth-century state of "crisis" in which industrial capacities had developed in the absence of social and intellectual unity. The twelfth and final stage—the necessary outcome of the preceding stages—would be a society in which industry and science were properly ordered. Physiology, as the basis for a kind of medical attention to the social organism, would take its rightful place alongside the science of "brute bodies" (*corps bruts*), directing all industry toward the increase of productive powers to improve the lot of "the poorest and most numerous class." In 1825, the year of his death, he made this the single commandment of his "New Christianity."[10]

Saint-Simon's followers, including Prosper "Père" Enfantin, Saint-Amand Bazard, Hippolyte Carnot, Michel Chevalier, Philippe-Joseph-Benjamin Buchez, and Pierre-Henri Leroux, created a full-fledged messianic movement of intellectual and industrial reform. In their published sermons of 1828 and 1829, they set the terms of critique and the agenda for reform that all later socialist movements had to respond to. The Saint-Simonian preachers identified a millennia-long history of class struggle and the different forms it had taken: the relation between slave and free, serf and master, and finally "industrials" and the "idle" owners. They also pointed out the harmful competition and spiritual disunity that characterized the present, denouncing the ideology of liberal individualism and its harmful moral and social effects. In their "historical series" they depicted a rising alternation between "organic," or unified periods, and "critical" periods, in which there was no common purpose. For these prophets, many of whom had trained as engineers at the École Polytechnique, the historical series was an ascending sine wave.

To "re-organize" society, they applied the classifying and serializing urge of natural history. Society would be divided into three main classes: scientists, workers, and priests. Priests coordinated the relations between the others, matching research to social needs and assigning people to their roles according to their capacities. The priest class was also aligned with artists, the literal "avant-garde" or advance troops of human progress, who depicted the advantages of the future state and appealed to the emotions. In addition to establishing the ideology of modern art, the Saint-Simonians were among the first modern feminists, with many women in their ranks, including Flora Tristan. Women were valued both as workers and for their emotional capacities, perceived as superior to those of men. Under the direction of Père Enfantin, the Saint-Simonians created an elaborate religious dogma based on a pantheist conception of divine matter, which they enacted with costumes, songs, and rituals. This "cult" culminated in their 1832 retreat to Ménilmontant, then a hamlet outside Paris, where they made a spectacle of the gospel of industry by growing their hair and beards and performing household labor: cooking, cleaning, and gardening.[11]

While the Saint-Simonians' view of progress drew upon their founder's "tableau physiologique," their writings also showed a new influence that also reinforced the importance of the animal series. The 1820 book, *Essai de palingénésie sociale*, by the liberal Christian philosopher Pierre-Simon

Ballanche was widely read in romantic-era Paris.[12] It depicted the Revolution as a divinely ordained "expiation," a painful period of transition required for a metamorphosis into a more just and more spiritual society. Ballanche took his central notion, palingenesis (rebirth), from the *Palingénésie philosophique* of the Swiss entomologist Charles Bonnet, a follower of the German philosopher Gottfried Wilhem Leibniz, whose doctrine of pre-established harmony held that this was the best of all possible worlds. According to the twentieth-century historian of ideas Alfred Lovejoy, Bonnet's work "temporalized the Great Chain of Being."[13] Bonnet depicted the animal series as a whole growing more perfect over time according to a pre-established plan, in harmony with shifts in the makeup of the earth's surface. Bonnet used the chrysalis as a metaphor for all life forms—both for the progressive material transformations of species and for the eventual "rebirth" of their "germ of restoration" at the last judgment. Bonnet was also one of the first to use the term "evolution" in a biological sense, applying it to the gradual unfolding of embryos.[14] Inspired by Bonnet and Ballanche's providential vision of embryological metamophosis in both animals and humans, the Saint-Simonians wrote: "the doctrine of Saint-Simon does not want to bring about an upheaval or a revolution. It comes to predict and to complete a transformation, an evolution."[15] Their teachings would bring about the transition to the next stage in the historical series of social organisms.

Even after the decline of the movement in 1833, the former followers of Saint-Simon propagated their own visions of social science and social reform. For Auguste Comte, the founder of positivism, who had been Saint-Simon's secretary in the 1820s, the animal series was a foundational organizing principle. This was true not only in his writings on biology and sociology. Comte's fundamental concept of the "hierarchy of the sciences," which ranked them by the moment when each left theology and metaphysics behind, as well as by the power each science granted humans over their environment, was a great chain of disciplinary being.[16] Likewise, the Catholic physician Philippe-Joseph Buchez—depicted as a member of the group of idealistic social philosophers called the "Cénacle" in Balzac's novel *Les illusions perdues* (1837–43)—made "series" central to his vision of social reform. In his *Introduction à la science de l'histoire*, Buchez argued that the inevitability of social progress was confirmed by recent findings in physiology, zoology and geology. Correlations between the developmental stages of organisms, species, and the earth were proof that humanity's presence in the world "was no accident," and that "labor, devotion and sacrifice" were part of the "universal order"; reasoning by analogy to mathematics, he saw the "series" of historical facts forming a "progression" that indicated the gradual appearance of a socialist republic in fulfillment both of scripture and of the promise of 1789. Buchez's fusion of the animal series, embryonic series, geohistory and human history provoked an attack from Cuvier as well as praise from Geoffroy Saint-Hilaire.[17]

A NEW TWIST IN THE CHAIN

In the wake of his much-publicized debate with Cuvier in 1830, Geoffroy and his work became a focal point for romantic artists and social reformers. He hosted a weekly salon attended by Victor Hugo, George Sand, Franz Lizst, Heinrich Heine, Balzac, and many former Saint-Simonians. The notion of a chain of increasing perfection among animals that was associated with Geoffroy's doctrine of "the unity of type" was crucial to Balzac's "Avant-propos" and inspired work by Sand and Jules Michelet. Thanks to Geoffroy's influence, the application of the animal series to social philosophy underwent a new twist in the doctrine of "Humanity" of Pierre Leroux.[18]

In 1830, the Saint-Simonians took over *Le Globe*, the journal that was the leading voice of liberal opposition and romantic arts, by recruiting its founding editor, Pierre Leroux, to their cause. After two years, offended by Père Enfantin's megalomania, Leroux broke away, launching a series of other journals with the help of other former Saint-Simonians as well as George Sand, who not only supported Leroux but also wrote several novels that exemplified his philosophy. Leroux's ideas embraced new developments in romantic literature, new scientific ideas, as well as the study of Asian and Middle Eastern languages, literatures and religions inaugurated by German poet and critic Friedrich von Schlegel. Leroux's social philosophy opposed both liberal "individualism" and the centralized, hierarchical "absolute socialism" (*le socialisme absolu*) of the Saint-Simonians. Instead, he saw progress as the development of the central ideas of the eighteenth century: liberty, fraternity, and equality. These were themselves the latest installments of a long tradition of "Humanity" running throughout history. For Leroux, Humanity was "an ideal being" that exists "in the virtual state," manifesting itself in specific social and intellectual forms. Any living human was a doubled being: "a real being in whom lives, in the virtual state, the ideal being called humanity." The combined history of religions, philosophies, and social orders recorded the stages of this ideal being's development.[19]

Leroux frequently cited Geoffroy as part of the promising new wave of sciences, many associated with German *Naturphilosophie*, which treated nature as a dynamic process with all parts affecting each other. But beyond this "developmentalism," there was a more direct connection between the ideas of Leroux and Geoffroy's "philosophical anatomy." Against Cuvier's idea that the organisms of the world can be divided into four distinct *embranchements*, Geoffroy argued for the "unity of composition." In his anatomical studies, he identified analogies among the parts of different animals, which led him to conclude that despite morphological variations, there was actually only one "universal animal plan," which underwent metamorphoses to produce all the diverse animal forms. In the vertebrates, the sterna (breastbones) were simply geometrical modifications of each other; making even greater analogical leaps, he argued that lobster shells, for example, were simply bones turned inside out. He contended that "there is only one animal—there is only one single being: Animality, an abstract being that is perceptible by our senses under different shapes." Despite the kaleidoscopic forms of animals on earth, a single form or plan united them all: birds, mammals, reptiles, invertebrates, and even insects. Thus Geoffroy's "philosophical anatomy" embraced both multiplicity and unity, along with the developmental processes through which individuals and new species were formed.[20]

Geoffroy's junior associate, the embryologist Étienne Serres, analyzed the steps through which embryos unfolded, forming symmetrical organs and other quasi-mathematical patterns in animals. His writings on "organogenesis" borrowed from the work of the *Naturphilosophe* Lorenz Oken, which had been translated into French in the 1820s. Along with Etienne's son Isidore Geoffroy Saint-Hilaire, Serres launched a new field of study, teratology, which examined developmental abnormalities and monsters as a means of illuminating normal processes of development (**FIGS. 16.3** and **16.4**). Although Geoffroy himself did not argue for the animal series, Serres, like Oken, argued for a graduated hierarchy of animals. Geoffroy's "unity of type" was the intellectual underpinning for this refigured animal series.[21] Likewise, Serres saw comparative embryology as an empirical confirmation of Geoffroy's doctrine of the unity of type. He derived what came to be known as the "Meckel-Serres" law, which held that the higher animals, as embryos, passed successively through the stages corresponding to each of the lower animals in the series. According to Serres, "lower species" were thus "frozen embryos" of the higher species.[22]

The revision of the animal series brought about by Geoffroy and his followers—a chain of beings united by an underlying plan, in constant development towards perfection, with teratological deviations along the way—had its sociological analogue in Leroux's concept of Humanity. Leroux's history traced an embryological unfolding of a single, simple ideal into diverse and more complex forms. Geoffroy's ideal, universal "animality," which he called

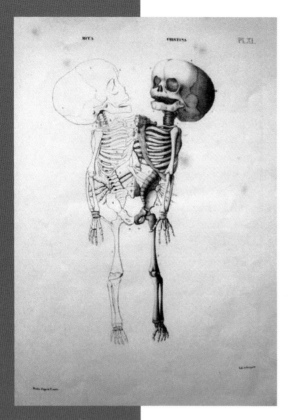

Figs. 16.3 and 16.4

Rita-Christina (conjoined twins) from Étienne Serres, *Recherches d'anatomie transcendante sur les lois de l'organogénie appliquées à l'anatomie pathologique* (Paris, 1827). Courtesy of Cambridge University Library

the "virtual conditions" for any individual, was an exact correlate to Leroux's notion of a virtual humanity. For Geoffroy and Serres, the endpoint of this process was never spelled out, but Leroux's series had a utopian destination. Throughout the universal "tradition" he identified—stretching from Vedism and Buddhism through Pythagoras and Plato, the Hebrew Bible and New Testament, and the *Encyclopédie*—the same great idea was expressed. This idea was the underlying identity between each individual and humanity and, therefore, our dependence on and responsibility for each other. Leroux saw this idea repeatedly expressed in ceremonies, including the recurrent ritual of the shared meal. According to Leroux, rites of communion were symbols and models for collective ownership of the means and fruits of production. For Leroux, a new, collective order of property—based on equality among individuals—would be the fulfillment of the series of human history.

SOCIALISM AS POLITICAL (BIO)TECHNOLOGY

In their writings of the 1830s and 1840s, romantic historians and social scientists such as Jules Michelet, Edgar Quinet, and even Karl Marx (who lived in Paris in the 1840s) came to portray the French Revolution as inevitable: the result of a natural necessity, a kind of "embryological force" demanding a continued evolution.[23] They also saw the revolutions of 1830 and 1848 as the results of crises in the social organism, produced by a disharmony that (once the spasms and fevers had passed) could be confronted and cured.[24] At the same time, however, notions equally indebted to the life sciences—such as "critical period" and "teratology"—suggested there might be unexpected ruptures and turns in this development. They also declared that humans would be able to direct it. Here, social science would intervene.

From this point of view, it should be no surprise that "sociology" emerged at the exact same moment as "socialism," and in many of the same texts. Social science was a tool for transforming the social organism. As Comte put it, "savoir pour prévoir, afin de pouvoir" (know in order to predict, predict in order to act).[25] The keys to remaking society were: identifying its anatomy, a task aided by concepts and methods from natural history; aligning the past stages in its development, in order to predict and bring about the next phase; and enacting that new order, not only by describing it, but by inventing new dogmas, new practices, and new rites to secure it. These historical and prophetic theories formed the intellectual backdrop for the Revolution of 1848 and the brief Second Republic that followed it.

While this paper has pointed out the importance of *biological* thought—and in particular, the notion of the "animal series"—for understanding early socialism, just as important was the role played by *technology*. For Saint-Simon, Comte, and Leroux, the series of stages of human history was determined in large part by the kind of technologies they employed. The human was thus presented in biological terms, but frequently defined as the *technological animal*—the creature that alters its environment (and itself) with tools. At the same time, these "children of the century" produced a forceful image of the human as the *ceremonial* animal: the being that undertakes repeated acts in collective gatherings in order to provide a direction for individual passions, arrange the givens of nature, and align the unfolding of time.[26] Such notions were later central for Émile Durkheim, who argued that emotional solidarity in an "organic" society such as the Third Republic required collective rites in consecrated public venues for the production and diffusion of knowledge.[27] Among such sites we can count the Muséum d'Histoire naturelle: a place where natural and social orders were made visible, and where they might also be transformed.

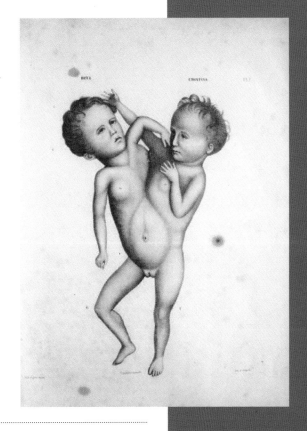

1 E. C. Spary, *Utopia's Garden: French Natural History from Old Regime to Revolution* (Chicago: University of Chicago Press, 2000); Richard W. Burkhardt, Jr., "La Ménagerie et la vie du Muséum," in *Le Muséum au premier siècle de son histoire*, ed. Claude Blanckaert, Claudine Cohen, Pietro Corsi, and Jean-Louis Fischer (Paris: Éditions du Muséum national d'Histoire naturelle, 1997).

2 Bernadette Bensaude-Vincent, "Un public pour la science: L'essor de la vulgarisation au XIXe siécle," *Réseaux* 11, no. 58 (1993): 47–66.

3 J. J. Grandville, *Scènes de la vie privée et publique des animaux* (Paris: Hetzel, 1840); J. J. Grandville, *Un autre monde* (Paris: H. Fournier, 1844); Philippe Kaenel, "Le Buffon de l'humanité: La zoologie politique de J.-J. Grandville (1803–1847)," *Revue de l'art* 74, no. 1 (1986): 21–28.

4 Judith E. Schlanger, *Les métaphores de l'organisme* (Paris: L'Harmattan, 1971); Claude Blanckaert, "La nature de la société: Organicisme et sciences sociales au XIXe siècle," in *Une histoire des sciences humaines*, ed. Claude Blanckaert and Laurent

Mucchielli (Paris: L'Harmattan, 2004); I. Bernard Cohen, ed., *The Relations between the Natural Sciences and the Social Sciences* (Princeton, N.J.: Princeton University Press, 1994).

5 Charles Fourier, *The Theory of the Four Movements*, ed. Gareth Steadman Jones and Ian Patterson (Cambridge: Cambridge University Press, 1996); Pierre-Joseph Proudhon, *De la création de l'ordre dans l'humanité*, 2nd ed., 2 vols. (Paris. Garnier Freres, 1849), 1:244.

6 Arthur O. Lovejoy, *The Great Chain of Being: A Study of the History of an Idea* (Cambridge, Mass.: Harvard University Press, 1976); Richard W. Burkhardt, Jr., *The Spirit of System: Lamarck and Evolutionary Biology* (Cambridge, Mass.: Harvard University Press, 1995).

7 Henri Daudin, *Cuvier et Lamarck: Les classes zoologiques et l'idée de série animale* (Paris: Éditions des Archives Contemporaines, 1983); Michel Foucault, *The Order of Things: An Archaeology of the Human Sciences* (New York: Vintage, 1994); William F. Bynum, "The Great Chain of Being after Forty Years: An Appraisal," *History of Science* 13 (1975): 1–28.

8 Stephen Jay Gould, *Ontogeny and Phylogeny* (Cambridge, Mass.: Belknap Press of Harvard University Press, 1967); Ann Fabian, *The Skull Collectors* (Chicago: University of Chicago Press, 2010).

9 Toby Appel, "Henri de Blainville and the Animal Series: A Nineteenth-Century Chain of Being," *Journal of the History of Biology* 13, no. 2 (1980): 291–319.

10 Claude-Henri Saint-Simon, "Mémoire sur la science de l'homme (1813)," in Prosper Enfantin and Claude-Henri de Saint-Simon, *Science de l'homme, Physiologie réligieuse* (Paris: Masson, 1858), 235–400; see also Saint-Simon, *Nouveau Christianisme* (Paris: Éditions de L'Aube, 2008).

11 Frank Manuel, *The New World of Henri Saint-Simon* (Cambridge, Mass.: Harvard University Press, 1956).

12 Pierre Simon Ballanche, *Œuvres complètes* (Geneva: Slatkine Reprints, 1967); A. J. L. Busst, "Ballanche and Saint-Simonism," *Australian Journal of French Studies* 9 (1972): 291–92.

13 See Lovejoy, *The Great Chain of Being*, chap. 9.

14 Charles Bonnet, *La Palingénésie philosophique, ou Idées sur l'état passé et sur l'état futur des êtres vivants, ouvrage destiné à servir de supplément aux derniers écrits de l'auteur et qui contient principalement le précis de ses recherches sur le christian* (Amsterdam: M.-M. Rey, 1769); Arthur McCalla, "*Palingénésie philosophique* to *Palingénésie sociale*: From a Scientific Ideology to a Historical Ideology," *Journal of the History of Ideas* 55, no. 3 (July 1994): 21–39.

15 "La doctrine de Saint-Simon, nous le répétons, ne veut pas opérer un bouleversement, une révolution; c'est une *transformation*, une *évolution* qu'elle vient prédire et accomplir." "Première année, 1828–1829: 7ᵉ Séance, Constitution de la proprieté.—Organisation des banques," in *Doctrine Saint-Simonienne: Exposition* (Paris: Librairie Nouvelle, 1854), 154; italics in the original.

16 Patrick Tort, "L'échelle encyclopédique: Auguste Comte et la classification des sciences," in Tort, *La pensée hiérarchique et l'évolution* (Paris: Aubier-Montagne, 1983).

17 ". . . il existe, dans la série historique, quelque chose d'analogue à ce que les géomètres appellent la raison, quelque chose qui sert, comme celle-ci, à reconnaître qu'une suite de faits forme un progression et non une succession d'actes sans rapport entre eux" (151–52); "C'est ainsi que l'état social devient une des causes les plus impulsives de la progression humaine" (164); "Cette considération n'est point sans importance philosophique. En effet, indépendamment de toute autre preuve, indépendamment de celles que nous avons fait précédemment valoir, elle suffit pour nous montrer que la présence de l'humanité, dans le monde actuel, n'est point un accident, ni un phenomène indifférent, mais un fait charactéristique appartenant à l'ordre universel" (177–78); "Elle [l'humanité] sait pourquoi le travail, le dévouement, et le sacrifice sont, aujourd'hui, les lois de son existence" (178–79); Philippe-Joseph-Benjamin Buchez, *Introduction à la science de l'histoire*, 2nd ed., vol. 1 (Paris: Guillaumin, 1842). See François-André Isambert, *De la Charbonnerie au Saint-Simonisme: Étude sur la jeunesse de Buchez* (Paris, Éditions de Minuit, 1966); on Cuvier's response to Buchez, see p. 32.

18 Franck Bourdier, "Le prophète Geoffroy Saint-Hilaire, George Sand et les Saint-Simoniens," *Histoire et Nature* 1 (1973): 47–66; Richard Somerset, "The Naturalist in Balzac: The Relative Influence of Cuvier and Geoffroy Saint-Hilaire," *French Forum* 27, no. 1 (2002): 81–111.

19 "L'homme est un être réèl dans lequel vit, à l'état virtuel, l'être idéal appelé humanité. L'homme est l'humanité dans une manifestation particulière et actuelle." Pierre Leroux, *De l'humanité, de son principe, et de son avenir, où se trouve exposé la vraie définition de la religion et où l'on explique le sens, la suite, et l'enchaînement du mosaisme et du christianisme*, 2 vols. (Paris: Perrotin, 1845), 1:256. See also Pierre Leroux, *Discours de Schelling à Berlin: Du cours de philosophie de Schelling: Du Christianisme* (Paris: J. Vrin, 1982); Armelle Le Bras-Chopard, *De l'égalité dans la différence: Le socialisme de Pierre Leroux* (Paris: Presses de Sciences Po, 1986).

20 "Pour cet ordre de considérations, il n'est plus d'animaux divers. Un seul fait les domine, c'est comme un seul être qui apparaît. Il est, il reside dans l'Animalité; être abstrait, qui est tangible par nos sens sous des figures diverses." Étienne Geoffroy Saint-Hilaire, *Principes de philosophie zoologique, discutés en mars 1830, au sein de l'Académie royale des sciences* (Paris: Pichon et Didier, 1830), 92. See Hervé Le Guyader, *Geoffroy Saint-Hilaire: A Visionary Naturalist* (Chicago: University of Chicago Press, 2004); and Toby Appel, *The Cuvier-Geoffroy Debate: French Biology in the Decades before Darwin* (New York: Oxford University Press, 1987).

21 Étienne Serres, *Recherches d'anatomie transcendante sur les lois de l'organogénie appliquées à l'anatomie pathologique* (Paris: Thuau, 1827); Lorenz Oken, *Elements of Physiophilosophy*, trans. A. Turk (London: Ray Society, 1848).

22 Edward S. Russell, *Form and Function: A Contribution to the History of Animal Morphology* (Chicago: University of Chicago Press, 1982); Elizabeth A. Williams, *The Physical and the Moral: Anthropology, Physiology, and Philosophical Medicine in France, 1750–1850* (Cambridge: Cambridge University Press, 1994).

23 The influence of embryology on Marx is suggested in Arno Wouters, "Marx's Embryology of Society," *Philosophy of the Social Sciences* 23, no. 2 (June 1993): 149–79, but with reference only to German sources, not the French sources Marx would have encountered in Paris.

24 David Bates, *Enlightenment Aberrations: Error and Revolution in France* (Ithaca, N.Y.: Cornell University Press, 2002).

25 This phrase of Comte's was an enduring slogan of positivism, as cited, for example, by his follower Émile Littré in *La Philosophie Positive: Revue* 27 (1881): 291.

26 Wendy James, *The Ceremonial Animal: A New Portrait of Anthropology* (Oxford: Oxford University Press, 2004).

27 Émile Durkheim, *The Elementary Forms of the Religious Life* (New York: Free Press, 1954).

DOMESTICATING THE EXOTIC: THE GIRAFFE CRAZE AND FRENCH CONSUMER CULTURE

DENISE Z. DAVIDSON

THE PRESENCE OF A GIRAFFE in France in the 1820s, the first such specimen to appear in Europe in hundreds of years, unleashed an explosion of interest unlike anything ever seen before. While earlier scientific fads—such as mesmerism in the eighteenth century, or the spectacle of elephants arriving in Paris in 1798—had certainly drawn the public's attention, the fascination with this animal took on new contours and new dimensions. To explore how and why the giraffe elicited so much excitement and enthusiasm among the French public, this essay focuses on three factors: the expansion of the press along with changing forms and practices in popular culture; the growth of consumption often labeled the consumer revolution, which dated from the eighteenth century but continued to evolve in the nineteenth; and new attitudes toward exotic others taking shape in the period, a set of practices and ideas that have been encapsulated in the term "Orientalism." These three trends combined to turn the giraffe into an early example of a modern fad, a phenomenon that only became possible once the press and popular culture had developed sufficiently to both stimulate and satisfy the public's curiosity.

When *la belle Africaine*, as she was often called, arrived in Marseille in October 1826, the French were ready for diversion.[1] More than ten years had passed since Napoleon had made his last-ditch effort to return to power, which ended in his defeat at Waterloo. The Restoration kings, Louis XVIII and then Charles X, were the younger brothers of Louis XVI. Hating all the Revolution stood for, they did everything in their power to return France to its pre-1789 condition. One cannot turn back the hands of time, however, and their efforts to erase all traces of the Revolution were courting the impossible.[2] In addition, neither king had the charisma nor the potential for the glorious victories that had enabled Napoleon to enrapture much of the French public. All they could promise—and that was a lot after twenty-five years of nearly constant warfare—was peace. While many French supported the returned Bourbon kings as the legitimate rulers of France, an increasingly vocal liberal opposition expressed frustrations with the regime's limitations on free speech and its highly restrictive voter franchise. Political tensions increased when Charles X ascended the throne in 1824, since he appeared even more committed than his brother had been to overturning the vestiges of revolutionary change.[3]

These political developments took place in the context of broader social and cultural transformations, among them the growth of the press and expanded literacy. During the Napoleonic Empire, strict censorship and limitations on the number of newspapers and theaters permitted to operate allowed the government to exercise near-total control over the press and most forms of cultural production.[4] At first the Restoration government loosened those restrictions, but legislation passed in 1827 reintroduced stricter controls. By that point, the number of newspapers had expanded considerably; in this context of political censorship, journalists were hungering for "safe" topics to fill their pages.[5] The giraffe satisfied that desire. From the moment the animal set foot in Marseille, newspapers all over the country published information about her behavior, stirring up curiosity and enthusiasm for the new arrival.[6] Daily reports then followed her progress as she crossed the country that spring. No similar reporting had taken place when two elephants traveled to Paris from the Netherlands in 1798. Although they too had become popular attractions for crowds visiting the Jardin des Plantes, they had not elicited the kinds of press coverage and consumer objects that would be produced around the giraffe motif thirty years later.[7] The evolution of journalistic methods, along with the public's ensuing demands for information and entertainment, help to explain this contrast.

The press was not the only way that information circulated among the public. Parisian amusements included a wide variety of options, including theaters, cafés, restaurants, and parks. One trend that marked the first decades of the nineteenth century was a desire to see and be seen in public. I have argued elsewhere that this inclination was a consequence of the Revolution's dismantling of earlier systems for marking social status. Uncertainty about how to display and read new behavioral codes made people seek out opportunities to mingle with heterogeneous groups and thus learn to decipher those markers.[8] The years from 1795 to the early 1820s were a high point of social mixing in public, particularly in the space known as the Boulevard, a neighborhood on the northeastern edge of Paris.[9] In 1791, the revolutionary government ended earlier restrictions that had limited Boulevard theaters to plays without dialogue, and a new genre emerged as a result: melodrama. First staged around 1800, melodramas combined spoken dialogue with music chosen to reinforce the emotional reactions of the audiences.[10] These plays drew huge, diverse crowds for about two decades, with audiences' reactions providing part of the spectacle. The juxtaposition of classes inside theaters put the new social order on display quite literally, as the wealthiest spectators in the loges above were able to look down at the lower-class audience members seated below them. This period represents the first step toward a modern approach to culture that views society as spectacle and spectacle as society.[11] The spectacle of the giraffe fits into this trend.

The arrival of "le bel animal du roi" (the king's beautiful animal), in Paris in 1827 coincided with a transition toward greater class segregation in Parisian public life, a tendency visible in discussions of the crowds that assembled to see the giraffe.[12] During the giraffe's time in Marseille, aristocratic visitors to the Préfecture, the government building whose courtyard served as her residence for six months, had the opportunity to observe the animal up close, while boisterous crowds jostled in the street to catch a glimpse during her daily walks.[13] Once in Paris, the giraffe attracted such large crowds that the administrators of the Jardin des Plantes began selling tickets to provide wealthier spectators a chance to approach the animal more closely. One study estimates that 600,000 people saw the giraffe in Paris during her first six months there, citing the large increase in tolls collected at the nearby bridge, the Pont d'Austerlitz.[14] The population of Paris in the 1820s was only about 750,000, but hundreds of thousands also visited Paris, as a booming tourist industry attracted both domestic and foreign travelers.[15] So it is possible that half a million people could have visited the

DENISE Z. DAVIDSON

giraffe during her first months there. An engraving from the period satirizes these crowds and their exaggerated interest in the animal by portraying well-dressed adults pushing and shoving each other, while ignoring the fact that they have knocked over a young child (**FIG. 17.1**).

Of course, theater owners and playwrights could not resist the temptation to profit from the giraffe's popularity. Soon after her arrival in Paris, a play entitled *La girafe, ou Une journée au Jardin du Roi* was staged at the Théâtre du Vaudeville. The dialogue included a conversation between a character named Madame Bertholin and her domestic servant, Fanchette, who expresses surprise that the newspapers were giving so much coverage to the giraffe. "Yes, my child," responds Madame Bertholin, "they have discussed her actions and gestures as though they were discussing an important person [*un grand personnage*]." At that point they break into song, which includes the line: "Les grandes bêtes pourtant à Paris ne sont pas rares" ("great beasts are not rare in Paris"), playing on the two meanings of *bête*: "animal" or "stupid (person)."[16] Playwrights used the giraffe craze to mock Parisians, even as they profited from the behavior they ridiculed.[17]

The large number of objects that appeared with images of the giraffe reflects new forms of production and consumption. Beginning in the eighteenth century, an explosion in consumption changed everyday life in Paris. Thanks largely to the influx of wealth arriving from the colonies in the Caribbean, more people had more disposable income than ever before.[18] Wealthy merchants in the port cities of Nantes, La Rochelle and Bordeaux built huge, elaborately furnished townhouses and then sent their sons to receive an education and aspire to prestigious posts in Paris, thus stimulating production and consumption there. The rise in consumption among this growing group of wealthy non-nobles expanded production and consumption among

Fig. 17.1

H. D. Plattel, *Les Quartiers de Paris, No. 6: Jardin des Plantes*, 1827, lithograph. Musée Carnavalet, Paris. © Musée Carnavalet / Roger-Viollet

LES QUARTIERS DE PARIS.   N.º6.

Jardin des Plantes.

Fig. 17.2

Brisé (Lacework) Fan
Painted with Two Giraffes,
ca. 1827, pale yellow
tortoiseshell with silk
ribbon and painted paper
appliqués. Musée Carna-
valet, Paris. © Musée
Carnavalet / Roger-Viollet

the lower classes as well, as more people could afford to buy more things: clothes, sheets, dishes, cookware, and furniture. Historians sometimes refer to this transition as the consumer revolution, since it impacted society, politics, and culture, along with production and consumption. Increased demand led to greater production of goods, along with stylistic innovations. The Revolution of 1789 disrupted these pathways to wealth, but did not end them altogether. By the early nineteenth century, the fashion press encouraged an obsession with novelty, thus facilitating consumer culture. The combined political, economic, and cultural changes visible in late eighteenth and early nineteenth-century France made possible the giraffe craze of 1827.

Press coverage made the giraffe a celebrity long before she arrived at the Jardin des Plantes and entrepreneurs sought to profit from the public's excitement. When the prefect in Marseille arranged for the giraffe to walk out-doors daily, a local circus operator got the idea of bringing his animals behind her to profit from the crowds already gathered to see the giraffe.[19] In Lyon, too, where the giraffe spent five days resting in the large central square, Place Bellecour, crowds gathered to watch her eat leaves off the trees and drink her milk. Local newspapers publicized her arrival and announced the hours of her scheduled morning and afternoon walks. People were impressed at the docility of this wild beast from the heart of Africa and flocked to see her, even after an incident in which she broke free, frightened some horses, and caused some injuries among the spectators.[20] As the giraffe continued her long march toward Paris, the inhabitants of villages and towns lined the route to catch a glimpse of this famous animal. Seeing her as an opportunity to improve busi-ness, several innkeepers even renamed their establishments in her honor.[21]

When the giraffe arrived in Paris, her celebrity provided an opportu-nity to make money and artisans responded enthusiastically. Details of those ventures shed light on the public's taste and on producers' creativity. The fact that the *Journal des dames et des modes*, a publication whose price limited its audience to wealthy women and men along with their servants, included fashion plates that referenced the giraffe attests to the animal's appeal among the upper classes, particularly the prosperous bourgeoisie.[22] The variety of

Fig. 17.3

Papier peint, motif de tapisserie à la girafe (Wallpaper sample with giraffe and Osages), 1827, printed wallpaper. © MNHN, Bibliothèque centrale

Fig. 17.4

Assiette représentant une girafe avec un palmier (Plate with giraffe and palm tree), 1827, "faience de Waly" (earthenware) with polychrome decoration. © MNHN, Bibliothèque centrale

Fig. 17.5

Bag with a Giraffe, ca. 1830–50, glass beads, leather and gilt metal. Museum of Fine Arts, Boston, The Elizabeth Day McCormick Collection. Photograph © 2011 MFA, Boston

objects produced with the giraffe's image similarly demonstrates the intensity of bourgeois interest in this exotic visitor, as they most likely were the ones buying these decorative pieces. We cannot know much about the buying habits of the lower classes during this period as they left few, if any, diaries or letters. Most lived on the edge of subsistence and had little money for anything but necessities. They could visit the giraffe, however, and they may have been tempted to buy little toy giraffes for their children, like the one George Sand mentioned her son playing with in a letter to her mother.[23] Artisans produced an amazing assortment of giraffe-inspired items, including all kinds of dishes, bowls, platters, and pitchers, as well as matchboxes, inkwells, toothpick holders, hairbrushes, and even wallpaper. They also made fireplace back plates, irons, children's toys, tobacco tins, aprons, and fans, all adorned with images of the giraffe (**FIGS. 17.2–17.5**; see also **FIG. 12.8**).[24]

Another element of the giraffe craze brings to mind the phenomenon of the modern fad: it was short-lived. For a few months, crowds flocked by the thousands to see the giraffe; they bought every imaginable object emblazoned with her image; they attended plays and wore clothes that made reference to her. Yet by the end of 1827, much of that enthusiasm had faded. In June 1830, Balzac wrote a short piece entitled "Étude de philosophie morale sur les habitants du Jardin des Plantes," in which he reflected on the fickle nature of public enthusiasm. He summarized the giraffe's place in French culture: "In her present situation, the giraffe is a great moral idea, an eloquent philosophical lesson. Everyone knows that, as a gift to the king, members of the Academy . . . served as her honor guard; for several months she was all anyone thought about and the Parisian crème de la crème [*le tout Paris*] visited her; two black slaves took her for walks among these audiences; literature, theatre, lithography, [and] fashion [all] took advantage of her fame." Three years later, however, she had been forgotten, and Balzac used her story to reflect on how "glory is only smoke." The giraffe, he wrote, is living proof of this fact. "For today, she is scorned, forgotten; she is only visited by backwards provincials, unoccupied child's maids, and simpletons."[25] As we are only too aware today, fads are, by definition, short-lived. Her story illustrates the first steps toward a modern culture of spectacle and consumption. The objects produced, the news coverage, and the crowds struggling to see the giraffe with their own eyes suggest that the giraffe was the first of many such fads in which celebrity itself inspires adulation.[26]

One important component of the giraffe's appeal lay in her exotic origins, specifically her connection to Egypt. Interest in Egypt had reached a high point in the 1820s. Jean-François Champollion had deciphered the hieroglyphics on the Rosetta Stone in 1822 to great acclaim and public fascination with that part of the world remained vibrant, as shown by the creation, in 1826, of a new department in the Louvre dedicated to Egyptian art and architecture.[27] This interest in exotic locations, objects, and people bubbled up in French popular culture, with plays, books, and art set in the Middle East. Fashion, too, reflected this trend, with jewelry inspired by Egyptian artifacts held in the Louvre, and the use of turbans to adorn women's heads, a popular practice since Napoleon's 1798 invasion of Egypt.[28]

As many of the giraffe-adorned objects and engravings suggest, it was not just the giraffe that interested the Parisian public, but also her Egyptian and Sudanese handlers (**FIG. 17.6**; see also Chapter 12). During the giraffe's few days in Lyon, the local newspaper commented on these exotic men: "four negroes the most negro imaginable walked at her sides. They formed a court [around her], thus contributing to the picturesque scene."[29] Two of these four "negroes" must have been Atir and Hassan, the Africans who had accompanied the giraffe across the Mediterranean. Another was probably Barthélemy Choquet, a man from Marseille hired to assist them on the cross-country journey. The fact that the journalist described him as a "negro" attests to the unfixed nature of racial categories in this period. The fourth was probably

Youssef (or Joseph) Ebed, a young boy hired to serve as a translator. He had spent his life in a refugee camp outside of Marseille that held several hundred Arabs who had assisted Napoleon during the invasion of Egypt.[30] Soon after arriving in Paris, Youssef returned to his family in Marseille and all trace of him disappeared. Hassan, the Egyptian, also returned to his native country in October 1827, pleading ill-health, but Atir, the Sudanese handler, remained in Paris with the giraffe he had cared for since she had been captured, only leaving France in 1838.[31] Étienne Geoffroy Saint-Hilaire commented on Atir's reputation as a ladies' man, news that even reached the ears of the Duchesse de Berry who asked the naturalist about Atir's amorous adventures.[32] *Le Figaro* used his reputation to publish racist humor that shocks modern ears: "Two ladies tried to kidnap Monsieur Atir, one of the giraffe's handlers. That would have been very black." The next day, the newspaper made a similar joke: "Young Atir has been studying music. Of all the notes, those he likes most are the black ones."[33]

Why was there such an interest in the exotic in 1820s France? Edward Said's influential study of Orientalism, by which he meant European dominance over the Middle East through intellectual and cultural means, begins to provide an answer. For Said, European interest in the Middle East sprung from a desire to understand European culture through building a contrast with an exotic "Other."[34] Knowledge of that other in turn facilitated its domination. Public interest in the giraffe and the men who accompanied her fits into the trends analyzed by Said. In a book on Orientalism in nineteenth-century French theater, Angela Pao found a sharp distinction between plays performed before and after 1830, the year that France invaded Algeria. Before 1830, melodramatic plays set in exotic locations tended to be far removed from real situations, relying instead upon imaginary characters to inspire emotional reactions among audiences. Pao labeled these kinds of plays "domestic exoticism." After 1830, a new genre of military or national drama emerged, with plays set in real locations in which military conquest, exploration, or colonization were dramatized.[35] The giraffe stood on both sides of this divide as a very real, yet thoroughly domesticated object in every sense of the term. She thus served to introduce the French to a kind of exotic realism in a form that was not in the least bit threatening. All the discussions of her behavior emphasized her docility and her easy-going manner, including one text that described the giraffe's "sweet expression."[36] Here was a truly exotic visitor, an object suitable for both scientific study and curious onlookers. It is not surprising that her image would have proven so appealing to such a broad range of the French public.

The giraffe craze of 1827 took place because of a combination of factors that include the nature of French popular culture, consumerism, and a fascination with the exotic. Together, they created a "perfect storm" around the giraffe, whose arrival served the interests of scientists, journalists, artisans, and the French public looking for amusement and distraction. The explosion of fashionable objects, plays, engravings, and other items produced at the time embody the first steps towards modern consumer culture, and the rapidity with which the giraffe craze ended reinforces this notion that the giraffe may have been among the first modern "fads." Interest in the giraffe was intense but short-lived as the fickle public soon found other attractions. Still, her presence lives on in these cultural artifacts, objects produced to satisfy the public's desire to feel a connection to this celebrity. The giraffe craze reveals modern consumer culture in its infancy.

1   The story of the giraffe's capture, the diplomatic and political motivations underlying Pasha Muhammad Ali's decision to send it to France, and the events that took place once it crossed the Mediterranean are covered in Gabriel Dardaud, "L'extraordinaire aventure de la girafe du pacha d'Egypte," *Revue des conférences françaises en Orient* 14 (1951): 1–72; Gabriel Dardaud, *Une girafe pour le roi* (Paris: Dumerchez-Naoum, 1985); and Olivier Lagueux, "Geoffroy's Giraffe: The Hagiography of a Charismatic Mammal," *Journal of the History of Biology* 36, no. 2 (2003): 225–47. A beautifully illustrated and readable account, which includes long excerpts from documents dating from the period, appeared recently: Olivier Lebleu, *Les Avatars de Zarafa, première girafe de France: Chronique d'une girafomania, 1826–1845* (Paris: Arléa, 2006). A less scholarly but nonetheless reliable account in English is Michael Allin, *Zarafa: A Giraffe's True Story from Deep in Africa to the Heart of Paris* (New York: Walker, 1998).

2   On this politics of *oublie* (forgetting), see Sheryl Kroen, *Politics and Theater:*

The Crisis of Legitimacy in Restoration France, 1815–1831 (Berkeley and Los Angeles: University of California Press, 2000).

3   The classic work on the Restoration is Guillaume de Bertier de Sauvigny, *The Bourbon Restoration*, trans. Lynn M. Case (Philadelphia: University of Pennsylvania Press, 1966). More recent work includes Emmanuel de Waresquiel, *Histoire de la Restauration, 1814–1830: Naissance de la France moderne* (Paris: Perrin, 1996).

4   André Cabanais, *La presse sous le Consulat et l'Empire, 1799–1814* (Paris: Société des études Robespierristes, 1975).

5   On Restoration censorship, see Robert Justin Goldstein, "France," in *The Frightful Stage: Political Censorship of the Theater in Nineteenth-Century Europe*, ed. Goldstein (New York: Berghahn Books, 2009).

6   Dardaud, "L'extraordinaire aventure," 20. On press coverage of the giraffe, see Michele Majer, "La Mode à la girafe: Fashion, Culture, and Politics in Bourbon Restoration France," *Studies in the Decorative Arts* 17, no. 1 (Fall–Winter 2009–10): 123–61.

7   See Louise E. Robbins, *Elephant Slaves and Pampered Parrots: Exotic Animals in Eighteenth-Century Paris* (Baltimore: Johns Hopkins University Press, 2002), 225–27; Richard W. Burkhardt, Jr., "La Ménagerie et la vie du Muséum," in *Le Muséum au premier siècle de son histoire*, ed. Claude Blanckaert, Claudine Cohen, Pietro Corsi, and Jean-Louis Fischer (Paris: Éditions du Muséum national d'Histoire naturelle, 1997), 481–508; and Michael E. McClellan, "'If We Could Talk with the Animals': Elephants and Musical Performance during the French Revolution," in *Cruising the Performative: Interventions into the Representation of Ethnicity, Nationality, and Sexuality*, ed. Sue-Ellen Case, Philip Brett, and Susan Leigh Foster (Bloomington: Indiana University Press, 1995), 237–48.

8   Denise Z. Davidson, "Making Society 'Legible': People-Watching in Paris after the Revolution," *French Historical Studies* 28, no. 2 (Spring 2005): 265–96.

9   Michèle Root-Bernstein, *Boulevard Theater and*

Revolution in Eighteenth-Century Paris (Ann Arbor, Mich.: UMI Research Press, 1984); Robert Isherwood, *Farce and Fantasy: Popular Entertainment in Eighteenth-Century Paris* (Oxford: Oxford University Press, 1986). On the press and political culture during this turbulent period, see Pierre Serna, *La République des girouettes (1789–1815 . . . et au-delà), une anomalie politique: La France de l'extrême centre* (Seyssel: Champ Vallon, 2005).

10 Peter Brooks, *The Melodramatic Imagination: Balzac, Henry James, Melodrama, and the Mode of Excess*, 2nd ed. (New Haven, Conn.: Yale University Press, 1995).

11 Denise Z. Davidson, *France After Revolution: Urban Life, Gender, and the New Social Order* (Cambridge, Mass.: Harvard University Press, 2007), chap. 3. See also Rebecca Schwartz, *Spectacular Realities: Early Mass Culture in Fin-de-Siècle Paris* (Berkeley: University of California Press, 1998) and Guy Debord, *The Society of the Spectacle*, trans. Donald Nicholson-Smith (New York: Zone Books, 1994).

12 Étienne Geoffroy Saint-Hilaire stated that this

was the name given to the giraffe during its voyage to Paris. *Sur la girafe* (Paris: C. Thuau, 1827), 4.

13 Dardaud, "L'extraordinaire aventure," 12–13.

14 Dardaud, *Une girafe pour le roi*, 68–69. On the Muséum d'Histoire naturelle and the Jardin des Plantes as social space, see Dorinda Outram, "New Spaces in Natural History," in *Cultures of Natural History*, ed. Nicholas Jardine, James A. Secord, and E. C. Spary (Cambridge: Cambridge University Press, 1996).

15 On tourism and guidebooks, see Victoria E. Thompson, "Telling 'Spatial Stories': Urban Space and Bourgeois Identity in Early Nineteenth-Century Paris," *Journal of Modern History* 75, no. 3 (September 2003): 523–56, and "Foreign Bodies: British Travel to Paris and the Troubled Self, 1789–1830," *Studies in Travel Writing* 15, no. 3 (September 2011): 243–65; Priscilla Parkhurst Fergusen, *Paris as Revolution: Writing the Nineteenth-Century City* (Berkeley and Los Angeles: University of California Press, 1994); and Davidson, "Making Society 'Legible.'"

16 Quoted in Dardaud, "L'extraordinaire aventure," 50–51. Majer discusses the play as well in "*La Mode à la girafe*," 150–51.

17 This kind of satire was common in the press and literature of this period. A similar mocking tone is visible in the fashion periodical *Le Journal des dames et des modes*, which ridiculed the public's desire to follow fashion at all costs while simultaneously profiting from such behavior. I make this argument in "Imaging the Readers of the *Journal des dames et des modes*," paper presented at the "More than Fashion: *Le Journal des dames et des modes* (1797–1839)" workshop at the University of Michigan (April 2009). See also Annemarie Kleinert, *Le "Journal des dames et des modes" ou la conquête de l'Europe féminine (1797–1839)* (Stuttgart: Thorbecke, 2001).

18 The literature on the commercial revolution is quite large. Two useful examples are Daniel Roche, *A History of Everyday Things: The Birth of Consumption in France, 1600–1800*, trans. Brian Pearce (Cambridge: Cambridge University Press, 2000); and Jennifer M. Jones, *Sexing La Mode: Gender, Fashion and Commercial Culture in Old Regime France* (Oxford: Berg, 2004). On luxury goods evolving into everyday items of consumption, see Colin Jones and Rebecca Spang, "Sans-Culottes, Sans-Café, Sans-Tabac: Shifting Realms of Necessity and Luxury in Eighteenth-Century France," in *Consumers and Luxury: Consumer Culture in Europe, 1650–1850*, ed. Maxine Berg and Helen Clifford (Manchester: Manchester University Press, 1999). A fascinating comparative study of how objects took on political significance is Leora Auslander, *Cultural Revolutions: Everyday Life and Politics in Britain, North America, and France* (Berkeley and Los Angeles: University of California Press, 2009).

19 Dardaud, *Une girafe pour le roi*, 46–47.

20 Lebleu, *Les Avatars de Zarafa*, 107–10.

21 Dardaud, "L'extraordinaire aventure," 20.

22 The composition and even existence of the French bourgeoisie in this period has been a subject of intense debate among historians. One provocative account argues that the French bourgeoisie only emerged as a self-conscious class in the 1820s, as a consequence of political, not economic developments. See Sarah Maza, *The Myth of the French Bourgeoisie: An Essay on the Social Imaginary, 1750–1850* (Cambridge, Mass.: Harvard University Press, 2003).

23 George Sand, letter dated October 5, 1827, in *Correspondance de George Sand*, vol. 1, ed. Georges Lubin (Paris: Garnier, 1964), 400–1.

24 Dardaud, *Une girafe pour le roi*, 79–82; Oliver Lebleu, *Les Avatars de Zarafa*. Majer also discusses many of these objects, including the toys, in "*La Mode à la girafe*," 143–44.

25 "La girafe est, dans sa position actuelle, une grande idée morale, un éloquent enseignement philosophique. Chacun sait que, envoyée en présent à notre roi, des académiciens allèrent à sa rencontre et lui servirent de garde d'honneur; pendant des mois entiers, elle occupa tous les esprits, fut visitée par tout Paris; deux esclaves noirs la promenaient dans ses audiences publiques; la littérature, le théâtre, la lithographie, la mode exploitèrent sa célébrité. . . . 'La gloire n'est que fumée.' . . . [L]a girafe en est un éloquent résumé, une preuve vivante; car aujourd'hui, on la dédaigne, on l'oublie; elle n'est plus visitée que par le provincial arrière, la bonne d'enfant désœuvrée et le jean-jean simple et naïf." Honoré de Balzac, "Étude de philosophie morale sur les habitants du Jardin des Plantes," *Œuvres complètes de H. de Balzac*, vol. 21 (Paris: Michel Lévy Frères, 1872), 222–23. On the "Tout-Paris," see Anne-Martin Fugier, *La vie élégante, ou la formation du Tout-Paris, 1815–1848* (Paris: Seuil, 1993).

26 For a discussion of fads related to natural history, see David Allen, "Tastes and Crazes," in Jardine et al., *Cultures of Natural History*, 394–407.

27 Todd Porterfield, *The Allure of Empire: Art in the Service of French Imperialism, 1798–1836* (Princeton: Princeton University Press, 1998), chap. 3.

28 Majer, "*La Mode à la girafe*," 126. See Eric Ringmar, "Audience for a Giraffe: European Expansionism and the Quest for the Exotic," *Journal of World History* 17 (2006): 375–79; Ian Coller, *Arab France. Islam and the Making of Modern Europe, 1798–1831* (Berkeley and Los Angeles: University of California Press, 2011), chap. 7; and Angela C. Pao, *The Orient of the Boulevards: Exoticism, Empire, and Nineteenth-Century French Theater* (Philadelphia: University of Pennsylvania Press, 1998). The classic work on this fascination with the exotic, focusing mostly on knowledge production and its relationship to power, is Edward Said, *Orientalism* (New York: Vintage, 1979).

29 "Quatre nègres les plus nègres qu'on puisse imaginer marchaient à ses côtés. Ils formaient une cour et contribuaient à un aspect pittoresque." *Gazette universelle de Lyon*, June 6, 1827, quoted in Lebleu, *Les Avatars de Zarafa*, 108.

30 Collier, *Arab France*; Lebleu, *Les Avatars de Zarafa*, 90–92. On the invasion and its eventual failure, see Juan Cole, *Napoleon's Egypt: Invading the Middle East* (New York: Palgrave Macmillan, 2007).

31 Lebleu, *Les Avatars de Zarafa*, 173.

32 Dardaud, *Une girafe pour le roi*, 71–72.

33 *Le Figaro*, 2 and 3 August 1827, quoted in Lebleu, *Les Avatars de Zarafa*, 151.

34 Said, *Orientalism*.

35 Pao, *The Orient of the Boulevards*.

36 M. L. D. Ferlus, *Nouvelle notice sur la girafe envoyée au roi de France par le Pacha d'Egypte* (Paris: Moreau, 1827), 5. Majer makes this point as well, and draws attention to notions of French cultural superiority as expressed in the depictions of the giraffe and her handlers. Majer, "*La Mode à la girafe*," 144–45.

AN EGYPTIAN GIRAFFE AND SIX OSAGE INDIANS: AN EXOTIC PLEA AGAINST THE CENSORSHIP OF 1827

ALAIN LESCART

WHO REMEMBERS THE YEAR 1827? Coming three years before the three decisive days of the July Revolution of 1830, the year 1827 marked a milestone in the fall of the Bourbons. The government of Charles X, represented by the ministry of Jean Baptiste de Villèle (president of the council), was regularly dragged in the mud by the Parisian press. The government therefore sought desperately to muzzle the freedom of the press, despite the guarantees of liberty assured by the Charte Constitutionnelle (Constitution) issued by King Louis XVIII in 1814. In February 1827, there were 132 newspapers or periodical publications in France, 84 of which circulated by mail.[1]

The story begins on December 29, 1826. On that day, Pierre Denis, Comte de Peyronnet, keeper of the seals and minister of justice, introduced a bill in the Chamber of Deputies on the freedom of the press that he called "the law of justice and of love."[2] The debate on this bill lasted from February 13 to March 12, 1827. Generally, the reasons for the application of censorship were related to religion, the throne, and morals. For the right-wing Ultras, only religion could assure social stability. The liberal faction reacted viscerally, stirring fears linked to the growing role of religious societies behind the scenes of French politics. Two groups were strongly incriminated: the Jesuits (normally banned in France, but who returned on the sly under cover of the Restoration) and the mysterious Congregation.[3] The left described these two groups as evil societies that functioned in the shadow of the king and followed undemocratic principles. Despite animated debate, the Chamber of Deputies voted on the bill on March 12, with 233 votes for the law and 134 opposing. The Deputies then sent the bill to the Chamber of Peers for another approval, where it faced more resistance. The Commission of Peers sent it back to the ministers, modified by twenty-one amendments. The exasperated government then decided to retract its bill on April 17, 1827.

The affair would have been closed if another historic event had not taken place twelve days later, on April 29. That day, the king reviewed the Garde Nationale in front of one hundred thousand spectators in Paris. During their passage, a few guardsmen cried, "Down with the ministers! Down with the Jesuits! Down with Villèle! Long live the Charter!" The next day, the irritated Villèle decided to terminate the entire force of fifty thousand men, which had functioned continuously since the French Revolution. The press reacted virulently, displaying a frank hostility towards the government. On June 24, the government decided on the provisional reestablishment of censorship with its own leader, creating a bureau of censorship as well as a bureau of surveillance.[4]

Thus, newspapers were trapped and unable to comment on current affairs when an important national cultural event took place in the late afternoon of June 30, 1827. After a journey on foot of more than forty-one days,[5] the first giraffe in France made a triumphal entry into Paris, escorted by the celebrated scientist Étienne Geoffroy Saint-Hilaire. During July, more than sixty thousand people filed through the Jardin des Plantes (then called the Jardin du Roi) to see the giraffe, and more than forty thousand visitors came during the month of August.[6] This political gift from Egypt, offered to King Charles X, soon began serving the opposition's own political interests.

At the beginning, the giraffe was just an object of curiosity. She quickly acquired the status of national treasure and generated very exotic fashions, from hairstyles and cravats mimicking the style of her long neck to an imprint in Marseilles soap. Small booklets (*notices*) appeared during the early days of July, at first offering naturalistic studies of the quadruped.[7] Then, the zoological emphasis on the great African animal faded rapidly into the background, clearing the way for a more subversive discourse (**FIG. 18.1**).

Fig. 18.1

Langlumé, *La plus grande bête qu'on ait jamais vue*, 1830 (caricature against Charles X), lithograph. BnF

On July 5, there was a small, innocuous insert in the newspaper *Le Constitutionnel* that associated the Pasha of Egypt with the supposed creation of a new newspaper in Alexandria:

> There will be a newspaper established in Alexandria, with M. Bousquet Deschamps, author of several works, as its editor. The Pasha, enchanted with this enterprise, strongly supports its realization. The freedom of the press is traveling; here it is fixed in Egypt.[8]

This news item arrived in Lyon on the same day that the ordinance reestablishing censorship appeared in that city.

On Saturday, July 7, the Théâtre du Vaudeville took up the subject of the beautiful African: "The Vaudeville has hastened to take advantage of the giraffe's arrival; as of tomorrow, Saturday, it will present a play designed to celebrate her," noted *Le Constitutionnel*.[9] The play in question, *La Girafe, ou Une journée au Jardin du Roi*,[10] was a light entertainment known as a *tableau d'à-propos* (a picture of the times), a term designating a one-time use of current events. The giraffe was first a cultural commodity. Emmanuel Théaulon and his co-authors counted on Parisian curiosity aroused by the giraffe's arrival at the Jardin des Plantes. The vaudeville developed around a pre-bohemian theme, typical of vaudevilles at the time. The giraffe, received with princely honors, only plays a minor role. She is, however, already serving the purpose of "beastifying" French and international politics: "Here comes all of Paris / What bizarre whims! / Tall [Big time] beasts [dummies] therefore / Are not a rare breed in Paris!"[11] This playlet is the first instance of the giraffe's transmutation into an agent for sublimating French politics. The play, presented from July 7 to August 15, 1827, was a minor success.

While articles against the government disappeared from the visible horizon of official newspaper publication, eyes were turned to a more open sky where the giraffe extended her long neck. As Narcisse-Achille de Salvandy wrote (in the giraffe's voice), "I see from far away and from on high... Everyone envies the wide scope of my gaze."[12] This feature of tangential geometry permitted her to become the emissary of free speech: "Illustrious beast, you who owe to your elevation the rare advantage of being able to carry the truth to the ears of kings without intermediaries, pray for us."[13]

Though the giraffe began as a mere diversion, she quickly became a topic in political pamphlets, which were not censored (unlike newspapers). The movement towards pamphlets was supported by the political events of the moment, notably the Greco-Turkish War. The Pasha of Egypt, donor of the giraffe, was allied with the Porte (the Turkish government) in the ongoing war against Greek independence. Every day during the summer of 1827, newspapers discussed the perilous situation of the Greek fighters. French opinion, encouraged by the press, supported the country of Leonidas I, hero-king of Sparta. This support permitted the first use of the giraffe for international politics, in an episode of pseudo-Turkish students who suddenly pretended to be Greek.[14]

Next, the giraffe's visit to King Charles X—a walk from Paris to the Château Saint-Cloud—on Monday, July 9, offered a pretext for another diversion, this time about domestic politics. This visit to the king is essential for understanding the evolution of the figure of the giraffe. Her supposed privileged relation with Charles X, as well as the spectacular security resources deployed by the government for her movements (she was treated like an invited foreign queen), made her an appropriate emissary for two writers of the opposition. Narcisse-Achille de Salvandy and François René, Vicomte de Chateaubriand, were members of a newly created society, the Amis de la liberté de la presse. Nearly simultaneously (between July 12 and 13), they printed two small brochures inspired by the giraffe's arrival.

Salvandy published his first *Lettre de la Girafe au Pacha d'Egypte* on July 12, 1827.[15] The giraffe here assumes the role of arbiter, indicating the distance or the republican disagreement between the people (France) and tyrannical authority (Villèle's government). Salvandy drew up a list of contradictions showing the deep fracture between the two factions. On one side were liberty, the Charter, industry, morality; on the other, censorship, the right of primogeniture, monasteries, lotteries, congregations, and absolute power. He also attacked the closure of public schools in favor of religious schools. After having savaged the Congregation, he took on all the projects of Villèle's ministry: the law of sacrilege, elections, censorship, and above all the inability of the Chambers to advise on the choice of government, which was left entirely to the king. Censorship was front and center: "France has had her tongue burnt out with the red-hot iron of censorship."[16]

This political allegory also allowed Salvandy to publish, as an addendum, French press clippings to "fill out" the so-called Egyptian newspapers of Alexandria (mentioned above in a notice from July 5). The giraffe suddenly became a journalist of record, a war correspondent from Paris to the Pasha of Egypt. This *Lettre de la Girafe* had an appendix attached: the *Journal Libre* (free newspaper) of political and literary affairs of Alexandria in Africa. This addendum had the mission of denouncing the ridiculous nature of censorship by showing the arbitrary nature of the cut texts. The rapid recovery, to the political profit of the giraffe, did not escape censorship. In the *Journal Libre* of July 12, we read, "censorship forbids little newspapers to make any jokes about the giraffe. The Lord Pasha is not unaware of this courtesy. Censorship has not permitted the announcement of the present delivery of the giraffe from the Pasha of Egypt. The Lord Pasha will demand explanations of this offense."[17] Thus, the giraffe herself became an object of censorship. Salvandy transgressed again on August 2, 1827 with a *Seconde lettre de la Girafe au Pacha d'Égypte*,[18] in which he denounced the government's supposed attempt to buy one-third of all newspaper space instead of devoting its budget to the arts.

Between July 12 and 14, 1827, a small theatrical entertainment appeared called *La Girafe, ou le Gouvernement des bêtes*.[19] By an anonymous hand, except that the author claimed to be sponsored by the animals of the Jardin du Roi, the "Lafontaine" on this occasion seems to have been Chateaubriand himself. For instance, he is cited in the epigraph, intended to give a playful tone to the entertainment: "In a representative monarchy, ministerial pleasure counts for nothing. Everyone is permitted to laugh or to be indignant about it. (M. the Vicomte de Chateaubriand, Speech on the Budget, June 18, 1827)."[20] The piece took a farcical tone in a tradition that borrowed from the fable and from another exotic precedent, the *Lettres persanes* (1721) of Charles de Secondat, Baron de Montesquieu. This literary caper evidently had the goal of deriding domestic politics. This government of the beasts overtly represents the ministerial government then in place, which had just imposed censorship on the press. It thus formed a sort of puppet show of the news, assuming the right to put the shift in government on stage. The giraffe here plays only a very minor role, only intervening through the intermediary of a goat "emissary of the giraffe," a very clear allusion to the important service the Ethiopian quadruped provided.

The play begins as the government of the animals, staged in a royal barnyard,[21] prepares for the giraffe. The two animal groups are the Turkeys (under the jurisdiction of the Hare, minister of war) and the Ducks (under the jurisdiction of the Duck, minister of the marine).[22] The presence of Foxes among the Turkeys creates a constant agitation. The minister of public instruction (the Bishop-Raven) at first denies their existence. Then seven are mentioned, and next four hundred. These Foxes seem to impose their will on the group of Turkeys, and end by devouring the fowls in the grand finale of the play. All these elements are intended to identify the Jesuits unmistakably, as Jean Berenger, the famous singer of popular songs, pointed out clearly in his poem/song on the Jesuits, "Les Réverends Pères":

Black men, where did you come from?
We come from underground.
Half foxes, half wolves,
Our rule is a mystery.
We are sons of Loyola:
You know why they exiled us.
We are returning; take care to keep quiet,
And see that your children follow our lessons.[23]

This anti-Jesuit poem, popular in 1827, directly inspired the use of foxes in the play. The number seven as applied to the Foxes refers to the seven small Jesuit seminaries in France, schools publicly declared in parliamentary session by Monseigneur Frayssinous, minister of religion, on May 25, 1826. Once again, the giraffe has only a very minimal role in the play, but she symbolizes the people on the move, a news item that attracts attention, and therefore perhaps also the press. This impression is confirmed when she is described as an exotic species that "walks without a bridle and without iron chains."[24] This attitude attracts the special interest of the minister, who proposes keeping the giraffe with the Turkeys in the Saint-Germain quarter of the Jardin du Roi. There she will be shut up and closely watched by them.

This parodic use of the giraffe, faithful to current news, was immediately and rapidly muzzled by censorship itself. At this point, another cultural event followed on July 27, 1827. Six Indians of the Osage tribe disembarked at Le Havre, newly arrived from Missouri. For the press, they were serviceable "savages" to be used in a manner similar to that of the giraffe.

The Osages arrived in Paris on August 13, creating a phenomenon of déjà vu. As he had done with the giraffe, the king received the Osages at Saint-Cloud on August 21, after which they had a meal of fruits. In the weeks that followed, they filled all the theaters and dance halls of the capital where they were invited free of charge. They rapidly became associated with the giraffe, as an article in *Le Constitutionnel* showed on August 6: "The giraffe begins to decrease in popularity; luckily, six savages have arrived to rekindle enthusiasm. We hope they will attract the crowd."[25] And on August 14, the paper noted:

> *The six savages arrived in Paris today. At one o'clock, they came by stagecoach as far as the city gate, where the prince and his entourage boarded a carriage; they went down the Rue de Rivoli to the Hôtel de la Terrasse. It is said that they will go successively to honor with their presence all the theaters of the capital, all the public establishments, and all the curiosities; they will begin with the giraffe.*[26]

The Osages in fact went to visit the giraffe on August 29 for three hours. This visit is important, because it inspired the writing of two anonymous pamphlets during the following weeks. Several caricatural lithographs also illustrate this encounter. The first pamphlet, entitled *La Girafe et les Osages*, is a brief text, light and mischievous in form (**FIG. 18.2**).[27] The second, a touch more serious, takes the title *Discours de la girafe au chef des six Osages (ou Indiens) prononcé le jour de leur visite au Jardin du roi. 15 septembre. Traduit de l'arabe par Alibassan, interprète de la girafe.*[28] This text was officially registered in the *Bibliographie de France* on September 15, 1827. The two pieces are written in the realistic, journalistic fashion of the street, with the reproduction of a grotesque pseudo-Osage language in the first. These *live* texts, supposedly taken from life, took the form of an exchange of impressions between tourists on French politics and customs. In *La Girafe et les Osages*, the giraffe warns the Indians that they are being fooled about the benefits of French civilization. The Osages are treated like unusual beasts, exploited by those who invite them. Here, the giraffe is a great animal that warns other brave animals of the misdeeds of civilization, in a Rousseau-like perspective that presents the good savage as the only carrier of simple truth.[29]

Fig. 18.2

G. Renou, *La Girafe et les Osages* (Paris, 1827), lithograph. BnF

The second pamphlet was printed by Honoré de Balzac, then a printer, and is in fact an invention of Balzac himself. Here also, the giraffe is a commentator on the times. Balzac made himself the interpreter of the giraffe, and not of the Osages as in the first pamphlet cited. In this work, she compares her royal visit with that of the Indians: she had received flowers to eat; they had received fruits to taste. The giraffe then asks for news of their great ruling chief in America: Does he have the virtue of a great king, does he like to hear truth, and does he take care of his subjects? Finally, she asks if the chief's ministers had established censorship so no that one would critique their administration.[30]

The long list continues. She likewise insists on the exploitation of the Osages and reports the gossip peddled about them. The end of the text is romantic in its desire: "Ah! Go back. Gentlemen, go quickly to your faraway lands, enjoy sweet liberty in the midst of your forests, on the banks of the Mississippi; leave the civilized people who could do you a bad turn."[31] This pamphlet, like the other, includes a lithograph representing the giraffe with the six Indians.

In that same second week of September, the theater put on a new play entitled *Les Osages en Goguette* (The Osages singing in a Goguette society). This vaudeville, overflowing with puns, turned the Osage Indians into Bretons disguised as Indians. The giraffe is cited as a "beast with a big neck." "We are accustomed to great blows," replies Marchartotatoongo, one of the Osages. In one of the conversations, Washingsabba, another Osage, alludes to political proposals linked to Chateaubriand's play about the giraffe:

> You know that among us are fine foxes whose black skin is spotted with blood. These foxes intrude into our wigwams, suborn our women, corrupt our children, and say they are sent by the Great Spirit to make all these kindnesses. [...] Soon the Black Spirit will stretch his candlesnuffer over the whole country of the Osages, like a vast skullcap.[32]

The farce's point of departure came from "Black Spirit," the real name of one of the Osages. The vaudeville took up this homonym to denounce the other black spirits, the Jesuits, "but the foxes who fear the paternal soul of the Great Chief held a consultation, and the Black Spirit decided unanimously that we will carry a yoke still more heavy than the one we have carried up to the present time. This yoke is called *saansühre*, and no one dares anymore to say a word without having asked and obtained permission beforehand."[33]

Then follows the grotesque chant of the Black Spirit in an imaginary Osage language, in which the only recognizable word is the repeated *saansühre* (a play on *censure*, French for censorship):

> *Kirabolama finachoroco*
> *Lopachataca lililisaansühre*
> *Borazalati Chosmaliroco*
> *Mestapaloca forcotosaansühre*
> *Kikissalora dalmokomroco*
> *Fofolatara pipichasaansuühre.*

The other Indian asks for and receives a translation of the text.

> *It means:*
> *One beautiful day the great Black Spirit*
> *Created the work of* saansühre;
> *It aids the Black Spirit*
> *Who owes his glory to* saansühre.

The end becomes even clearer, with domestic politics combining this time with international politics in Greece.[34]

Irritation against government censorship underwent still more metamorphoses, this time through the medium of lithography. In the days that preceded October 6, 1827, artist Achille Devéria deposited in the Cabinet des Estampes (Print Cabinet) of the Bibliothèque nationale a lithograph published by Mantoux entitled *Objets Précieux de la Curiosité Parisienne* (FIG. 18.3). The caption read: "Diogenes with his lantern seeking a man in broad daylight. / Great Gods! You see them and do not laugh."[35] This lithograph marvelously sums up the fight against censorship using the giraffe and the six Osage Indians. The subject undoubtedly found its origin in a celebrated Italian painting, *The Adoration of the Magi* by Bernadino Luini (a disciple of Leonardo da Vinci), in the church of Serrano. This was the first painting to represent a giraffe, as the Florentines had had the privilege of owning the first giraffe in Europe in the 1480s. In the lithograph, three giraffes replace the three Magi, and the six Osage Indians contemplate the scene from the balcony. Diogenes searches in vain for an honest man in a world peopled with animals. The comic character Punchinello and flying dragons represent the folly of the present situation.

The exotic gaze of the giraffe and the Indians, whose extranational, foreign perspective created an out-of-the-ordinary "other" space of discourse, focused attention on the "unspoken" void created by censorship. That "unspoken" space then became the principal subject of discourse, quickly contributing to the emergence of a social malaise that ultimately generated the 1830 revolt against the king. In other words, the social pandemonium created by the exoticism of the giraffe and the Indians produced a derailment of political life and a redirection of energies through plays, pamphlets, and visual imagery that indirectly repossessed what censorship had suppressed. These exotic "Others" were ironically the last republicans capable of questioning the well-founded nature of a "civilization" that behaved like a savage animal.

Fig. 18.3 Mantoux (?), *Diogène avec sa lanterne cherchant un homme en plein midi: "Grands Dieux! vous les voyez et vous n'en riez pas,"* 1827 (?), lithograph. BnF

Translated from the French by Jane E. Boyd

1 Jacques Vivent, *Charles X, dernier roi de France et de Navarre* (Paris: Le Livre contemporain, 1958), 304–5. The most prominent newspapers in 1827 were *Le Journal des Débats, La Quotidienne, La France Chrétienne, La Pandore, Le Constitutionnel, Le Figaro, Le Journal du Commerce, Le Courrier Français,* and *Le Moniteur.*

2 The king had put the project in *dépôt* (in deposit) on December 12, 1826. Chateaubriand would call this proposal "la loi vandale" (the vandal law).

3 Sometimes called *le Parti-Prêtre* (the Priest Party).

4 François-René de Chateaubriand, "Du rétablissement de la censure par l'ordonnance du 24 juin 1827," in *Œuvres complètes de M. le Vicomte de Chateaubriand,* vol. 27 (Paris: Ladvocat, Librairie, 1828), 69.

5 She had left her winter quarters in Marseille on May 20, 1827.

6 Michael Allin, *La Girafe de Charles X: Son extraordinaire voyage de Khartoum à Paris* (Paris: J. C. Lattès, 2000), 240.

7 *Le Courrier Français,* 1 July 1827, p. 3, col. 1–2. See, for instance, Louis Saint-Ange, *Notice sur la Girafe: Observations curieuses sur le caractère, les habitudes et l'instinct de ce quadrupède,* 1st ed. (Paris: Moreau, 1827).

8 "On va établir à Alexandrie un journal dont M. Bousquet Deschamps, auteur de quelques ouvrages, sera le rédacteur. Le pacha, enchanté de cette entreprise, tient infiniment à son exécution. La liberté de la presse voyage; la voilà fixé en Égypte." *Le Constitutionnel,* 5 July 1827, p. 3, col. 1–2.

9 *Le Constitutionnel,* 7 July 1827, p. 3, col. 2.

10 Emmanuel Théaulon, Théodore Anne, and Jean-Baptiste Gondelier, *La Girafe, ou Une journée au Jardin du Roi, tableau-à-propos, en vaudevilles* (Paris: Barba, 1827).

11 "Ici tout Paris se rend / Quels caprices plus bizarres ! / Les grandes bêtes pourtant / À Paris ne sont pas rares!" Ibid., 11.

12 "...je vois de loin et de haut, ...cette portée de regard que tout le monde m'envie." [Narcisse-Achille de Salvandy], *Lettre de la Girafe au Pacha d'Égypte, pour lui rendre compte de son voyage à Saint-Cloud, et envoyer les rognures de la censure de France au journal qui s'établit à Alexandrie en Afrique* (Paris: A. Sautelet, 1827), 1.

13 "Illustre bête, vous qui devez à votre élévation le rare avantage de pouvoir porter la vérité sans intermédiaire à l'oreille

des rois, priez pour nous." Théaulon et al., *La Girafe, ou Une journée au Jardin du Roi,* 17.

14 Ibid., 13–15.

15 Salvandy, *Lettre de la Girafe au Pacha d'Egypte.*

16 "... la France avait eu la langue brûlée avec le fer rouge de la censure." Ibid., 12.

17 "La censure a interdit aux petits journaux toute plaisanterie sur la girafe. Monseigneur le pacha ne sera pas insensible à cette courtoisie.—La censure n'a pas permis d'annoncer le présent envoi de la girafe au pacha d'Égypte. Monseigneur le pacha demandera des explications sur cette offense." Ibid., 39–40.

18 [Narcisse-Achille de Salvandy], *Seconde lettre de la Girafe au Pacha d'Égypte, en lui envoyant son album enrichi des*

dernières noirceurs de la censure (Paris: A. Sautelet, 1827).

19 [François-René, Vicomte de Chateaubriand], *La Girafe, ou le Gouvernement des bêtes, divertissement interrompu, donné par MM. les animaux du Jardin du Roi comme un témoignage de leur reconnaissance envers le Pacha d'Egypte, à l'occasion de l'arrivée de la Girafe à la Ménagerie de Paris* (Paris: Ambroise Dupont, Haut-Cœur; Ponthieu, Palais-Royal; et les marchands de nouveautés, 1827).

20 François René, Vicomte de Chateaubriand, *Discours de M. le Vicomte de Chateaubriand, pair de France, contre le budget de 1828, Prononcé à la Chambre des pairs le 18 juin* (Paris: Chez Ladvocat, 1827). This text was published in the days preceding June 23.

21 This was an almost treasonous allusion. The representation of a country barnyard (not an exotic zoological garden) referred to the ministers' base actions. The choice of French animals mixed with exotic ones (monkeys, giraffe, and so forth), serves the purpose of a local polemic examined from a foreign point of view.

22 In nineteenth-century Parisian *argot* or slang, *le dindon* (the turkey) represented a simpleton, one easily fooled, or a deceived husband. *Le canard* (the duck) was a faithful husband. See Lorédan Larchey, *Dictionnaire de l'argot parisien* (Paris: Polo, 1872; reprint, Paris: Éditions de Paris, 1996).

23 "Hommes noirs d'où sortez-vous? / Nous sortons de dessous terre. / Moitié renards, moitiés loups, / Notre règle est un mystère. / Nous sommes fils de Loyola: / Vous savez pourquoi on nous exila. / Nous rentrons; songez à vous taire, / Et que vos enfants suivent nos leçons."

Pierre-Jean de Béranger, "Les Révérends Pères," in *Toutes les chansons de Béranger* (Brussels: F. Verteneuil, 1843), 204–5.

24 "...marche et sans bride et sans fers." Ibid., 8.

25 "La giraffe commence à baisser; heureusement il nous arrive six sauvages pour réchauffer l'enthousiasme. On espère qu'ils attireront la foule." *Le Constitutionnel*, 6 August 1827, p. 3, col. 1.

26 "Les six sauvages sont arrivés à Paris aujourd'hui. À une heure; ils sont venus par la diligence jusqu'à la barrière, où le prince et sa suite sont montés en fiacre; ils sont descendus rue de Rivoli, hôtel de la Terrasse. On dit qu'ils vont successivement honorer de leur présence tous les théâtres de la capitale, tous les établissemens publics et toutes les curiosités. Ils commenceront par la giraffe." *Le Constitutionnel*, 14 August 1827.

27 *Le Girafe et les Osages* (Paris: Paul Ledoux, 1827).

28 "Alibassan" [Honoré de Balzac], *Discours de la girafe au chef des six Osages (ou Indiens) prononcé le jour de leur visite au Jardin du roi. 15 septembre. Traduit de l'arabe par Alibassan, interprète de la girafe* (Paris: Hautecœur-Martinet, 1827).

29 *Le Girafe et les Osages*, 6–7.

30 Balzac, *Discours de la girafe*, 4–6.

31 Ibid., 8, 10, 11.

32 "Vous savez qu'il y a parmi nous de fins renards dont la peau noire est tachetée de sang, lesquels renards s'introduisent dans nos wig-wams, subornent nos femmes, corrompent nos enfans, et se disent envoyés par le grand esprit pour faire toutes ces gentillesses. Or ils ont commencé par gagner l'esprit du grand chef de la tribu. Quoiqu'ils aient tué son grand-père, il est tellement bon, il aime pardonner, qu'il a oublié que sa sûreté et celle des Osages dépendaient de

l'extermination de cette race maudite. Plus on les tolérait, plus ils prirent de pouvoir, jusqu'à ce qu'enfin ils se rendirent maître de tout. Bientôt l'esprit noir étendit son éteignoir sur tout le pays des Osages, comme une vaste calotte." "Cadet-Roussel," *Les Osages en goguette, ou bien encore: Voici ce qu'on dit et voici ce que c'est; Les Indiens ne sont pas ce qu'un vain peuple pense; Ne vous y fiez pas, gobe-mouche de France; Imitation de Lamartine; Vous êtes tous des imbéciles; Henriade* (Paris: Librairie française et étrangère, 1827), 16–17.

33 Ibid., 17.

34 "Cela veut dire: / Un beau jour le grand esprit noir / Créa l'œuvre de la saansühre; / Elle secourut l'esprit noir / Qui dut sa gloire à la saansühre." Ibid., 18–19. The end of the text reads, in part, "So when does a minister have for all power / Hands to take all, eyes to see nothing? / Ignorant Osage! What! The greatest marvels / Resound in your long ears without teaching you anything. / Indians, does it remind you of progress… / The Greeks abandoned, and their arms usurped. / The Greek Revolution and the intervention of European nations. / Reason is trampled under the feet of bigots; / With a party's anger the Charter is burned" ("Quand donc un ministère eut-il pour tout pouvoir / Des mains pour prendre tout, des yeux pour ne rien voir ? / Osage ignorant! quoi! les plus grandes merveilles / Résonnent sans t'instruire à tes longues oreilles. / Faut-il, Indiens, faut-il vous rappeler le cours… / Les Grecs abandonnés, et leurs fers usurpés. / La Révolution grecque et intervention des nations européennes. / Sous les pieds des cagots la raison est foulée ; Au fureur d'un parti la Charte est immolée"). Ibid., 27.

35 "Diogène avec sa lanterne cherchant un home en plein Midi / Grands Dieux! vous les voyez et vous n'en riez pas." Département des Estampes et de la photographie, Bibliothèque nationale de France, Paris.

PART V

NATURAL HISTORY AND FRENCH CULTURE

SYMPOSIUM COMMENTARY

ANDREA GOULET

Each of the talks in this interdisciplinary session, which takes us from geology to giraffes, reflects in some way on the relation between the natural sciences and that which is precisely *not* natural: the sociopolitical order of things—and more specifically, of France. John Tresch's essay shows how scientific discourse provided models for social reform movements; Claudine Cohen explains that new fields of geology and paleontology gave nineteenth-century thinkers new ways to visualize human history; Alain Lescart and Denise Davidson tell us how an African giraffe in Étienne Geoffroy Saint-Hilaire's Jardin des Plantes was turned into a discursive screen for governmental opposition. That *esquive* or stratagem to dodge censorship recalls a later text that also relies on fanciful detours to make a controversial point: Pierre Boitard's *Paris avant les hommes* (Paris Before Man).[1] Boitard's antediluvian fantasy, published

posthumously in 1861, was a fictionalized account of "fossil man," but because the Académie des sciences sided officially with Georges Cuvier's dismissal of human prehistory, Boitard had to come up with a comically convoluted framing device in which an extraterrestrial demon, the *diable boiteux*, takes the author on a dream journey to the deep past. One well-known illustration from the novel shows the narrator and his grinning guide astride a meteor, preparing to visit prehistoric times.[2] The image demonstrates the link between science and imagination that Cohen signals in her essay, as well as the displacement to avoid censorship exemplified by the allegorical "Gouvernement des Bêtes" discussed in Lescart's essay. The fact that Boitard had to avoid censorship by a *scientific* academy, rather than the imperial government of Napoleon III, reminds us (as have Michel Foucault and others) that the "natural" sciences were never actually natural or neutral, but rather that scientific discourse is always already political and institutional.

Göran Blix, for his part, suggests that the impulse to allegorize is tempting, not only for nineteenth-century authors, but also for us as critics and readers—as when attempts are made to map Honoré de Balzac's views of the debate between naturalists Georges Cuvier and Geoffroy Saint-Hilaire onto his political conservatism. I have made a similar move in my own work, for example reading Cuvierian catastrophism and Lamarckian transformism into the politics of Second Empire catacomb crime fictions by Élie Berthet and Constant Guéroult. But when it comes to Balzac, I fully agree with Blix that we cannot take his stated systems of classification as successful—or even fully earnest—guides to his writing. There is always a gap between the "social species" model of the "Avant-propos" of *La Comédie humaine* and the rich disorder of Balzacian language, which splendidly spills out of any container of classificatory schemes. In the 1970s and 1980s, poststructuralist readers of Balzac saw that gap as exceeding the author's intention; for them, the social species model revealed a realist ideology of totalizing knowledge that only the slippery play of language itself could undercut. Blix cleverly sends the ball of play back into Balzac's court by allowing him to enjoy both the will to classify *and* the delights of that will's disruption. Françoise Gaillard, too, has presented Balzac as taking the scientific model merely as a useful fiction, one that allowed him not only to impose a provisional order but also to embrace the chimerical monstrosities that escape that order.[3] Giving in once more to the allegorical impulse, I will connect that idea back to politics, because for all of Balzac's nostalgic conservatism, he could not have written *La Comédie humaine* without the social mobility of his post-revolutionary age, without the possibility that *l'épicier* (the grocer) could become a *Pair de France* (peer of the realm).

At least two of our speakers have written elsewhere about the association between Cuvier's geological term "revolutions" and the violent cycles of political revolution in early nineteenth-century France.[4] This analogy between geological and political revolutions deserves further discussion. Who in the nineteenth century used it? To what ends? And how far can that analogy be taken? I conclude by bringing back the stratigraphic geological model that Cohen described and asking whether we can visualize the *splendeurs* and *misères* of Balzac's social order according to the Cuvierian, catastrophist model of terrain, with *La Comédie humaine's* social climbers jutting upwards, puncturing layers of hierarchy like seismic upthrusts—and his victims of financial failure falling through the suddenly crumbling strata that had held firm for centuries before.

1   Pierre Boitard, *Paris avant les hommes: L'homme fossile, etc.; Histoire naturelle du globe terrestre* (Paris: Passard, 1861). On this and other nineteenth-century French fictions of prehistory, see Marc Angenot and Nadia Khouri, "An International Bibliography of Prehistoric Fiction," *Science Fiction Studies* 8, no. 1 (March 1981): 38–53; and Claudine Cohen, *The Fate of the Mammoth: Fossils, Myth, and History*, trans. William Rodarmor (Chicago: University of Chicago Press, 2002), 12 (originally published as *Le Destin du Mammouth* [Paris: Seuil, 1994]).

2   The book's illustrations can be seen at http://www.trussel.com/prehist/boitardf.htm.

3   Françoise Gaillard, "La Science: Modèle ou vérité; Réflexions sur l'avant-propos à *La Comédie humaine*," in *Balzac: L'invention du roman*, ed. Claude Duchet and Jacques Neefs (Paris: Belfond, 1982), 57–83.

4   Cohen, *The Fate of the Mammoth*; Göran Blix, *From Paris to Pompeii: French Romanticism and the Cultural Politics of Archaeology* (Philadelphia: University of Pennsylvania Press, 2009).

NATURAL HISTORY AND FRENCH CULTURE

INDIVIDUAL PAPERS

14. "THE QUEST FOR "LOST WORLDS":
INTELLECTUAL REVOLUTIONS AND MUTATIONS
OF THE IMAGINATION AT THE TURN OF THE
NINETEENTH CENTURY
Claudine Cohen (CC)

Question: I was wondering if you could account for the enormous admiration and respect by artists and writers for natural scientists that was developing through the whole romantic period. It's really remarkable—what accounts for that hold over the imagination in the domain of the arts and literature?

CC: This is a very broad question. A general answer is that this was the age of what is called positivism in France, founded by Auguste Comte. Science was revered absolutely, not only by the scientific world, but also by philosophers, by the general public, and by artists. And it's very interesting to see how science was integrated into the artistic dimension and discourse. For example, in literature, Balzac was quoting science all the time not only as a general justification of his novels; he also quoted Franz Joseph Gall to explain the physiognomy of people and their various psychological features. He used the phlogistic theory of chemistry and all kinds of science that are now obsolete as justification for his fiction and for his writing. And all through the century there was a very strong presence of the sciences.

And speaking of Flaubert, *Bouvard et Pécuchet* is a wonderful novel concentrated on the sciences. These two people do all the sciences—chemistry, paleontology, medicine—and everything fails. At the end of the century, it was the reverse of August Comte's ambition, that the sciences were going to succeed in giving us a general idea of the world. But the importance of science in society in this period was enormous, and that's why it is reflected in the arts.

Cuvier remains fascinating, although his ideas are obsolete; he was a fixist, he was a catastrophist, and then it appeared that one should think about evolution, and catastrophes were not the way to think of geology. But Cuvier brought this very interesting image of the parts and the whole. This paradigm, going from a little tiny bit to reconstruct a totality, from the footprint to the whole animal: I wrote a book on that called *La Méthode de Zadig* (Zadig's Method). And all the time in the nineteenth century, everyone referred to that. When Flaubert wrote *Salammbô*, which is about Carthage, archaeologists reproached him, saying, "Well, you have invented everything, there are not many things left that can explain what Carthage was, how do you know?" And he said, "I did the same as Cuvier, I took little pieces and I made a whole world." So this endured all through the century, this model, the paradigm: what I call the synecdoche, the part for the whole. I think the whole century was reflecting this very strong vision of Cuvier.

15. SOCIAL SPECIES IN THE *COMÉDIE HUMAINE*: BALZAC'S USE OF NATURAL HISTORY
Göran Blix (GB)

Question: Obviously Balzac was not alone in using classification as a literary method—I'm thinking of all the physiognomies of the period and so on. The question is not so much what Balzac hoped to achieve, or his other contemporaries who were using similar methods, but it obviously was viewed as a very effective style. Do you have any sense of why this would have been so appealing to the readers at the time?

GB: You're right that it definitely was, because you have this gargantuan project of *Les français peints par eux-mêmes*, for example, by Louis Curmer in the 1840s, which was a huge compendium of several hundred literary physiologies of ten or so pages, to which everyone who was a writer contributed, including Balzac himself. It was doing on a collective scale to some extent what the *Comédie humaine* was doing within the framework of one person's work. The project of mapping the new social types produced by mobility, capitalism, and diversification in the post-revolutionary period was one of the major literary enterprises at the time. Why they would have chosen to adopt the language of *la physiologie*, for example, I'm not sure—maybe because it conferred some sort of legitimacy or credibility or scientific prestige on the enterprise. But as we've heard, science was a model for literary enterprise not just for Balzac, but for all the writers of the period.

Many people have said this before, there was a great deal of anxiety as well about—given a person you encountered—what class did they belong to, what profession? All these things were no longer so clear, so semiotically transparent, as they had been in the ancién regime. So in order to be able to identify people properly, you needed a roadmap, a code, some sort of a text, so in that sense this is also pedagogical literature that reassures people and says, "well, that's a *femme comme il faut*, that's a *lorette*, that's a *gamin de Paris*." It allows you to name people that somehow potentially pose a threat.

CC: I agree with you about the metaphorical use of these words. You stress the notion of heredity at some points, and this may be one parameter, but there is another thing that you mention at the end, the notion of "milieu." And I think all these types take their meaning in their milieu, and that's why Balzac's descriptions are so important. People say they are boring, but they are really what gives meaning. For example, the *pension* Vauquer, in the beginning of *Le Père Goriot*, is exactly the milieu that the people are going to fit into, not only to fit in but to use the colors of the walls and transform themselves as creatures of that milieu. And Paris also is a milieu, so this is not only a biological notion, but it becomes a social one. And I think Balzac invented the social notion of milieu, after Lamarck. So this is at least as important as classification and perhaps even heredity.

GB: Thank you very much for mentioning that. I actually wanted to address the importance of the milieu, but in twenty-five minutes it would have taken too long, and you wrote about the milieu as Balzac co-opted it from Lamarck, so I didn't want to repeat that train of thought again. But it is important, and it's also an ambiguous thing, because you would think that his reference to the milieu as the formative influence that finally shapes and sets different characters and turns them into species actually implies that there is no prefabricated or hereditary form. In other words, that would avoid the unhappy political consequences of positing species that are innate, that are born in the way they are, because they are simply produced contextually by the environment.

But I think it's often quite ambiguous in Balzac whether everyone is born with a universal potential that seemingly gets shaped because they're thrust into the machinery of the bureaucracy, and *voilà*, finally months later, they're a bureaucrat. And it raises other questions, such as: Well, what if the bureaucrat moves into a different walk of life? Does he remain a bureaucrat forever or does he suddenly turn into another species? So these are questions that he doesn't quite address and which makes the issue of the milieu unable to fully respond to the political problem presented by his language, his rhetoric of classification.

And there is something in the *Physiologie de l'employé* (which I cited) where he talks about the bureaucrat, and he says, the bureaucrat is perfectly outfitted to occupy this shell of a *bureau*, with *le plume* and *la table*, because he is produced by it. And then Balzac says, but maybe he was a *crétin* to begin with and then went in there because he had an elected affinity to that place. So he also turns that milieu idea on its head, and we don't know which is the cause and the consequence, so his thinking about that is fuzzy as well.

Question: Was the notion of type used by biologists in the 1830s?

GB: Not as far as I know.

Alain Lescart (AL)

Question: Where does the name "Zarafa" for the
giraffe come from?

AL: Everybody thinks that the name of the giraffe
was Zarafa, but I have never found that name
quoted anywhere. Michael Allin wrote a book in
1998 and he called her Zarafa, because in Arabic
zarafa is the word for giraffe. But nowhere have I
found any source in newspapers of the time where
that name is used. Everybody calls her this today,
but I have found no evidence that she was called
this at that time.

END-OF-SESSION DISCUSSION

GB: Andrea Goulet brings up an excellent point
about the analogy between political and geological revolutions. Nothing that I've seen in Balzac
comes to mind immediately. I'm sure that he
referenced geological language as much as many
of his contemporaries did, and it's something that
I'd love to look into. But the person I think of
foremost is the historian Jules Michelet, who was
quite explicit in his use of geological and fossil
language and the imagery of volcanic eruptions.
Notably, in the preface of 1869 to his *Histoire de
France* and also in the preface of *Histoire de la
Révolution française*, he likened the advent of the
Revolution, not surprisingly, to a volcanic eruption
that has been long in coming. That's a trope of the
period as well, because the sentiment was that
things were about to break through the surface in
the culture, and he really made major use of that
trope of the volcano. And of course, Michelet
thought of social classes in terms of geological
strata. So he said *la chaleur*, the warmth, is in the
lower strata, and that's what's going to regenerate
and rejuvenate our culture. So that metaphor was
all over the place in Michelet. And you can also
look in his *Histoire romaine* from 1829, where he
talks about the prehistoric revolutions that formed
and shaped the geographical terrain of Italy, which
seem to find a political and social continuation
in the early political revolutions of the Roman
landscape, as if there were no solution of contin-
uity between the two.

CC: Well, I think the concept of cataclysms and
ruins did not begin with Cuvier. It is something
that really was pervasive since the end of the
seventeenth century. Seeing the earth as a heap
of ruins, and the mountains as some remains of
a gigantic event—some people attributed that to
the deluge, but others were catastrophists well
before the French Revolution. So it's not really a
new imagination; there were actually two opposite
visions. There was the slow change, and the water,
and the immersion, and the decrease of the water.
And the other one was the fire and the cataclysms
that could have happened.

But I think that the word "revolution" was
not very much used in the eighteenth century in
the sense that Cuvier and the French Revolution
used it, so it's certainly a new use. In Cuvier's
prose, there was really a rhetoric of catastrophes
and immense upheavals which certainly spoke to
the imagination of the people. It had happened not
so long before he was writing in 1812. So I think
the association is certainly very tangible. I don't
know if people think of Cuvier when they delve
into this imagery of ruins and the world in ruins;
but if you read, for example, the preface to *La confession d'un enfant du siècle*, by Alfred de Musset,
it's an absolutely wonderful text, in which Musset
explains that they are the sons of a generation that
lived through the Revolution, the Empire, and now
everything is in ruin. He wrote, "Then came to
the earth a race of children with gray hair," a very
striking image. I think this imagination was part
of a paradigm, an intellectual and imaginary paradigm, which explains its success.

AL: You refer to Pierre Boitard's use of the demon,
the *diable boiteux*. This comes from Alain-René
Lesage's *Le Diable boiteux*, written in the eighteenth century, which was the prototype of the
new literature that happens just after the French
Revolution that we call *le tableau des mœurs*. *Le
Diable boiteux* is the story of a man who goes to an
attic in Paris, and it's the bedroom of a magician.
And there are different jars, and one has a devil
in it. It's a kind of Aladdin story, and the devil tells
the man, "Please, let me go," and says, "I'll give
you something wonderful if you let me go." He
promises that he's going to open up all the roofs
of Paris and show him all of what people do in
private. So it's the entrance into privacy which,
to me, *le tableau des mœurs* represents, and Balzac
of course, all that, even the giraffe curiosity. It is

the idea that you cannot restrain people anymore, you have to open up the roofs now. We have entered a new world, there's no way we can go back to the old systems, the ancién regime.

John Tresch (JT): To go back to the first question, about revolution and its relation to politics and geology, there is a really interesting text from 1848 by one of Pierre Leroux's disciples, Ange Guépin. It's called the *Organ of Genesis of the Earth*, and it was an attempt to tell the history of the earth using the language of embryology. So there are huge transformations in the surface of the earth, but we shouldn't see these as catastrophes, as unnatural, as changes in the laws of nature, rather we should see them as the same kind of development, which is predictable, and necessary, as we see in embryology. That's one of many attempts— Michelet does the same—to make the Revolution, as catastrophic as it may have appeared, to seem like a natural and necessary process.

CC: If I may add something on this French desire to speak of catastrophes and revolution, this may be part of the reason why Cuvierian dogma remained influential for so long in France. From the 1830s in England, by contrast, Lyell had put forward other means of thinking about the history of the earth, in which there was a continuous causality. Lyell insisted that slow causes were the core of geological processes. So maybe there are deeper reasons, but there is perhaps something here that belongs to the French imagination.

Question: About the giraffe as a fad—it's interesting that Charles X was the Duc d'Artois and in the eighteenth century he knew very well how to make fads. He was one of the fashion masters of the eighteenth century, for example, at the game of bagatelle. So I'm wondering how you adapt someone who was quite libertine in the eighteenth century to be the opposite in the way that we're talking about in politics in the 1820s.

Denise Z. Davidson (DZD) :
I don't really see Charles X as the opposite by the 1820s, but there's a very big difference between being king and being the Duc d'Artois. One of the stories that circulated widely involved the protocol that the Duchesse d'Angoulême insisted be followed. The giraffe had to be brought to Charles X at Saint-Cloud even though Geoffroy wanted

Charles X to go to the Jardin du Roi (it was obviously called the Jardin du Roi at that time). I think the king was willing, but it was the Duchesse d'Angoulême who insisted that the giraffe had to be presented to the king, that the king couldn't go to the giraffe. So there was not that much of a break; I don't see that he would have in any way been opposed to the construction of the giraffe as a fad. It was his giraffe, so whatever admiration was expressed for the giraffe reflected on him.

Question: I would like to come back to the first question raised earlier about how we can account for the tremendous presence of science in French literature. And it seems to me that the usual answer that Claudine Cohen took, about the ranking influence of positivism, is not quite satisfactory. I would say it's the other way around. Positivism was the expression of this overarching presence of science in French culture, and when positivism was first coined by Comte in 1844 he continuously tried to confine the influence of science. When he created spiritual power, he tried to balance the power of science with the power of women and workers.

My second point comes from the last talk, by Denise Davidson. I think one major reason of the overarching influence of science is consumer culture, and science was really a driving force in the development of this consumer culture. There were science columns in the popular press and in newspapers, and especially before, at the time of the Cuvier-Geoffroy controversy, journalists were accepted at the Académie des sciences, and they even had a heated room next to the big room where they could write their papers after the session.

In 1830, because Geoffroy didn't want to argue with Cuvier in front of the journalists, he said in this case we will stop the controversy, and Arago, who was then the secretary, decided that the Académie would have its own weekly column. So every week there was a special science column together with the theatre column and the exhibition column in all newspapers. It's this presence of science in print culture, or this pocket *encyclopédie*, and the newspaper and all this consumer culture—and popular courses, which Comte himself was teaching—that seem more related to this emergence of mass consumption and commodification of science. What is your opinion of that?

CC: Well, we can talk of positivism even if the word was not invented then. What I named positivism is this attitude that put science at the top of any human activity. I think this idea was formulated by Auguste Comte quite early in his career, but it certainly also derived from the fact that many sciences emerged at the turn of the nineteenth century. The word biology is invented at that time. Geology, paleontology, cosmology—all kinds of sciences that were not yet formed in the eighteenth century happened to be really formalized at that time—not only the sciences themselves, but also the technology, the techniques. And there was an abundance of novelty created from the improvement of techniques all through the nineteenth century.

So science popularization alone doesn't explain why literature or art used and embodied the sciences. For example, when Flaubert said he wanted to create a science of writing, he wanted to write scientifically in some way; this was quite a goal for a writer. It seems that literature had the sciences as a model, and it was more than just having an ear to popular journals. I think it's really that science became a social ideal—which it was not previously, even in the eighteenth century—so I think this was really a novelty in the nineteenth century, and literature really became a servant of science. It embodied the sciences, it narrated the science, and its ideal was to become a science itself. So I think it's a bit more complicated than just saying popularization of science induced the writers to write about science. I think this impoverishes the possibility of analysis.

GB: It seems something might be gained by thinking about literature as aspiring to create truth effects as well. That wouldn't be something new in the nineteenth century; certainly, you can go back to the eighteenth century and talk about all sorts of novel prefaces that attempt to say that this was a manuscript found and then translated, et cetera. But with the resurgence or emergence of all these disciplines and sciences in the early nineteenth century, it seems that the bar for truth was being set higher and higher. To produce truth effects, you had to borrow from these fields.

And that also goes concurrently with the devalorization of rhetoric that happened with the romantic revolution. The Romantics notoriously felt that if they were engaging in acts of rhetoric, following genres and conventions, they were speaking falsely. So they had the conceit that to speak truly, you had to break through the hollow shell of rhetoric. Well, how can you do that better than by borrowing your truth effects from science? As you go further and further into the nineteenth century, the bar to achieve those same truth effects gets set ever higher. When Flaubert set about recreating a historical novel in Carthage in *Salammbô*, he was no longer being bound by the same vague criteria that Hugo used when he wrote *Notre-Dame de Paris*. He engaged in a lot more research. By a similar token, the scientific rhetoric really gets amped up later in somebody like Zola, but isn't it actually the same phenomenon as the pseudo-erudition that we find in some of the romantic writers?

DZD: I would add that seeing the giraffe represented was also an opportunity not just to view this novel exotic creature that's arrived, but to feel as though one was participating in science, even indirectly.

AL: Like you said, even the romantic order, wherein everything is based on imagination, fulfilled the need to read science. I work on *grisettes* and representations of courtesans, and everybody based their work on work by Parent du Châtelet on prostitution in Paris. This was the most serious study that had ever been made on prostitution, with graphics—statistics was a new science. And everybody read that, and it was transferred into novels, so it had become the new approach. I'm wondering how much Napoleon sparked that also, because you know he was also a member of the science academy, and he pushed science enormously. I think it's already present in Robespierre, in the Temple of Reason and what happened after the French Revolution. And certainly it's coming from the eighteenth century.

JT: The idea that science is everywhere because it's being commercialized is not necessarily in opposition to the idea that science is being championed as a new spiritual power, which Saint-Simon and Comte are saying. People in literature have written that romantic authors saw themselves as taking on the mantle of the priest, replacing the priesthood. In parallel with that is the *sacre du savant*—I don't know if the bar has been set higher, but it's been displaced. We can't look to the church for truth about the cosmic order, instead poetry as well as science is going to give us those truths. And interestingly that goes hand in hand with commercialization of both of those genres, both science and literature.

Question: How do you think that the interaction between science and art during the periods that you're discussing may have had something to do with the development of French imperialism? For example, you talked about the colonies in the Caribbean, you talked about the invasion of Algeria, then you brought up Napoleon and the fact that he launched these incredible invasions in Egypt, so I know that that impetus is present there, but could you elaborate on that a little bit?

DZD: Science and art certainly did contribute towards the push to the new colonialism that we'll see develop in the nineteenth century. And the argument that I'm trying to develop here is that one of the reasons that the giraffe was so appealing was that she served to offer a lesson about the exotic world in a way that made it seem less threatening and potentially civilizing. If the giraffe could be brought to France and could be so docile and willing to go along with what everybody is asking her to do, well then maybe when we go to other parts of the world we'll find something similar. Judging by the images that we have and the texts and the way that the press covered the giraffe upon her arrival, this was the case. I found a book by Angela Pao, about how exotic accounts or plays set in exotic locations changed so drastically with the invasion of Algeria, to be very useful. This is a hypothesis, that the giraffe may have prepared the way for this new approach to the rest of the world that will come as the nineteenth century goes on.

JT: Back to the Saint-Simonians: They're all for it. Clearly people who've told the history of the social sciences say anthropology goes hand in hand with imperialism. You want to map all these populations, find their weak spots, figure out who they are and how to put them into a unified order. The Saint-Simonians are part of that, the birth of the social sciences, but I was trying to emphasize that it's not just about objectively studying, but also about trying to orchestrate a peaceful imperialism that is not seen as imperialism, but as a new civilization that will merge the East and the West. And so Saint-Simonian imagery, their new religion, is all about taking imagery and symbolism from Western traditions and merging them with Islam, and also the detritus of Orientalism, just weird imaginings from all the traditions of religion that are entering French culture at the time.

FRENCH NATURAL HISTORY: REFLECTING BACK, LOOKING FORWARD

PART VI

FRENCH NATURAL HISTORY:
REFLECTING BACK, LOOKING FORWARD

Previous page and detail, left Sèvres Porcelain Manufactory, Vase with African Birds, 1822, porcelain, ormolu,
and bronze; vase by Evariste Fragonard, birds by Pauline
Knip, ornaments by Didier, gilding by Boullemier *l'aîné*.
Hillwood Museum and Gardens, Washington, D.C., Bequest
of Marjorie Merriweather Post, 1973. Photo by E. Owen

THE POWER OF OBJECTS

BERNADETTE BENSAUDE-VINCENT

HISTORICAL STUDIES BASED ON MUSEUM COLLECTIONS invite historians to reconstruct the life stories of objects: who made them, where did they come from, how they were shipped, how they were used, and so forth. In paying attention to material culture, object-centered history leads to the revision of a number of popular clichés. In particular, two standard concepts about the period under study might be reexamined in light of the papers delivered at this symposium: the view of natural history as the most popular science in the age of romanticism, and the view of 1789 as an epochal break in French culture that marked the beginning of a new era.

NATURAL HISTORY ON THE MAP OF KNOWLEDGE

What is special about natural history? To what extent was it unique? Indeed, there is factual evidence that natural history in general and botany in particular enjoyed a particular status in the period under study. Among the two hundred volumes of the *Encyclopédie méthodique* published between 1782 and 1832, fifty-one were dedicated to natural history, with six volumes on zoology and thirteen on botany. The volume of plates for the *Tableau encyclopédique et méthodique des trois règnes de la nature*, which began publication in 1788, included a thousand engravings for botany alone (versus 108 plates for all of natural history in Denis Diderot and Jean Le Rond d'Alembert's famed *Encyclopédie*).

The *Encyclopédie méthodique*, however, is not a good indicator of popularity. It was a commercial failure and the encyclopedic "landscape" shaped by Diderot and D'Alembert was replaced by disciplinary dictionaries that mirrored the increasing influence of academic science.

It is often claimed that the popularity of natural history in this period was due to the overarching influence of Jean-Jacques Rousseau's *Les rêveries d'un promeneur solitaire*, which propagated the view of botanical practice as a kind of direct and easy contact with nature.[1] In fact, at the end of the eighteenth century natural history was already an academic science practiced by professional scientists. The term "history" in natural history referred to arid descriptions of morphological features with Latin names, rather than to pleasant narratives. This practice of nomenclature and taxonomy, which

Carolus Linnaeus had introduced, was nevertheless opened to amateurs like Rousseau. They collected specimens and actively corresponded with people all over the world. Rousseau propagated Linnaeus's views in France and himself wrote a *Dictionnaire de botanique*, in which he discussed the merits of the Comte de Buffon's and Linnaeus's systems. Botany was the core of an active network of amateurs, who exchanged letters and specimens across national borders and social boundaries.

Amateur practices of natural history did not result in a romantic view of nature as a refuge for solitary *promeneurs*. The Jardin des Plantes played a crucial role in the diffusion of scientific culture, setting the standards for the practice of natural history and at the same shaping its image as a science between curiosity and utility.

The Muséum remained a teaching site providing free public lectures and demonstrations; its auditoriums were always full. Natural history was tightly linked with chemistry at the end of the eighteenth century, especially in Antoine de Fourcroy's lectures. The audience included amateurs as well as people attending for occupational reasons: pharmacists who needed to extract active ingredients from plants sat alongside gentlemen farmers.

As pointed out in this symposium, the Muséum contributed to the aura of democratic science surrounding natural history. It survived the attacks on academic science during the Terror because the Jacobins presented natural history as a science for the people, within everyone's reach and existing for the public good. Natural history even benefited from the Revolution, as the Muséum's collections were hugely amplified by the private collections confiscated from aristocrats and by the collections that the revolutionary armies "liberated" throughout Europe. As a result twelve chairs were established in natural history, enabling tremendous advances in comparative anatomy and the invention of "biology" as such (a term coined by Jean-Baptiste Lamarck). In the hands of Georges Cuvier and Étienne Geoffroy Saint-Hilaire, paleontology no longer consisted of dry descriptions of minute morphological details. Rather, it provided grand narratives about the history of life on earth. Science popularizers, who helped shape science as a new religion, substituted this secular view of the creation for the traditional biblical view.

THE MUSÉUM AND THE GIRAFFE IN THE HISTORY OF POPULARIZATION

Is the term "popularization" relevant for our period? Historians of popularization suggest that it is just one form of the relationship between science and the public that developed over the course of the nineteenth century.[2]

The intense activity of collecting instead characterizes the "culture of curiosities." The *cabinet de curiosités* or *Kunstkammer* brought together objects from the world of nature, scientific instruments, and works of art. They were not static collections; the exhibits were actively used and the collections were linked with laboratories and libraries. This notion blurred the boundaries between art and science, the natural and the artificial, and between contemplating the spectacle of nature and investigating nature.

With the wide diffusion of print culture and provincial academies in the eighteenth century, a different culture of science developed. Science was by and large considered a communal activity, shared by amateur scientists who felt a duty to transmit knowledge rather than advancing it. Typical enlightened amateurs were reading scientific literature, attending public courses, conducting laboratory experiments and field work, having discussions with experts, teaching, and forming their own collections. They occasionally wrote their own textbooks by compiling others' works, as there were no intellectual property laws at the time. Though there were tensions between the academy and amateurs, there was no real gap between science and the public.

The phrase "popularization" emerged in the nineteenth century, referring to a new trend of the mass diffusion of science.[3] It was the result

BERNADETTE BENSAUDE-VINCENT

of a complex and contingent process involving many factors: the creation of engineering schools (the École Polytechnique in 1793, the École Centrale des Arts et Manufactures in 1830) that propagated the engineering ideal of science for public welfare and practical applications; revolutionary educational reforms and the inclusion of science in the secondary school curriculum; the Loi Guizot of 1833 for primary schooling, which increased the number of potential readers in the French population; the emergence of a popular press, enabled by new printing and engraving techniques, which sold newspapers and magazines for the price of a loaf of bread; and the creation of large publishing houses that commercialized school textbooks and popular books. These publishers developed marketing strategies to segment the readership into social categories that could have been inspired by Honoré de Balzac's social types: astronomy or chemistry was tailored for ladies, gentlemen, entrepreneurs, workers, farmers, the clergy, and above all, for children. Lastly, popular science presupposes changes in scientific practice, with the creation of university chairs and diplomas. The term "scientist," referring to the professional practice of science, emerged in 1830 and gradually replaced "natural philosopher." Amateurs were no longer legitimate unless they collected data or samples for the benefit of professional scientists and under their control.

The practices of natural history described in this symposium are of particular interest because they confound all genres. Josephine Bonaparte's passion for exotic specimens is typical of the culture of curiosities. To a certain extent, she recalls Rousseau's correspondent, Margaret Cavendish Holles Harley Bentinck, the Duchess of Portland, who owned famous botanical collections. Although Josephine developed the utilitarian dimension of natural history with her merino sheep farming, she never became a realistic or successful entrepreneur. The giraffe craze also testifies to the permanence of the culture of curiosities. It is reminiscent of similar episodes that occurred much earlier, such as the journey of an elephant from Lisbon to Vienna in 1551.[4] The novelty in 1827 was the role of media—namely newspapers and theaters—and the explosion of a consumer culture of souvenirs.

The giraffe nevertheless also belongs to popular science in many respects. In particular, it proved a double-edged political instrument. It distracted the readers' attention from what was no longer made public and at the same time was turned into a literary weapon to criticize the regime. The connection between science popularization and press censorship for political reasons is a typical feature of the history of popularization. Popular science journals flourished in France when Napoleon III decreed strict censorship of political subjects. Science popularization became a refuge for socialist journalists in the 1850s, as it would be again in the Soviet Union under Stalin during the twentieth century.

"CIVILIZING SPECIMENS AND CITIZENS"

To return to the beginning: the phrase "civilizing specimens and citizens" took on several meanings over the course of the symposium. The Jardin des Plantes was a microcosm of the entire world, providing a well-ordered image of nature and society. With neatly kept flowerbeds of labeled plants, caged animals, and visitors walking along the broad, clean, and straight footpaths, the Jardin constructed an ideal communal world, a space to be shared by plants, animals and humans with strict demarcations, each one in its place.

The arrangement of specimens of the mineral, animal and plant kingdoms was also civilized, instantiating the eighteenth-century vision of nature as the "tableau de representations" that Foucault described in *Les mots et les choses* (The Order of Things).[5] Civilizing nature by imposing taxonomic rationality on the proliferating diversity of living species, however, required more than classifications designed by the illustrious professors and curators now standing as statues in the Jardin. It required crowds of invisible technicians, workers, and keepers who took care of the plants and animals, for civilizing also means care.

The Muséum was also a place of domestication and acclimatization of plants and animals. It imposed the Parisian climate and seasons on exotic plants and animals, along with specific dietary regimes. Civilizing in this case meant imposing norms and policing. The surveillance and discipline extended to the Parisian population. The Jardin was not only a recreational space where the bourgeois and workers' families could stroll while entertaining and educating their children for free; it was also an instrument of social control.

Finally, civilizing ironically consisted of altering boundaries, for instance in the use of music to encourage the elephants' mating or in the *bestiaire* of Balzac's *Comédie humaine.* Just as the culture of curiosities blurred the lines between the natural and artificial, the French culture of natural history in the early nineteenth century played with the borders between nature and culture.

1   For comments on Rousseau's actual practice of botany, see Robert Thiery, ed., *Jean-Jacques Rousseau: Le philosophe botaniste* (Montmorency: Musée Jean-Jacques Rousseau, 1996); Jean-Marc Drouin, "Les herborisations d'un philosophe: Rousseau et la botanique savante," in *Rousseau et les sciences,* ed. Bernadette Bensaude-Vincent and Bruno Bernardi (Paris: L'Harmattan, 2003), 77–92; and Alexandra Cook, "Rousseau et les réseaux d'échange botaniques," in ibid., 93–114.

2   James A. Secord, "Knowledge in Transit," *Isis* 95, no. 4 (December 2004): 654–72; Jonathan R. Topham, "Introduction" to "Focus: Historicizing 'Popular Science,'" *Isis* 100, no. 2 (June 2009): 310–18; Bernadette Bensaude-Vincent, "A Historical Perspective on Science and Its 'Others,'" *Isis* 100, no. 2 (June 2009): 359–68.

3   Bernadette Bensaude-Vincent and Anne Rasmussen, eds., *La science populaire dans la presse et l'édition* (Paris: Éditions du CNRS, 1997).

4   José Saramago, *The Elephant's Journey,* trans. Margaret Jull Costa (Boston: Houghton Mifflin Harcourt, 2010).

5   Michel Foucault, *Les mots et les choses: Une archéologie des sciences humaines* (Paris: Gallimard, 1966); translated as *The Order of Things: An Archaeology of the Human Sciences* (New York: Pantheon Books, 1970).

IMAGES AND POLITICS

ANNE LAFONT

IT IS NOT EASY TO SUMMARIZE such an ambitious interdisciplinary symposium, which Sue Ann Prince has conceived in so many dimensions. During these three days, we have been presented with much new material, many points of view, and many new research directions from different academic disciplines. This wide variety also makes the symposium very relevant. Here, I will point out some topics that will not be representative of everything we discussed (an impossible task), but which seem significant to me as an art historian and in the context of the wonderful exhibition *Of Elephants & Roses*.

The first argument deals with the interdisciplinary tools needed for natural history studies, especially when dealing with the subject at the end of the eighteenth century and in the first half of the nineteenth century. Whether one is interested in paleontology, botany, mineralogy, anthropology, anatomy, physics, or the arts, the same actors reappear, whatever their expertise: Georges Cuvier, Étienne Geoffroy Saint-Hilaire, Pierre-Joseph Redouté, Nicolas Maréchal, Josephine Bonaparte, Jean Hoüel, and so on. I would like to compare our essays with Bruno Latour's idea in his *Essai d'anthropologie symétrique* that "we have never been modern."[1] His writings are often controversial and have been contested by some historians of science, but considering what he tries to prove—the belief that keeping nature and culture, humans and objects, science and humanities, and knowledge and arts in separate mental chambers is a sign of progress or civilization (to refer to Richard W. Burkhardt's keynote lecture)—and examining this belief in the very French context of the revolutionary and post-revolutionary eras might be helpful and productive.

The new institutions of science, namely the Muséum d'Histoire naturelle and the Institut de France, both founded in the mid-1790s, might be signs of the fact that we have never been modern. If it is obvious that the distribution of tasks in the natural history field grew precisely around 1800, we can assert that by the same time, the growing power of the dominant and unique institutional voice reaffirms what Latour calls the *non-lieu* (no-place) of modernity, or the so-called division of expertise in a strict, tight manner.[2] On the contrary, the need for all these scientists, visual artists, and politicians to gather in the same institution tells us how, in order to improve their science—in a broad understanding of this word—they asked to be linked to one another and to have a greater circulation of their activities and research results. Thus, Paris became temporarily the natural science capital of the world. Elise Lipkowitz's essay on the confiscation of natural history collections recalls the violence this centralization process entailed.

All the essays presented here show that there was an expressed need for a deepening of the specific knowledge at the same time that a narrowing and a gathering (both intellectually and spatially) of the individuals leading these researches took place. This specialization did not separate the scientists; their practices, through the process of institutionalization, evolved in shared spaces and served common purposes. Modernity organized the community of future laboratories and did not, as Latour explained it, tighten and individualize scientific expertise. In other words, in my view, Latour's thoughts on supposed modernity (believed to be based on separate and specialized expertise) are fair. We have never been modern, in the sense that the separation of knowledge and expertise never took place. The institutions that emerged from the French Revolution prove this point; they attempted to gather researchers in the same place despite this purported division, in order to take advantage of the circulation of knowledge and to create more links among the disciplines. I believe, as Latour has stated, that modernity is not synonymous with expertise and specialization.[3]

Another theoretical reference I would like to introduce in this query about methods of interdisciplinary research is Lorraine Daston and Peter Galison's *Objectivity*, published in 2007.[4] I think it would be very useful to approach the images we have seen by historicizing the formal way they were presented to their contemporaries (namely French society around 1800) as reliable documents, or borrowing the authors' expression, as "truth-to-nature" documents. At that time, as never before, people felt they could trust images to answer questions such as: What does this exotic plant look like? What is the original milieu of such an animal? Or, what is under the flesh of living animals and what are the cranial differences between the races (scientifically speaking, of course)? To express this thought another way, we could further explore the conventions of image-making and of the gaze in this particular era, in order to understand how scientists attempted to make reliable documents, supposedly to found scientific researches that could not be suspected of transforming reality. Historicizing the ways each epoch creates its own objectivity is another step in understanding the social conventions and implications of natural history and of science in general.

The second argument, which was explicit or implicit in almost all of the essays and comes directly from the preceding one, is the evidence of the political issues of science and the political goals assigned to it by politicians and scientists themselves. At this time, the Napoleonic conquests began (with the natural history collections of the Dutch Stadtholder as an example) and the programmatic French colonization of different territories in the world was underway (as seen in the Egyptian campaign and diplomatic gift of the giraffe, and in Josephine's capture of specimens at the port of Lorient when Baudin's scientific expedition returned from Australia, and so on). The participants in this symposium assigned different names to these processes of domination and spoliation; but are civilization, acclimatization, and naturalization all the same thing? The partisans of the deportation of art objects from different European capitals to the Louvre during Napoleon's reign even used the term "naturalization" to justify those actions. What kind of euphemism disguises the idea of acclimating someone, or some animal, or some natural plant? Is it the same for all three? And how can we explain, in the terms used at the time, that *nature* needed to be *civilized* by French savoir-faire at the same time that *artifacts* needed to be *naturalized*? Why were these two regimes of thought used to explain and to justify morally (benefiting the propaganda efforts of the French government) the processes of theft, violence and denial that actually happened to Hans the elephant, Constantine the lion, the giraffe and her keeper Atir, the "Hottentot Venus" Sarah (Saartjie) Baartman, and others?

ANNE LAFONT

The opponents of the spoliation of art masterpieces are well known, as are the individuals who collaborated with the depredations.[5] But who were the opponents in the natural sciences? Were there numerous petitions against spoliations? Who were the Quatremère de Quincy, Jacques-Louis David, or Anne-Louis Girodet of natural history who argued that it was impossible to have a faithful comprehension of nature, animals, plants, or human beings if they were uprooted? Bernardin de Saint-Pierre, for example, did not really appear in the symposium papers. What was he thinking? These important questions deserve further study.

As a third point, I would like to raise the question of the role of art history in this field. Dorothy Johnson's paper on Pierre-Joseph Redouté revealed the amazing presence of precise botanical knowledge in history painting around 1800 in works by Girodet, François Gérard, and Pierre-Paul Prud'hon, among others. Many art historians have recently discovered the advantages of working with all images, instead of just the fine arts, in a theoretical manner. Most of the very fruitful works stemming from these inter-disciplinary visual culture studies question precisely the scientific illustration, that is, the image situated between art and natural science. I count myself among the art historians who try to demonstrate that the visual arts (objects, models, and images) participated in social life, contributed extensively to the shaping of knowledge and to the shaping of society in general, and were not dedicated solely to a privileged elite. Johnson shows how scientific knowledge penetrated Art with a capital A: how history painting (the highest level in the hierarchy of academic genres) and *nature morte* (still life), which supplied the luxury market of eighteenth-century France, were affected by scientific discoveries and the natural specimens displayed in new museums. One cannot speak here of a simple iconography, but of a renewed, more informed iconology that pays greater attention to influences beyond the conventional, traditional literary sources.

In conclusion, I would like to signal another idea present in our discussion, but not directly addressed: the status of the image in the realm of the natural sciences. Claudine Cohen underlined how scientific images are polarized between interpretation and proof. She put forward the extremes on a horizontal scale of possibilities, and I would like to add an argument to this proposal. Each image, whatever its function (pedagogical aid, work-in-progress, marginal note, comparative scheme, table, diagram, and so on) has to be understood through the prism of the different temporalities included within it. This is the case for all images, but the scientific ones in particular have to integrate the time of the experience represented; the time in nature (raising again the question of studying nature from life or from dead specimens and what kinds of results those studies yield); the time when the images were made; the time of the writing and reading of the text that accompanies most of them; and so forth. Since Nelson Goodman has definitively demonstrated in *Languages of Art* that images are not transparent and unambiguous documents,[6] we must reconstitute these multiple temporalities for the foundations of a deep interpretation, not merely a simple surface reading.

1 Bruno Latour, *Nous n'avons jamais été modernes: Essai d'anthropologie symétrique* (Paris: La Découverte, 1991).

2 Ibid.

3 Ibid.

4 Lorraine Daston and Peter Galison, *Objectivity* (New York: Zone Books, 2007).

5 See especially Édouard Pommier, *L'Art de la liberté: Doctrines et débats de la Révolution française* (Paris: Gallimard, 1991).

6 Nelson Goodman, *Languages of Art: An Approach to a Theory of Symbols* (Indianapolis: Bobbs-Merrill, 1968).

Baruch S. Blumberg (1925–2011), Committee Chair
President (2005–2011), American Philosophical Society

France

Dr. Dominique BRÊME
Directeur, Domaine de Sceaux,
Parc et Musée de l'Île-de-France

M. Bertrand-Pierre GALEY,
followed by M. Thomas GRENON
Directeur général du Muséum
national d'Histoire naturelle

M. Amaury LEFÉBURE
Conservateur général du patrimoine
Directeur du Musée des châteaux de
Malmaison et de Bois-Préau

M. Jean-Marc LÉRI
Conservateur général du patrimoine
Directeur du Musée Carnavalet

M. Bruno RACINE
Président de la Bibliothèque nationale
de France

M. Daniel ROCHE
Professeur au Collège de France
Chaire d'Histoire de la France des
Lumières (Éméritus)

United States

Dr. James BILLINGTON
The Librarian of Congress

Dr. Baruch S. BLUMBERG
President, American Philosophical
Society

Ms. Ellen FUTTER
President, American Museum of
Natural History

Dr. Amy GUTMANN
President and Christopher H. Browne
Distinguished Professor of Political
Science
University of Pennsylvania

Mr. Philippe de MONTEBELLO
Director Emeritus, Metropolitan
Museum of Art
Fiske Kimball Professor in the History
and Culture of Museums, Institute of
Fine Arts, New York University

Dr. Neil RUDENSTINE
President Emeritus, Harvard
University
Chairman, ARTstor

Of Elephants and Roses: Encounters with French Natural History, 1790–1830
With abbreviations used in checklist

ANSP	The Academy of Natural Sciences of Drexel University, Philadelphia, Ewell Sale Stewart Library
APS	American Philosophical Society, Philadelphia
Arader	Arader Galleries
Beaune	Musée des Beaux-Arts, Beaune, France
BnF-Mus	Bibliothèque nationale de France, Paris, Département de la Musique
BnF-Phil	Bibliothèque nationale de France, Paris, Département Philosophie, histoire, sciences de l'homme
BnF-Rés	Bibliothèque nationale de France, Paris, Réserve des livres rares
BPL	The Trustees of the Boston Public Library / Rare Books
Brind	David Brind
Carnavalet	Musée Carnavalet–Histoire de Paris, France
FLP	Free Library of Philadelphia
Hagley	Hagley Museum and Library, Wilmington, Del.
Hillwood	Hillwood Estate, Museum & Gardens, Washington, D.C. Unless noted, all items Bequest of Marjorie Merriweather Post, 1973
LoC	Thomas Jefferson Papers, Manuscript Division, Library of Congress, Washington, D.C.
Malmaison	Musée national des châteaux de Malmaison et de Bois-Préau, France
MFA	Museum of Fine Arts, Boston
MNHN-Bib	Bibliothèque centrale du Muséum national d'Histoire naturelle, Paris
MNHN-Col	Collection du Muséum national d'Histoire naturelle, Paris
Princeton	Department of Rare Books & Special Collections, Princeton University Library, Princeton, N.J.
Sceaux	Département des Hauts-de-Seine / Musée de l'Île-de-France, Sceaux (France)
Twinight	The Twinight Collection

Fig. C1 Everard Home, Drawing of American Mastodon (*Mammut americanum*, "The bones of Mr Peale's mammoth"), 1804, ink and watercolor on paper. © MNHN, Bibliothèque central, photo by Florent Jakubowicz

Music for Elephants

SPECIMENS

African Elephant Molar Tooth (*Loxodonta africana*), collected in present-day Central African Republic before 1957. Gift of the heirs of Gatean Mollez, 2000. MNHN-Col

American Mastodon Partial Lower Jaw (*Mammut americanum*, "Mammoth") collected by William Clark at Big Bone Lick, Kentucky in 1807, gifted to the Institut national (Paris) by Thomas Jefferson in 1808. MNHN-Col

American Mastodon Molar Tooth (*Mammut americanum*, "Elephas Americanus"), probably collected by Pierre Chouteau near Osage River in present-day Missouri in 1796, sent by B. S. Barton to Georges Cuvier in 1806. MNHN-Col

Fragment of Skull of Asian Elephant Named Hans (*Elephas maximus*), captured in present-day Sri Lanka around 1784, died in 1802. MNHN-Col

Woolly Mammoth Molar Tooth (*Mammuthus primigenius*, "Sebirian Eliphant"), collected by William Clark at Big Bone Lick, Kentucky in 1807, gifted to the Institut national (Paris) by Thomas Jefferson in 1808. MNHN-Col

PAINTING, DRAWINGS, & PRINTS

J. A. Alavoine, *La fontaine de l'éléphant, place de la Bastille* (*Elephant Fountain, Place de la Bastille*), ca. 1810, watercolor on paper. Gift of Mathieu Meusnier, 1881. Carnavalet

B. S. Barton, Drawing of Mastodon Tooth (*Mammut americanum*), Crown View, n.d., graphite and watercolor on paper. APS

Georges Cuvier and/or assistants, Drawings of Mastodon Jaw (*Mammut americanum*), pencil and ink on paper, ca. 1821, mockup for *Recherches sur les ossemens fossiles* (*Researches on Fossil Bones*) by Cuvier (Paris, 1821). MNHN-Bib

Georges Cuvier and/or assistants, *Grand mastodonte, pl. III* (Great Mastodon, Plate 3), ca. 1821, engraving with manuscript additions, proof from *Recherches sur les ossemens fossiles* (*Researches on Fossil Bones*) by Cuvier (Paris, 1821). MNHN-Bib

Georges Cuvier and/or assistants, Drawing of Mastodon Lower Jaw (*Mammut americanum*), after 1807, graphite on paper. MNHN-Bib

Everard Home, Drawing of American Mastodon (*Mammut americanum*, "The bones of Mr Peale's mammoth"), 1804, ink and watercolor on paper. MNHN-Bib (**FIG. C1**)

Rembrandt Peale, Sketch of Mastodon Skeleton (*Mammut americanum*), ca. 1801, ink on paper. APS

PRINTED MATERIALS

Ah! ça ira, dictom [*sic*] *populaire* (*It'll Be Fine, A Popular Phrase*), music composed by Bécourt (Paris, 1790). BnF-Mus

Ah! ça ira, dicton populaire (*It'll Be Fine, A Popular Phrase*) (London, n.d.) (rotation). FLP

Georges-Louis Leclerc, Comte de Buffon, *Histoire naturelle* (*Natural History*), vol. 28 (Paris, 1800), engravings by Bacquoi and others. APS

Georges Cuvier, "Suite du mémoire sur les éléphans vivans et fossiles" (Continuation of a Memoir on Living and Extinct Elephants), in *Annales du Muséum national d'Histoire naturelle*, vol. 8 (Paris, 1806). APS (see **FIG. 2.6**)

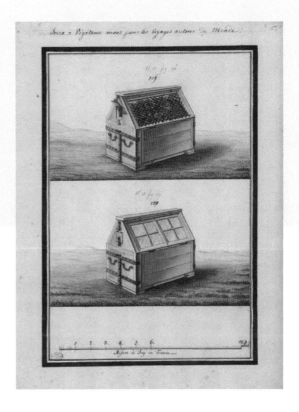

J. P. Hoüel, *Histoire naturelle des deux éléphans* (*Natural History of Two Elephants*) (Paris, 1803). ANSP (**COVER AND FRONTISPIECE; FIGS. 2.5, 8.1, 10.4, 10.5; INDEX**)

Édouard de Montulé, *Voyage en Amérique en Sicile et en Egypte* (*Travels in America, Sicily, and Egypt*), atlas vol. (Paris, 1821). APS (**FIG. 1.4**)

MANUSCRIPTS

B. S. Barton, Postscript to a letter to Georges Cuvier about the mastodon, 14 October 1805, ink on paper. MNHN-Bib

Georges Cuvier and J. B. Delambre, Letter to Thomas Jefferson acknowledging fossil donation to the Institut national, 14 November 1808, letter-press and ink on paper, in bound volume. APS

Everard Home, Letter to Georges Cuvier describing Peale's mastodon shown in London, 17 August 1804, ink on paper. MNHN-Bib

Thomas Jefferson, Letter to Comte de Lacépède about fossil bones, with list of box contents, 14 July 1808, ink on paper. LoC

James Mease, Letter to Georges Cuvier about the mastodon, 8 May 1802, ink on paper. MNHN-Bib

C. W. Peale, Letter to Georges Cuvier about mastodon excavation, 16 July 1802, ink on paper. MNHN-Bib

Hunting for Trees

SPECIMENS

Packets of Chestnut Oak Acorns (*Quercus prinus*), collected by André Michaux in the United States, 1786–96. MNHN-Col (**FIG. 1.10**)

Franklinia (*Franklinia alatamaha*, "Gordonia franklenia dicta"), collected by André Michaux in United States, 1786–96, herbarium sheet (with rotation). MNHN-Col

Acorns of Scarlet Oak (*Quercus coccinea*), collected by André Michaux in the United States, 1786–96. MNHN-Col

White Oak (*Quercus abietum*, "Quercus alba virginiana"), collected by André Michaux in United States, 1786–96, herbarium sheet. MNHN-Col

Red Oak (*Quercus rubra*), collected by André Michaux in North Carolina, 1786–96, herbarium sheet (rotation). MNHN-Col

PAINTINGS, DRAWINGS, & PRINTS

Serre à Végétaux vivans pour les voyages autour du Monde (*Live Plant Greenhouse for Voyages Around the World*), late 18th or early 19th century, watercolor on paper. MNHN-Bib

William Bartram, Franklinia (*Franklinia alatamaha*), ca. 1786, engraved by James Trenchard. APS

Fig. C3

Pauline de Courcelles Knip, "Colombi-Galline Goura, *Columba coronata* Lath." (Blue Crowned Pigeon, *Goura cristata*), from Pauline Knip and C. J. Themminck, *Les Pigeons*, plate I (Paris, 1809–11). ANSP

DECORATIVE ARTS

Sèvres Porcelain Manufactory, *Seau à glace forme Hébée* (Ice-Cream Cooler), with Franklinia (*Franklinia alatamaha*, "Gordonie pubescente") and Blue Water Lily (*Nymphaea nouchali* var. *caerulea*, "Nénuphar bleu"), from Service of Plants of Malmaison and Lilies, 1804–5, hard paste porcelain with colored enamel and gilded decoration. MFA, Gift of Mr. and Mrs. Henry R. Kravis (**FIG. 1.6**)

PRINTED MATERIALS

William Bartram, *Travels through North & South Carolina, Georgia, East & West Florida*, 1st ed. (Philadelphia, 1791). APS

H. L. Duhamel Du Monceau, *De l'exploitation des bois* (*On the Use of Trees*), vol. 2 (Paris, 1764). APS

A. D. Fougeroux de Bondaroy, *Art du tonnelier* (*Art of Cooperage*) (Paris, 1763), illustrations by Patte and others. APS

François-André Michaux, *Oaks of the United States and Canada*, stipple engravings printed in Paris, ca. 1816, engravings after P. J. Redouté, H. J. Redouté, and Pancrace Bessa. Gift of F. A. Michaux, 1816. APS

François-André Michaux, *The North American Sylva*, vol. 1 (Paris, 1819), stipple engravings by Bessin, Gabriel, and others after drawings by P. J. Redouté and others (2 copies). APS

MANUSCRIPTS

Thomas Jefferson, Manuscript Subscription List Put Forward by Jefferson to Support a Proposed Scientific Expedition under André Michaux, 1793, ink on paper. APS (**FIG. 7.7**)

André Michaux, Botanical Journal in North America, 1793–95, pamphlet-bound manuscript notebooks. APS (**FIG. 7.4**)

Black Swans for an Empress

SPECIMENS

Black Swan (*Cygnus atratus* or *Chenopis atrata*), collected in Australia ca. 1802, sent to Josephine Bonaparte at Malmaison in 1803, died 1814. MNHN-Col (**FIG. 1.7**)

Blue Crowned Pigeon (*Goura cristata*), collection date unknown, died 1844. Gift of Captain Félix Favin-Lévêque, 1844. MNHN-Col

Blue-Headed Quail-Dove (*Starnoenas cyanocephala*, "Tourterelle de la Jamaïque"), collection date unknown, died 1804. Gift of Josephine Bonaparte, 1804. MNHN-Col

PAINTINGS, DRAWING, & PRINTS

Les cangourons [sic] *à la Malmaison / Les cygnes noirs à la Malmaison* (*Kangaroos at Malmaison / Black Swans at Malmaison*), n.d., etching. MNHN-Bib

Pauline de Courcelles Knip, Cloven-Feathered Dove (*Drepanoptila holosericea*, "Colombe Vlouvlou"), gouache on vellum, study for *Les Pigeons* by Pauline Knip and C. J. Themminck (Paris, 1809–11). Arader

François Peron and C. A. Lesueur, Title Page Illustration, engraved by Frères Lambert, from atlas vol. of *Voyage de decouvertes aux terres australes* (*Voyage of Discovery to the Southern Lands*), by C. A. Lesueur and N. M. Petit (Paris, 1807). MNHN-Bib (**FIG. 2.7**)

Fig. C4

Sèvres Porcelain Manufactory, Plate with Cape Sand Lily (*Veltheimia capensis*), from Service of Lilies for Louis XVIII, 1821, hard paste porcelain (plants after P. J. Redouté). Museum Purchase, 2006. Hillwood. Photo by E. Owen

DECORATIVE ARTS

The following are by the Sèvres Porcelain Manufactory:

Square Dish with Rufous-Tailed Rock Thrush (*Monticola saxatilis*, "Le merle de roche"), from Yellow Service with Birds, 1793, soft paste porcelain. Hillwood

Plate with Half-Moon Conure (*Aratinga canicularis*, "Perruche à front rouge, du Brésil"), from Yellow Service with Birds, 1793, hard paste porcelain, painted by E.-F. Bouillat *père* and Fumez. Hillwood

Plate with Paradise Tanager (*Tangara chilensis*, "Septicolor"), from South American Birds Service, 1819–20, hard paste porcelain; bird by Pauline Knip, border and perch by J. F. C. Leloi. Hillwood (**FIG. 1.8**)

Plate with Violaceous Euphonia (*Euphonia violacea*, "Euphone teïté"), from South American Birds Service, 1819–20, hard paste porcelain; bird by Pauline Knip, border and perch by J. F. C. Leloi. Hillwood

Vase with African Birds, 1822, porcelain, ormolu, and bronze; vase by Evariste Fragonard, birds by Pauline Knip, ornaments by Didier, gilding by Boullemier *l'aîné*. Hillwood (**PP. 229–30**)

PRINTED BOOKS

Pauline de Courcelles Knip and C. J. Themminck, *Les Pigeons* (Paris, 1809–11), illustrations by Pauline Knip, engraved by César Macret, color-printed by Millevoy. ANSP

A Flower Blooms

SPECIMENS

Venus Flytrap (*Dionaea muscipula*), collected by André Michaux in North Carolina in 1797, herbarium sheet (with rotation). MNHN-Col

PAINTINGS, DRAWINGS, & PRINTS

The following are by P. J. Redouté:

Austrian Yellow Rose (*Rosa foetida*, "Rosier Eglantier, Rosa eglanteria"), watercolor on vellum, study for *Les Roses*, vol. 1 (Paris, 1817). Arader

Blush-Colored Crinum (*Crinum erubescens*, "Crinum rougeâtre"), 1802–5, watercolor on vellum, study for *Les Liliacées*, vol. 1 (Paris, 1805). Arader (**FIG. 1.9**)

Josephine's March Lily (*Brunsvigia josephinae*, "Amaryllis de Joséphine, Amaryllis Josephinae"), 1802–5, watercolor on vellum, study for *Les Liliacées*, vol. 7 (Paris, 1813). Brind (**FIG. 3.5**)

Bulb of Josephine's March Lily (*Brunsvigia josephinae*, "Amaryllis de Joséphine, Amaryllis Josephinae"), 1802–5, graphite on vellum, study for *Les Liliacées*, vol. 7 (Paris, 1813). Brind

Paarl Roosvygie (*Erepsia lacera*, "Mesembryanthemum carinatum"), stipple engraving by Allais (*noir* or uncolored proof), for *Jardin de la Malmaison* by É. P. Ventenat (Paris, 1803). Malmaison

Slender False Garlic (*Nothoscordum gracile*, "Ail Parfumé, Allium Fragrans"), watercolor on vellum, study for *Les Liliacées*, vol. 2 (Paris, 1805). Arader

CHECKLIST OF THE EXHIBITION

245

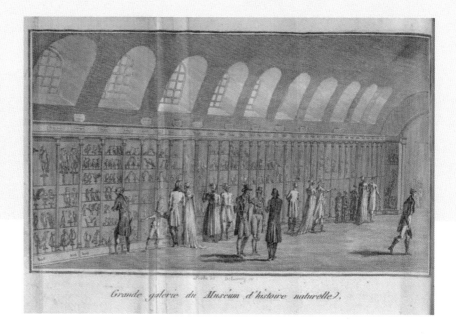

Fig. C5

Jean-Baptiste Pujoulx, *Promenades au Jardin des plantes, à la ménagerie et dans les galeries du Muséum d'histoire naturelle*, 1803. The Academy of Natural Sciences of Drexel University, Ewell Sale Stewart Library (not in exhibition)

Grande galerie du Muséum d'histoire naturelle.

William Bartram, Venus Flytrap (*Dionaea muscipula*), ca. 1803, colored engraving by I. H. Seymour, after engraving by James Roberts, after drawings by John Ellis. APS (**FIG. 1.11**)

Venus Flytrap (*Dionaea muscipula*), stipple engraving by A. Chapponnier (*noir* or uncolored proof), for *Jardin de la Malmaison* by É. P. Ventenat (Paris, 1803). Malmaison

DECORATIVE ARTS

Sèvres Porcelain Manufactory, Plate with Mourning Iris (*Iris susiana*, "Iris de Suse"), from Service of Plants of Malmaison and Lilies, 1802–5, porcelain (plants after P. J. Redouté). Malmaison

Royal Porcelain Manufacture, Berlin (KPM), Plate with Paarl Roosvygie (*Erepsia lacera*, "Mesembryanthemum carinatum"), from Exotic Plants Service, 1807, porcelain (plants after P. J. Redouté). Malmaison (see **FIG. 3.1**)

Royal Porcelain Manufacture, Berlin (KPM), Plate with Venus Flytrap (*Dionaea muscipula*), ca. 1809, porcelain (plants after P. J. Redouté). Twinight (**FIG. 1.12**)

Sèvres Porcelain Manufactory, Plate with Flower Bouquet, from Dessert Service for Josephine, 1809, porcelain. Malmaison

Dagoty Manufacture, Plate with Purple Anemone ("Anémone pourpre"), ca. 1815, hard paste porcelain. Malmaison

Sèvres Porcelain Manufactory, Plate with Cape Sand Lily (*Veltheimia capensis*), from Service of Lilies for Louis XVIII, 1821, hard paste porcelain (plants after P. J. Redouté). Museum Purchase, 2006. Hillwood (**FIG. C4**)

PRINTED BOOKS

John Ellis, *A Botanical Description of the Dionaea Muscipula, or Venus's Fly-Trap, A Newly Discovered Sensitive Plant*, in *Directions for Bringing over Seeds and Plants* (London, 1770). ANSP

J. B. Lamarck, *Flore française (French Flora)*, 3rd ed., vol. 1 (Paris, 1815). APS

P. J. Redouté and A. P. de Candolle, *Plantarum historia succulentarum–Histoire des plantes grasses (History of Succulent Plants)*, vol. 1 (Paris, 1799–1805). APS

P. J. Redouté and C. A. Thory, *Les Roses*, vol. 1 & part of vol. 2 (Paris, 1817–21). ANSP (**COVER** and **FIG. 3.3**)

MANUSCRIPTS

Josephine Bonaparte, Letter to Gérard Cazeaux (Assistant Commissioner in Portsmouth, N.H.) about North American seeds, 23 November 1803, ink on paper. Malmaison

E. I. du Pont de Nemours, Letter to Josephine Bonaparte about North American seeds, 20 January 1802, ink on paper. Hagley

E. I. du Pont de Nemours, List of seeds sent to Josephine Bonaparte and others, ca. 1802, ink on paper. Hagley

A. L. de Jussieu, *Catalogue des plantes démontrées en 1782 au Jardin du Roy (Catalogue of Plants Exhibited in 1782 at the King's Garden)*, 1783, bound manuscript volume. APS

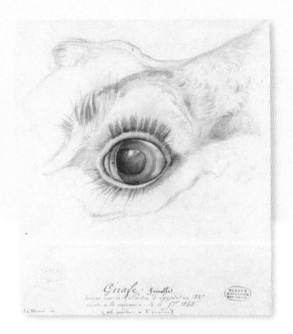

Fig. C6

J. C. Werner, *Girafe femelle
donnée par le Pacha
d'Egypte en 1827, œil
gauche*, 1845, graphite on
paper. © MNHN,
Bibliothèque centrale

Everything Giraffe

PAINTINGS, DRAWINGS, & PRINTS

Billet d'entrée, Muséum royal d'histoire naturelle
(Muséum admission ticket for giraffe), 1827,
signed by Louis Bosc, letterpress and ink on paper.
MNHN-Bib

. . . . et la Giraffe, ou ici on Rumine (Charles X
and the Giraffe, Or Here We Ruminate), ca. 1827,
colored etching. Carnavalet

La Girafe à la mode, air à la façon de Barbari
(*Giraffe in Fashion: Air in the Manner of Barbari*,
song sheet), 1827, colored engraving. Carnavalet
(**FIG. 17.6**)

J. R. Brascassat, *Passage de la girafe à Arnay-le-Duc*
(*The Giraffe Passing Through Arnay-le-Duc*), 1827,
oil on canvas. Beaune (**FIG. 2.1**)

Langlumé, *Ah! soyez notre grand maman… Belle
Girafe* (Ah! Be Our Grandma [literally, "Tall
Mother"]… Beautiful Giraffe), 1827, lithograph.
Carnavalet (**FIG. 12.9**)

H. D. Pattel, *Les Quartiers de Paris, No. 6: Jardin
des Plantes* (*The Districts of Paris, No. 6: Jardin
des Plantes*), 1827, lithograph. Carnavalet (**FIG. 17.1**)

J. C. Werner, *Girafe femelle donnée par le Pacha
d'Egypte en 1827, museau à poils de lèvre* (*Female
Giraffe Given by the Pacha of Egypt in 1827, Hairy
Muzzle*), 1845, graphite on paper. MNHN-Bib

J. C. Werner, *Girafe femelle donnée par le Pacha
d'Egypte en 1827, œil gauche* (*Female Giraffe Given
by the Pacha of Egypt in 1827, Left Eye*), 1845,
graphite on paper. MNHN-Bib

DECORATIVE ARTS

Bag with a Giraffe, ca. 1828, glass beads, leather and
gilt metal. MFA, The Elizabeth Day McCormick
Collection (**FIG. 17.5**)

Brisé (Lacework) Fan Painted with Two Giraffes,
ca. 1827, horn with silk ribbon and painted paper
appliqués. Bequest of Madame Francisque, 1907.
Carnavalet (**FIG. 17.2**)

Clothing iron with giraffe motif, 1827, cast iron.
MNHN-Bib

Encrier à la girafe (Giraffe inkstand), ca. 1827, tin
or pewter and cut crystal. Sceaux

Papier peint, motif de tapisserie à la girafe (Wallpaper sample with giraffe and Osages), 1827,
printed wallpaper. MNHN-Bib (**FIG. 17.3**)

Petit plat "à la girafe" (Small plate with giraffe and
attendant), ca. 1827, *faience des Islettes* (ceramic)
with painted decoration. Carnavalet

Plat à barbe, décor à la girafe (Shaving bowl with
giraffe and attendant), ca. 1827, earthenware.
MNHN-Bib (**FIG. 12.8**)

Assiette représentant une girafe avec un palmier
(Plate with giraffe and palm tree), 1827, *faience de
Waly* (earthenware) with polychrome decoration.
MNHN-Bib (**FIG. 17.4**)

Plate with Giraffe and Attendant, ca. 1827,
earthenware. Sceaux

*Vase en forme de cornet orné de branchages portant
sur son socle une girafe* (Vase in form of a cornet
with branches, with a giraffe framed by vegetation), ca. 1827–28, hard porcelain. Sceaux

A. L. Barye, *Statuette de girafe debout* (Statuette of
standing giraffe), ca. 1827–28, bronze. Sceaux

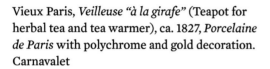
Fig. C7

La Girafe, from
Georges Cuvier, *Le
règne animal distribué
d'après son organiza-
tion: Les mammifères*
(Paris, ca. 1836–49).
APS

Vieux Paris, *Veilleuse "à la girafe"* (Teapot for
herbal tea and tea warmer), ca. 1827, *Porcelaine
de Paris* with polychrome and gold decoration.
Carnavalet

BOOKS

A la girafe: Invocation en chœur et couplet (*To the
Giraffe: Invocation in Chorus and Verse*) (Paris,
1827), words and music by F. G. BnF-Mus

Journal des Dames et des Modes (*Ladies' Fashion
Journal*), no. 50 (Paris, September 1827). BnF-Rés

Journal des Dames et des Modes (*Ladies' Fashion
Journal*), no. 50 (Paris, September 1827) (rotation).
BPL

La Girafe et les Osages (*The Giraffe and the Osages*)
(Paris, 1827). BnF-Phil (**FIG. 18.2**)

Le petit chansonnier des dames et des demoiselles
(*Little Songbook for Ladies and Young Ladies*) (Lille,
1828). MNHN-Bib

*Messager boiteux de la girafe parisienne … l'arrivée
de la girafe à Paris* (*Lame Messenger of the Parisian
Giraffe … The Giraffe's Arrival in Paris*) (Paris,
1828). BnF-Phil

Georges Cuvier, *Le règne animal distribué d'après
son organisation: Les mammifères* (*The Kingdom
of Animals Distributed According to its Organization: Atlas of Mammals*) (Paris, ca. 1836–49). APS
(**FIG. C7**)

Émile de l'Empesé (pseud.), *L'Art de mettre sa
cravate de mille et une manières* (*The Art of Wearing
One's Cravat in 1,001 Ways*), 8th ed. (Paris, 1828);
attributed to H. de Balzac or E. M. de Saint-Hilaire.
Princeton

G. L. Leclerc, Comte de Buffon, *Natural History,
General and Particular*, vol. 8 (London, 1812). APS

Allin, Michael. *La girafe de Charles X: Son extraordinaire voyage de Khartoum à Paris.* Paris: J. C. Lattès, 2000.

———. *Zarafa: A Giraffe's True Story from Deep in Africa to the Heart of Paris.* New York: Walker, 1998.

Auricchio, Laura, Elizabeth Heckendorn Cook, and Giulia Pacini, eds. *Invaluable Trees: Cultures of Nature, 1660–1830.* SVEC 2012:08. Oxford: Voltaire Foundation, 2012.

Auslander, Leora. *Cultural Revolutions: The Politics of Everyday Life in Britain, North America, and France.* Berkeley and Los Angeles: University of California Press, 2009.

Baglione, Gabrielle, and Claude Blanckaert. *L'Autre: Les naturels vus par l'Occident (1800–1804).* Le Havre: Éditions du Muséum d'histoire naturelle, 2008.

Baglione, Gabrielle, and Cédric Crémière. *Charles-Alexandre Lesueur, Peintre voyageur, un trésor oublié.* Paris: Éditions de Conti, 2009.

Barreto, Christina, and Martin Lancaster. *Napoléon et l'Empire de la mode.* Milan: Skira, 2010.

Bensaude-Vincent, Bernadette. "A Historical Perspective on Science and Its 'Others.'" *Isis* 100, no. 2 (June 2009): 359–68.

———. "Un public pour la science: L'essor de la vulgarisation au XIXe siécle." *Réseaux* 11, no. 58 (1993): 47–66.

———, and Bruno Bernardi. *Rousseau et les sciences.* Paris: L'Harmattan, 2003.

———, and Anne Rasmussen, eds. *La science populaire dans la presse et l'édition.* Paris: Éditions du CNRS, 1997.

Berg, Maxine, and Helen Clifford, eds. *Consumers and Luxury: Consumer Culture in Europe, 1650–1850.* Manchester: Manchester University Press, 1999.

Blanckaert, Claude, Claudine Cohen, Pietro Corsi, and Jean-Louis Fischer, eds. *Le Muséum au premier siècle de son histoire.* Paris: Éditions du Muséum national d'Histoire naturelle, 1997.

Blix, Göran. *From Paris to Pompeii: French Romanticism and the Cultural Politics of Archaeology.* Philadelphia: University of Pennsylvania Press, 2009.

Blunt, Wilfrid, and William T. Stern. *The Art of Botanical Illustration,* rev. ed. London: Antique Collectors Club, 1994.

Boyer, Ferdinand. "Le Transfert à Paris des collections du Stathouder (1795)." *Annales historique de la Révolution française* 43 (1971): 380–404.

Bruson, Jean-Marie, and Anne Forray-Carlier. *Au temps des Merveilleuses: La société parisienne sous le Directoire et le Consulat.* Paris: Paris-Musées, 2005.

Bultingaire, Léon. "Les Peintres du Muséum à l'époque de Lamarck." *Archives du Muséum,* série 6 (1930): 49–58.

Burkhardt, Richard W., Jr. "Constructing the Zoo: Science, Society, and Animal Nature at the Paris Menagerie, 1794–1838." In Henninger-Voss, *Animals in Human Histories,* 239–41.

———. "The Leopard in the Garden: Life in Close Quarters at the Muséum d'Histoire Naturelle." *Isis* 98, no. 44 (December 2007): 675–94.

———. "La ménagerie et la vie du Muséum." In Blanckaert et al., *Le Muséum au premier siècle de son histoire,* 481–508.

———. *The Spirit of System: Lamarck and Evolutionary Biology.* Reprint. Cambridge, Mass.: Harvard University Press, 1995.

Casid, Jill H. *Sowing Empire: Colonialism and Landscape.* Minneapolis: University of Minnesota Press, 2005.

Chassagne, Annie. *La Bibliothèque de l'Académie royale des sciences au XVIIIᵉ siècle.* Paris: Éditions du Comité des travaux historiques et scientifiques, 2007.

Chevallier, Bernard. *Malmaison: Château et domaine des origines à 1904.* Paris: Éditions de la Réunion des musées nationaux, 1989.

——, and Christophe Pincemaille. *Douce et incomparable Joséphine.* Paris: Payot, 1999.

——. *L'Impératrice Joséphine.* Paris: Payot et Rivages, 1996.

Chinard, Gilbert. "André and François-André Michaux and Their Predecessors: An Essay on Early Botanical Exchanges between America and France." *Proceedings of the American Philosophical Society* 101, no. 4 (1957): 344–61.

Cohen, Claudine. "De la biologie au roman: Le modèle morphologique et ses variations." *Romantisme*, no. 138 (May 2007): 47–59.

——. *Le Destin du Mammouth.* Paris: Seuil, 1994.

——. *The Fate of the Mammoth: Fossils, Myth, and History.* Translated by William Rodarmor. Chicago: University of Chicago Press, 2002.

——. *La Méthode de Zadig: La trace, le fossile, la preuve.* Paris: Éditions de Seuil, 2011.

Coller, Ian. *Arab France: Islam and the Making of Modern Europe, 1798–1831.* Berkeley and Los Angeles: University of California Press, 2011.

Cook, Alexandra. *Jean-Jacques Rousseau and Botany: The Salutary Science.* Oxford: Voltaire Foundation, 2012.

Dardaud, Gabriel. *Une Girafe pour le roi.* Paris: Dumerchez-Naoum, 1985.

Daston, Lorraine, and Peter Galison. *Objectivity.* New York: Zone Books, 2007.

Daudin, Henri. *Cuvier et Lamarck: Les classes zoologiques et l'idée de série animale.* Paris: Éditions des Archives Contemporaines, 1983.

Davidson, Denise Z. "Making Society 'Legible': People-Watching in Paris after the Revolution." *French Historical Studies* 28 (2005): 265–96.

——. *France After Revolution: Urban Life, Gender, and the New Social Order.* Cambridge, Mass.: Harvard University Press, 2007.

Farber, Paul Lawrence. "The Development of Taxidermy and the History of Ornithology." *Isis* 68, no. 4 (December 1977): 550–66.

——. *Finding Order in Nature: The Naturalist Tradition from Linnaeus to E. O. Wilson.* Baltimore: Johns Hopkins University Press, 2000.

Foucault, Michel. *Les mots et les choses: Une archéologie des sciences humaines.* Paris: Gallimard, 1966.

Foucault, Michel. *The Order of Things: An Archaeology of the Human Sciences.* Reprint. New York: Vintage, 1994.

Fox, Robert, and George Weisz, eds. *The Organization of Science and Technology in France, 1808–1914.* Cambridge: Cambridge University Press, 1980.

Gaillard, Françoise. "La science: Modèle ou vérité; Réflexions sur l'avant-propos à La Comédie humaine." In *Balzac: L'invention du roman*, edited by Claude Duchet and Jacques Neefs, 57–83. Paris: Pierre Belfond, 1982.

Gillispie, Charles. *Science and Polity in France at the End of the Old Regime.* Princeton, N.J.: Princeton University Press, 1980.

——. *Science and Polity in France: The Revolutionary and Napoleonic Years.* Princeton, N.J.: Princeton University Press, 2004.

Henninger-Voss, Mary J., ed. *Animals in Human Histories: The Mirror of Nature and Culture.* Studies in Comparative History. Rochester, N.Y.: University of Rochester Press, 2002.

Héran, Emmanuelle, ed. *Beauté animale, de Dürer à Jeff Koons.* Paris: Réunion des musées nationaux–Grand Palais, 2012.

Hoage, Robert J., and William A. Deiss. *New Worlds, New Animals: From Menagerie to Zoological Park in the Nineteenth Century.* Baltimore: Johns Hopkins University Press, 1996.

L'Impératrice Joséphine et les sciences naturelles. Rueil-Malmaison: Musée national des châteaux de Malmaison et Bois-Préau; Paris: Éditions de la Réunion des musées nationaux, 1997.

Jacobsohn, Antoine. "De l'accroissement des variétés, ou 'sortes,' de fruits au 16ᵉ et 17ᵉ siècles." In *Le patrimoine fruitier: Hier, aujourd'hui, demain; Actes du colloque de La Ferté-Bernard (Sarthe), 16-17 octobre 1998*, ed. Michel Chauvet, 109-110. Paris: AFCEV, 1999.

———. *Fruits du savoir: Duhamel Du Monceau et la pomologie française*. Versailles: École nationale supérieure du paysage; Saint-Épain: Lume, 2007.

Jardine, Nicholas, James A. Secord, and E. C. Spary, eds. *Cultures of Natural History*. Cambridge: Cambridge University Press, 1996.

Johnson, Dorothy. *David to Delacroix: The Rise of Romantic Mythology*. Chapel Hill: University of North Carolina Press, 2011.

Joyaux, François. *Les Roses de l'Impératrice: La rosomanie au temps de Joséphine*. Brussels: Éditions Complexe, 2005.

Kemp, Martin. *The Science of Art: Optical Themes in Western Art from Brunelleschi to Seurat*. New Haven, Conn.: Yale University Press, 1990.

Kiefer, Carol Solomon. *The Empress Josephine: Art and Royal Identity*. Amherst, Mass.: Amherst College, 2005.

Kusukawa, Sachiko. "The Uses of Pictures in the Formation of Learned Knowledge: The Case of Leonhard Fuchs and Andreas Vesalius." In *Transmitting Knowledge: Words, Images, and Instruments in Early Modern Europe*, edited by Sachiko Kusukawa and Ian MacLean, 73-96. Oxford: Oxford University Press, 2006.

Lacour, Pierre-Yves. "Les amours de Mars et Flore aux cabinets: Les confiscations naturalistes en Europe septentrionale." *Annales historique de la Révolution française* 4 (2009): 71-92.

Lafont, Anne, ed. *L'artiste savant à la conquête du monde moderne: Formes et savoirs*. Strasbourg: Presses universitaires de Strasbourg, 2010.

Laissus, Yves. *Les Vélins du Muséum*. Paris: Palais de la Découverte, 1967.

———, and Jean Jacques Petter. *Les Animaux du Muséum, 1793-1993*. Paris: Muséum national d'Histoire naturelle and Imprimerie nationale, 1993.

Latour, Bruno. *Nous n'avons jamais été modernes: Essai d'anthropologie symétrique*. Paris: La Découverte, 1991.

———, and Peter Weibel, eds. *Iconoclash: The Image Wars in Science, Religion, and Art*. Karlsruhe: ZKM; Cambridge, Mass.: MIT Press, 2002.

Lazlo, Pierre. "Buffon et Balzac: Variations d'un modèle descriptif." *Romantisme* 58 (1987): 67-80.

Leavelle, Tracy N. "The Osage in Europe: Romanticism, the Vanishing Indian, and French Civilization during the Restoration." In *National Stereotypes in Perspective: Americans in France, Frenchmen in America*, edited by William L. Chew, III, 89-112. Amsterdam and Atlanta: Rodopi, 2001.

Lebleu, Olivier. *Les Avatars de Zarafa, Première girafe de France: Chronique d'une girafomania, 1826-1845*. Paris: Arléa, 2006.

Lipkowitz, Elise. "Seized Natural History Collections and the Redefinition of Scientific Cosmopolitanism in the Era of the French Revolution." Forthcoming in *British Journal for the History of Science*.

Lovejoy, Arthur O. *The Great Chain of Being: A Study of the History of an Idea*. Cambridge, Mass.: Harvard University Press, 1976.

Majer, Michele. "*La Mode à la girafe*: Fashion, Culture, and Politics in Bourbon Restoration France." *Studies in the Decorative Arts* 17, no. 1 (Fall-Winter 2009-10): 123-61.

Martin, Meredith. *Dairy Queens: The Politics of Pastoral Architecture from Catherine de' Medici to Marie-Antoinette*. Cambridge, Mass.: Harvard University Press, 2011.

McClellan, James E., III. "André Michaux and French Botanical Networks at the End of the Old Regime." *Castanea: Occasional Papers in Eastern Botany* 2 (December 2004): 69-97.

McClellan, James E., III. *Colonialism and Science: Saint Domingue in the Old Regime.* Reprint. Chicago: University of Chicago Press, 2010.

———, and François Regourd. *The Colonial Machine: French Science and Overseas Expansion in the Old Regime.* Turnhout: Brepols, 2012.

Meyers, Amy R. W., ed. *Knowing Nature: Art and Science in Philadelphia, 1740–1840.* New Haven, Conn.: Yale University Press, 2011.

Michel, Marianne Roland. "La botanique est-elle un art? Is botany an art?" In *The Floral Art of Redouté,* edited by Marianne Roland Michel, 13–26. Greenwich, Conn.: Bruce Museum of Arts and Science, 2002.

Outram, Dorinda. *Georges Cuvier: Science, Vocation and Authority in Post-Revolutionary France.* Manchester: Manchester University Press, 1984.

———. "Politics and Vocation: French Science, 1793–1830." *British Journal for the History of Science* 13, no. 1 (March 1980): 27–43.

Parrish, Susan Scott. *American Curiosity: Cultures of Natural History in the Colonial British Atlantic World.* Chapel Hill: University of North Carolina Press, 2006.

Pieters, Florence. "Notes on the Menagerie and Zoological Cabinet of the Stadholder William V of Holland, Directed by Aernout Vosmaer." *Journal of the Society for the Bibliography of Natural History* 9 (1980): 539–63.

Pinault, Madeleine. *The Painter as Naturalist, from Dürer to Redouté.* Paris: Flammarion, 1991.

———. *Le peintre et l'histoire naturelle.* Paris: Flammarion, 1990.

Pinault Sørensen, Madeleine. *Le Livre de Botanique, XVIIe et XVIIIe siècles.* Paris: Bibliothèque nationale de France, 2008.

———. "Portraits of Animals, 1600–1800." In Senior, *A Cultural History of Animals in the Age of Enlightenment,* 157–96.

Pincemaille, Christophe. *Il y a 200 ans, Joséphine achetait Malmaison.* Rueil-Malmaison: Société des amis des Malmaison, 1999.

Porterfield, Todd. *The Allure of Empire: Art in the Service of French Imperialism, 1798–1836.* Princeton: Princeton University Press, 1998.

Potts, Alex. "Natural Order and the Call of the Wild: The Politics of Animal Picturing." *Oxford Art Journal* 13, no. 1 (1990): 12–33.

Prince, Sue Ann, ed. *Stuffing Birds, Pressing Plants, Shaping Knowledge: Natural History in North America, 1730–1860.* Philadelphia: American Philosophical Society, 2003.

Quellier, Florent. *Des fruits et des hommes: L'arboriculture fruitière en Île-de-France (vers 1600–vers 1800).* Rennes: Presses universitaires de Rennes, 2003.

Qureshi, Sadiah. *Peoples on Parade: Exhibitions, Empire, and Anthropology in Nineteenth-Century Britain.* Chicago: University of Chicago Press, 2011.

Rheinberger, Hans-Jörg, Peter McLaughlin, and Staffan Müller-Wille, eds. *Conference: A Cultural History of Heredity I: 17th and 18th Centuries.* Preprint 222. Berlin: Max-Planck-Institute for the History of Science, 2002.

Roche, Daniel. *A History of Everyday Things: The Birth of Consumption in France, 1600–1800.* Translated by Brian Pearce. Cambridge: Cambridge University Press, 2000.

Roger, Jacques. *Buffon: A Life in Natural History.* Ithaca: Cornell University Press, 1997.

Rudwick, Martin J. S. *Scenes from Deep Time: Early Pictorial Representations of the Prehistoric World.* Chicago: University of Chicago Press, 1992.

Senior, Matthew, ed. *A Cultural History of Animals in the Age of Enlightenment.* Oxford and New York: Berg, 2007.

Sharpley-Whiting, T. Denean. *Black Venus: Sexualized Savages, Primal Fears, and Primitive Narratives in French.* Durham, N.C.: Duke University Press, 1999.

Sliggers, Bert, and A. A. Wertheim, eds. *Een vorstelijke dierentuin: De menagerie van Willem V; Le zoo du prince: La ménagerie du stadhouder Guillaume V.* Zutphen: Walburg Institute, 1994.

Somerset, Richard. "The Naturalist in Balzac: The Relative Influence of Cuvier and Geoffroy Saint-Hilaire." *French Forum 27*, no. 1 (Winter 2002): 81–111.

Spary, E. C. *Utopia's Garden: French Natural History from Old Regime to Revolution.* Chicago: University of Chicago Press, 2000.

Stafford, Barbara Maria. *Body Criticism: Imaging the Unseen in Enlightenment Art and Medicine.* Cambridge, Mass.: MIT Press, 1991.

Tort, Patrick. *La pensée hiérarchique et l'évolution.* Paris: Aubier-Montagne, 1983.

Van Heiningen, Teunis Willem. "Le vol et la restitution des objets d'histoire naturelle du Stathouder Guillaume V ou Les péripéties des collections du Stathouder Guillaume V entre 1795 et 1815." *Archives internationales d'Histoire des sciences* 56 (2006): 21–42.

Vézin, Luc. *Les artistes au Jardin des Plantes.* Paris: Herscher, 1990.

Williams, Roger L. *Botanophilia in Eighteenth-Century France: The Spirit of Enlightenment.* Archives internationales d'histoire des idées, 179. Dordrecht: Kluwer, 2001.

Principes de Dessin, from J. P. Hoüel, *Histoire naturelle des deux éléphans* (Paris, 1803), plate V. The Academy of Natural Sciences of Drexel University, Ewell Sale Stewart Library

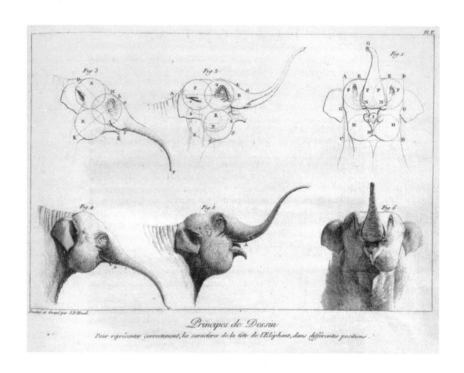